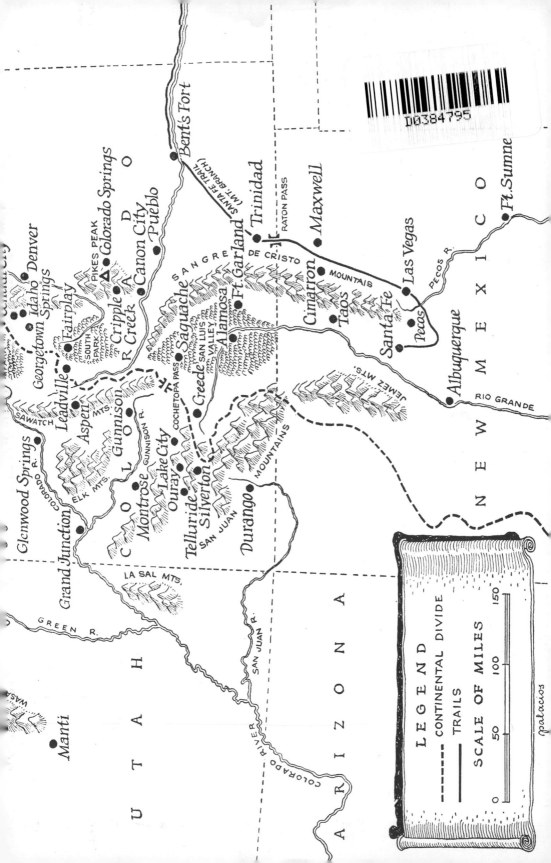

THE BIG DIVIDE

By David Lavender

Non-Fiction

THE BIG DIVIDE

ONE MAN'S WEST

Fiction

ANDY CLAYBOURNE

Juveniles

GOLDEN TREK

MIKE MARONEY, RAIDER

TROUBLE AT TAMARACK

THE
BIG DIVIDE

David Lavender

CASTLE BOOKS

This edition published in 2001 by

CASTLE BOOKS
A division of Book Sales, Inc.
114 Northfield Avenue
Edison, New Jersey 08837

Published by arrangement with and permission of
DOUBLEDAY, a division of The Doubleday Broadway
Publishing Group, a division of Random House, Inc.,
1540 Broadway, New York, New York 10036

PRINTED IN THE UNITED STATES OF AMERICA.

ISBN: 0-7858-1376-4

FOR BROOKIE AND DAVID

CONTENTS

ILLUSTRATIONS

THE BIG DIVIDE

COSMOS IN WEATHERED ROCK

A ND evil days were on the land. Wicked spirits from countries by the sea, unable to overcome the chosen people of the Manitou in fair fight, went among them with forked tongues, whispering lies. The sunshine vanished, snows came, neighbor struck down neighbor. And the Manitou grew wroth. His rains fell and a great flood swept the world.

In terror the people fled toward the western gate of heaven, bearing in their hands soil and sticks and rocks with which to build a better world. But the Manitou saw their evil and selfishness and fear, and the gate was barred. Then, as the floods swept them away, the people cursed the Manitou and flung at the heavens the stones they carried. And from these materials grew a vast mountain which later men would call Pikes Peak. High it towered, far above the flood, pointing the way to heaven but shutting out heaven's light until such time as man did penance before the throne where sits the Manitou.

Such is the legend of the Utes who lived in the mountains behind the great peak, and of the Utes' cousins, the Shoshone and Comanches, and even of those enemies of the Utes, the Arapaho and Cheyennes, who fought the mountain people on the piedmont plains and sometimes raided their mountain fastnesses. And in the legend is all the essence of all the things that men have felt for the mountains since time began: terror and mystery and hope.

First, of course, there was mystery. Indians from the plains, having watched storm clouds cannonading among the peaks, would not venture into the defiles without first placing on rocks or trees propitiatory offerings for the lords of the high places. Strange things abounded there. From the time of Lewis and Clark onward explorers reported hearing, even during the clearest of weather, a distant booming like thunder. Probably it was the echo of falling rocks, but some men attributed the noise to the bursting of rich veins of silver in the frozen heart of the mountains, or to the "disengagement of hydrogen" from subterranean beds of coal. Other legends grew. Trappers told tales of the fearsome carcagne, half wolf and half bear, of giants living on islands in the Great Salt Lake, of white Indians, called Munchies, who dwelt in towns of solid gold (an Anglo-Saxon re-creation, obviously, of Coronado's Seven Cities).

Familiarity ended the folk mysteries, but solid terrors took their places. Avalanches roared, floods hammered, the grizzly prowled. Mountain-dwelling Utes and Snake Indians, though not so tall, clean, or bold as the aborigines of the plains, proved capricious enough. For nearly four centuries men fought, froze, starved, and thirsted. Yet still they came, some because they wanted to break through the barrier of the stony peaks to reach the lotus fields by the Pacific, others because the Rockies themselves beckoned as the land of fulfillment.

During most of those centuries each wave of men was a wave of un-bridled exploitation, originally the Spanish, and after them four suc-cessive though somewhat overlapping surges of Anglo-Americans. As with the *conquistadores*, gold in one form or another was the dream of each new rush: first, the gold of beaver pelts; second, the glittering trade of Santa Fe; third, the precious metals themselves; and last, the golden seas of ripened grass.

Then, as some of the exploiters fell in love with the land and settled, as cities grew and men saw their children also looking toward the promise of the peaks, a reaction set in. Unchecked exploitation must end; the good things of the land must be preserved. With sound and fury the battles of conservation and of reclamation were joined. The echoes still roll, the clouded fights still rage. Meanwhile a new, less vicious form of exploitation has been found in mining the pocketbook of the tourist, the sportsman, the summer and winter vacationist.

The span of the story, both in miles and in years, is far too enormous for one man or one book to cover completely. The Rockies are not just a chain of mountains; they are many separate mountain ranges, plus the vast basins, plateaus, and even deserts which lie cupped among them. Reluctantly, therefore, this account has had to draw a boundary about those sections of the Rockies which lie inside Colorado, Wyoming, eastern Utah, and northern New Mexico, with a tacit understanding that the regions which border the Big Divide on east and west are too closely integrated with mountain economy to be entirely ignored. Likewise there have been unavoidable compressions in subject matter. A few well-known towns and rivers, persons and places have occasion-ally been skimmed over in favor of granting more space to less familiar topics. Other subjects, such as "bad men" and sheriffs, which seem not to make a valid contribution to the picture as a whole, have been largely disregarded.

These, then, are the threads. And the first to draw a lusty pattern across the mountains, to set the design for nearly everything that was to follow, were the mountain men.

CHAPTER I

THE TWIG IS BENT

AT THE headwaters of the Yampa in north-central Colorado, where the rounded hills bask voluptuously and the gleam of aspens mocks the darkling spruce, a ruined cabin stood. Here a small party of wayfarers stopped. And melancholy touched the man named Kelly, who had built the cabin several years before.

"The mountains were rich then," he told his journal-keeping companion, Thomas Jefferson Farnham. "The [buffalo] bulls were so bold that they would come close to the fence there at night, and bellow and roar until I eased them of their blood by a pill in the liver. . . . Now the mountains are poor. . . . No place for a white man now. Too poor, too poor."

The year of this dolorous plaint was 1839. By that time Kelly and a thousand other mountain men had tramped the Rockies from end to end and in the process had nosed out nearly every one of the vaunted resources which in future years would bring hot-eyed hordes of new "discoverers" panting up their forgotten trails. They had taken the first wagons across the Continental Divide, had found gold and oil. They had aided in cracking open the Spaniards' jealously guarded trade marts at Santa Fe, had recognized the stock-fattening possibilities of lands which were dismissed by official explorers as hopeless desert. They anticipated the Mormons' introduction of irrigation, helped scientists to classify and artists to reproduce the New World's newest marvels, cashed in on the recreational profits involved in guiding big-game hunters, and introduced health seekers to the climate.

They were also the first despoilers of a great natural resource. In their rush to reap but not to sow, they trapped themselves right out of business, debauched the Indians, and set the pattern for the unbridled ferocity that soon would spill its red horror from one end of the Rockies to the other.

And now, in 1839, they were sad. The good old days were gone; the mountains were washed up. Too poor, too poor.

Who were these designers of destiny? Where did they come from? How did they live?

First whites to see the Rockies were, of course, the Spaniards, but although these exuberant exploiters dwelt at the edge of the big divide, it would be a mistake to call them mountain men. Lustful, lazy, avaricious, yet possessing in the face of the unknown a cool contempt for danger, they preferred to get rich quick by letting slaves pick money for them right out of the ground. When that did not work and New Mexico's fabled cities of gold turned out to be pueblos of mud, the *conquistadores* were content to sink back into well-worn feudal modes of life with primitive agriculture as its base. Using enslaved Indians for the dirty part of the work, they irrigated a few fields, bred good horses and poor sheep, instituted a crude textile industry, prospected desultorily for metals, found turquoise and copper, and even mined a little gold and silver, though nowhere near as much as they had hoped for. The peculiar fortitude and the peculiar patience required for trapping, most of them did not possess. What skins they procured were won by barter with the Indians, and their only ventures into the mountains, aside from a few aimless trips taken for the love of adventure, were made by occasional prospectors and by military expeditions chasing runaway workers, looking for new slaves, or trying to chastise marauding bands of Utes and Comanches.

The New World French were different. Merry, pliable, quick-witted, and patient as oxen under burden, they swarmed up the northern rivers in ever-increasing flotillas and came back to civilization not only with valuable cargoes of furs but with such a fund of expansive yarns that Father Charlevoix, visiting the French settlements in Illinois in 1721, remarked that "traveling in the distant West seemed to unfit men for telling the truth."

These happy-go-lucky *voyageurs* did not always know where they were. One common misassumption was that they were treading the eastern boundaries of Asia. Another was that they could reach Santa Fe by way of the Yellowstone River. Distance lends enchantment. The French, primarily traders rather than trappers, supposed that Santa Fe was fully as rich as the Spanish wished it were. They kept fumbling from the Mississippi toward the legendary city, and finally, after Arikara Indians on the upper Missouri had set their geography straight, the brothers Mallet, leading a party of eight, reached the New Mexico capital in 1739. The Spanish let them in, but after that the door was slammed hard, one prime reason, aside from military considerations, being that the dons who controlled the arduous trade route to Old Mexico did not want to lose their monopoly to goods brought in via easier roads from the east.

Power politics spared the Spaniards worry. In 1763 the Treaty of Paris booted the French Government out of North America. But it did not boot out the Frenchmen. Adaptable as cats, they stayed where they were, mingled with the Indians as no other Caucasians were quite able to do, begot innumerable half-red progeny, roamed among the tribes with handfuls of gaudy trade goods, collected a few plews and hides, bobbed up for brief roisters in the Mississippi River towns, and then vanished again into the wilderness. To what extent they made the mountains their own—or rather, to what extent the mountains claimed them—is impossible to say. Certainly they had reached the Rockies before 1763 and quite possibly had crossed them. But the wanderings were haphazard. No government existed to inspire expeditions, no company channeled energies, no clerks wrote down records in their crabbed hands. For forty years the central Rockies existed in a kind of historical vacuum.

But the French were there. When the United States acquired Louisiana Territory and rushed out expeditions to see what kind of pig they had bought in the poke, up the *voyageurs* bobbed. It was a man named Charbonneau who sat at the foot of the passes with his squaw Sacagawea as Lewis and Clark toiled up the Missouri. It was a Pierre Dorion whom Hunt hired as interpreter for the 1811 overland expedition to Astoria, and it was a man named Bijeau who led Long to the Colorado Rockies in 1820. Other nameless hundreds of them were on hand to do the chores as the great fur companies rediscovered the upper Missouri. Even the language of the trade was French: *cordelle, voyageur, engagé; bourgeois, pelu, fanfaron* (which in English became booshway, plew, and foofaraw). The early mountain man's title of approbation was *hivernant*, one who had wintered out. The slur of contempt: *mangeur de lard*, pork eater, greenhorn. Long after the United States had shouldered out the English companies with an 1816 law that forbade foreigners' operating on American soil, French names bulked large: Sublette, Larpenteur, Chouteau, Fontenelle, Basil Lajeunesse, and Alexis Godey (Frémont's stalwarts), Robidoux, which the phonetic-spelling Americans wrote in a dozen ways, and a score of others.

Another heritage from the old French fur companies was the custom of trading from fixed posts scattered throughout the wilderness. The system worked well so long as there was only one outfit in the field, as in the case of the Hudson's Bay Company, and the Indians, smeared with ocher and bedecked with bangles, needs must swarm into its "forts" to trade off their furs for three-point blankets (the number of stripes or "points" woven into a blanket indicated its quality), for galena pig lead and powder, for tobacco, vermilion, and looking glasses. Profits to the trader ranged from 300 to 1900 per cent, unless, unknown to him in his newsless post, the market price sagged on a once popular fur or a cargo was lost to the rapids or to pirates, red or white.

With the advent of the Americans and their disruptive ideas of free competition, things changed. To beat a rival to a customer, a man had to leave his fort and follow the trade. Some of these reckless entrepreneurs were salaried employees of the companies. Others were "free traders" who procured goods under whatever credit arrangements they could wangle and took off into the unknown to barter at their own risk.

Typical of those footloose trail blazers was James Purcell. In 1802, before the United States owned Louisiana, he and a few other whites bought some goods from traders in the Mandan villages on the Missouri, packed the plunder on a string of horses, and headed south with a group of "Padouca [Comanche] and Kioway" Indians. The party's horses were soon stolen, and when Purcell later saw a Kansa buck riding his former mount, he brazenly demanded it back. The Kansa, armed with a rifle, refused, whereupon Purcell drew his knife, darted forward, and ripped open the horse's bowels. The astonished Indian fired at point-blank range, but the spasm of the dying animal threw the bullet wide. With a triumphant yowl Purcell brandished his knife and chased the buck right back through his own village.

The audacity so delighted the Kansa chiefs that they gave the party fresh horses, but somewhere along the South Platte, not far from present-day Denver, these animals, too, were stolen. In an effort to return to the Missouri, the men built a raft. It sank, and at this juncture along came a war party of Sioux. The traders took to their heels, wormed a way through the river's gloomy canyon, and so reached South Park, the first whites (unless some unknown Frenchman had preceded them) to see one of Colorado's four lush, mountain-rimmed basins. From the summer of 1803 to the spring of 1805 they stayed there, and sometime during that interval James Purcell washed from the sands of one of the creeks several nuggets of gold. For many weeks he carried them in his shot pouch. But they were only a burden to him there in the wilderness, and eventually he threw them away.

Meanwhile the party had fallen in with a group of Utes who wanted to trade with the Spaniards to the south. The whites went to Santa Fe as emissaries and worked out arrangements, whereafter all but Purcell headed back for the States. He liked the lazy town and hung around, picking up a good living as a carpenter. To the New Mexicans he said nothing of his gold discovery, for by some whisper along the moccasin telegraph he had learned that the United States now owned the Louisiana Territory and he was patriotic enough not to reveal his secret to foreigners. However, when explorer Zebulon Pike was brought as a prisoner to Santa Fe, Purcell sought him out and passed on the news.

All this was duly recorded in Pike's journal (wherein the discoverer was misnamed Pursley) and published to the world in 1810. The effect? Exactly nothing. The Rockies were too far from civilization; the nation's mind had not yet been prepared by the California strikes, which came after Frémont and a thousand others had left the West looking less like the ends of the earth.[1]

Purcell was not primarily a trapper; he was a trader. So far the onerous business of collecting pelts had been left largely to the somewhat inefficient Indians, but as competition grew keener the notion of sending large brigades of whites directly to the streams took hold. Most of the companies clung to the Missouri, trapping its mountainous headwaters and using its turbulent current as a highway for their keelboats. But this was too circuitous a route for men eying the less crowded beaver streams of the central Rockies. Soon they were striking directly overland (giving future food for thought to a certain rugged "gentleman of credit" named William Ashley), and the minute they reached the Colorado mountains they ran into temptation.

Southwest lay the goods-hungry New Mexicans of Santa Fe, where the governor might be cajoled into granting licenses to trap the virgin streams that lay just beyond the international boundary. Southwest, too, lay Taos, which mountain men called Touse, where winters were mild, codes lax, the señoritas—and the señoras—willing.

The combination was irresistible. As early as 1804 Baptiste la Lande skipped across the border with goods entrusted to him by his employer, William Morrison, sold them at dizzy prices, and settled down in Santa Fe with Morrison's profits burning holes in his unfaithful pockets. By 1814 Phillebert's hired French trappers were wintering in Taos, thus starting it off on its boisterous career as the mountain man's favorite

---

[1] Purcell was not the only mountain man to discover gold in Colorado. During the thirties, also in South Park, Du Chet picked up richly mineralized specimens. In the forties Antoine Robidoux spent considerable time and money trying to develop some placer diggings he had located in the southwestern part of the state. And in 1848, again in South Park, the year of the first California strikes and eleven years before the Colorado rush, Old Bill Williams dug up several nuggets, but that solitary eccentric had no intention of laboring for a living with pick and shovel.

resort; and during the next two years Auguste Chouteau and Jules de Munn, wealthy fur traders from St. Louis, persistently knocked at the governor's gate in a futile effort to win a license for trapping Spanish waters.

Chouteau and De Munn would have done better to have made themselves less conspicuous. In May 1817, just as the party was starting home with bales of furs collected in American territory in central Colorado, up clattered a troop of Spanish dragoons. Off to Santa Fe went the trappers. Furs, horses, goods, and supplies were confiscated; the men were fettered and tossed into the *cárcel*. Forty-eight days later the two leaders were tried by a court-martial of six members, only one of whom knew how to sign his name.

The Spanish governor, De Allande (so wrote De Munn in a letter to explorer William Clark, who was governor of Missouri Territory at the time), "entered into such a rage that it prevented his speaking, contented himself with striking his fist several times on the table, saying, 'Gentlemen, we must have this man shot.' . . . When mention was made of the Mississippi, he jumped up saying . . . that Spain had never ceded the west side of it. It may be easy to judge of our feelings to see our lives in the hands of such a man. . . .

"We were dismissed, and Mr. Chouteau and myself put in the same room. Half an hour afterward the lieutenant came in with a written sentence; we were forced to kneel to hear the citure of it, and forced, likewise, to kiss the unjust and iniquitous sentence that deprived harmless men of all they possessed—of the fruit of two years' labors and perils."

The trial concluded, the entire party was ordered out of New Mexico by the shortest route, "each with one of the worst horses we had." Eventual redress: none. Cracking the gates of New Mexico would have to wait for revolutions and for later mountain men.

Northward, in 1822, William Ashley and Andrew Henry started for the sources of the Missouri with the one hundred "enterprising young men" who, with their successors, were destined to die violently at the rate of one every ten or twelve days, to give the country some of its household names and most hair-raising legends, and to tear from the Rockies nearly every one of their secrets. Fortunately for history, this ribald and unwitting band of history makers did not stay long on the Missouri. Competition from Astor's American Fur Company was a tough nut to crack; furthermore, in 1823, the Assiniboins and Blackfeet stung Henry hard on the Yellowstone, and the Arikaras pounced on Ashley's second hundred youths, killed thirteen, and sent the rest reeling backward.

Disgusted, Ashley determined to quit the bloody Missouri and travel overland as the trappers to the south had been doing for nearly a score of years. But if the overland idea wasn't new, the refinements Ashley added were. Chief among these was his development of the annual rendezvous into a mountain-wide fair and a mountain-wide clearing-house for information garnered by "the most significant group of continental explorers ever brought together."

America has known no gayer, noisier, busier, more drunken, or more lecherous scenes than those that took place each summer at some varying but carefully selected crossroads convenient to the entire mountain area, where enough game abounded to feed thousands of persons, enough grass to feed thousands of horses. Thousands—because not only Ashley's men came to the gatherings to deposit their furs, collect their wages, and outfit themselves for the following season. There were also free trappers and trappers bound to other companies, out to pick up what they could. And Indians from all the tribes of the West, adding their own furs and robes to the growing bales in exchange for blankets, hawk bells, brass kettles, vermilion, and rotgut whisky. It is no wonder that in the early days of the trade the company partners reaped fortunes in spite of the high risks involved. Between 1823 and 1826, when he sold out to Jedediah Smith, David Jackson, and William Sublette, Ashley is said to have netted close to one hundred thousand dollars, a very tidy sum for those times.

The workaday trapper, however, was nearly always behind the game. First of all, he had to supply his own equipment. It sounds simple enough: a horse (which he often lost to the Indians), saddle and bridle, a sack containing six traps, a rifle and perhaps a pistol, a blanket, a buffalo robe, a hatchet, a powder horn, and a bullet pouch for the bullets he ran with his own hands. If he was flush he wore a flannel shirt and a felt hat. Otherwise his clothes were entirely homemade of leather, except perhaps for leggings devised from strips of blanket which would not draw tight after a wetting in the streams, as buckskin was wont to do. Around his neck he might wear a pipe case lovingly sewn by the squaw of the moment, and on his belt hung his Green River knife and a wooden box containing foul-smelling beaver castor for bait, tobacco, and implements for making fire.

Meager though these goods were, he generally had to put himself in hock to the company for all or part of them. When Tom (Broken

Hand) Fitzpatrick signed up young Kit Carson at Taos in September 1830, this was the bill:

1 saddle mule	30 plews
1 Spanish saddle	40 plews
1 capote, Hudson's Bay	8 plews
Galena lead pigs (for bullets)	1 plew
3 feet of twist tobacco	1 plew
6 traps	24 plews

In other words, to get out of debt Kit had to catch and deliver at the rendezvous the next summer 104 beaver pelts. He also had to have enough left over to outfit himself for the following season. Any excess was profit—but profits weren't likely to last long when the men sat down to gamble at the Indian game of hand, to buy alcohol over the company's plank counters, or company gewgaws for red maidens who were willing to sell themselves overnight for a silver-studded Spanish belt or a piece of scarlet strouding, generally with the connivance of their menfolk. (But not always. Milton Sublette, to whom many a gory legend clings, is said to have been stabbed nearly to the heart by a chief who suspected Milton's intentions regarding his daughter.)

A few men managed to escape the company's financial bondage. These were the free trappers, the vainest of the whole vain lot, the quickest to fight, the gaudiest dressers, the freest spenders. They furnished their own supplies, trapped where they liked, sold to whomever they pleased. Some of them journeyed in small groups, tempting prey for Indians. Others, like the brigade that gathered around Kit Carson after he became a free agent, banded together for protection, shared such labors as camp making, horse herding, and night guarding, but retained individual ownership of the furs that were caught. Once in a while a group of free traders tried a completely communal experiment, but the efforts seem not to have been successful. And in the end, however the free trappers operated, the rendezvous generally scooped in the fruits of their toil.

When the rendezvous drew to its sodden end, the season for exploration began. Off the men went to pick out next year's trapping ground, frequently traveling in large groups under the command of a seasoned leader known as the "booshway." Discipline was exact. Behind the booshway came the pack train and the camp keepers, each one responsible for three animals. At the end of the column rode the "little booshway," who, when a halt was made, assigned each man his place in the circle, inspected the backs of the animals for sores. Until dark the horses and mules grazed loose under guard; then they were picketed or hobbled inside the circle of lodges and baggage.

The squaws (generally there were several along) threw up the lodges, and the camp was divided into messes. When meat was butchered, some chance bystander called out, sight unseen, what particular piece was to go to each man, including the booshways, thus preventing squabbles over favoritism. Night guards were appointed, and soon the camp was dead quiet under the stars. At the first crack of dawn the little booshway roused the sleepers by bawling out, "*Levé, levé!*" and five minutes later drew them from the lodges with a hoarse, "*Leche lego, leche lego*—turn out, turn out!" The horses were grazed; breakfast, which, like the other meals, consisted principally of meat, was prepared; scouts made sure no Indians lurked about; packs were replaced; and the cavalcade moved on.

When the trapping area was reached, the trappers split into small groups to work the streams. Autumn came early to the mountains: air like a polished knife blade, scuffs of snow on the peaktops, riot of gold among the aspens. The hardest kind of labor now was wading the icy pools, setting traps, skinning the catch, always with one eye peeled for Indians who might be lusting for a white man's hair or a white man's horse. So the days sped until the cold bit bone-deep, the streams froze, and deep snow made travel difficult. Then came the retreat to winter quarters.

This might be in beguiling Taos or in one of the forts that had sprung up on the prairies just east of Colorado's Front Range, preferably at the huge establishment of the Bent brothers and St. Vrain on the Arkansas River.

Storied ground here, a sort of no man's land where buffalo roamed in plenty and the red tribes swarmed along intersecting trails that led to Wyoming and Santa Fe, across the mountains and through the plains. The Arkansas, Spain's northern boundary, had lured traders ever since 1762, when Frenchmen built a temporary post on its banks. Since then the stream had known more crude stockades than history probably records, but it remained for the Bent brothers and courtly Ceran St. Vrain really to cash in on the region's mercantile possibilities.

There were four Bents, grandsons of a man who had been at the Boston Tea Party and sons of the presiding judge of the St. Louis Court of Common Pleas. When young William Bent first went West as an employee of the American Fur Company, he was only fifteen years old and the Sioux called him Little White Chief. For a time after

Mexico revolted from Spain and opened her doors to American traders, the brothers worked the Santa Fe Trail—an undersized sixteen-year-old runaway apprentice named Christopher Carson (reward for his return, one cent) first saw the mountains in 1826 as horseherder for one of Charles Bent's wagon trains—but Santa Fe's fat profits weren't fat enough. William and Charles Bent, with St. Vrain's help, decided to build a post of their own where they could batten not only on the Santa Fe hauling but also on trade with the Indians and the mountain men.

Except possibly for Fort Laramie in eastern Wyoming, the mountain area never saw the equal of that feudal castle, Western style. Imported Mexican laborers spent four years (1828–32) building it out of adobe mud mixed with wool. Its walls, four feet thick and fifteen high, embraced an area somewhat larger than half a football field and were guarded at the northwest and southeast corners by circular bastions full of loopholes and musketry. As a further deterrent to Indian attack, the tops of the walls were planted thick with cactus. A massive gate sheathed with iron gave ingress to a graveled patio surrounded by two-storied rooms that served as dwelling quarters, warehouses, saddlery, and blacksmith shops. To the rear a walled corral held stock and wagons. Outside was a garden irrigated by water from the Arkansas and an icehouse filled each winter with river ice. When younger brothers Robert and George Bent joined the establishment, by now a favorite recreation spot for big-game hunters and invalids, they added a billiard room and a bar, often dispatching riders far into the mountains to get mint for juleps; and when Francis Parkman visited the fort in 1846 he was gratified to be served meals off china and white tablecloths. Two captive eagles inhabited the belfry, and the kitchen was in charge of a Negress named Charlotte who was known throughout the mountains for her slapjacks and pumpkin pies and who claimed to be "de only lady in de whole damn Injun country."

William Bent married a Cheyenne Indian beauty, Owl Woman, and thus helped cement the concern's hold on the tribe. Even more important in maintaining friendly relations, however, was the scrupulous—and, in those days, unusual—fairness with which the Indians were treated. (It is significant, perhaps, that during the uprisings of the sixties William Bent's sons fought not with the whites but with the Cheyennes.) At a great council in 1840, Bent induced the antagonistic tribes of the central plains to cease warring on each other, and thereafter during the trading season thousands of peaceful Indians sometimes pitched their lodges around the fort.

By 1840 the Bents' retainers numbered more than a hundred, and never was a more colorful group assembled within one set of walls. There was Sol Silver (his real name he never knew), who had been carried off from his home in Old Mexico by Comanches and sold to the Kiowas. Beaten and abused until he was fourteen or so, he finally cut the throat of the fat bully who had been assigned to watch him, ran away, threw in with some Osages, led them on a raid against the Kiowas, and there found revenge in lifting the scalp of his former owner.

Another was Blackfoot Smith, who won his name by feeding knock-out doses of laudanum to five Blackfeet warriors who had captured him up on the Missouri. Two more warriors chancing by, he killed both in a vicious fight, scalped all seven, and fled south with a party of Sioux. An adept linguist and a canny trader, he married a Cheyenne woman, became a leading figure in the tribe, and exacted tribute from the New Mexicans who drifted up from Santa Fe to barter with the Indians. Rufus Sage, who wandered through Colorado with the trappers in 1841–44, has left us a picture of one of these motley Mexican groups "escorting a caravan of pack-horses and mules, laden with flour, corn, bread, beans, onions, dried pumpkin, salt and pepper, to barter for robes, skins, furs, meats, moccasins, bows and arrows, ammunition, guns, coffee, calico, cloth, tobacco and old clothes . . . A more miserable gang of filthy, half-naked ragamuffins I never before witnessed." To Blackfoot Smith similar traders paid as much as one robe out of every three for the privilege of moving through "his" country, but autocrat though he was, he, too, joined the Bents.

When the fur trade declined toward the end of the thirties, Kit Carson, Lucien Maxwell, Old Bill Williams, and others signed on with the fort as hunters for a dollar a day. It was no sinecure. A hundred employees and their families, plus innumerable visitors, ate a lot of meat. Far and wide the hunters ranged after the herds, killed buffalo cows in preference to anything else, rolled the dead prey on its belly, cut off the hump, split the hide along the back, and, pulling the skin down the sides, spread it on the ground to keep the meat clean. Bones were severed with a hatchet. The tongue and *boudins* (that part of the intestines containing the chyme) were carefully saved as delicacies. The butchered meat, wrapped in the hide, was packed to the hunters' camp and immediately cut, always with the grain, into thin strips for jerking. These dried, smoked sheets, stiff as boards, were then transported to the fort either on mules or in wagons.

The end of Bent's Fort was as flamboyant as its existence. During the war with Mexico the adobe castle fell within the withering orbit of the Army. In the panting hot summer of 1846 General Stephen Watts Kearny let his ragtag volunteers rest beside the Arkansas while he pondered plans for seizing Santa Fe. The fort's brass cannon fired a salute—and burst. Perhaps it was an omen. The establishment was turned into a military storehouse and hospital; and after the war had been won, the government, realizing the fort's strategic location for cowing the Indians of the plains, dickered for its possession. Their offer for a concern which housed an annual one-hundred-thousand-dollar business was a paltry sixteen thousand dollars. But the brass hats were trifling with the wrong man. Tired of haggling, William Bent loaded his goods into twenty large wagons, hauled them out onto the plains, went back to the fort, staved in the tops of several powder kegs, set the buildings afire, and blew the place sky high. Later he must have regretted the spectacular display of petulance, because after a year of freighting government supplies he built a new but much smaller fort some forty miles farther west, and in 1859 leased it to the United States. The Army eventually rechristened it Fort Lyon. Here Kit Carson died in May 1868; almost exactly a year later Kit's friend, William Bent, passed away on the nearby Purgatoire River.

The Bent brothers' fort and its satellites (such as Fort St. Vrain on the South Platte) were not the only ones where mountain men holed up during winters. Deep in the mountains free traders had tossed up establishments of their own in an effort to nibble away at the business of the big fur companies. Travelers did not find these spots very prepossessing. Joseph Williams, Oregon-bound in 1842, looked down his nose at Robidoux's Fort "Winty" in Utah's Uinta Mountains "on account of the wickedness of the people and the drunkenness and swearing, and the debauchery of the men with the Indian women." Wislizenus in 1839 described Fort Davy Crockett at Brown's Hole in northwestern Colorado as "the worst thing of the kind we have seen on our journey. It is a low one-story building constructed of wood and clay with three connecting wings and no enclosure . . . known to the trappers by the name of Fort Misery." Be that as it may, several hundred trappers and Indians camped at Davy Crockett during the winter of 1839–40, whiling away the time with games, dances, horse races, hunting trips, and a fight with some raiding Sioux.

Forts lacking, the trappers created their own camps in one of the innumerable "holes" or parks that dot the Rockies. Life was good in these lovely mountain-sheltered basins: game abounded, winds were rare, temperatures comparatively mild. Most of the men had squaws, taken sometimes in real affection, sometimes for convenience. The ladies talked their mates' ears off, used language and cracked jokes that would, as Bernard De Voto puts it, blister an oak, and often filled the lodges with their none-too-clean relatives. But they also prepared animal sinews for thread, sewed whangs of buckskin down the seams of the leather trousers (later these tabs could be cut off and used for patching clothes), decorated hunting shirts with beads and porcupine quills, prepared jerky and pemmican, cut firewood, and cooked meals.

The men made daily hunts, often on snowshoes, and wrestled with the daily problem of hanging meat where marauding wolverines could not get at it. The rest of the time they lolled around the lodges, smoking, eating, and picking up from the interminable yarns the thousand bits of lore which might help keep them alive through one more season. All too soon the spring breakup came, and there was another rush for the streams before the fur lost its prime. Then on to the rendezvous, where the hundred lonely trails were knit together. When the official "explorers" came and behind them the settlers, the routes would be known, the guides ready.

Carrying goods into and furs out of the rendezvous was a man-sized transportation feat that at first was accomplished with pack trains. But by 1830 the route to Wyoming was well enough known for Ashley's successors, Smith, Jackson, and Sublette, to try mimicking the wagon trains that for several years now had been rolling clear to Santa Fe. Although Bill Sublette led the trip, the results were reported to Congress in a letter signed by all three partners. Not the least portentous part of the document is that which mentions cattle:

" . . . In the month of April last, on the 10th day of the month, a caravan of ten wagons, drawn by five mules each, and two dearborns, drawn by one mule each, set out from St. Louis . . . up the Great Platte river, to the Rocky mountains, and to the head of Wind River, where it issues from the mountains. This . . . was as far as we wished the wagons to go, as the furs to be brought in were to be collected at this place, which is, or was this year, the great rendezvous of the persons engaged in that business. Here the wagons could easily have crossed the Rocky mountains, it being what is called the Southern Pass . . . "

(Two years later Bonneville's twenty wagons did cross South Pass, over which Ashley already had hauled, six years before, an Indian persuader in the form of a small wheeled cannon. Bonneville's men also touched on another matter of import to the field of transportation, though they had no way of knowing it. On the Popo Agie they discovered some black, viscous seeps which they and later mountain men set on fire for the fun of watching the greasy smoke billow. Also they bottled some of the ooze and carried it along with them to rub on their rheumatic joints. What else was there to do with oil in those days?)

Sublette's letter continues: " . . . For our support, at leaving the Missouri settlements, until we should get to the buffalo country we drove twelve head of cattle, beside a milk cow. Eight of these only being required for use before we got to the buffaloes, the others went on to the head of Wind river. . . ."

But what good was a beef animal in buffalo country? The cattle and the milk cow were sold and the purchasers drove them all the way back to the States! The fact that the creatures made the round trip with only native grasses for sustenance (grasses which both Pike and Long ignored when they dismissed the region east of the Rockies as worthless desert) went unnoticed.

It was not the only experiment with cattle. In 1833 Robert Campbell, another fur trader, took four cows and two bulls across the Continental Divide to the rendezvous at Green River, then drove them back through South Pass to the Big Horn Mountains in northern Wyoming. There one of the bulls and three men were bitten by a rabid wolf. The bull went mad and died; one of the men tore off all his clothes, ran naked into the wilderness, and never was seen again. The remaining cattle limped on to the mouth of the Yellowstone River, a total trip of some fourteen hundred miles, during the latter part of which they were so sorefooted that they had to be shod with raw buffalo hide. But, says Charles Larpenteur, a member of the expedition, they "added a great deal to our good living: as we had no coffee, milk was a great relish." Thus another trail had been blazed, but it, too, came ahead of its time, and Wyoming's cattle industry did not develop until after the close of the Civil War.

The tapestry also had its dingy spots. As competition increased, the fur companies used every possible device to lure the Indians' trade away from rivals. The most potent method was raw alcohol. At first, apparently, the Indians despised the fiery stuff. But one trader among the Cheyennes, knowing the tribe was ravenous for sugar, sweetened his liquor and thus inveigled the Indians to drink it. Soon the Cheyennes (and the same tale is told of the Arapaho) were a nation of drunkards.

An Indian's whole concept of liquor was to get as soused as he could in the shortest time possible. The appearance of a keg in a village was a signal for a mass debauch that continued until the last drop was gone. The wildest excesses took place—dances that ended in orgies, fights that ended in murder, lusts that ended in broken families. The women were as bad as the men, biting, cuffing, pulling hair, open to every advance. Soberness brought no remorse; if a trader appeared among a particularly debased group, the Indians, even in the dead of winter, would barter their last robes to obtain liquor.

The government tried to stop the traffic. From the time of the Louisiana Purchase traders were required to operate under license (one of Pike's orders on his expedition in 1806 was to apprehend unlicensed traders), but to watch two thousand miles of frontier with no more troops than the infant nation possessed was an impossibility. The impious trade grew so outrageous that in 1832 Congress forbad the taking of any spirits into Indian country for any purpose whatsoever, even for the preservation of natural-history specimens. Another paper law. That same year William Sublette obtained permission to take 450 gallons of whisky to his "boatmen," an unmitigated sham, for he traveled overland every mile of the way to the rendezvous in Pierre's Hole. Mexicans slipped across the border from Taos to establish a notorious depot for smuggled liquor at the Pueblo, seventy-five miles upriver from Bent's Fort on the Arkansas. When the searching of boats on the Missouri became more vigilant, the American Fur Company imported corn to Fort Union and opened a distillery! (This same company later became ardently prohibitionist for the reason that small companies were using liquor to advantage, and it was hoped that a drying up of the trade would run them out of business.)

Competition also led to some companies indiscriminately arming and stirring up Indians against rival traders. Before the advent of the whites, war had been largely an exhilarating sport among the tribes, entailing a great deal of excited maneuvering, dances, and talk, but relatively little bloodshed. The mountain men changed that. Partly because they were outnumbered in a hostile land, they fought with a calculating ferocity which filled the "savages" with so sullen an awe that rarely would the Indians attack unless odds were overwhelmingly in their favor. But when they did, the red men repaid ferocity with more ferocity, breeding retaliations that led through a mounting circle of viciousness to fearful fruition in the uprisings of the sixties.

Long before this ugly heritage was reached the fur trade was dead. By the late thirties the main streams had been trapped out. Scarcity, however, did not bring high prices, for silk had replaced beaver felt in the making of hats. Though the American Fur Company continued operations in the north, the central Rockies watched their last skeleton rendezvous flicker out in 1840. For a time thereafter prices rose somewhat, but only a few men were left to comb, in greater danger and under greater privations than ever before, the last untouched streams of the high meadows. An era had ended, but already the gates of Santa Fe had been broached and the mountains' second great rush of exploitation was pounding southwest toward the silver pesos of trade-starved New Mexico.

CHAPTER II

MEXICAN DOLLARS

THE lieutenant was lost and had been lost ever since leaving the Arkansas River to strike directly into the Colorado foothills. For an official explorer this was an unfortunate situation. His commanding general had given him a watch, a compass, and certain crude instruments for ascertaining latitude, plus a telescope for determining longitude by noting "with great nicety the periods of immersion and emersion of the eclipsed satellites" of Jupiter. These gadgets, however, "were ruined in the mountains by falling of the horses from precipices," and anyhow Lieutenant Zebulon Pike was not adept at using them. So with little more than his nose for a guide, he blithely led his starving, ill-clad party of fifteen across the snow-covered ridges which border what is now known as South Park, Colorado, and in due time struck a frozen river some forty yards wide.

This, he decided, must be the Red, whose headwaters were among the things he had been sent out to find. Accordingly he poked around it for a while and then laid off for a day to celebrate Christmas, "not one person properly clad for winter, many without blankets, having been obliged to cut them up for socks and other articles; lying down, too, at night on the snow or wet ground, one side burning whilst the other was pierced with the cold wind." As recompense, however, the party was able to feast on eight badly needed buffalo that had been killed the day before, and on December 26, 1806, they headed downstream in good spirits.

It took them ten days to go forty-five miles, and to their dismay the river plunged into a towering canyon they could not negotiate. The worn horses giving out, the discouraged soldiers put the packs on their own backs or on improvised sleds and split into segments to climb over the barricading ridges by whatever means they could devise. It was January 9, 1807, before the last stragglers came limping out of the foothills, only to find to their mortification that the river was not the Red and that they had followed their old friend, the Arkansas, right back to where they had left it nearly a month before.

"I now felt," confided Zebulon Pike to his journal, "at a considerable loss how to proceed."

A Wyoming sheepherder at the foot of the Absaroka range. Endless hills of grass have been Wyoming's gold mines, have resulted in stampedes, violence, and legends as colorful as any in the mining towns.

The Taos Indian Pueblo, New Mexico, boasts a longer history of bloodshed than any other spot in America. Here Po-pé found recruits for his 1680 defeat of the Spaniards; here, in 1847, American soldiers and mountain men gruesomely avenged the murder of Governor Charles Bent.

It was a loss shared by many a later biographer. Exactly what was Pike's underequipped expedition trying to do?

High treason can be and has been made out of this first official scouting trip to the central Rockies, newly acquired through the Louisiana Purchase. Ostensibly Pike was to carry out certain assignments among the Indians, clamp down on any unlicensed traders he found, study the "geographical structure, the natural history, and population of the country," and explore the headwaters of the Arkansas and Red rivers, all the time being most circumspect not to tread on Spanish soil or otherwise give offense to Spain, with whom the United States was all but at war.

Pike's orders, unlike those of Lewis and Clark, came not from the President or from Congress, but from James Wilkinson, commanding general of the Army of the West. And Wilkinson was involved in the notorious Aaron Burr conspiracy to set up a private domain somewhere in the Mississippi Valley. Part of the "plot" (just how far Burr's machinations actually extended seems a moot point) perhaps envisioned a seizure of Spanish lands, in which case Wilkinson would need data on New Mexico's geography, garrisons, resources, etc. What better way of spying it out than through an expedition supposedly exploring Mr. Jefferson's new, vaguely defined territories? Accordingly, as a key figure in this grandiose enterprise Wilkinson selected a mere lieutenant not yet out of his twenties, Zebulon Montgomery Pike, recently returned from a successful mission to the then little-known sources of the Mississippi. Or so the sleuths after treason would have us believe.

Be that as it may, the Spanish were instantly suspicious. Their agents along the Mississippi knew about the expedition long before it started and promptly sent warnings to Mexico. Out from Santa Fe rode Don Facundo Malgares with 100 dragoons, 500 mounted militia, and 2075 beasts of burden to intercept the minuscule party of invaders. No trace of Pike was found for the simple reason that he had not yet appeared on the scene. Consequently, after exhorting a grand council of Pawnees to be on the *qui vive* for interlopers, Malgares went home via the Colorado Rockies, but not without dispatching scouts through the foothills just in case his quarry had somehow slipped by unnoticed.

All this Pike learned both from the Indians and from the tracks of the Spaniards themselves. Nonetheless, he pushed resolutely on, as a good spy would—or like an ambitious young soldier obeying orders. The probabilities are that at worst he was but an untreasonable dupe whom Wilkinson was using in the hope that he might stumble on valuable information during the normal course of his mission.

Still, Pike did some strange things.

When in January he unexpectedly found himself back on the Arkansas, his horses were incapable of further travel and his exhausted men, equipped only for a summer trip, were utterly unprepared to weather a mountain winter. Logic might have suggested retreat or at least a holing up where he was. But not to Pike. He erected a crude breastwork and left two of his fifteen men there in charge of the horses and baggage. The remaining sockless, blanketless, cotton-clad soldiers each shouldered some seventy pounds of food, arms, and ammunition, and on foot struck due west through the canyoned ranges in another effort, Pike says, to find the Red River—which, incidentally, rises some two hundred and fifty miles southeast of where they then were.

This foolhardy venture was almost his last. Provisions gave out. For four days of intense cold the party tasted no food; only the lucky killing of a lone buffalo saved them from starvation. The feet of two men froze so badly that they could not travel; two others were able to hobble along only minus their packs and with sticks for crutches. In this extremity Pike furnished the totally disabled pair with meat and ammunition and left them, "not without tears."

Eventually, after enduring a furious blizzard, the travelers killed four buffalo, dried the meat, cached it, and left one more "frozen lad" behind to guard the deposit. The others then forced a heroic crossing of one of Colorado's most rugged ranges, the Sangre de Cristo, and stumbled south by west into the San Luis Valley. Here they encountered a southward-flowing river. It was El Rio del Norte—the Rio Grande—and the explorers were deep within Spanish territory. But once again Pike thought he had found the Red.

Or did he? After following the stream some distance south, he swung five miles up a western tributary, the Rio Conejos, and there spent two weeks building a stockade thirty-six feet square. This was no crude log breastwork such as he had erected on the Arkansas. Sharpened stakes protruded over walls twelve feet high, the whole was surrounded by a water-filled moat four feet wide, and a gunnery platform enabled the occupants to shoot from numerous loopholes placed eight feet above the ground.

"Thus fortified," the lieutenant wrote in his journal, "I should not have had the least hesitation in putting the hundred Spanish horse at defiance."

What Spanish horse, ask the suspicious, if he really believed he was on the Red River in American territory? Well, having seen Malgares's many tracks on American land, he knew the Spanish were not paying close heed to boundaries in their search for him. And he was a rather bombastic young man. Perhaps the words were a kind of fanciful figure of speech to let patriotic readers know just how dauntless he was.

Meanwhile an event had occurred which is a little harder to swallow. On February 6, the "volunteer" surgeon of the party, Dr. John Robinson, took off for Santa Fe. His excuse: to collect for William Morrison of Kaskaskia, Illinois, those trading profits which the unfaithful Baptiste la Lande, mentioned in the preceding chapter, had neglected to return to Morrison from the New Mexico capital. Now Santa Fe is a long way from the Red River, which lay in the hostile heart of the Comanche nation. It was midwinter and the doctor had to travel afoot. Yet he set off completely alone. The presumption that he knew perfectly well he was not on the Red but on the Rio Grande, only two or three days' march from the city, is inescapable. Furthermore, Pike admits that the claim on La Lande was largely a pretext to enable Robinson "to gain a knowledge of the country, the prospect of trade, force &c." But to jump from this to a conclusion that Pike himself was a deliberate spy of Wilkinson is a rather large-scale feat of mental acrobatics—which leap, however, various detractors have made with ease.

On the day after the doctor's departure Pike at last dispatched a small squad to retrieve his cached baggage and the abandoned soldiers. Two of the men, however, were still unable to travel. When the rescuers left them to return to the stockade, the distraught pair sent on to Pike "some of the bones taken out of their feet, and conjured me by all that was sacred not to leave them to perish far from the civilized world. Oh! little did they know my heart, if they could suspect me of conduct so ungenerous!" So wrote the beset and busy lieutenant, though he had been on the Conejos a full week before he got around to sending out relief.

On February 26 fifty Spanish dragoons and fifty mounted militia appeared at the fort. These hundred horse Pike did not put at defiance. After evincing considerable surprise when informed that he was not on the Red River, he left word of the turn of events for the men still out with the disabled soldiers (later they all reached New Mexico) and suffered his party to be led as semi-captives to Santa Fe, where his bedraggled band of history makers created a profound impression on the sympathetic natives. Soon he was moved on to Chihuahua, Mexico, seat of the Spanish government for the Internal Provinces.

There all his records were confiscated, except a few which he concealed in the rifle barrels of his soldiers, and after a searching cross-
examination he was released on the condition that he never return to
New Mexico. Six years later, a brigadier general, he was killed while
storming a British fortification outside Toronto in the War of 1812.
An honorable end, but not completely unclouded. Zebulon Pike died
without ever having received from a suspicious Congress those official
rewards for meritorious service which had been extended the other
explorers of Louisiana, Lewis and Clark.

Publication of Pike's journal in 1810 rewoke old fables of Santa Fe
as a center of riches—Yankee style. No cities of gold this time. Rather it
was a rainbow of dry goods that Pike revealed: high-grade cloth selling
at twenty dollars a yard, ordinary linen at four dollars. Although his
whole experience was a loud warning that Spanish officials discouraged
intercourse with outsiders, a mere hint in 1812 that Mexico had won
her independence from Spain was enough to send Robert McKnight
and twelve traders scurrying to the Southwest. Unfortunately the
revolt had foundered, and the men were promptly clapped into prison
at Chihuahua, where they remained for nine long years. While Mc-
Knight's group languished in prison, fur trappers Chouteau and De
Munn suffered confiscation of their goods and ejection from New
Mexico; and when other would-be emissaries of mercantile enlighten-
ment fared no better, interest sagged.

Nonetheless, there were always a few who were willing to take a
chance. In 1821 three parties edged toward the unfriendly border. Of
these three, the only one that seems deliberately to have intended
bearding the lion in his den was a party led by irascible Thomas James
and containing as a member John McKnight, bent on rescuing his imprisoned brother if he could. The second, composed of eighteen hired
French fur trappers from the Arkansas, was managed by a self-styled
"colonel," Hugh Glenn, and his second-in-command, keen-eyed
"Major" Jacob Fowler, the world's champion manhandler of the
English language.[1]

---

[1] Sample extract from Fowler's diary: " . . . a Snow fell about one foot deep and
the Weather is now Cold the [Arkansas] River frosen up the Ice a great thickness
and the Indean Children that is able to walk and up to tall boys are out on the Ice
by day light and all as naked as the came to the World . . . all tho the frost is
very seveer . . . I am shure that We Have Seen more than one thousand of these
Children on the Ice at one time and Some that Ware too young to Walk Ware
taken by the larger ones and Soot on a pece of skin on the Ice and In this Setua-
tion kicks its [legs] Round and Hollow and laff at those Round it at play."

The third and most significant group was led by William Becknell, who had advertised in the *Missouri Intelligencer* for seventy men to venture westward "for the purpose of trading for Horses and Mules and catching Wild Animals of all descriptions," each man to outfit himself and chip in a certain amount toward the common expenses of the company. Though only four men seem to have answered this sanguine appeal, Becknell cheerfully loaded their trifle of goods on a few mules, led them up the Arkansas, swung south, and tackled the Rockies at what later became famous as Raton Pass. It was rough going. For two days the party chopped trees and rolled boulders, but at last they gained the top, and the golden loveliness of northern New Mexico spread out before their eyes.

To their acute apprehension they also saw, shortly thereafter, a troop of Mexican cavalry. Astonishingly enough, however, the soldiers welcomed them with grins, not rifles. A new revolution had succeeded, Mexico was free, and after a century of rebuff foreign traders were at last welcome. In triumph the dazed Becknell party rode on November 16, 1821, into joy-drunk Santa Fe.

Quickly news of the extraordinary turn of events seeped across mountains and plains. Thomas James and John McKnight heard it far out south of the Arkansas and came panting into the city a few weeks behind Becknell. Up in Colorado, Hugh Glenn learned it from wandering Mexican traders and went off with four men to investigate. Fowler, being suspicious, retreated with the rest of the party to the north shore of the Arkansas and there built "a Strong Hous and Hors Pen on the Banks of the River Wheare it Will not be In the Powe of an Enemy to aproch us from the River Side—and shold the Spanierds apeer In a Hostill manner We Will fight them on the Ameraken ground." The precaution was needless. The New Mexicans were celebrating independence with an abandon that curled Thomas James's puritanical hair; Robert McKnight and his men, released from prison, also hurried to Santa Fe (they eventually returned to the States with the Fowler party), and all three groups sold their pittance of goods at the wildest of prices.

Becknell, first to arrive in Santa Fe, was the first back home. When he opened the sacks he brought with him, handfuls of Mexican dollars tumbled into the dusty streets of Franklin, Missouri, and the rush was on. Again Becknell pioneered it. When he left Franklin in the spring of 1822, he had with him three wagons, the first wheeled vehicles to cross the Western plains. Two years later, while he was off on a trapping venture in Colorado, Augustus Storrs and M. M. Marmaduke showed just how big the killings could be: their twenty wagons, having trundled westward with $30,000 worth of dry goods, notions, and hardware, returned with $180,000 in gold and silver, $10,000 in furs.

Profits of 600 per cent or better, of course, could not last, but they remained high enough for Yankee traders to push from Santa Fe clear down to Chihuahua and still undersell their native competitors. The Mexicans, likewise recognizing a good thing when they saw it, promptly imposed staggering import duties on goods and an export tax on specie. This latter duty the traders avoided by false bottoms in their wagons, so that Dr. Wislizenus, answering questions about the annual gold production of Nueva Méjico, remarked dryly, "As nearly all the gold is bought up by traders and smuggled out of the country to the United States, I believe a closer calculation of the gold produced in New Mexico could be made in the different mints in the United States than in Mexico itself."

One form of import duty was Governor Armijo's flat tax of $500 on every entering vehicle, regardless of size. Partly because of this the wagons grew, for that day of bridgeless streams and gradeless hills, to enormous size. With beds deep enough to hide a standing man and mounted on iron-sheathed hind wheels eight inches wide and sixty-four inches tall, they could carry up to three tons each, pulled by five to ten yoke of oxen. Generally (though there was no attempt at standardization) they were painted blue and arched with a double thickness of white canvas between whose layers smuggled blankets could be hidden. The equipment, the dress, the arms, and the varying languages of attendants and hangers-on made one of the weirdest potpourris of humanity that the already heterogeneous West had ever seen.

Until the freighting fell largely into the hands of such professional carriers as the Bents, the wagons were owned and the wagoners paid by individual traders, called proprietors. Early in the spring these proprietors banded into caravans, elected a captain whom they seldom obeyed, and traveled in loose columns of four so that the train could swing quickly into a defensive square at the first sign of Indian hostilities. When the rocky passes of the mountains at last drew near, the proprietors sprinted ahead under cover of darkness to rent stores and to deal, mostly by bribery, with customs officials.

Behind them the train lost all cohesion as the various outfits began an eager race for the prestige and profits involved in being first to reach the city. Today it sounds like a vast exertion for a piddling trade; in 1843, after twenty years of growth, there were only 230 wagons carrying 450,000 pounds of merchandise, hardly a good load for a small freight train. But to isolated New Mexico it was an annual miracle, a lone contact with civilization that they hardly dared believe until it happened again. All Santa Fe poured out in welcome. *"Los americanos! Los carros!"* What a day it was—the women dancing with excitement; the native men in their outlandish clothes, half friendly, half jealous; soldiers strutting, Indians swarming. The *bailes*, the gambling halls, the barrooms—the end of the trail.

But not quite the end for some. There was Chihuahua. And southern California. The short line to the latter place, of course, lay due west, and as usual trappers were the first to blaze the trail. Pattie blundered as far as the Colorado River in 1826, and Ewing Young covered the rest of the distance in '29, taking with him as a member of his ragged crew a twenty-year-old wanderer whose name everlastingly bobs up in Western annals, Kit Carson. But the desert was fearsome that way, the Apaches worse. When later mountain men, turned trader, headed for California with a few notions lashed to the backs of their pack animals, they generally followed the safer but much longer Old Spanish Trail. This veered off through western Colorado into Utah and then swung south again in a great, looping curve. Actually it wasn't so old, though Escalante had pioneered the first part of it in 1776. Escalante, however, never reached the coast. That remained for Manuel Armijo in 1829, and for the mountain men who, beginning with William Wolfskill in 1830-31, smoothed out the kinks and filled it full of mule tracks.

California overflowed with mules—huge, fine mules such as the Santa Fe wagoners were calling for but could not find until the mountain men obliged them. Sometimes the traders swapped for the creatures; sometimes they simply stole them. Either way it was a large and profitable traffic. Peg-leg Smith, who once supervised the amputation of his own leg with a hunting knife and a keyhole saw, is reputed, possibly with exaggeration, to have made off with three thousand head in a single swoop. Peg-leg, however, was a patriotic man; when California entered the Union he ceased stealing and paid for his mules. By that time, one presumes, he could afford the gesture.

Some seventy miles north of Santa Fe, on a high benchland at one of the spraddling toes of the Sangre de Cristo Mountains, was the smaller but only slightly less important trading center of Taos. It is an art colony now, a hangout for tourists, and one would never guess from looking at its tiny, sleepy plaza that it has probably had a longer history of raw violence than any other village in America.

Its earliest inhabitants were, of course, Pueblo Indians, dwelling in those terraced "apartment houses" that have been pictured on so many brassily colored post cards. Then along about 1600 Spanish colonists arrived, accompanied by their thin-lipped priests and their fanatical swords. At first the swords were not needed and the newcomers settled peacefully around the Pueblo, but so many additional colonists kept arriving and there were so many intermarriages that the displeased Indians ordered the Spaniards to move "a league away." The resultant flat-roofed hamlet was called Don Fernando de Taos, and this is generally what is meant when New Mexicans speak of Taos. The term, however, is generic and sometimes includes the Indian Pueblo, San Geronimo de Taos, and the Indian farming center, Ranchos de Taos, a short distance south of Don Fernando.

The whole Taos district boasted good sheep, good grain, good water. It was convenient to the mountain Utes, to the Navajos and the Comanches, and even to the Arapaho of the plains—horribly convenient when any of those tribes happened to be in a raiding mood. As a result, a century before the Santa Fe Trail was known, the Taos "fairs" were flourishing. As the exciting day drew near, up out of nowhere bobbed the ubiquitous French with goods from the East. Along the trail from Chihuahua creaked the solid-wheeled *carretas* laden with fine mantillas and *rebozas*, with casks of El Paso wine and kegs of huge, soft Mexican silver dollars, beloved by the decorative Navajos. Down from the hills crept donkey-pulled travois bearing hides and wool. Indian lodges and Indian lances flashed on the flats.

"The governor comes . . . and people from all over the kingdom to those fairs, which they call ransoms. They bring captives to sell, buckskins, many buffalo hides and booty that they have taken in other parts —horses, guns, muskets, ammunition, knives, meat and various other things." There were dances and gambling and the game of *gallo*, where an Indian on a racing horse plucked a live rooster by its head from the sand and sprinted away while the rest of the contestants tried to wrench the trophy from him. There was also, until as late as 1867, slavery for debt, in case a man (or woman) bought beyond his means.

These fairs endured until 1800 or so; thereafter, for a short time, the little town of perhaps five hundred souls dozed in the sun. Then the trappers found Taos and, following Mexico's independence, wintered there in droves. By 1824 a distillery was turning out for their consumption that apparently inimitable brand of liquid fire which became famous throughout the Rockies as Taos Lightning. Barefooted girls padded across the dusty plaza in flimsy *camisas* that tantalized rather than concealed. Everyone came to the fandangos, according to eye-brow-raised Albert Pike (no kin to Zebulon), who watched one in 1833: "well-dressed women (they call them ladies), harlots, priests, thieves, half breed Indians—all spinning around together in the waltz. Here a filthy, ragged fellow with half a shirt, a pair of leather breeches and long dirty woolen stockings and Apache moccasins was hanging round with the pretty wife of Pedro Vigil; and there the priest was dancing with La Altragarcia, who paid her husband a regular sum to keep out of the way and so lived with an American. I was disgusted."

American traders discovered Taos almost as soon as did the mountain men. Their road, branching west across the Sangre de Cristos from the main Santa Fe Trail, was wide open to ambush, so the town tried to help them. When a wagon train was expected, a sentinel carrying a cross for protection slipped down the trail looking for Indian sign; on a strategic hill other scouts stood vigil. If danger threatened, these men built a fire where the village but not the raiders could see the wavering column of smoke, and out from Taos charged a relief party.

Much of the Taos trade came over the so-called northern or mountain branch of the Santa Fe Trail, thus avoiding the dreaded Cimarron desert and also offering a chance for recuperation and repairs at Bent's Fort on the Arkansas. Naturally the Bent brothers and St. Vrain were soon in the thick of the lucrative commerce. In 1832 Charles, the eldest, opened a branch store at Taos for the firm, and there he was soon joined by Ceran St. Vrain.

Both men took Mexican wives—not peasant girls. The Jamarillo family, into which Charles Bent married, were powers in Nueva Méjico, and Maria Jamarillo brought Bent an ample dowry. Maria also had a younger sister, Josepha. Josepha was only fifteen years old when Charles Bent's friend and employee, Kit Carson, saw her in 1842 or so, fell head over heels in love, and married her. But the Spanish mature early. An enthusiastic observer, Lewis Garrard, who saw Josepha Carson four years later, describes her in one vivid sentence: "Her beauty was of the haughty, heart-breaking kind—such as would lead a man with the glance of an eye to risk his life for one smile."

Other Bent associates also married into Taos aristocracy, Tom Boggs for one and also Lucien Maxwell, who had hunted with Kit at the fort and had gone with him on Frémont's early expeditions. Maxwell's wife was Luz Beaubien, daughter of Carlos Beaubien, born a French Canadian but by now so thoroughly Mexican that in 1841 he and Guadalupe Miranda won from slippery Governor Armijo a huge grant of mountain land two and a half times the size of the state of Rhode Island.

This is not mere genealogy we are dealing with here. These are the actors in as grisly a tragedy as the blood-spattered Rockies have ever known.

Always Taos was explosive; always the mercurial Mexicans and the Pueblos, sullen with their age-old superstitions of torture and cruelty, had resisted tampering. In 1837, for example, they revolted when General Santa Ana sent in an outsider named Albino Perez to be governor of New Mexico, chopped off Perez's head, and elected in his place one José Gonzales, an Indian of Taos Pueblo and "a good buffalo hunter." José, however, did not last long. Explorer Manuel Armijo, a slippery opportunist who at first had encouraged the Taos rebels, switched allegiance and led an avenging army of Mexican regulars in a reconquest of the province.

Rewarded with the governorship, Armijo ordered the captured Gonzales brought before him. The buffalo hunter was a simple soul. He remembered Armijo as a friend and greeted him with outstretched hand. "How do you do, *compañero?*"

Armijo shook hands. "How do you do, *compañero?* Confess yourself, *compañero.*" He turned to his soldiers. "Now shoot my *compañero.*"

So ended that revolt. But the spirit of intransigence still smoldered in Taos. Ten years later it would shift with almost insane fury to the new masters who came marching arrogantly in from the east.

In 1845 a rampant newspaper editor with a flair for words coined a phrase—Manifest Destiny—thus neatly packaging in two words Oregon in the Northwest, New Mexico and California in the Southwest. Eventually the English compromised in Oregon, but after the rape of Texas, Mexico was in no mood to dicker. War came in 1846. General Stephen Watts Kearny's bedraggled Army of the West straggled past Bent's Fort, blistered under 120° heat, gorged themselves until they vomited on the cool mountain waters of the Purgatoire, labored over Raton Pass, and finally limped into Las Vegas, New Mexico. There Kearny made a speech annexing New Mexico to the United States and promised the inhabitants, among other things, protection from the Indians, a security Mexico had never been able to provide—and neither would the United States for a few more decades to come.

In Santa Fe, Governor Armijo roared and rattled his saber, but Kearny's emissary, trader James Magoffin, got to him on the side; although breastworks were thrown up in Apache Canyon, no stand was made. Armijo scampered south and his province fell without a shot being fired. It was easy—too easy. The gratified Kearny attended a ball or two, delivered a few speeches, appointed Charles Bent (who, incidentally, was a graduate of West Point) governor of the new territory, left a few garrison troops behind to maintain order, and marched on toward California. Unfortunately for the Americans in Taos, he took Kit Carson with him as scout.

Under the genial surface discontent bubbled. No need to elaborate here on the frictions; they were much the same as those that always appear between conqueror and conquered. Kearny had scarcely headed west before a revolt was planned for Christmas Day, 1846. However, the mulatto girl-wife of one of the conspirators learned of the plot and ran tattling, so one legend goes, to Santa Fe's most notorious madam, Gertrude Barcelo, better known as La Tules or Doña Tules.

If the story is true, the little mulatto knew what she was doing. The once beautiful La Tules, her hands heavy with diamonds and her coarsening neck circled by three chains of gold, had influence where it counted. A monte dealer in her own gambling house, she had amassed a fortune; and when Colonel D. D. Mitchell appealed to her for a loan with which to outfit his Missouri Volunteers, she granted it—on condition that Mitchell squire her to a grand ball attended by the cream of Santa Fe society. This the colonel did. Society gagged but buckled, and the Missourians marched off with the supplies they needed. Thus there was a mutual debt between La Tules and the Army, and her relaying of the mulatto's story brought quicker action, perhaps, than if the warning had come through stodgier channels. The revolt was nipped in the bud.

The disaffection which had germinated it, however, was not nipped, particularly in Taos. There the Mexicans and the Indians of the Pueblo planned a new uprising for sunrise on January 19, 1847. Their chief target: Charles Bent.

Forming a new government is hard work. Bent was tired. His desk finally cleared and the Christmas revolt out of the way, he went home to Taos to rest. He was warned. But he would not leave, nor would he accept a guard. The people of Taos were his friends. He had married there, had lived among them for years. Surely he was in no danger.

All night long on the eighteenth Taos was in an uproar. Nonetheless, Bent put his household to bed just as though the village were as quiet as ever. In addition to his own family he was sheltering two frightened visitors, Tom Boggs's wife and Kit Carson's Josepha, not yet out of her teens. In another part of town Lucien Maxwell's young brother-in-law, Narcisse Beaubien, just back from college, was being careful not to show his nose on the streets. A question inevitably arises:

how much difference would it have made if just three cool fighters had been in Taos that night? Carson, Boggs, Maxwell, hard-trained on the fur streams of the Rockies, where the odds were never in a man's favor. . . . But they weren't there.

At dawn a mob surged up the street to Bent's door. When his wife Maria tried to thrust a pair of pistols in his hands he shook his head. Resistance would only madden the mob and engulf the women; besides, he still could not believe his former friends meant him personal violence. In his night clothes he went to the door and tried to talk to them. Behind him the terrified women, using a poker and an iron spoon, started digging a hole through the adobe wall into the house next door.

The mob howled Bent down. He slammed the heavy door in their faces, and his ten-year-old son Alfredo came to him lugging a shotgun. "Let's fight them, Papa." Gently Bent laid the gun aside, well knowing that if one of the mob died now, his whole family would be massacred in retaliation. Unarmed, he faced the quivering door while the women, shielded by his back, clawed at the wall.

A panel splintered. On the other side of the breach bows twanged. One arrow struck Bent in the chin, another in the stomach. Still he held his feet, trying to talk. Behind him the women pushed five-year-old Teresina Bent through the hole, then Alfredo, then each other. The door fell with a crash and Bent stepped to the threshold. The mob struck him down, knifed off his scalp. And still he lived. Somehow he broke free, staggered to the hole, and crawled through, holding one hand to the top of his bleeding head.

Years later Teresina Bent told the rest of the story: " . . . It was too late. Some of the men came after him through the hole and others came over the roof of the house and down into the yard. They broke down the doors and rushed upon my father. He was shot many times and fell dead at our feet. The pleading and tears of my mother and the sobbing of us children had no power to soften the hearts of the enraged Indians and Mexicans.

"At first they were going to take the rest of us away as prisoners, but finally decided to leave us where we were. They ordered that no one should feed us, and then left us alone with our great sorrow. We were without food and had no covering but our night-clothing, all that day and the next. The body of our father remained on the floor in a pool of blood. . . .

"At three o'clock the next morning some of our Mexican friends stole up to the house and gave us food and clothing. That day also they took my father to bury him. A few days later we were allowed to go to their house. Mrs. Carson and Mrs. Boggs were sheltered by a friendly old Mexican, who took them to his home, disguising them as squaws and set them to grinding corn on metates in his kitchen."

Nearly every American or American sympathizer in Taos died that day, including Narcisse Beaubien and his body servant, who were dragged from their hiding place in a stable manger, killed, and scalped. Then on to Turley's mill and distillery, twelve miles away, roared the insurgents. For two days Turley and nine mountain men held them off, but finally the attackers succeeded in setting fire to the building. The besieged broke for safety; only Turley and one other made it. They separated. Seeking shelter, Turley went to a neighbor whom he had befriended. The man hid him in a deserted house, rode to the mill, and betrayed him.

When news of the disaster reached Bent's Fort on the Arkansas, the Cheyenne chiefs offered to send the entire tribe against New Mexico. With tears in his eyes William Bent refused. He could not set loose a horror like that, but he hit the trail himself at the head of twenty-three volunteers from the fort. Beside him rode Tom Boggs and Lucien Maxwell. But the January snows were deep, the winds bitter. They could not get to Taos in time for the pay-off.

In Santa Fe, Colonel Sterling Price called in some of his scattered garrisons. With him, grim as death, rode Ceran St. Vrain and his Santa Fe Volunteers, many of them mountain men to whom Charles Bent had been a personal friend. On the twenty-fourth a rabble of fifteen hundred Mexicans and Pueblos challenged the avengers near Santa Cruz. A quick, sharp battle killed thirty-six of the insurgents, sent the rest flying. They re-formed at Embudo Canyon. St. Vrain's volunteers and a company of regular troops charged up the snowy slopes, outflanked them, swept them aside.

Taos was found deserted amid the knee-deep snow. The rebels had barricaded themselves in the squat, massive church at the Pueblo, two miles beyond. Price wheeled up his cannon, but the thick adobe walls absorbed the shells like a sponge. Next, under cover of grapeshot, sappers fired the roof and with axes and crowbars hacked a small hole in one wall. Through this gap they tossed improvised bombs which dealt wicked carnage inside the crowded house of peace. Then cannon ran up within a few yards of the hole, blasted it wider, and now attackers stormed the breach while other squads rushed the great front doors with battering-rams and axes.

Inside the reeking church a hundred or more men lay dead or wounded. Panic swept the Pueblos. As the huge front doors crashed down, they bolted from the back, fleeing for their lives. At their heels rode St. Vrain and his men, clubbing them down. One huge buck fell, shamming death. When St. Vrain stooped over him, the Indian seized him, tried to stab him with an iron-pointed arrow. It might have been a close thing had not Uncle Dick Wootton chanced by with a tomahawk.

Those participants in Bent's murder who had not already died were tried almost on the spot. Undoubtedly they deserved it, but not on the charge leveled—treason—and not by the jury that was sworn in. It was completely prejudiced. James Hatcher, one of its members, summed up their attitude when he said, speaking of himself in the third person as the mountain men were wont to do:

"This hoss has a feelin' for poor human nature in most any fix, but for these palous [the defendants] he doesn't care a cuss. This coon has made Injuns go under some, wagh! but he's never sculped 'em alive [referring, of course, to Bent] . . . and he says it's onhuman, again nature, an' they ought to choke."

Choke they did. Sixteen of the defendants were found guilty and hauled under the gallows in a single wagon drawn by two mules. Cannon bristled on the hills to preclude attempts at rescue, Sheriff Metcalf entered a charge at the store "To soft soap for greasing nooses . . . 12½ ¢," someone hit the mules a lick, and that was that.

There were other heritages of trouble which Mexico left her conquerors. In the long run none caused more headaches than the huge land grants, and of these grants none proved more vexatious than Lucien Maxwell's 2680 square miles of land in northern New Mexico and southern Colorado. Half of these juicy mountain miles of cattle, sheep, and horse lands, of grain and hay fields, of gold and coal deposits, the one-time fur trapper inherited through his father-in-law, Carlos Beaubien. The rest he purchased from the other heirs after he had driven several thousand sheep from New Mexico to California and had sold them at a fantastic profit in the mining towns.

The vitality in Maxwell's great-muscled frame was as limitless as his acres. Life was enjoyment. So it had been on the beaver streams; so it was now in the huge stone house he built at Cimarron and stuffed with ornate furniture hauled over the Santa Fe Trail he knew so well. He drank hard, gambled prodigiously, entertained with baronial magnificence. Yet essentially he was a simple, openhearted man. The Apaches and the Utes, whose agent he was, trusted him implicitly, came to him for counsel; the dark cult of the Penitentes knew that he would not persecute them.

Had he wished, he might have been far richer than he was. There was gold on the grant, and he knew it. But he did not want it—or the heartaches he sensed would come with it. The most he did was put a handful of nuggets in a buckskin sack and give them to his six children, shiny baubles to play with on the ranch-house floor. Yet in the end it was gold that broke him.

Inevitably the mineral discoveries in Colorado led prospectors to push south, during the sixties, along the high ribs of the Sangre de Cristos onto Maxwell land. They were not the first interlopers. Settlers had also been edging in, hoping to obtain "squatters' rights" to home-steads in spite of the fact that the Mexican grants had all been legally recognized, in principle at least, by an 1860 congressional "Act to Confirm Certain Private Land Claims in New Mexico Territory." Bucking these trespassers had caused Maxwell some trouble, but nothing like that which followed the gold strikes in the mountains above Taos and brought a stampede of ten thousand people to Elizabethtown and Red River, to Moreno Valley, Ute and Willow creeks.

In self-defense Maxwell turned belatedly to mining ventures of his own, but his proverbial luck deserted him and he lost heavily while almost at his elbow trespassers reaped fortunes off his land. Drive them away? An army could not have done it. He did try to assert ownership by claiming royalties on the output of the mines, but the vindictive bitterness and legal snarls which met the attempt were not the kind of battle which Lucien Maxwell, mountain man, could stomach. There were private troubles too. Against his wishes his daughter secretly married a certain Captain Keyes; in a passion Maxwell sought out the minister who had performed the ceremony and threatened to rawhide him; then, cooling down, he followed the girl to New York, gave her ten thousand dollars—and, according to legend, never saw her again.

By 1870 the piling harassments were too much and he sold the grant, lock, stock, and barrel, for a niggardly $650,000. Three months later the purchasers resold it for twice that sum. But perhaps he was well out of the mess. Though the gold-mining boom faded away, the rush of settlers swelled. Maxwell's successors waged an endless war of eviction that in time led to the enlistment of company militia, the importation of hired gunmen, the formation of vigilante committees by the "anti-grant" people, and the turning of all Colfax County into such a hornets' nest that "the sheriff . . . and his deputies were of necessity men who had made out their last wills and testaments."

The attention of the entire United States was drawn to the battle and to the complex legal actions which ended with the Supreme Court's confirmation of the grant's title. As a result of the uproar a Court of Private Land Claims was instituted in 1885 to bring order out of the whole land-grant chaos. However, titles remained so cloudy, until surveys and hearings were completed about 1903, that settlement of southern Colorado and northern New Mexico by Anglo-Americans was severely retarded. Since then, of course, the Maxwell grant and its gargantuan cousins have been whittled down by private sale.

Meanwhile, what of Lucien Maxwell? He went to Santa Fe, founded New Mexico's first bank (his previous experience having consisted of keeping his loose change in an old cowhide trunk on the ranch), and issued bank notes that bore a picture of him smoking a fat cigar. It was no business for a mountain man. Neither was the Texas and Pacific Railroad, in which he lost a quarter of a million dollars. Restless, yearning for the days that were gone, he tried to re-create the old life by buying from the Army the abandoned buildings at Fort Sumner in eastern New Mexico. (Here, in 1881, in the bedroom of the house he remodeled and passed on to his son Peter, Billy the Kid was shot down in the darkness by Sheriff Pat Garrett.) As of old, he gambled hard, raised race horses, entertained with a lavish hand. But the taste was gone. Time had caught up with Lucien Maxwell, just as throughout the Rockies it was overtaking and shattering the men and the things he had lived by. In 1875, heartbroken, almost in poverty, he died.

CHAPTER III

GET US THROUGH!

BEAVER PELTS and Mexican dollars were not enough. Always, for some men, fulfillment lay beyond the horizon, and to their eyes the Rockies loomed as a heart-stopping barrier. "Get us through!" During more than two centuries kings, ministers, and presidents passed the fruitless order on to their explorers. England's Drake circumnavigated continents looking for the Straits of Anian and a salt-water passage to India. Rumors that he had found it so frightened Spain that in 1598 Oñate's colonists were sent into New Mexico to assert dominion over the mountainous lands through which the passage supposedly led. Slowly it dawned on the caballeros that there was no strait, at least none they could reach, and that the crossing would have to be made by land. Yet in spite of their being first on the backbone of the continent they never did attain the Pacific by shank's mare from New Mexico. Escalante, who tried in 1776, could push the unknown no farther back than the southern end of Great Salt Lake Basin.

Even before Escalante's time vague Indian tales of the Salt Lake had given a new twist to the old myth. Surely a body of salt water as vast as the one described must be connected to the sea. In far-off Europe romantic cartographers etched onto their maps a Buenaventura River flowing west from the inland lake to the Pacific. French trappers, picking up the legend and at times confusing the Buenaventura with still another "River of the West" (the Columbia of today), paddled up the Missouri with fresh heart, sublimating the dream of a salt-water passage to one of fresh water. But the Missouri fingered out into baffling tributaries, and no matter which way the *voyageurs* turned, there the Rockies of Wyoming and Montana loomed, shining, aloof, impenetrable.

Strangely enough, the first traverse of the continent was completed far north in Canada by Alexander Mackenzie in 1793, but as a commercial route the zigzag river trails were impossible: cold, wild, fit only for half-breed *coureurs de bois* who could wolf out the winters like Indians on a handful of pemmican. Surely there was a better way farther south, if only it could be found.

That upstart among nations, the United States, discovered one. In the summer of 1805 Lewis and Clark breasted the passes between the Missouri and the Columbia and trundled triumphantly down to the Pacific. Americans were elated, none more so than a New York fur merchant named John Jacob Astor. Almost immediately, however, the Lewis and Clark route proved impractical. It, too, looped far north of the settlements along the Mississippi, and, even worse, it was dangerous. Blackfoot Indians soon scattered the trappers who risked its rigors, and when Astor's overland expedition, led by Wilson Price Hunt, came poling up the Missouri in 1811, they were warned by three of the survivors to find another route. And they did. Led by the very mountain men who had warned them, the Hunt party swung south across the Wind River Mountains of Wyoming, only to plunge to disaster in the canyon of Idaho's Snake River on one of the grimmest treks in the long, grim annals of the West.

Three breaches made and not one of them feasible! In the whole breadth of America was there no easy pass by which this merciless divide could be pierced?

Indian-borne rumors of such a gap reached the ears of young Robert Stuart. He had journeyed by ship to Astor's new post on the Columbia and in 1812 was ordered with six survivors of the Hunt party to return overland to St. Louis with dispatches for the anxious owner of the post. Southeastward Stuart's tiny party struck, following a broad Indian trace that offered great promise. Then hostile Crows bobbed up in the party's way, and the seven frightened men scurried northward, hoping to escape over Hunt's old crossing through the Wind Rivers. It was no use. Not far west of the Tetons the pursuing savages struck, and the whites lost every horse they had. On foot they straggled east, racing winter in a dreadful journey filled with quarrels, sickness, starvation, and whispered threats of cannibalism which Robert Stuart silenced with a cocked rifle.

Finally, on the eighteenth of October 1812, somewhere along the watershed of Wyoming's Green River the derelicts encountered a village of Snake Indians who, like themselves, had been raided by Crows. In return for a few trinkets these companions in misery gave the wanderers a little meat, some desperately needed leather for moccasins, and, best of all, one lame, ancient horse, all skin and bones. For half a year this sorry beast served Stuart's men, packing what it could and sharing their long winter bivouac, where it dieted on cottonwood bark. The next spring, on reaching the Missouri, it was traded off for a canoe.

During that trek the historic creature followed its footsore masters around the southern end of the Wind River Mountains, over a broad pass so gradual that its exact apex could not be discerned, and down the then unnamed Sweetwater Creek to the Platte. Quite by accident Robert Stuart's returning Astorians had stumbled on the gateway to the West, South Pass, the storied heart of the Oregon Trail.

Though the breach had been made, the times were not right. Dogged by disaster, war, and treachery, Astor's distant outpost on the Columbia passed into the hands of Britain's Northwest Fur Company, and there was no need for American supply caravans to use the trail Stuart had blazed. South Pass was forgotten.

But not for long. Gradually the East struggled out of the doldrums caused by the War of 1812, British intrigue among the tribes of the Northwest slacked off for a time, and when Manuel Lisa came floating down the Missouri with thirty-five thousand dollars' worth of beaver pelts there were men who sat up and took notice, among them Andrew Henry and William Ashley. Straightway the two launched themselves into such a hornets' nest of Indian troubles that in 1823 Ashley vowed to quit the Missouri and work overland. To test the plan, a group of trappers was dispatched cross-country to the Shining Mountains, their leader a Bible-packing, twenty-four-year-old youth named Jedediah Smith, probably the greatest explorer the United States has known.

On this trip Jed Smith ran afoul of a grizzly bear that all but scalped him alive. Small matter. Jim Clyman sewed the frayed scalp and mangled ear back into place, and on the party went, bumping hard against the ice-clean peaks of Wyoming's Wind River Mountains in midwinter. Shivering, the men swung south and, in March 1824, stumbled on Robert Stuart's pass. Did any· among them recognize it? No record says so, yet Stuart's feat was of a kind likely to be remembered in the tale-loving taverns of St. Louis and along the lonely rivers.

Never again would South Pass be forgotten. During the next dozen years many another crossing was found, but none like this one. Broad, rolling, grassy, it contained good camp sites and good water—so good that the creek at its eastern approach was called the Sweetwater (though one contrary tale says the name came when a pack horse dumped a load of sugar in the stream). By 1830, South Pass was the focal point of the fluid West. Trails of countless trappers funneled into it from both sides; Indian tepee poles furrowed its sod as whole nations journeyed to the annual fur rendezvous. Experimental wagons inched up and over. Grades were so easy that generations of Americans refused to believe the truth. Even using instruments, Frémont in 1842 could not fix the summit, and hundreds of amazed wayfarers bound for Oregon or California corroborated the observation in their diaries and letters; yet today the notion still persists of a rugged defile pitching sharply up to a knife-edged ridge whereon the fabled but never-yet-seen drop of water could split itself in twain, one half rolling to the Atlantic, the other to the Pacific.

At long last the way was known; the guides were ready. When the new cry came, "Can you get us through?" the mountain men would answer, "Yes!"

Oddly, the first to ask were Oregon-bound missionaries, Jason and Daniel Lee's small band in 1834, and then, two years later, a man of tremendous import to the entire Pacific Northwest. He was Marcus Whitman, a lay physician who in 1836 accompanied Dr. Samuel Parker, the stiffly dignified fifty-six-year-old former head of a girls' school, to the mountains on a sort of scouting trip for the American Board of Foreign Missions. At the turbulent rendezvous on the Green River in southwestern Wyoming, Whitman impressed himself forever on Western folklore by slicing loose a three-inch iron arrowhead which for the past three years had been embedded in Jim Bridger's horny back, a heroic open-air operation that promptly became legend among the mountain men.[1]

At the same rendezvous Whitman and Parker were given a rousing welcome by a delegation of Flatheads and Nez Percés, or, more properly, Salish Indians. Innately religious, the Nez Percés were also motivated by an inarticulate notion that in embracing the white man's gods they would also embrace, as a corollary, such items of white medicine as glass beads, tin kettles, guns, powder, and perhaps even a bit of whisky. Quite probably Whitman and Parker did not then detect this

---

[1] There were others. Kit Carson, running away from Missouri with one of Charles Bent's wagon trains, helped cut off and cauterize with a heated bolt the injured arm of a teamster. Peg-leg Smith's amputation of his own leg is said to have been duplicated by Milton Sublette, although Bernard De Voto doubts the tale. Be that as it may, the Sublette legend helped name a Wyoming county. Legislator Perry Jenkins, having laid out the tract, suggested to the lawmakers that it be named after Wyoming's five fur-trading Sublette brothers. Another legislator, so Jenkins told me with fiery scorn, dared object: why call a county which might endure forever after a bunch of forgotten Creoles?

Fiercely Jenkins turned on the objector and told how Milton Sublette, wounded by a poisoned arrow while seventy-five miles from camp, sat on a log and chipped saw teeth into the blade of his Green River knife. With another knife a companion sliced through the flesh to the bone. Milton tied up the arteries, then sawed through the bone and seared the stump with a red-hot hatchet.

"When your waistline is that big," Jenkins snapped at his adversary, "we'll name a county after you."

Objection withdrawn.

quirk of the savage mind, but the enthusiastic reception convinced them that here was a fertile field for sowing. While Parker, attended by an ecstatic escort of red devotees, traveled north to Pierre's Hole with Jim Bridger, Whitman returned East for more workers, more supplies, more everything—including a wife, the lovely Narcissa, her soft red-gold hair and clear sweet voice an incongruous target for the tomahawks which would strike her and her husband down some years later.

Among the zealots who the following year accompanied the newly-weds back across South Pass were Henry Spaulding and his dark, dour Eliza. As Whitman and Parker had done the year before, the cavalcade traveled with a fur-trade supply caravan. They had a wagon with them (which eventually they had to abandon in the rocky wilderness of Idaho), plus several milk cows; and along the way the women tried to preserve the amenities. At halting places they would spread an India-rubber sheet on the ground, polish up sticks for forks, and invite various astounded mountain men to "tea."

Triumph, Rocky Mountain style. When the Whitman party dropped down South Pass to the rendezvous on Horse Creek, several hundred yearning, grease-stained, whisker-bristling males put on the most thunderous welcome any females ever experienced. The Indians, who had heard that whites saluted their women with kisses, all but smothered the pair under noisome embraces. Bashful trappers bobbed into their tents, ostensibly to get religious tracts, and bobbed out again with a strange restlessness gnawing at their hearts. Joe Meek, mightiest bear hunter of them all, spun his yarns to Narcissa by firelight and began to dream of a farm in Oregon.

For a week the party rested on the Green. When the women of the Sublette County Historical Society commemorated the event a hundred years later, one of them said wryly, "They ought to be remembered; they were the only women who were ever able to rest in Wyoming." Then on the little troop went, conscious of history making. Narcissa Whitman and Eliza Spaulding were the first white women to cross the Big Divide. And women meant homes. In 1838 four more came with their missionary husbands. Jim Bridger's men, drunk, howling, smeared with ocher and vermilion, welcomed them with so uproarious a scalp dance that their dog plunged into the Popo Agie and swam across for dear life.

Women . . . Where a missionary's wife could go, could not a farmer's wife go as well?

It was a haunting question in the minds of many a woman during the late 1830s. Eastward, depression lay like a blight on the land. Meanwhile rumors of abundance in Oregon were trickling across the mountains—letters from the Whitmans and from Jason Lee, and finally Lee himself, painting pictures from Midwestern lecture platforms of fertile fields for the taking, of unlimited wheat markets in the Orient, of sea-otter pelts and lumber. Mortgaged farmers stirred. Oregon. The end of the world. But if a man had nerve enough . . .

In 1841 fifty-five of them found their nerve, and of that restless number five had wives who refused to stay behind. They joined forces with eleven Catholic missionaries under famed Father Pierre-Jean de Smet; and in late July one of the greatest of the mountain men, Tom "Broken Hand" Fitzpatrick, guided their thirteen wagons and four Red River carts across the Green, up Bear River Divide. Decision now. Along the fork to the right lay the blazed trail to Oregon; leftward wound the untried way to California.

Destiny's pattern revealed itself. The party split. Sixteen men and four women chose Oregon. The Bidwell-Bartleson group, including Nancy Kelsey, chose California. Nancy Kelsey . . . The name should be better known. After the wagons had been abandoned in the terrible deserts of the Great Basin, she rode and walked with her baby in her arms down the alkali wastes of the Humboldt, over the Sierra to the sunny Sacramento, eating the oxen that died, subsisting once on the entrails of coyotes, half naked, barefoot. Had not Joel Walker's wife come down from Oregon a few weeks earlier, Nancy Kelsey would have been the first white woman to reach California by land.

Far behind on Blacks Fork of the Green, Jim Bridger, now known to his cronies as Old Gabe, stared at their tracks and pondered. "Get us through!" And the fur business had collapsed. Old Gabe started to build a trading post, first with one partner, later with another, and taking time out whenever he felt like it to ramble off over half the West, either on his own or as a guide for anyone who wanted to go anywhere. Critical wayfarers found Jim's carelessly tended "fort" shabby enough, but to many a man in need it spelled, during the years, salvation. And Old Gabe was pleased. He borrowed a letter writer from some passing train and relayed the news to Pierre Choteau in St. Louis. "In coming out here they [the emigrants] are generally well supplied with money, but by the time they get here they are in need of all kind of supplies, horses, provisions, etc." Old Gabe, first on the ground, knew what to do about that.

The wheels were rolling now, the cry swelling. "Get us through!" Information—that was the need. Accurate maps to replace the crude drawings of Gallatin and Bonneville. Guidebooks to give detailed instructions concerning water holes, camp grounds, equipment, game, Indians, stream crossings, passes. In addition there were such secret considerations as the location of sites for forts and the surveying of a military road to the West, just in case Great Britain, then exercising joint sovereignty with the United States over Oregon, got expansionist notions of her own.

Compiling these facts would be a man-sized job, but back in Washington, Senator Thomas Hart Benton of Missouri thought he knew the person who could do it: his own handsome, brilliant, erratic son-in-law, John Charles Frémont, since called the "Pathfinder." It was high time for a little scientific pathfinding. When Kit Carson guided Frémont's first expedition into South Pass on August 5, 1842, Langford Hastings was already on the road with 160 Oregon-bound emigrants. The next year, as Frémont's second expedition labored toward the Cascades, it shared the way with the celebrated Great Migration of Northwest history, a mass hegira of nearly 1000 men, women, and children, 121 wagons, 694 draft oxen, and 773 loose cattle, fortunately guided not by Frémont but by Marcus Whitman, who was returning from an emergency winter trip to Washington.

On the face of it, as some historians have tirelessly pointed out, all this makes Frémont's title sound a little silly. Well, the Pathfinder tag wasn't Frémont's idea, and the criticism overlooks the fact that, although many people preceded him nearly everywhere he went, he was the first competently trained cartographer to touch the crest of the Rockies. On his two earliest expeditions he conscientiously and thoroughly did what he had been sent out to do: mark trails (not find them) and tie them together with exact observations. More important, he described those trails in readable prose which any farmer bound West could understand.

When Frémont's report was issued in 1845 it met as receptive an audience as any book has ever had. Among its avid readers was a group of religious zealots who had been harried first out of Missouri, then out of their hopeful new settlement at Nauvoo, Illinois. Their prophet murdered, their homes aflame, the first panic-stricken bands of them stumbled across the ice of the Mississippi on February 6, 1846 and headed West. Where in the West? Not Oregon. Too many emigrants were already there; too good a chance existed that the region would become part of the United States. But California belonged to Mexico:

The Upper California, O that's the land for me—
It lies between the mountains and the great Pacific sea.

The Saints can be protected there, and enjoy their liberty
In Upper California, O that's the land for me.

"Upper California" was then a vague geographical term embracing a vast territory. Where in California? As a whole people marched into the unknown with their gods and their pathetic dabs of goods, with their bickerings and their magnificent faith, Brigham Young pinpointed their destination. "This is the place"—Utah. Two years were spent by the first army of Mormons in toiling fearfully across the plains and over South Pass. When finally they reached their promised land, the war with Mexico was over and the government they had thought to escape ruled all the country between the mountains and the great Pacific sea. Flight into irony. For weal or woe, destiny lay under the Stars and Stripes.

More thousands poured in to share that destiny. Many of them came from overseas, and to aid these converts in reaching Utah the "Perpetual Emigrating Fund for the Poor" was devised. Unfortunately many of its beneficiaries failed to keep their promise about repaying loans, and by 1856 the fund was in parlous state. Meanwhile hundreds of destitute newcomers begged at the edge of the plains, "Get us through!"

The answer was a two-wheeled wooden handcart mounted on a wooden axle and capable of carrying from four to five hundred pounds of baggage. Motive power was furnished by the emigrants themselves, who stood in pairs between the cart's forward-protruding shafts and pushed against a crossbar. The average company numbered five hundred persons. In theory, though practice often brought variations downward, there were four handcarts and one tent for each twenty emigrants, plus an occasional wagon (roughly one to a hundred persons) for hauling provisions. It was an arduous way to travel. But it was cheap. One party journeyed the thousand miles at a cost of $22.30 per person; and enthusiasm, reinforced by military discipline, made the method effective. A day's march of thirty miles was not uncommon, and in four years some three thousand Saints handcarted themselves almost a third of the way across the continent to Utah.

Some must push and some must pull
As we go marching up the hill
As merrily on the way we go
Until we reach the Valley Oh!

"Merrily" was at times an exaggeration. On October 18, 1856, a blizzard caught the Willie Company in South Pass. By the time rescuers rushed out from Utah the emigrants had been without food for forty-eight hours and a sixth of its nearly five hundred members were dead, fifteen of them in the pass itself. Wrote one rescuer: "The train was strung out for three or four miles. There were old men pulling and tugging at their carts, many of which were loaded with sick wives and children. We saw little children, six and eight years old, struggling through the snow and mud. As night came on the mud and snow froze to their clothes." The relief party fed them, hauled in firewood, but it wasn't quite soon enough. Nine more died before shelter was reached at Jim Bridger's fort. And behind them a worse tragedy was shaping up for 576 English converts led by Captain Howard Martin. In nine snowbound days at Devil's Gate, at the eastern foot of the pass, a hundred people perished and were buried in a single trench.

Drops in the bucket. Gold had been discovered in California. By 1849 the rush through South Pass reached such proportions (one estimate for the year '49: 8000 wagons, 80,000 draft animals, 25,000–30,000 people) that the popeyed Indians, believing the East depopulated, seriously discussed going there and seizing the vacated lands. And still the tide grew. They came in elaborately equipped companies, in destitute handfuls. They rode horses and mules, prodded oxen, walked with packs on their backs. Invariably they overloaded their vehicles, wore out their animals, and, when it was too late to help matters, discarded their useless possessions. From Fort Laramie, Wyoming, to the Sierra so many creatures died that journals of the trip complain continuously about the unending stench. Though the hordes' greatest fear was of Indians, more died from accidents with their own weapons than from redskin attacks. Cholera, dysentery, sore eyes, scurvy, exhaustion, exposure, drowning, hunger, and ineptness—those were the villains of this mighty drama that has been told too many times to need retelling here.

"Get us through!" The cry was a thunder now, but of all the vehicles that annually crossed the mountains there was not one, during the 1850s, that offered transportation to the general public! The first stagecoaches to reach California went nineteen thousand miles around Cape Horn in ships; and although for years Asa Whitney had been lobbying in Congress for a railroad to the Pacific, no rails had been laid toward the Continental Divide. The reason, of course, was politics. North and South were heading pell-mell toward disaster, and neither side dared strengthen the other by letting it tie itself to the burgeoning empires on the coast.

Still, the cry was too loud to ignore completely. In 1848, John Frémont, smarting under a recent court-martial, tried to salvage his reputation by finding a railroad pass over the Colorado Rockies. Working on his own and financed in part by men interested in a Pacific railroad, he deliberately tackled the mountains in the dead of winter, saying he wanted to learn firsthand the most difficult conditions under which a railway might have to operate.

He learned.

When his cavalcade of thirty-three men and one hundred and twenty pack mules clattered through Bent's Fort in mid-November 1848, the mountain men told him he was crazy. None would serve as guide, but Frémont pushed on to Pueblo and there hired Old Bill Williams. Red-headed Bill was a good trapper, but eccentric—to put things mildly. North Carolina-born and Missouri-raised, he had started his career as an itinerant preacher, trying to convert the Osage Indians. Before long the Indians converted Bill, and after his Osage wife had died, he headed his unwashed, grease-glazed body West. Tall, gaunt, as tough and hump-backed as a barrel stave, he had covered the entire Rocky Mountain area, sometimes with other trappers but more often alone, riding his crowbait horse with such short stirrups that his knees appeared, grasshopper-like, to reach almost up to his hunched shoulders. The Indians liked him, but eventually his love of liquor made him betray their trust. A few months before Frémont appeared on the scene Bill misappropriated a bale of furs some Utes had given him to sell for a monstrous drunk in Taos, and then topped off the treachery by leading a punitive expedition of soldiers against a combined band of Utes and Apaches. In the battle that followed thirty-six Indians were killed and Old Bill received a bullet-shattered arm. He had just convalesced from the wound when he hired out to Frémont as a guide.

Pushing over the Sangre de Cristo Range into the San Luis Valley gave the expedition a foretaste of what lay ahead—deep snow, below-zero temperatures, frozen hands and feet, short rations, and starving mules. Reaching the Rio Grande River on December 11, the leader and his guide fell into a bitter quarrel. Three routes were open: a northward swing to ninety-two-hundred-foot Cochetopa, the Ute "Pass of the Buffaloes"; a southward detour through the easier and milder terrain of New Mexico; or a course due west via Wagon Wheel Gap, an opening on the Rio Grande which Williams claimed to have discovered some years earlier. Finally they started up the Rio Grande, then unaccountably veered into the La Garita Hills, where no pass at all existed. Whose fault? Frémont blamed Old Bill: "The error of our journey was committed in engaging this man. He proved never to have known, or entirely to have forgotten, the whole region," an observation later supported by various of Frémont's men but scoffed at by trappers in Taos, who held a high respect for Old Bill Williams's abilities. Moreover, others of Frémont's party insisted that their leader ignored their guide's advice entirely and himself selected the route. Probably the tension between them led both men to make angry mistakes, and out of those mistakes stalked the grim specter of death.

After a hideous ordeal the party floundered onto the treeless top of the Continental Divide, twelve thousand feet high. Twice Frémont attempted to force a way down the other side. Twice screaming blizzards and bottomless drifts drove the men back. Starving mules dropped dead; living ones, in a frenzy, devoured their tie ropes, the blankets that were used to cover them at night, even one another's manes and tails. The situation of the men was scarcely better. In despair Frémont ordered four of the party, including Williams, to hasten to the New Mexico settlements for succor. Slowly the rest followed after them, cruelly hampered by Frémont's order that they take all the expedition's baggage with them.

Sixteen days passed and no relief appeared. By now one of the party had frozen to death; the others had eaten the last of the mules and were boiling rawhide ropes and parfleches for soup. In this extremity Frémont and four men hurried ahead down the Rio Grande. Six days later they found Old Bill and two of his companions, tottering skeletons who, for some inexplicable reason, had in three weeks advanced only fifty miles from their starting point. The fourth man, King, was dead; subsequent charges of cannibalism, never definitely proved, were leveled at the survivors, whom Frémont put on some emaciated horses he luckily obtained from a band of Utes. Four days later the gaunt group reached the settlements. From Rio Hondo and Taos, Frémont dispatched relief to the main party. All but snow-blind and with one leg frozen, he did not return with the rescuers, though some of the men who had come down the river with him did.

Meanwhile the remnants of the party had been creeping southward, subsisting—those who did live—on dried buds, water bugs, and the carcass of a dead wolf. They straggled out for miles, vomiting, crawling on bleeding hands and knees, some of them raving mad. By the time rescue arrived, eleven of the expedition's original thirty-three members had died.

Nursed back to health by Kit Carson at Taos, Frémont re-formed the broken party and continued on to California. To salvage the records and instruments that had been left behind in the drifts he chose the very man he accused of the disaster—Old Bill Williams. But Old Bill never made it. During the search, as he and a companion were hunched over one of their campfires, they were shot down by vengeful Utes and died without ever knowing what had hit them.

So glaring a failure could hardly further the cause of a railroad through the central Rockies. The emigrants, however, were becoming so vociferous that to appease them the government in 1850 instituted a wretched once-a-month mail wagon traveling from Independence, Missouri, over South Pass to Salt Lake City, where it was joined by a mule train operating from Sacramento. Finally, in 1853, surveys for a railroad were authorized, one south through Texas, one north through Montana, and a potentially compromissary middle route along Frémont's fatal thirty-eighth parallel in Colorado. The Wyoming path was deemed well enough known not to require additional surveying at this time.

All routes proved feasible. Captain John Gunnison, whose party included several survivors of the Frémont disaster, took twenty wagons over Cochetopa Pass and on to Sevier Lake in western Utah. There Gunnison and six of his men were massacred by Indians and their mutilated bodies so gnawed by wolves that only a few fragments could be found for burial. Gunnison's second-in-command, Lieutenant E. G. Beckwith, carried the caravan on to California, but a survey is not necessarily a commitment. The government still refused to provide any sort of transportation to the West—until suddenly the so-called Mormon War of 1857 startled Congress out of its internecine North-South bickerings.

Relationships between the Saints and the government from which they had once tried to flee were strained. Though Brigham Young had been appointed governor of the new territory of Utah, the rest of the officials were sent out from Washington. Men of poor caliber, they made bad matters worse by lecturing the Mormons on morals, legal practices, and ethics in general. The Saints, believing that isolation made them invulnerable, retaliated by being intransigent. A string of frustrated officials went back to Washington in a huff; and certain apostate Mormons, grinding axes of their own, spread enough wild tales to convince hotheads in the East that the territory was in revolt. One rumor, for example, insisted that both Gunnison and a territorial secretary named Babbitt, killed in 1856, had been slain not by Indians but by Mormons in disguise.

In final anger the government removed Brigham Young as governor and dispatched Albert Sidney Johnston with a sizable army to restore order. Brigham promptly summoned out the Utah militia and fortified the passes leading into the basin. In public "The Lion of the Lord" breathed fire; in private, however, he ordered Lot Smith to spill no blood while harrying Johnston's supply columns.

Smith was notably successful. He destroyed several of Johnston's wagons, and the Army was forced to go into camp near the remains of Jim Bridger's fort, which the Mormons had recently burned to the ground on the probably justifiable suspicion that Old Gabe was selling guns to the Utes.

Fearing himself cut off, Johnston, on November 24, 1857, sent Captain R. B. Marcy and forty men scurrying south to Fort Union, New Mexico, for supplies. The march came within an ace of duplicating Frémont's tragedy. In crossing Cochetopa Pass the men had to crawl on hands and knees to break trail and soon were eating their own starved mules, sprinkling the steaks with gunpowder in lieu of salt and pepper. However, rescuers reached them and, in March 1858, Marcy was able to leave Fort Union with the necessary supplies and reinforcements. Near the present site of Denver a spring blizzard scattered the column's stock and froze one man to death. While the soldiers were recuperating, an Army teamster panned gold from the South Platte River. Harbinger of history. Having received his discharge a short time later, the teamster went to Missouri, showed his dab of dust, and thus contributed one more mite toward starting the Colorado gold rush of 1859, which, among other things, increased the West's transportation crisis.

Back in northern Utah, the beleaguered Saints abandoned cities and towns in preparation for another flight. Then a compromise was effected. In June 1858, Johnston's army marched through the deserted streets of Salt Lake, and slowly the Saints straggled back, sullen, ready for trouble. Its troops now located in the heart of "enemy" country, Congress decided that rapid communication was a military necessity. John M. Hockaday, a twenty-one-year-old law student from Missouri, was authorized to establish weekly stage service between St. Joseph and Salt Lake City. George Chorpenning, pioneer California stager, linked the route to the coast, and the long-delayed transcontinental service was at last a fact.

Soon Hockaday and Chorpenning found themselves facing a powerful rival. In 1857, at a yearly cost to the government of $150,000, a

semi-monthly, thirty-days-on-the-road mail had been instituted between—only God and Southern politicians knew why—the adobe
hamlets of San Antonio, Texas, and San Diego, California. This was the
ill-famed Jackass Mail, leading "from no place through nothing to nowhere." St. Louis, Santa Fe, Salt Lake City, and San Francisco protested
violently. What happened? The new million-dollar Butterfield stage
line was instituted—with Memphis as its eastern terminus, El Paso and
Tucson as way stations, and half the length of California as a last lap to
San Francisco. St. Louis, where most overland traffic originated, and
Santa Fe, heart of the rich New Mexico trade, were served by branch
lines.

To quiet the North's vociferous objections to this route, John
Butterfield, operator of the line, performed prodigies in whisking his
passengers over the 2792 roundabout miles from St. Louis to San Francisco in twenty-four days. ("Hell?" groaned one sleepless, joint-
petrified passenger on dismounting. "I've just been there for three and
a half weeks.") Apologists for the southern route crowed in triumph.
Let the central route, for all its thousand-mile advantage in distance,
beat *that* time! Promptly Hockaday's and Chorpenning's under-
nourished, underequipped stepchild of a line did beat it. The Postmaster General merely sniffed. Wait till winter blocks the South Pass
roads.

Winter did come, and a three-way race was arranged among the
new Tehuantepec steamers (which connected their sea lanes by a
short land hop across Mexico), the Butterfield line, and Hockaday and
Chorpenning, who pooled eight thousand dollars of their dwindling
funds for this climactic proof of their route's advantages. Batons in the
cross-country relays were to be transcripts of President Buchanan's
message to Congress, delivered simultaneously to each competitor at
its eastern terminus. But no official copy ever reached the Hockaday
starter, and there seems little doubt that government officials, pre-
ponderantly Southern in sympathies, were responsible for the sleight of
hand. For eight days the central-route man waited, finally obtained a
copy of the speech from a newspaper, and took off. Although he
reached San Francisco well after Butterfield's arrival, his running time
shaved two full days off that of the southern route, and it was done
over roads swept by incessant blizzards. (The steamships, incidentally,
were never in the running.)

The feat added up to exactly nothing. The ax fell on Chorpenning,
young Hockaday went broke, and the eastern half of the line eventually fell into the hands of the great freighting firm of Russell, Majors

& Waddell, which in 1858 was employing 3500 wagons, 40,000 oxen, 1000 men, and 1000 mules to supply Johnston's army in Utah and to conduct a few side ventures down to Santa Fe. Each of these thousand workers, at the stern behest of Alexander Majors, signed an amazing pledge: "I, John Doe, do hereby swear, before the Great and Living God, that during my engagement, and while I am an employee of Russell, Majors & Waddell, I will under no circumstances use profane language; that I will drink no intoxicating liquors; that I will not quarrel or fight . . . So help me God." So frightening was the dour visage of Mr. Majors that most of the workers were careful to maintain at least the appearance of compliance. A tale is told of one freighter, exhausted in a battle with a bogged team, who wired Majors for permission please to cuss just once. The request was granted on condition that the single outburst be delivered from a point where neither man nor mules could hear it.

When the contracts to supply Johnston's army fell off, the firm decided on a mighty half-million-dollar advertising stunt to impress the entire nation with the central route's lightning-like time advantages and so win the post office's lush mail contracts away from Butterfield. The stunt was the pony express, which wrought almost as many marvels as it has been credited with. Floods, blizzards, and Indians never halted its diminutive riders, and its only loss of mail occurred during the dark of the moon one balmy July night in 1860, when an ox went to sleep on a bridge over the South Platte River. Up charged the pony with the semi-weekly mail for Denver. There was a thud, a startled yell, a splash. Though the rider climbed out, horse and letters were never recovered. What happened to the ox, history saith not.

But the dazzling experiment was fruitless. The pony express, operating no more than eighteen months, made fewer than 150 round trips to the coast, earned not half the enormous sum it cost, and accomplished nothing—unless an incalculable addition to the romance, the literature, and the legends of the nation be also tossed into the scale. For by the time the pony had proved its point, the point no longer needed proving. With the outbreak of the Civil War the central route became the only practicable route for the embattled North.

Work on the transcontinental telegraph, already authorized in June 1860, was redoubled, and the pony's doom was sealed. Ed Creighton's shovelmen, ten to a squad, trudged across the plains and over the Wyoming desert digging an endless row of four-foot holes. Teamsters distributed poles that sometimes were hauled more than a hundred miles. Other freighters rushed in wire, insulators, and brackets while sweating cooks and camp movers leapfrogged in pursuit.

The Indians were baffled. Wily operators often lured several savages to touch a wire, then administered a hair-stiffening shock that for months afterward kept the bucks at a respectful distance. When Washakie, chief of the Wyoming Shoshone, discovered the use of the devilish instrument, he called it the "long tongue," and the speed with which it flashed from station to station reports of the tribes' movements filled the aborigines with dread. In due time, however, familiarity blunted awe; during the uprisings of the sixties marauding war parties burned down poles faster than the beleaguered operators could replace them.

Buffalo were another trouble. On the treeless plains the poles looked like heaven-sent hide scratchers; and when some unsung maintenance expert, enraged by the way his poles were being rubbed down, tried to discourage the practice by embedding sharp spikes in the timbers, he merely added to the delight of the shaggy beasts. Every upright became a congregating point. The sighting of a lone bull far east of the herds' normal range prompted a Wyoming wag to remark that the creature had heard rumors of a vacant pole and was hurrying off to stake out a claim.

The stepping up of stage service and the awarding of million-dollar mail contracts brought cutthroat competition to the Rockies. Wells, Fargo took over the western half of the central route. On the eastern half Russell, Majors & Waddell, their strength sapped by the failure of the pony express, went to the wall, and in stepped Ben Holladay, "Napoleon of the Plains," whom Henry Villard found "illiterate, coarse, pretentious, boastful, false, and cunning," but who was described by John Donaphin as "brave, strong, aggressive, talented and generous . . . one of God's gifted children."

In March 1861, Holladay was awarded the central route's first overland mail contract. Citizens of the two-year-old town of Denver were enormously excited, especially when Holladay implied that if they could guarantee him a crossing through the Colorado Rockies as good as South Pass he would put Denver on the main line to the coast. Ebullient Denverites promptly whooped up a monster mass meeting, where funds were subscribed for a survey to be headed by Captain E. L. Berthoud, one-time construction engineer on the Panama Isthmus Railway. Assistant to Berthoud was no less a personage than Jim Bridger, Old Gabe himself. With the huzzahs of the town ringing in their ears, they struck due west. But the season was early spring, and

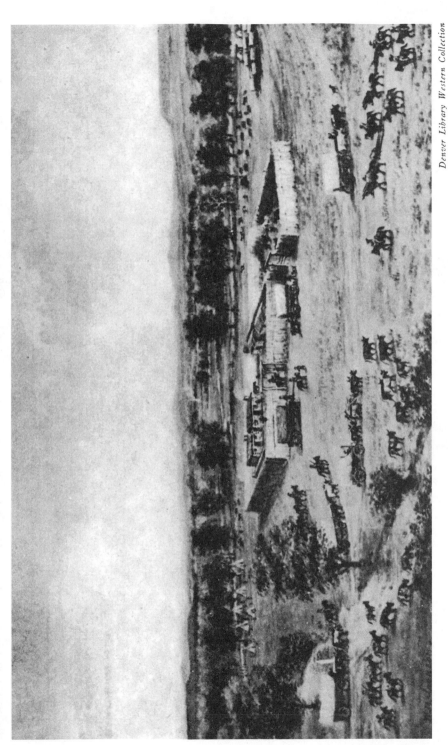

Jim Bridger's fort on Blacks Fork of the Green, southwestern Wyoming, 1843. Built by Old Gabe after the collapse of the fur trade, the crude post was a vital way station on the Overland Trail. (Reproduced from a painting by W. H. Jackson.)

Behemoth of the 1890 highways. The skinner rode the off-wheel animal, controlled the leaders with a jerk line. This five-span outfit with its high-sided trailers plied between Laramie, Wyoming, and Walden, in Colorado's North Park.

the snow in the upper Clear Creek canyon was deep. No all-year road, Old Gabe grumbled, could possibly exist in that country, so he went around by South Park. But Berthoud struggled stubbornly on over the pass which today bears his name and joined Bridger on the other side. The rest of the way to Salt Lake City, they reported in due time, offered no serious obstacles to a first-class wagon road. As for Berthoud Pass, with a little time, luck, and money . . .

That was enough for Ben Holladay. Profit, quick and big, was the sole criterion for his steamship companies as well as for the thirty-five hundred miles of stage lines he ran from New Mexico to Idaho and Montana, from Salt Lake to the Missouri River. Though there was enough business in Denver to warrant running a cutoff line to the Colorado city, South Pass would remain his crossing.

Even there winter snows and spring floods wrought havoc enough. So did the Indian outbreaks which accompanied the withdrawal of Federal troops to the battlefields of the Civil War. Stations were raided, coaches trapped and burned. The kind of driver who would undertake staging under such circumstances was not apt to be the sort who would radiate pride in his craft. Many of Holladay's division agents were men almost too brutal to be believed—for one, that warped killer, Jake Slade, whose bloodthirsty accomplishments so awed Mark Twain in *Roughing It*. Service was abominable. Traveler after traveler complained to no avail of disgusting food, filthy stations, shabby equipment. Newspapers screeched against failures to maintain schedules and deliver mail.

Not all the attacks on the line, growled Holladay's many enemies, were the work of Indians. After a blockade by blizzards, floods, or savages had left mail piled to the rafters of the Wyoming stations, a cryptic order would go out from the division agents to "clean up the line." Often then "Indians" would raid a particularly clogged point and destroy the accumulation. In the single month of May 1862, 53,000 letters alone were reported lost. How much of this was unavoidable and how much might have been traced to the active connivance of Big Ben Holladay is, of course, impossible to say.

There were, however, enough real attacks to make him abandon twenty-six stations along the Sweetwater and over South Pass in favor of a safer, more direct, but bone-dry route through Bridger's Pass and the Red Desert, just north of the Colorado-Wyoming border. This new line roughly paralleled the desolate route where, in a few more years, several of General Grenville Dodge's surveyors would die of scalpings and thirst as they staked out the line of the Union Pacific.

The end of the Overland Mail (though not of its multitudinous branches) was in sight. But it did not catch Ben Holladay. In November 1866 he sold out to Wells, Fargo in a $1,800,000 deal which gave the latter company control of every stage line between the Missouri and the Pacific.

Like the transcontinental telegraph and the Overland Mail, the Union Pacific was a war baby, born when Lincoln signed the Pacific Railroad Bill on July 1, 1862. But it fumbled its start. The war was over and Lincoln dead before the road had built its first paltry forty miles of track. Then late in 1865 the management was reshuffled, financial juggling through the ill-famed Crédit Mobilier brought a brief economic breathing spell, and three tough ex-soldiers, Grenville M. Dodge and the Casement brothers, Jack and Dan, were put in charge of construction. From then on the Union Pacific lunged westward in ever-lengthening strides.

During all this time Denver tried frantically to assure itself a spot on the main line. Berthoud boomed his pass, and half a dozen tunnel sites for piercing the divide were proposed. At first the Union Pacific seemed to listen. After all, Colorado's mineral resources were more tempting bait than anything the territory farther north could offer. But no amount of statistics on ore tonnage could quite dispel the chill of the towering mountains at Denver's back, and by now the Union Pacific was in a headlong race for land grants with the eastward-pushing Central Pacific. After years of coyness the road announced that it was going through Cheyenne, whereupon most of Denver migrated north, many merchants even tearing down their stores so they could load the lumber on wagons and take it with them. A Union Pacific official, surveying the dismal scene, announced that the Colorado city was too dead even to bury.

West of Cheyenne, however, loomed another mountain poser, the rugged Black Hills. The Union Pacific's charter forbade more than a 2-per-cent grade, and matters looked glum until a war party of Sioux chased Grenville Dodge and his surveyors down a ridge they had previously neglected to explore. An easy grade, Dodge noted, as he marked a locating tree between uneasy glances at the Indians. Surveys soon corroborated his eye-squint estimate: the climb was only ninety feet to the mile. Thus Sherman Pass was found, and Laramie (not to be confused with old Fort Laramie farther north on the Oregon Trail) was fixed as the goal of the next spurt of construction work.

Of all the Union Pacific's wild-and-woolly construction camps, none was tougher than Laramie, where corruption and lawlessness became so rampant that the Federal courts had to assume jurisdiction. It was under the aegis of these courts in March 1870 that the first women in the world were empaneled to serve on a grand jury. The revolutionary move led King William of Prussia to cable congratulations to President Grant, while Western newspapers in coarse delight cartooned veiled jurors dangling infants before the bench, and dashed off such jingles as

> *Baby, baby, don't get in a fury,*
> *Your mama's gone to set on the jury.*

If Denver was ignored by the Union Pacific, so, too, was the old gateway to the coast, South Pass. The iron horses, not needing to follow northward-angling Sweetwater Creek to find a drink, struck due west. At times they wished they hadn't. On the stretch between Rawlins and Green River, water was so alkaline that it destroyed boiler flues faster than they could be repaired. "This dope," grumbled one early engineer, "had the appearance of water until it was . . . subjected to heat, when it became a law to itself and . . . would shoot out the smoke-stack like a miniature geyser." Engines and engineers arrived at round-houses looking as if they had been whitewashed. Eventually, however, the drilling of artesian wells and the use of chemical softeners obtained moisture that would "perform the uses that nature intended."

It was on this bleak stretch that Dodge waged his closing sprint with the Central Pacific, a household story whose heroes and villains all America knows: the Scandinavian tie hacks who swarmed through the Medicine Bow and Wind River mountains to hew the 2640 cross ties needed for each mile of rail, who chucked whole forests into the rivers, followed them down in roistering drives—then fell in love with the lonely vales of the mountains, came back and settled; the burly Irish-men with their clanging hammers and boisterous fights; the roustabouts sweating over tangles of freight; surveyors, graders, and bridgebuilders obeying Dodge's orders never to run when attacked; gunmen, gamblers, and prostitutes padding through the fantastic "hell-on-wheels" towns which sprang into lurid life at every railhead.

These last Brigham Young watched with a jaundiced eye. No such antics for Utah. He himself took a contract for grade work through the rugged Wasatch canyons, where the earth froze so hard it had to be blasted like rock and where construction camps were so sober that wives and daughters of the workers could come in to run the boarding-houses and laundries. Other Mormon contractors duplicated the grading chore for the eastward-scurrying Central Pacific, and the fat fees they earned helped console them for the fact that in swinging around the north end of the Salt Lake the rails entirely missed their capital city.

On May 10, 1869, at Promontory Point, the golden spike was driven. At last the desperate cry had found its answer: those who wished to get through the Rockies could now do so with maximum speed, minimum effort. From now on our story will concern those who chose to stay. And the first to leave a permanent scratch on the mountains' high flanks were, of course, the miners.

CHAPTER IV

POOR MAN'S DIGGINGS

THIS is not a yarn of gold, but it leads to gold, simply because a Spanish caballero was not content to tell the truth.

The caballero was Álvar Núñez Cabeza de Vaca, royal treasurer of a three-hundred-man colonizing expedition that came to grief in Florida in 1528. Butchering their horses and making boats of the hides, the survivors set sail along the Gulf coast toward Mexico. Two of the craft were eventually wrecked on the east shore of Texas. Only four men escaped: Vaca, two other Spaniards, and a Negro named Estevan. For six years they wandered among the Indians, sometimes as drudging slaves, sometimes as venerated medicine men. In such fashion they toiled across southern Texas and Old Mexico to the Pacific coast, where they at length fell in with their countrymen and were conducted in triumph to Mexico City. Surely they had wonders enough to relate without inventing more. But no. The Spanish *conquistadores*, inflamed by the mines of Peru and Mexico, wanted to hear only of treasure. Vaca obliged. Rumormongers, aided by Indian captives bent on pleasing their masters, touched up his crude strokes and, lo, the Seven golden Cities of Cibola glimmered on the northern horizon.

In 1540 off went Francisco Coronado and a resplendent retinue of adventurers. The Seven Cities turned out, of course, to be various poverty-stricken pueblos of mud scattered throughout southern Arizona and New Mexico. But a new horizon loomed and beyond it, to the northeast, the opulent land of "Quivara." Thither rode a company of the now desperate Spaniards, guided by a foxy Indian opportunist called El Turko, who led them off through present-day Kansas to a desolate village of prairie Indians. Disgusted, the Spaniards strangled El Turko, rejoined the main body of the Army in New Mexico, and in 1542 went home to disgrace.

No gold. And yet—it is too entrancing a legend to die. Today, four centuries later, you can still pick up echoes of it in the Rockies. Here is one version which stems back to a full-blooded heir of chieftains, presently employed by the United States Indian Service. This man, on evidence deemed by him to be sufficient, believes that the Pueblos did

possess gold, laboriously mined and laboriously wrought into sacred
images. Forewarned by the moccasin telegraph of the Spaniards' desires
and rapacious natures, the caciques, the high priests, disguised the priceless relics by daubing them with mud, and ever since then their location
has been known only to upper-caste members of the tribes, who occasionally and in great secret produce them for certain awesome ceremonies.

For half a century after Coronado's fiasco the Spaniards, except for
sporadic and inconclusive expeditions, left Nueva Méjico alone. Then
in 1598 along came Juan de Oñate's colonists, intending to farm and to
proselyte the Indians rather than to mine. Yet records show that during
the next two centuries their successors did mine: turquoise, silver, gold,
lead, copper. Insuperable difficulties in the way of supply and ore reduction kept these known deposits from being particularly productive,
but prospectors, with the unquenchable fervor of their kind, kept on
looking. Traces of their probings are numerous in southern Colorado,
and far north in Wyoming are some mysterious ruins known to old-
timers as "the Spanish diggings," though archaeologists doubt the ac-
curacy of the name.

The French, too, contributed a titillating bit of lore. In 1790, so the
tale runs, a carefully organized expedition of three hundred Frenchmen—skilled miners, mechanics, geologists, and laborers officered by
soldiers—crossed Wolf Creek Pass to Treasure Mountain in southern
Colorado, not far from present-day Pagosa Springs. Here in a single
summer they dug out and refined no less than five million dollars' worth
of gold bullion. This was in Spanish territory; so when winter struck,
the Frenchmen hid the treasure in three caches, made detailed maps,
and beat a retreat to Taos. On their attempted return the next spring,
luck went sour. Starvation, disease, and Indians wiped out all but
seventeen, who fled eastward, lunching off each other according to
lot. Only two wasted skeletons reached what is now Leavenworth,
Kansas, then a trading outpost on the Missouri. From there they mailed
their charts to France, then died. Since Napoleon was busy with other
matters, the maps were chucked in the archives and forgotten.

Pure fantasy—except for one thing. During the latter part of the last
century a man named William Yule obtained what purported to be
tracings of the maps. After considerable delving, Yule and three other
substantial citizens of southern Colorado (Asa Poor, A. T. Stolsteimer,
and Leon Montroy, superintendent of Senator Bowen's famous Little
Annie Mine at nearby Summitville) discovered at least two of the
markers shown on the map, an inscribed stone and an old grave. These

markers they destroyed, then gophered madly about the vicinity, all to no avail, until a Mr. Crouse appeared with a patent gold-detecting rod. The rod vibrating hopefully, the quintet flew to their shovels and un-earthed an ancient walled shaft twenty feet deep. Though empty, the hole was encouraging. Assiduously the treasure hunters dug up quanti-ties of the adjoining landscape, found nothing, and gave up. Neverthe-less, they remained convinced of the map's authenticity and decided that the cache must have been rifled long ago by curious Indians or by Spaniards who had picked up the trail from one of the wine-relaxed Frenchmen in Taos. But what about the other two caches? Perhaps a few million dollars' worth of bullion still molders in them. You can look for yourself if you like. Some people still do.

Farther south in New Mexico at least two diggings, El Real de Dolores and the "Old Placers" in the Ortiz Mountains near Santa Fe, produced several hundred thousand dollars' worth of gold during the early 1830s. Many Americans knew this, yet no rush developed. These Nueva Méjico placers were a jealously guarded home industry. Under no circumstances could a foreigner obtain license to mine, a restriction which bothered the Santa Fe traders not one whit. They got the gold anyhow, swapping Yankee gimcracks for it and smuggling it through the customs back into the States, where knowledge of it sank into the national consciousness with scarcely a ripple.

Other vague rumors of gold in the Rockies trickled back to the Mississippi Valley with the mountain men. But California and Oregon were the magic words in those days, and it was not until gold talk was associated with them that the great stampede developed. Over South Pass the hordes streamed, with nary a glance for the mountains to the right and left. That is, most of them did not glance, nor would their untrained eyes have recognized mineral even if they had. But there were a few exceptions, among them a party of Georgians, mostly of Cherokee Indian blood, who hailed from the old gold fields around Dahlonega, Georgia, and knew what they were about. This party, headed by the Ralston brothers, worked their way up the Arkansas River to the Front Range, then swung north toward the Overland Trail, panning the streams along the base of the mountains as they went. They turned up color, not enough to distract them, but enough that memory of it was still sticking in their minds eight or nine years later.

Slowly the California excitement died down and many of the argo-nauts drifted home, some rich, some poor, some still with itching feet. Among them were William Green Russell and his two brothers of Lumpkin County, Georgia. Green Russell, who on state occasions wore his luxuriant beard braided in two neat plaits, was married to a Cherokee. From the gossip source thus opened, he learned both of the Ralston party's discoveries along the Front Range and of another mixed band of Cherokees, half-breeds and squaw men, who in 1857 had gone from Indian Territory (now Oklahoma) into the Rockies to hunt buffalo. The group had found traces of gold, and some of them, led by Baptist preacher John Beck—a full-blooded Indian, despite the name —were planning to return in the spring of '58 to try their hands at mining. The three Russell brothers and nine Georgia friends proposed joining forces with the Cherokees, and a rendezvous was agreed upon.

As the Georgians journeyed westward they met more men talking gold, excited in part by the dust which Marcy's Army teamster, George Simpson, had sent from Cherry Creek back to Missouri. The expansive Georgians invited those who wished to come along. By the time the combined parties reached the foothills, they numbered 104 men, a motley but not inexperienced mixture of Georgians, Missourians, and Indians.

Back in Leavenworth, Kansas, John Easter, the village butcher, was working himself into a state over a small quill full of yellow dust shown him by Fall Leaf, a Delaware Indian who promised to lead Easter and thirty other bemused grangers to the source of the metal. On the eve of their departure, however, Fall Leaf was sorely battered in a drunken brawl and, rather than wait for him to heal, the Kansans went on without a guide.

All through the border states the passage of the Russell and Easter parties was watched with speculative eyes. A wild-goose chase? Or maybe . . . The powder which might have detonated at any time during the past two decades was at last beginning to sputter.

By September of 1858 both bands of adventurers had come together where Cherry Creek joins the South Platte. No one had had much luck—indeed, Green Russell's party had almost disintegrated through discouragement and fear of the Arapaho—but bloated rumors of their doings had drifted back to the Kansas towns. Speculation mounted. From here, there, and everywhere a few hardy souls, ignoring the lateness of the season and the dangers of blizzards, headed west. Among them was William Larimer, who was interested not in mining but in selling building lots in the boom metropolis he hoped to found.

On reaching Cherry Creek on November 16, 1858, Larimer discovered to his dismay that practically everyone else in the region had hit on the same profitable idea, including a couple of local squaw men, John Smith and William McGaa, alias Jack Jones, reputed son of the

Lord Mayor of London. The only claims these would-be city fathers had to their land were vague "pre-emption" rights deriving from certain United States land laws which allowed squatters to purchase land from the government, provided that the lands were "open." But these Cherry Creek townsites were not open; the entire piedmont area had been awarded by treaty to the Arapaho Indians. This difficulty, however, the pioneers resolved by giving a small band of Arapaho a barbecue of three tough oxen, and industriously went on building small cabins on both sides of Cherry Creek and up and down the Platte.

Following this came a period of surreptitious claim jumping by the dark of the moon, stuffed ballot boxes, amalgamations, and involved financial deals in which entire "cities" changed hands for a few hundred dollars. Nor were political considerations overlooked. Though there were less than two hundred inhabitants in the district, the "Territory of Colona" was proclaimed and a representative sent dusting off to sit in Congress at Washington. Meanwhile, to be on the safe side in case Congress ignored the gesture, the boys also incorporated the same region as Arapaho County, Kansas, and elected delegates to the Kansas legislature. This made them a legal entity of some sort, though no one was quite sure what, and to confuse the issue still further local politicos with senatorial ambitions began agitating for the full-fledged "State of Jefferson."

In between plebiscites and referendums the boys amused themselves as best they could. "You have no idea of the gambling," tut-tutted William Larimer in a letter home. "They go it day and night, Sundays and all, and Oh, how they drink!"—a supply problem which had been taken care of on Christmas Eve, when Uncle Dick Wootton rolled in from New Mexico with several barrels of Taos Lightning in his wagons. As for mining, very few bothered with it. The nearby colors had proved to be nothing more than a flicker, and most of the quondam prospectors were waiting for spring, when they would either go home or, if they felt like it, perhaps try their hands farther afield.

Poor fodder, all in all, to feed a gold rush. But the people back East did not know that. Definite news lacking from isolated Cherry Creek, the wildest exaggerations took its place and fell on ears made wistful by the virulent land-boom depression of '57. Throughout the Midwest in particular bankrupt farmers and small-town merchants looked at one another. Remember California? The mountains there had been full of gold, so why not Pikes Peak? And it was an easy trip to the "Kansas fields." Why, a person could scoot out in no time, shovel up a few sacks of the shiny stuff, and be home before snow flew. Poor man's diggings! Let's go!

It wasn't logic, it was hope, and the sudden spark of it blew the powder keg sky high. Long before the snows melted, the first wave hit the border towns, each of which began stridently proclaiming itself the logical outfitting center for the easy, get-rich-quick trip to the mountains. Numerically speaking, the rush which developed was greater than that which had trampled off to California in '49. And though the distance was shorter and the trail easier, the sum total of suffering was equally enormous. The hopefuls simply would not prepare themselves. This was a lark, a picnic. Though there were multitudes of ox-drawn covered wagons and strings of pack animals, there were also thousands who set out on foot with no more supplies than they could carry on their backs; who pushed wheelbarrows or pulled handcarts; who even rigged up sails on wagons and planned to waft to the mountains on the prairie breezes.

Pikes Peak or Bust!

Hub-deep mud, raw winds, and no grass greeted those who started before May. Searing heat and thirst met latecomers. Electric storms shook the earth. Six hundred empty miles are not a short journey by foot or by wagon. Game was scarce, and the provisions which so many of the innocent had planned to procure along the way from traders or Indians failed to materialize. Hunger. Dysentery. Blistered feet. And suddenly, devastatingly, a growing trickle of men headed east, sullen-faced and bitter-tongued. Go home! There are no diggings. It's a promotion scheme, a humbug. Turn back!

Busted, by God!

Thousands wheeled around. More thousands, with no home to go back to, stopped beside unnamed streams and in desperation began breaking the sod which someday—but not for many years—would bloom into the vast wheat fields of western Kansas and Nebraska. The rest, hoping against hope, trudged on into shabby Denver and looked around. No mountains for miles yet—and they had supposed the streets pitched like ladders. Where is Pikes Peak? Hell, way off yonder to the south, barely visible. Somehow even this revelation seemed part of the monstrous hoax. More thousands auctioned off their brave new equipment for what little it would bring and pointed back toward the Mississippi, Jeremiahs crying in the wilderness, "Go home!" But the very inertia of the tide kept fresh thousands rolling westward.

The pessimists were correct. No riches existed in Cherry Creek, or in the Platte, or in any of the other streams that wound sandily along the foot of the mountains. Fortunately for the future of Colorado, however, there were a few weather-defying individuals who had not spent the winter in the scheming rival towns of Denver and Auraria, and by May they were ready to talk.

George Jackson first. Missouri-born, a fine figure of a man, he had lived for a time in New Mexico with his cousin Kit Carson and had worked in the California gold fields before knocking around the whole mountain area as a guide, trapper, and fly-by-night Indian trader. In the fall of '58 he had drifted down to Cherry Creek from Fort Laramie to swap trinkets with the Arapaho. During the first part of January he left the cabin on the site of present-day Golden, where he was wintering with two friends, one an Indian, and wandered alone up Clear Creek, hunting and prospecting as fancy moved him. Where then unnamed Chicago Creek empties into the main stream, he thawed out a frozen gravel bar with a bonfire and dug into the warm sands with his hunting knife. His findings he revealed only to his two close-mouthed partners and then calmly went off to Fort Laramie on business with an unsavory character known as Big Phil the Cannibal. By May he was back in Denver. There he met a company of twenty-two Chicagoans with a little loose change in their pockets. A deal was struck, and George Jackson led the group back to his discovery bar. They knocked their wagons apart, made sluice boxes, and within a week had taken out $1900 worth of dust.

John Gregory next, a sandy-haired, ill-favored Georgia cracker whose vocabulary consisted mainly of oaths. Stranded in Fort Laramie on his way to the gold excitement in British Columbia, Gregory had sold most of his outfit and had made his solitary way south, panning the mountain streams as he went. In January, shortly after Jackson had left the vicinity, he hit the north fork of Clear Creek, separated by a towering ridge from Jackson's bar, and there had turned up some good colors. But a blizzard drove him out, and in May, during a moody fit of discouragement, he would have pulled stakes had not ten men from South Bend, Indiana, grubstaked him and persuaded him to lead them to his discovery. Within four days Gregory's lode had produced $972.

Lastly, also in May, a small group from Nebraska City were hurrying up Boulder Canyon to exploit a sparkle of color they had located during that same fateful January at Gold Hill, some thirty miles north of the Jackson-Gregory finds. The news of all three discoveries electrified the despondent argonauts in Denver at approximately the same time.

Meanwhile, far to the east, so many conflicting reports about the

Pikes Peak gold fields were pouring into the offices of the New York *Tribune* that Horace Greeley shrugged into his old white coat, picked up his umbrella, and decided, in the interests of journalistic truth, to "go West, young man" and see for himself the conditions of all the land from Kansas to the Pacific. It was an eyeful. The stages he rode turned over twice, once on the plains east of Denver, where he skinned his face and lamed his leg, and later beside Wyoming's Sweetwater Creek, where a trunkful of his manuscripts went floating off beyond recovery. The activities of the freighting firm of Russell, Majors & Waddell strained his adjectives: "Such acres of wagons! Such pyramids of extra axletrees! Such herds of oxen! Such regiments of drivers!" Those in the Denver House disturbed his sleep: "The drinking room was occupied by several blacklegs as a gambling hall, and their incessant clamor . . . became at length a nuisance. Then, the visitors . . . had a careless way, when drunk, of firing revolvers, sometimes at each other, at other times quite miscellaneously."

Denver had reason for jubilation. New finds were being reported daily, notably that of Green Russell and his brother. Just returned from a winter trip to Georgia, where they had recruited 170 hot-eyed prospectors, the Russell brothers hopped a few miles upstream past Gregory Bar and opened glittering new gravels of their own. Within a week four thousand people had swarmed after them into the Clear Creek diggings, where Idaho Springs, Central City, Blackhawk, and half a dozen other towns soon would take root.

Zipping along behind the horde came Greeley and two colleagues, Henry Villard of the Cincinnati *Commercial Enquirer*, later to achieve renown as a rail tycoon, and Albert D. Richardson of the Boston *Journal*. The miners took the somewhat skeptical trio into a prospect hole (which, one legend says, had been judiciously salted) and let them wash out a few grains for themselves. Duly awed, the journalists next collected production statistics from nearby workings, sat themselves down under a tree, and composed their famous joint report to the nation. To its alluring figures they appended a sober warning about the difficulties of the trip across the plains, the backbreaking labor of mining, Denver's scanty resources and high prices, and the suffering which winter would bring to the ill-prepared. Newspapers were solemnly adjured not to distort these truths, a behest which many fulfilled by not printing them at all. Indeed, optimism had so completely replaced the discouragement of a few scant weeks ago that by June 18 the two-month-old *Rocky Mountain News* saw fit to jeer at the faint of heart in an editorial entitled "The Gobacks": "We hope this class are all again safely at home to their Pa's and Ma's, their sweethearts, and 'Nancy and the babies'. . . . They have had their day and soon will be forgotten."

Meanwhile, the stampeders along the creeks were being faced with acute problems of organization. The attributes of legal sovereignty—jails, judges, land offices, and all the rest—were hundreds of miles distant. Who was to maintain order? How were these lands, to which no one had any recognized right, to be fairly apportioned?

Again there bloomed that phenomenon of spontaneous social adjustment which had manifested itself ten years before in California. As each new field was opened the miners assembled at an open-air meeting to adopt constitutions and elect officials. Criminal codes came directly to the point and were designed to operate with a minimum of inconvenience for the prospectors, who had neither time nor facilities to bother with prisoners. The laws of the Gregory district declared:

> Sec. 1.   Any person guilty of murder upon conviction thereof shall be hanged by the neck until he is dead.
> Sec. 3.   Any person shooting or threatening to shoot another, except in self-defense, shall be fined a sum not less than Fifty nor more than Five Hundred Dollars and receive in addition as many stripes on his bare back as a jury of six men may direct, and be banished from the district.

To prevent any twisting of or quibbling with these clear mandates, many districts forbade the presence of lawyers in court; if, however, one litigant happened to be a lawyer, his adversary might then seek legal aid. In time, of course, these restrictions were removed and provisions made for pleadings. The final court of appeal was, in many cases, a meeting of the entire district, where the populace approved or disapproved the verdict by passing between a couple of wagons or stepping across a line. Under this procedure a preponderance of rogues in a district obviously could and sometimes did nullify justice. During the early months of 1860 Denver's primitive legal system broke down so completely that on February 29 the *Rocky Mountain News* asked sadly, "We are curious to know how long this reckless and promiscuous firing of pistols, cutting, and stabbing will be permitted." It was not long. In October vigilante committees were formed, and after a few bodies had been found dangling from various points of vantage the town again became comparatively quiet.

Land laws were equally pragmatic: first come, first served. The discoverer of a district was entitled to two claims, others to one, their size depending on their nature. Gulch, or placer, claims were one hundred feet long and from bank to bank in width. Lode claims extended a hundred feet along the vein and twenty-five feet on either side of it. Provisions were also made for water, timber, mill-site, and cabin claims. The furnishing of water to dry gulches, incidentally, was often more profitable than mining itself. The one-hundred-thousand-dollar Consolidated Ditch, by which Green Russell and other stockholders brought water to the Russell diggings, was the first "big business" venture in the new territory; and soon dripping, mossy flumes clinging to the sides of cliffs were a standard part of the mountain scene.

In all cases a claimant had to stake clearly the corners of his claim and within a specified time file notice of its location with the district's elected recorder. He also had to expend a certain amount of work on the holding. These provisions complied with, his title became vested and could be disposed of as he saw fit. In the more thriving districts there was a continuous bartering of claims and parts of claims, many of which were filed simply in hopes of sale to some sucker and which were often salted by such methods as firing a shotgun load of gold dust into the dirt. During Central City's speculative boom in 1864, the recorder had to hire a large force of extra day-and-night help to keep up with the frantic changes of title. He probably did not mind, however, as the fees paid him for each transaction totaled, according to one estimate, some forty thousand dollars for the year.

All this was absolutely illegal. Every claim was a trespass on the public domain, and Congress did not know quite what to do about it. Some legislators thought the United States should derive revenue from the mines by selling them; others thought the land should simply be given away. There was no doubt what the miners felt. From the Pacific to the Rockies they translated belief into action so thoroughly that the Federal Government was in effect presented with an unbreakable *fait accompli*. Still, so long as titles remained clouded, the free flow of capital was restricted, and by 1866 the hue and cry had reached such proportions that Congress passed the first national mining law. Modified in 1872, this allowed anyone to obtain "patent" to a claim fifteen hundred feet long and six hundred feet wide by fulfilling certain minimum requirements. Colorado miners found this too liberal! A territorial law promptly whittled down the width to three hundred feet —even to one hundred and fifty feet in some counties—and miners for years after continued to pass their own independent legislation. The Creede, Colorado, code of 1892 contained, for example, such pointed provisions as "stakes in snow don't go," and "prospecting shall be done with a pick and shovel, not with a penknife and lead pencil."

By midsummer of 1859 every foot of the Clear Creek diggings had been appropriated. Disgruntled latecomers either had to go home, as many did, or look somewhere else. Quickly the tide slopped over into South Park, prized summer hunting ground of the Utes, a trespass which caused Kit Carson, their agent, to cluck warningly, "The Utahs will be dissatisfied." Let 'em be! Soon the South Park camps of Tarryall, Fairplay, and Buckskin Joe were flourishing mightily, while by 1860 the town of Breckenridge on the Blue River, another favored Ute preserve directly across the Continental Divide from Clear Creek, boasted a reputed eight thousand inhabitants. But the richest of all these mushrooming camps was Oro City, center of six-mile-long California Gulch near the headwaters of the Arkansas River. Here many a claim yielded as much as sixty thousand dollars a season. Illiterate, unwashed Jack Ferguson and Pete Wells thrived so well that a saloon and gambling house was built next to their sluice boxes and reaped astronomically on their trade alone.

Within five years lonely prospectors, riding one animal and packing their picks, pans, blanket rolls, and coffeepots on another, had penetrated all but the most remote of the state's mountain fastnesses. And still the ripples spread. In 1867 flakes of gold clinging to the hoof of a bogged mule contributed to the short-lived rush which swept northern New Mexico and broke Lucien Maxwell. In that same year, phenomenally enough, gold was discovered in South Pass, where thousands of heedless forty-niners had rushed past it on their way to California, and immediately Wyoming's only sizable mineral stampede was on. In South Pass in 1869, Mrs. Esther Morris became the first woman justice of the peace in the world (a claim since disputed). Here, too, in the wild-and-woolly camp of Miners Delight, another socially minded woman picked off the streets a dirt-encrusted, loud-swearing orphan named Martha Jane Canary and took the girl to New York to be educated. By day Martha Jane roamed the streets of the metropolis in a buckskin suit and by night did those things which were better left undone. Fleeing back West, she amazed her friends in Miners Delight with the extent and variety of her "larnin'," then drifted up to Dakota's Black Hills, served (according to her story, though Army records do not reveal it) as scout for General Custer, and became inextricably linked in legend with Wild Bill Hickok. Pulp-story readers will readily recognize her by her *nom de guerre—* Calamity Jane.

The endless roamings of the prospectors were often fraught with horror. For one example, take the story of William Doyle, partner of a Dutchman named Joe Hahn, who in 1866 led fifty men to the placer diggings at Hahn's Peak in the extreme northern part of Colorado. As winter came on, all but three of the men—Hahn, Doyle, and George Way—drifted back to the settlements. These three, determining to wolf out the winter, sent Way for supplies to the Clear Creek towns, more than a hundred miles distant. He never returned. Nonetheless, Hahn and Doyle stayed where they were, whipsawing lumber for flumes in snow twelve feet deep. Finally, on April 27, 1867, their provisions dwindled to a few handfuls of coffee, the half-starved pair decided to leave. On the high, bleak plains of Middle Park a blizzard struck them. Hahn grew delirious. Leaving him bundled up in a deserted cabin they had passed, Doyle pushed on for help. He swam the icy Troublesome River, and on the opposite bank, as his clothing froze to his body and snow blindness began to sear his eyes, he yelled his desperation to the wilderness. No sound answered. Unable to go on, he struggled back across the stream to the cabin, where he found Hahn stone-dead and frozen solid. Hunkered by the corpse, Doyle made some coffee and wrote his own name and the names of his relatives in an old memorandum book. But he did not die—quite. Two men out hunting cattle found him, almost unconscious and totally blind. "If it hadn't been for that experience I might have made a fortune out of the Hahn's Peak mines. As it is, I am a poor man. It spoiled my life."

Out of such ordeals, in which discoverers died before they could file the locations of their claims, or suffered to the point that they were unable to remember where they had been, come the stories of the lost mines. The most famous one in the Rockies is perhaps the Lost Cabin mine of Wyoming's Big Horns. There are several versions, all dealing with Indians. One says that Allen Hulbert and two other ex-forty-niners made the strike in the summer of 1863 and washed out half a bushel of gold apiece. Winter coming on, they built a cabin. Then Indians killed all but Hulbert, who escaped by hiding in a tree. That night he packed as much gold as he could carry in a knapsack and fled across unknown country to the North Platte, eighteen days away. There he showed his take to stampeders bound up the Bozeman Trail to the gold strikes in Montana; and with 140 wagons and 550 excited men, women, and children at his heels, he turned back into the Big Horns. But he could not find the trail he had so carefully hidden from the Indians and was nearly lynched by his disappointed followers.

After that men continually looked for the telltale cabin. Again the mystic number three appears. An unnamed trio re-discovered it. Their tools and supplies giving out, they built a raft and floated down the Little Bighorn River—straight into the clutches of Sitting Bull's Sioux. Two were killed. The third escaped with a few nuggets, but the ordeal left him a babbling idiot and he could reveal nothing.

Even in the most populous camps living was harsh. These were poor man's diggings, placer beds that could be stripped to bedrock with no other resources than hard work, ordinary tools, and limited capital. That very concept precluded any notion of permanence. The first houses in a camp were mere tents, evergreen lean-tos, or open-fronted cavities dug in the hillside and roofed by boughs covered with dirt. If the gravels promised to last more than a single season, log cabins appeared during the fall; and though enough lumber might be whip-sawed for a door frame and single window sash, it was a rare hut that possessed the luxury of a plank floor. Sawdust six inches deep was often spread through the cabin's interior and covered with a peg-fastened gunny-sack carpet through whose loose weave dirt sifted and made cleaning easy. If a sawmill arrived in time, unpainted shanties of milled lumber were, of course, constructed.

For furniture a miner might possess a hand-hewn table, a chair with its seat woven out of rope or rawhide, a few three-legged stools, and a board nailed to the wall as a shelf. Bedsteads, too, were fastened against the walls in corners, to do away with the necessity of making more than a single leg, and mattresses were of hay, either piled up loose or contained in a canvas ticking. Dishes, invariably of tin, were limited, and cooking was done in iron pots over an open fireplace, bread being baked in a frying pan set up edgewise before the blaze. A flutter of calico at the window or wallpaper contrived from old newspapers generally indicated a woman's hand.

The towns were filthy. Refuse was pitched out the door, to be trampled into the snow and mud. Huge numbers of horses and mules added to the mess, and local butchers, unless persuaded otherwise by popular sentiment, simply let their offal lie beside their place of business. Personal cleanliness was little better. Indian squaws or the ambitious wife of an argonaut might wash shirts at three dollars a dozen, but many a miner wore his clothes until they rotted off. Needless to say, reminiscences frequently speak of outbreaks of skin diseases and internal disturbances.

Nor was the daily diet conducive to health. Hunters peddled game, and oxen, worn out by their trip across the plains, generally ended up in unsuspecting cook pots, but the great staples were salt pork, flour, and coffee. Dried fruit was a luxury; to impress this fact on the minds of his patrons one boardinghouse keeper in the Gregory district nailed to his wall a sign that bluntly stated, "Any man who won't eat prunes is a son of a bitch." Members of the gentler sex giving dinner parties found their ingenuity taxed. Taffy pulls were favored as providing both entertainment and a fillip to the palate, while a vile "lemonade" concocted out of a white powder of citric acid helped disguise the taste of the water which was hawked through the streets at ten cents a bucket or six bits a barrel.

Although there were women in the mining camps, during the earliest days of the rush they were outnumbered by an estimated thirty to one. But by 1861, when Colorado was admitted as a territory, a tentative census (inaccurate since many prospectors were in the mountains) revealed 20,758 males and 4484 females. The majority of the latter, contrary to popular opinion, were legitimately there with their husbands.

"Hurdy-gurdy girls"—the term "dance-hall girls" is of later derivation—were, of course, a staple item. Flossed out in several hundred dollars' worth of gay ribbons, kids, silks, and laces, these butterflies sold five-minute dances to all comers for from fifty cents to a dollar each, half of which sum they kept and half of which went to the house. The orchestra generally consisted of from one to three fiddles. To their jig time the miner, who seldom bothered to remove his hat, hurled his partner around with more exuberance than skill, then resuscitated himself and her with a friendly shot of redeye at the bar. Other entertainment was, of course, available for a fee.

One such girl, whose twinkling slippers had brought her the name Silver Heels, was the toast of Buckskin Joe. When a smallpox plague swept the town in the fall of 1861 all the other females fled. But not Silver Heels. She was the camp's sole nurse, until she, too, was stricken. After a desperate illness she recovered. One lonesome afternoon, a pale wraith now, she rose from her bed, dressed herself in all her finery, and asked for a mirror.

Shortly thereafter a delegation of miners called at her house. The grateful camp had subscribed a purse of, legend says, five thousand dollars, and the boys were grinning sheepishly as they mumbled their rehearsed speeches. But no one answered their knock. Silver Heels had disappeared. One tale says she was never again seen in the district; another, that many years later a heavily veiled woman began making annual pilgrimages to the graveyard where the plague victims were buried. Be that as it may, the boys left one enduring monument to "The Angel of Mercy of South Park": brooding over the deserted town of Buckskin Joe (now called Alma) is a peak known as Mount Silverheels.

Hurdy-gurdy girls notwithstanding, the early camps were surprisingly decorous. For one thing, they were hard for parasites to reach. It was not until the advent of railroads that the famed orgies of the silver towns became so marked. Besides, most of the first prospectors seem to have been interested in business, not play. Nearly all the Clear Creek diggings imposed stiff fines on gambling establishments and bawdyhouses; and at Gold Hill the miners, in a local-option election, overwhelmingly rejected saloons! Debating and literary societies, though not exactly robust, were features of many camps, while at Black Hawk there was a singing club of thirty-two male members.

As a matter of fact, life was rather monotonous. The men worked hard, often for small returns, and the only amusements they could afford were a drink or two in the evening and a sociable game of cards with a deck so grease-smeared that only close scrutiny could differentiate the king from the jack. Conversation, as one Breckenridge miner put it, was largely built around the Warm Stove Mine in the back of George Watson's store, where solid gold was taken out by the ton, shipped to Fairyland, and treated by the Hot-Air Smelter. Dances of the non-professional variety were, when they could be arranged, the favorite recreation, a circumstance which brought fulminations from the Reverend John L. Dyer, who was regularly vexed by Breckenridge revelers' stealing the harmonium from his church and carting it off in a wagon to their bacchanals.

He was an amazing man, this Dyer. In 1861, when he was nearly fifty years old, he walked seven hundred miles across the plains to become one of the tiny handful of itinerant preachers who, during the early sixties, spread the Gospel from mining camp to mining camp with almost no support from their poverty-stricken churches. On the September Sunday that he reached Washington Gulch "one man was cutting and selling beef; others rolling logs down the hill; others covering their cabins; another building a chimney, and still others selling provisions and whiskey in a tent. . . . I stepped into the center of the camp and cried: 'O yes! O yes! O yes! there will be a preaching at half-past ten o'clock wherever the most people can be found together.' The time arrived and . . . I got in front of the tent, under the shade of a pine, and read the hymn beginning 'Alas! and did my Savior bleed?' and as I tried in the old way to sing it, a number joined in." Eventually a hundred men drifted up; during the service a mule reached his head in the tent and distracted the audience by making off with a loaf of bread.

On he went, preaching in bars, marrying and burying, was snowed in, shoveled snow for three and a half days to go three and a half miles, and "by the Grace of God made the riffle." During those first two months "I traveled near 500 miles on foot, by Indian trails, crossing logs, carrying my pack, and preaching three times a week. I received $43 in collection at different places . . . and spent about $50 of my own resources, as I had worked through the week." Thus for more than twenty years, supporting himself by delivering winter mail across the Continental Divide on skis, by serving as a guide, teaching school, locating claims for others, hauling logs, and building houses. During the so-called Lake County War, an involved vendetta that terrorized the upper Arkansas Valley during 1874–75, his crippled son, Probate Judge Elias Dyer, was brutally murdered. Though the case caused an uproar throughout Colorado, no one was brought to trial. On his deathbed "Father" Dyer forgave the murderers, whose identity he had apparently long suspected without ever having been able to stir up official action against them.

Quickly the placer gravels were stripped and the boom camps began to die. Those where lodes, or veins, had been discovered clung on a little tighter. So long as the gold was "free" the ore could be ground between horse-drawn stones called arrastras, or crushed in stamp mills, and the mineral recovered by the usual sluicing devices and by amalgamation with mercury. But gold in combination with other elements called for smelting, a technique imperfectly known during the sixties. Moreover, deep mining called for capital, and capital was chill toward the Rockies. One reason, aside from the refractoriness of the ores, was the Civil War; another was the collapse of Central City's speculative boom in 1864. But the greatest deterrent was the growing restiveness of the Indians.

Fear of the Utes was keeping all but the most intrepid prospectors away from Colorado's western slope. On the plains, uprisings of increasing ferocity were cutting communications with Denver for weeks at a time. Whenever Sioux, Arapaho, Cheyennes, or Crows suffered reverses in Wyoming, they consoled themselves by raiding the South Pass mining towns, where the long-suffering citizens guaranteed themselves ten years of bloody reprisals by slaughtering an unarmed band of Arapaho who were traveling peacefully to Fort Brown to trade.

For three centuries the Indian problem had defied solution. Now the West must end it or strangle.

CHAPTER V

THE FATHER'S BACK IS TOWARD US

THE Spaniards were unprepared for the terror which swept the northern Rio Grande in 1680. For upward of three quarters of a century their colonists and their friars had been happily ensconced in New Mexico, saving Indian souls with one hand and subjugating Indian bodies with the other. Docile Pueblos labored from the government in mines and fields, wove cotton *mantas* for the church, and paid tribute to whoever appeared with strong enough force to collect it. Spiritually, too, the Indians were rewarding. One of the first padres, Geronimo de Zarate Salmeron, reported gleefully that in eight years he had baptized eight thousand heathens, and by 1626 the province boasted forty-three churches and thirty-four thousand converted savages.

Miracles furthered the good work, as in the case of the lightning bolt that ended polygamy at Taos. There a certain "sorceress" (i.e., a recalcitrant), "under pretext of going to the country for firewood, took out four other women with her" and endeavored to win them back to the old ways of indiscriminate mating. Whereupon, says Fray Alonzo de Benavido, "a thunderbolt fell and slew that infernal mistress of the Demon, right between the good Christians . . . and they remained very confirmed in the truth of the Holy Sacrament of Matrimony. Directly all the pueblo flocked thither; and seeing that rap from heaven all those who were living in secret concubinage got married and believed. . . ."

Thunderbolts lacking, the *conquistadores* had other methods. Whipping, imprisonment, slavery, or hanging were standard penalties for an Indian's refusing to give up his religion, for participating in an uprising, or for indulging in "superstitious practices." On this last score the authorities in 1675 rounded up from Taos, San Juan, and Picurís pueblos forty-six medicine men, hanged three, and subjected the others to various indignities. Dangerous tampering. These caciques had been high priests of a religion which had ruled the Indians for considerably longer than three quarters of a century. When a Tewa medicine man named Po-pé preached revolt to the grieving Pueblos, the inhabitants, who did not like their Spanish overlords anyhow, nodded agreement.

Thus encouraged, Po-pé made alliance with the Apaches and began extensive preparations. Too extensive, perhaps. Word of them leaked out to Governor Otermín at Santa Fe, whose frantic couriers scurried in every direction, warning loyal citizens to fly for shelter to the presidio.

For most of the colonists north of Santa Fe the alarm came too late. Learning they had been anticipated, Po-pé's forces launched their attack in the pre-dawn hours of August 10, 1680. No Spaniard found mercy, but at least laymen died easier than did the priests. At Jémez, west of Santa Fe, an aged padre was dragged from bed, stripped naked, and paraded through the streets on a hog. Next he was forced to crawl on his hands and knees while members of the howling mob rode him like a horse, beating and spurring until he dropped dead.

A thousand panic-stricken men, women, and children fortified themselves in the plaza at Santa Fe. Outside, three thousand Indians roared with victory. Two crosses were sent to the governor, one white and one red. A return of the white one to the Pueblos meant that the Spanish promised to leave New Mexico and their lives would be spared. Don Antonio de Otermín, however, was as stiff-willed as only a Spanish hidalgo can be. Back went the red cross, and the town braced itself for a siege.

By August 20 food and water had been exhausted. But Santa Fe's defenders were trained warriors; the long-suppressed Indians were not. Otermín led a hundred and fifty men in a sudden charge. Twice that number of surprised Indians went down before superior weapons and superior discipline. The others wavered long enough for the Spaniards to hack a way through and, with their women and children and a few pitiful possessions, begin a shambling, fear-tormented flight to Old Mexico.

In the vacated city the savages smashed everything they could move. They fired the churches, burned records, annulled all Christian marriages, pranced obscenely in the befouled vestments of the priests. They turned the Palace of the Governors into a pueblo and made a kiva of its chapel. Undoubtedly they thought they were extirpating every trace of their oppressors. But they were wrong. Frenzy such as that cannot be maintained forever, and the Spanish were stubborn people. Twelve years later, after several attempts at reconquest had failed, Don Diego de Vargas marched back into Santa Fe, and the first of the major Indian wars, which for three centuries would crimson the soil of the Rockies, was over.[1]

Blame that blood, or at least a large share of it, on a single Spanish importation—the horse, which, as nearly every schoolboy knows, transformed Western Indians from skulking, half-starved root diggers into a self-sufficient people almost as formidable as later dime novelists painted them to be.

Consider four essential items: locomotion, transportation, warfare, and food getting.

First, mobility. By simply looping around his horse's under jaw a light noose to the bottom of which was attached a single long cord, an Indian could speed his mount over any sort of ground in almost any sort of weather. During a single season adventurous young bucks could go, and did go, from the heart of Mexico in the South to Canada in the North, and it is difficult to believe that knowledge was not exchanged on these travels.

New modes of transportation altered living habits. Before (and after) the advent of the horse, dogs had been used to a limited extent in the North as beasts of burden, either carrying packs on their backs or pulling light travois over the snow. One Ute crossing of the Continental Divide, at an altitude of twelve thousand feet, near the present Trail Ridge Road in Rocky Mountain National Park, was known as the "Dog Trail" because of its adaptation to this kind of moving. With the coming of the horse the travois idea spread far and wide, and dogs were relegated chiefly to the cooking pot. For by lashing dismantled tepees and skin containers, called parfleches, to the travois's dragging poles, an entire village could mobilize itself. Primarily important because it allowed the Indians to follow migrating game, the horse-drawn travois further improved living standards by enabling the savages to seek cool mountain vales during summer and sheltered lowlands by winter. It also confounded later white settlers, who never knew from which direction a whole town might appear, and who, when they wished to punish the same town for a depredation, were often unable to find it.

In warfare the horse made possible the famed circling charge, further refined when the warriors learned to knot handhold loops in the shaggy manes of their ponies. This support enabled the rider to lean almost flat against the side of his mount, offering little of himself as a

[1] Actually the wars lasted 372 years, if one also counts the minor skirmishes that began with Coronado in 1540 and ended with Posey's Piute uproar in southeastern Utah in 1912.

target while he discharged his own arrows or bullets under the neck of the racing horse.

It was in the field of food getting, however, that the horse wrought the most revolutionary changes. Primitive agriculture (the runty maize, beans, squash, and pumpkins that were grown along the creek bottoms) all but disappeared, and buffalo became the irreplaceable essential not only of Indian economy but also of Indian sport. Today we can only guess at the sweeping exultation of that chase. Naked man on a naked horse. Single rein in left hand, bow in right, a few arrows in a quiver over his back. Fog of dust, crash of stampeding hoofs. One of the shaggy beasts separates ever so little from the central mass of the herd. A pursuer darts in. Close. If he is much more than two feet distant when he attacks, his arrow or lance may miss the vital spot above the heart. Yet the moment the blow is struck the wounded creature will likely turn at bay, and two feet leave the thinnest of margins. No matter. This is the instant of the kill, and caution is obliterated by a thrill as purely savage as man has ever known. The bow twangs; the trained horse veers. Generally the maneuver is successful, but once in a while miscalculation results in a hideous collision. Screaming horse and rider are catapulted over the bison's maddened head, either to be gored where they land or trampled by the tons of flesh that follow.

Thus for small parties, as hunting was usually conducted. The ordinary band of Indians, until white pressure forced amalgamation, seldom consisted of more than one hundred persons. Larger numbers were hard to feed, and quarrels proved disruptive. At times, however, particularly in the fall, several bands might join for a "surround." Men, boys, squaws—sometimes as many as a thousand Indians, according to that notorious exaggerator, Jim Beckwourth—would form a circle six miles in diameter around a herd which the scouts had selected. Slowly the net tightened. Warriors darted out, set the bewildered beasts to milling. While some riders kept the herd in its blind, circling run, others began the slaughter. After rifles were introduced the killing became tremendous. Each hunter (the braves alternated chasing and killing) carried several round lead bullets in his mouth. After every shot he took the barrel of the gun in his left hand, poured in powder from a horn slung around his neck, spit a bullet down the muzzle, and seated the charge by slapping the stock with his hand—all at full gallop.

Soon the plain was littered with carcasses. Now jubilation. A hundred Indians required approximately four hundred pounds of meat per day, and here were vast lumps that would average a thousand pounds each. Great was the strutting, warm the plaudits of the maidens, raucous the jeers for anyone unfortunate or inept enough not to have made his kill. That night there was a glorious surfeit of tender humps and tongues, of dances and stories, of love-making.

The next day the squaws went to work, a job that lasted two or three weeks. Before the meat spoiled it must either be smoked into jerky or dried, pounded into powder, mixed with berries, and, known now as pemmican, be sealed with fat into skin bags where it would keep sweet throughout the winter. Hides were saved for the making of moccasins, robes, tepees, and bullboats for navigating rivers. Sinew furnished thread. There was delicious marrow in the bones, the smaller of which could be utilized for ornaments, linked into defensive breastplates, or even made into musical instruments and needles. The skulls had cere-monial adaptations; bladders served as containers; horns might hold powder or decorate a headdress.

Food, shelter, mobility, safety, leisure—the horse furnished it all, but not in a twinkling, as casual historians sometimes seem to imply. Although Coronado brought the first horses into the future United States in 1540, he took most of them back home with him, and any that escaped could hardly have impressed the unimaginable emptiness of the plains. Besides, what could an earth-bound Indian who never before had seen a horse do with the beasts? No, history waited until 1598, when Oñate's colonists appeared on El Rio del Norte (the Rio Grande) with five thousand sheep and goats and two thousand head of "other stock."

Unlike Coronado, Oñate meant to stay. With iron swords, lances, and a few firearms his soldiery quickly convinced the Pueblos of the fact. But north of Santa Fe was a more troublesome tribe protected by mountain ridges and not bound to one spot by houses of mud. These were the Utes, and they were accustomed, when hungry or desirous of a fresh supply of maidens, to raid the more stable economy of the Pueblos.

Naturally the Pueblos appealed for protection to their new masters, who likewise were being annoyed by the sneak attacks. But the Utes would not stand and fight. And how can one colonize if he must ever-lastingly chase shadows through the hills? The Spanish tried to buy peace. In so doing they piled up infinitely greater harassments for them-selves, because among the bribes they offered to the eager Utes and to the Utes' dangerous cousins, the Comanches, were horses.

Slowly, during a century or more, the snowball grew. Horses escaping from their owners reached the flatlands east of the Sangre de Cristos and procreated lustily on the nutritive plains.[2] Indians already mounted by the obliging Spaniards could catch these animals by stampeding small herds of them into crude brush-and-pole corrals. A second device was to station riders at strategic points, chase the wild herds in relays, overhaul the exhausted beasts, and snare them with another Spanish importation, the *lazo*, a word since Anglicized to lasso. Animals could also be taken by creasing—shooting a nerve in the top of the neck with an arrow or bullet and so stunning the creature long enough for the hunter to seize it. This feat, however, dear though it became to later fiction writers, was far too difficult to be frequently successful. A much easier method than corralling, creasing, or chasing was simply to steal horses from someone who already had them. Accordingly the Utes and Comanches, riding Spanish mounts, stole more Spanish stock. In turn these Indians' neighbors stole from them, and so on and so on, until, in the words of Edgar McMechen, "The greatest horse-thief trail in history ran red at the eastern base of the Rockies."

By the time the fur trappers reached the mountains, horse stealing had become an honored Indian profession, relished both for the fun and the profit it provided. The white man's more rigid views of property failed to appreciate these motives, and early Western history is full of frictions caused by the divergent mental attitudes regarding horseflesh.

Take one isolated instance in the year 1824. In St. Louis beaver pelts were selling for six dollars a pound. Fifteen hundred miles away Tom Fitzpatrick's trappers, having made the first east-to-west crossing of South Pass, were pyramiding a dizzy fortune in the valley of the Green. Then one night a band of Snakes whooped down on the camp, waving hide robes and screeching like fiends. Away went the whites' twenty-five panicked horses, and so did the Snakes.

It was late spring now, and the time for taking prime pelts would soon pass. Coolly Fitzpatrick kept his stranded men busy at their traps until they had collected twenty full packs of plews. Now for the horses to transport that wealth. After caching their furs and equipment in a pit over which the sod was carefully replaced to prevent discovery, Fitzpatrick's fourteen men followed the Snakes' trail up the Green. For five days they walked. Then sign freshened, and for the next three nights the stalkers sneaked along under cover of darkness, until at last

---

[2] The process was duplicated, of course, in Texas with horses escaped or stolen from Spanish ranches along the lower Rio Grande.

they reached a village of twenty lodges. Above the village, near a dense stand of brush, a hundred horses grazed.

Slinging their rifles over their backs with buckskin thongs, the men crept forward. A horse snorted; a dog barked. "Go it, boys!" And God help any man who fell. Each sprang for the closest horse, caught its mane, swung aboard. No saddles, no bridles. Just hang on, howl, and hope for the best. Straight through the middle of the village the herd stampeded, tippling tepees, Indians, and frenzied dogs.

All that night the horses ran down the valley. Exhausted toward dawn, they became more manageable. Though several escaped, the mountain men reached their cache three days later with forty head, fifteen more than had been stolen from them. Fearing pursuit, they dug up the furs and fled cross-country, nearly dying of thirst in the desert before they reached the Sweetwater. There Fitzpatrick transferred the precious plews into bullboats—and lost most of them when rapids wrecked the frail craft near the stream's junction with the North Platte.

These skirmishes over horseflesh were only one of the many aggravations between the two races. Root of the trouble, of course, was the clash for land, but even this does not account for the incredible ferocity which both sides later injected into their battles. Power politics must be blamed in part. The Spaniards stirred up the Utes and Comanches against the French, who retaliated in kind. Later the Hudson's Bay Company armed Blackfeet against American trappers, and profit-hungry Yankee traders armed anyone against everyone. Meanwhile the various tribes did their bloody best to prevent guns from reaching enemy redskins, and out of all this jockeying many an unhappy tangle resulted.

Disease, too, was a factor. All the mountain tribes must have heard of the smallpox epidemics which in 1780 reduced Pecos Pueblo in New Mexico from perhaps two thousand inhabitants to one hundred and eighty, and of a similar outbreak which in the 1830s destroyed the Mandan villages and crippled the Blackfeet. Cause of disease, to Indians, was an evil spirit, and although they couldn't attack a spirit, they could kill the whites who harbored it. Thus an outbreak of measles among the Cayuses led to the grisly deaths of Marcus Whitman and his lovely Narcissa at their mission in Oregon; similarly, smallpox underlay Utah's hit-and-run Black Hawk War during the sixties.

Southward, the Spanish, by buying slaves from Utes and Comanches, reaped a whirlwind of their own. Not only did these two tribes raid their red neighbors for choice merchandise to barter to the whites, but they also decided that the trade ought to work both ways. Following out this principle, the Comanches, for example, in 1760 carried away fifty women and children from Taos. True, a punitive expedition slaughtered four hundred Indians in revenge, and henceforth Taos was given wide berth by raiders. But the fifty captives were never recovered, and the rest of New Mexico suffered continuously.

Notorious leader of the Comanche attacks was Cuerno Verde, Green Horn, so named either because he wore a green (new-grown) deer horn as a headpiece, or because deer, when their horns are green, grow unusually bold. In 1779, outraged by the depredations of this "cruel scourge of this kingdom," Governor Anza, who three years before had founded a California hamlet called San Francisco, cornered Cuerno Verde's band on a creek in southern Colorado. (Hence today's Greenhorn Creek and Greenhorn Mountain, and not because they are associated with tenderfeet, as many suppose.) Outnumbered, the Indians forted up behind their dead horses and won Anza's grudging admiration with "a defense as brave as it was glorious." Nevertheless, "the aforesaid Cuerno Verde perished with his first-born son . . . four of his most famous captains, a medicine man who preached that he was immortal," and thirty-two others. "A larger number might have been killed, but I preferred the death of this chief to more of those who escaped."

For a time peace followed, maintained by treaties and bribes. But it was an uncertain calm. One night in 1824 while James Pattie, his father, and their party of 116 Americans were in Santa Fe trying to inveigle trapping permits from the governor, "the drum and fife and French horn began to sound in a manner that soon awakened and alarmed the whole town." Comanches had raided several estates on the Rio Pecos to the southeast of the city, had robbed and murdered the occupants, and had made off with five women, among whom was Jacova, beautiful young daughter of a former governor. Asked to aid in the pursuit, the Pattie party succeeded in getting ahead of the Indians, who had stripped their captives and were forcing the naked women to herd a large flock of stolen sheep across the snowy ground.

At the first fusillade the women darted forward. Three fell, pierced by Comanche spears. Young Pattie and another man (echoes of all the Indian stories ever written!) leaped into the field of fire, rescued the remaining two maidens, and carried them to cover, where James Pattie wrapped the trembling Jacova in his hunting shirt. Later, in Santa Fe, after thanking her rescuer in a speech of which he did not understand a syllable, "Jacova, showing me a bed prepared for me, placed herself between me and the door. I showed her that my clothes were not clean. She immediately brought me others. . . . She then brought my leather hunting shirt . . . put it on, to prove to me she was not ashamed of it." But alas for romance. The governor, who likewise had been softened by the rescue, granted the trapping permit and the party rode away from Santa Fe to the high adventures so engagingly—and, one suspects, somewhat decoratively—told in *The Personal Narrative of James O. Pattie of Kentucky*, published first in 1831 and later reprinted in Thwaite's indispensable *Early Western Travels*.

In that battle with the Comanches the Pattie party lost ten men before the Indians broke and fled. Returning from the pursuit, the Americans found the Spanish soldiers, who had been of no use whatsoever during the fray, riding their horses back and forth over the bodies of the fallen Indians and spearing those who happened still to be alive. Savage? Well, not long before, James Pattie had been equally horrified to see Indians put wolf skins over their backs, crawl on all fours up to the bodies of some slain enemies, cut out the hearts, chew them up, and spit the pieces on the corpses to show contempt. As exaggerated tales of such atrocities spread, excitable members of each race soon deemed the other completely barbaric and accordingly fought with abandoned fury, neither giving nor expecting quarter.

Further proof of an Indian's barbarism, so the settlers thought, was the way in which he would attack without provocation. A band might one day exchange gifts with every appearance of friendliness and the next week come a-scalping. Quite naturally the whites called this treachery, though an Indian would have been surprised by the epithet. He was simply impulsive. Also he was vain. Counting coup, whether it be the hair of white man or red, was a glorious achievement; when he saw a chance to manage the feat without undue risk to himself, temptation grew overpowering.

Another side of vanity was face-saving. A defeated war party would ride scores of miles hunting for defenseless scalps with which to assuage their bitterness. In time the fur trappers learned to guard against such attacks, but later settlers rarely did. To them the unexpected raids were both baffling and infuriating—just as the communal-living Indian, himself generous with food, clothing, and liquor, was violently exasperated by the whites' refusal to share items that apparently were possessed in abundance, a refusal indicative, to the savage, of complete lack of civilization.

An illustration of seemingly senseless Indian brutality—and of white man's brutal retaliation—occurs in a yarn spun by Norris Griggs, pioneer

Wyoming settler, to the Linn Sargents, who live on the lonely, lovely Hoback Rim, not far from the scene of the grisly tale.

A long time ago (it must have been in the 1870s), a man whom Griggs knew only as Jack settled down with an unnamed partner for a winter of trapping near the confluence of Grays and Snake rivers. One morning, their hobbled horses having strayed high on the brushy hillside, Jack's partner went to fetch them. As he paused for breath, inconspicuous among the boulders and brush, a group of Indians, traveling with their travois and squaws, rode up to the cabin.

Jack came to the door. After a flurry of talk and gesticulation one of the bucks let out a whoop, galloped wildly around the cabin, and, on repassing the door, knocked Jack's hat from his head. As the man stooped to pick it up several of the Indians, including squaws, hurled themselves on him. Why? Perhaps he refused to give them something they wished; perhaps, being alone, he looked like easy recompense for some previous humiliation. At any rate, screaming and leaping in passion, they threw him in the river, hauled him out, clubbed him in the belly, and threw him in again. And again. Eventually, of course, he didn't revive, but that kind of dying is a slow process.

Expecting every minute to be detected, the unarmed watcher on the hillside wriggled up to one of the horses, fashioned a crude bridle from the rope hobbles, and fled across the mountains for help at Fort Hall in southern Idaho. On the way he encountered a couple of cowboys who left off gathering beef to summon a posse. But soldiers beat the riders to the Indian village. When the cowboys arrived they found among the still-warm carcasses of several horses twenty or more slain Indians, including eight or nine papooses.

Says Griggs, "We took what we wanted from the dead Indians. I took some buckskin, some blankets, and an Indian packsaddle. I also took a needle gun. It was a single-shot, four-inch shell, breech load . . . I prized this gun highly."

The dark story of Indian hostilities is further complicated by population shifts which occurred during the late eighteenth and early nineteenth centuries. Made possible by the horse and inevitable by the pressure of white settlers pouring across the Allegheny Mountains, the complex wanderings are beyond the scope of this work, save as they touch the Rockies of Colorado and Wyoming.

In the latter state a group of horse-riding, numerically inferior Shoshone Indians were jammed into hill-rimmed basins and surrounded by mortal enemies. Though related to the despised Snakes of fur-trapper days (a timid, primitive people who ranged westward as far as Oregon), these later Shoshone seemed to have lifted themselves by their own bootstraps. Bitterly they fought for and held their ground against Sioux and Crows, Cheyennes and Arapaho, sometimes pouncing on these gun-armed raiders in early days with no better weapons than bow, lance, and pogamoggan, a two-foot stick to which was attached a leather-covered stone.

Out of this welter emerged a magnificent Shoshonean chief, Washakie. Because he knew how to hit and then run, to be patient in avoiding strong parties, and to attack careless ones with a maximum of surprise, he managed to wage a score or more of defensive wars without suffering a major defeat; and as emigrants began pouring westward he became, through circumstance and inclination, the stanchest Indian ally our Rocky Mountain settlers had.

Washakie did not, of course, inaugurate Shoshonean friendship with the whites. That tradition stems back to Sacagawea, wife of the French trapper, Touissant Charbonneau, who strapped her newborn son to her back and helped lead Lewis and Clark across the mountains of Montana. The expedition's journal sums her up in two inclusive sentences: "With her helpless infant she rode with the men, guiding us unerringly through mountain passes and lonely places. Intelligent, cheerful, resourceful, tireless and faithful, she inspired us all."[3]

Somewhere in Montana, Washakie was born. Perhaps he saw Sacagawea on her trip with Lewis and Clark, though both the place and the

---

[3] The mystery of Sacagawea's death adds a piquant footnote to mountain history. On December 20, 1812, William Luttig, fur trader, noted in his journal, "This evening the wife of Charbonneau, a Snake squaw, died of putrid fever." Evidence inconclusive. Charbonneau had three wives. However, on August 11, 1813, the court in St. Louis appointed Luttig guardian of Baptiste, Sacagawea's son, and of Touissant, Charbonneau's offspring by another squaw. Later William Clark assumed Baptiste's guardianship; the explorer had loved the papoose since expedition days, calling him Pomp, the dancer. And it was Clark who let Prince Paul of Württemberg take Baptiste to Europe for schooling. Would this have happened while Sacagawea lived and no mention be made of her? Indian authority Clark Wissler thinks not.

Now skip sixty years or so. A withered crone appears on the Shoshone reservation in Wyoming. She is Sacagawea, she says. Long ago she left Charbonneau, married a Comanche, lived in what is now Oklahoma. Her husband having died in battle, she returned to her people. An adopted son, Bazil, who had not seen her for half a century, accepted her. So did famed missionary John Roberts, who understood the Shoshone better than any other man; and when the woman died in 1884, she was buried in the queer little Indian cemetery outside Fort Washakie, where many of the graves are now surrounded by iron bedsteads and decorated on Memorial Day with paper flowers. Her tombstone reads "Sacagawea." You can decide its authenticity as you choose.

date of his birth are uncertain. Probably the event occurred between 1798 and 1804, but some authorities set the time even earlier. Blackfeet destroyed his native village; his mother, with her three sons and two daughters, wandered helplessly through the mountains until she found refuge with the Lemhi in Idaho. Washakie early distinguished himself as a warrior; in his youth a Blackfoot arrow left under his cheek the deep scar which he carried to his death. By 1843 he had joined a small band of Shoshone located near Bridger's fort and had become its chief. Here it was, after the Mormons had burned Old Gabe's establishment and had erected their own Fort Supply nearby, that Washakie picked up a Colt revolver and made his famous remark, laden with all the wistfulness of every Indian who has lost his hunting ground:

"The white man can make this [the revolver] and a little thing that he carries in his pocket, so that he can tell where the sun is on a dark day, and when it is night he can tell when it will come daylight. This is because the face of the Father is toward him, and his back is toward us. But after awhile the Great Father will quit being mad and will turn his face toward us. Then our skins will be light, then our minds will be strong like the white man's, and we can make and use things like he does."

Don't assume from this that the man wasted time in wishful dreaming. To save his outnumbered, enemy-encircled tribesmen he repeatedly had to resort not only to high diplomacy and skilled warfare, but also to a kind of cold nerve that is seldom possessed by the ordinary Indian.

Picture the year 1851. All the tribes of the plains had been summoned to a great council at Fort Laramie by Tom Fitzpatrick, one-time fur trader who had hired himself out to the United States Government and had become a rarity of Western history, an honest Indian agent. Among other things Fitzpatrick was trying to induce the tribes to grant Oregon- and California-bound emigrants certain transit privileges and also to accept definite territorial limitations for themselves.

The Shoshone were nervous. "All the tribes of the plains" meant every enemy they had, gathered into one spot—ten thousand, if figures on the conference can be trusted—and although peace would prevail at the talks, there was grave risk in exposing themselves to the heavily armed bands traveling to and from the fort. Shortsighted wisdom counseled staying away.

But not Washakie. He rode to Fort Laramie, so reports say, at the head of a thousand warriors. If the figure is correct, he must have drained nearly every able-bodied male from his now defenseless villages. If he ran into a major battle and was defeated . . . The significant thing about

Washakie, chief of Wyoming's Shoshone, was a long-time ally of the whites and the mountain Indians' most able defensive warrior. This photograph was taken in 1884, when he was eighty or more years old.

A fair tourist on the Silverton road, first of Otto Mears's tight-spiraling narrow-gauges, is briefed on the scenery of the San Juans. Mears himself stands inconspicuously by the cowcatcher.

the bluff is that one Indian could impose such iron discipline on other Indians, for the mountain tribes were notoriously disorganized and individualistic.

Down they came. Full panoply, of course. Standards grisly with skulls and horns, lances fluttering with ribbons and coyote tails. Vermilion, blues, yellows, greens. Swirls of eagle feathers. Sunbursts of beadwork and porcupine quills against white buckskin. So, too, the assembled Sioux, Cheyennes, Arapaho, Crows. But these Shoshone, for all their yelling and breakneck horsemanship, swept by the log fort with the precision of trained cavalry. Moreover, through the machinations of their good friend, Jim Bridger, most of the Shoshone were armed with rifles. Whites and Indians stared agog. Afterward, at the dog feasts and during the interminable oratory of the council, Washakie, his lithe six feet clad in a chief's magnificent regalia, was equally impressive, equally efficient. When the Shoshone went home again, the Sioux knew that here was a man to be reckoned with.

And so did the whites.

Though it is doubtful whether Washakie or any Indian recognized at the outset how irresistible the palefaces would become, the Shoshone chief was shrewd enough not to add their enmity to the load he was already carrying. Moreover, his early contacts with the interlopers were fortunate. One of his friends was Jim Bridger. Another was Brigham Young, whose religion taught that the red men were offspring of Israel's lost tribes and hence better dealt with by missionaries than by soldiers. Thus Washakie's natural kindliness, linking friendship to expediency, left Wyoming's section of the Overland Trail freer from bloodshed than other stretches. One legend even says that he offered the breasts of his own squaw for thawing the frozen feet of a Mormon freighter.

He was, however, an Indian dealing with Indians. When the Civil War caused withdrawal of Federal troops throughout the West, one of his turbulent sub-tribes, the Bannocks, thought they recognized opportunity. Reinforced by malcontents from Washakie's own band, they fell on the South Pass stage stations, burning, plundering, murdering; and because the whites were used to Shoshonean friendship, the attacks were doubly paralyzing. For a time the Oregon Trail was closed (a feat no other tribe accomplished), and Ben Holladay's stagecoaches scurried southward to safer routes near the Colorado-Wyoming border.

For this triumph the Bannocks paid a fearful price—just as their fathers had thirty-six years before when Bannock raids roused 250 fur trappers, led by twenty-year-old Jim Bridger, to slaughter 488 Indians in a dreadful battle of vengeance. (Figures supplied by James Beckwourth, probably with characteristic exaggeration, though he was present at the fray.) Now retribution visited the Bannocks again. In January 1863, General Patrick Connor, that abrupt and uncompromising man who bludgeoned Utah open to mining, marched against the marauders with 300 soldiers. Snow and sub-zero weather crippled seventy of the troopers. To the others a Bear River settler named Petty brought word of the Indians' location in a deep gully on the Utah-Idaho line. Connor gave Petty five dollars for the information and deployed his forces, some to guard the north end of the ravine while others marched along it from the south. Two hundred and twenty-four Bannocks died in that trap; of those who escaped, several were shot down while trying to swim the icy river. Federal casualties: fourteen dead, forty-nine wounded.

The Shoshone nation was in an uproar. A tremendous conclave met on Bear River, war drums boomed, hotheads cried for blood. But Washakie was there too. Whatever he may have felt inside himself, he knew futility when he saw it. His counsel prevailed; though sporadic raids continued, there was no general uprising.

Elsewhere Indian affairs were marching toward the horrible years 1864–67. Only a few of the causes can be touched on here: Denver, founded squarely on an Arapaho camp site; hordes of covered wagons, stagecoaches, handcarts, wheelbarrows chewing ruts into the hunting grounds and reducing the Fort Laramie treaty of 1851 to meaninglessness; retaliations that bred new retaliations. Additional treaties solved nothing. Scarcely had the Arapaho and Cheyennes signed one in 1861 than they insisted they had not understood its terms and would not obey its provisions. As garrisons were drawn into the vortex of the Civil War, Chief Little Crow of the Sioux began to preach a word new to Indian ears—unity. In the proverbial nick of time Colorado's Elbridge Gerry, husband of a Cheyenne squaw, discovered a plot for a general uprising, and his warning undoubtedly forestalled a hideous massacre. Meanwhile cattle raids, horse raids, and minor skirmishes kept nerves on trigger edge until, in June 1864, uneasiness exploded into terror with the murder of the Hungate family twenty-five miles east of Denver.

The mutilated bodies of the settler, his wife, and two children were exhibited in the capital city. The next night a strange sound sent the town's women and youngsters pell-mell into barricaded buildings and brought out patrols under full arms. The frightening noise, it developed, was caused by Mexican cowboys singing to their cattle, but the incident is not comic, for it illustrates the mental state of terrified people who felt their government had abandoned them in a hostile land.

Meantime in New Mexico the territorial legislature prepared a frantic memorial for Congress: during the fifteen months previous to 1864, 99 residents of the territory had been killed, 47 wounded (more deaths than wounds is always a weather vane on ferocity), 18 taken captive. Stolen were 821 horses, 4809 cattle, 98,448 sheep, 641 mules, 3437 goats, 83 donkeys, the whole calculated with implausible meticulousness to be worth $448,638.92. Help!—and the best Indian fighter of them all was sent to the rescue with a handful of men. The Mescalero Apaches were whipped first, and then Kit Carson, lately as honest an Indian agent as Tom Fitzpatrick and now a colonel in the United States Army, led 14 officers and 375 men against 7000 Navajos. The snow was deep that January of 1864; three days were spent in making what was normally a one-day march. Such weather plus Kit Carson proved too much for the savages. Starved and outmaneuvered, they were finally trapped in Cañon de Chelly. If blood makes for triumphs, Kit Carson had his chance then. But after his early baptism of gore during trapper days Kit had lost his taste for blood. In what has been called "the greatest feat of Indian warfare ever accomplished by an American soldier," he forced a peaceful surrender and took the Navajos on their "long walk" to Bosque Redondo, a strange and enemy-haunted reservation in eastern New Mexico, where the government's efforts to make farmers of them broke their spirits and came close to breaking the tribe.

Unfortunately there were no Kit Carsons in Colorado, where, after the Hungate massacre, some eight hundred Cheyennes and Arapaho heeded the advice of Territorial Governor John Evans and voluntarily surrendered at Fort Lyon. After being fed for a time by the government, the Indians were allowed to go to Sand Creek for their annual fall hunt. Apparently the band caused no untoward trouble. But elsewhere there were atrocities, real and rumored. "For three hundred miles west of the Big Sandy in Kansas every building had been burned, all movable property taken, and about eighty of the settlers massacred." Throughout Colorado opinion grew that the Indians needed "summary and unmistakable chastisement"—a not unreasonable attitude among people whose communications had been shattered, whose living costs had been shot sky high because of freighting difficulties, and many of whose acquaintances or relatives had been brutally murdered. In obedience to this attitude, and apparently to nothing else, Colonel John M. Chivington, hero of the Union's stand against a Confederate attack in

New Mexico's Apache Canyon, set out in late November against the Indian encampment on Sand Creek.

At sunrise 950 men, supported by four cannon, attacked the village on the broad, brush-and-water-flecked valley bottom. Surprise was complete; the howitzers were frightful. To no avail Chief Black Kettle raised in front of his lodge an American flag and under it a white one of truce. Arms raised in surrender, Chief White Antelope fell dead. So did Left Hand, standing immobile, refusing to fight his "friends." Those few Indians who managed to collect enough wits and weapons to fight back killed ten soldiers and wounded forty. Chivington estimated that Indian casualties reached five hundred. Other reports range from seventy-five to three hundred, most of whom "were old men, women, and children."

If the whites previously had had horror to inflame them, now the red men had it. What difference that Chivington was censured by the War Department and removed from his command; that the families of the slain Arapaho and Cheyennes were given reparations? After Sand Creek all the plains east of the Rockies, from Mexico to Canada, burst into warfare. It is neither possible nor pertinent here to unravel that bloody skein, except for one crimson strand that leads, by indirection, back to Washakie.   •

Exacerbation in the flesh of the Sioux was a trail which scarred their lands along the eastern foot of Wyoming's Big Horn Mountains. Built in the early sixties by J. M. Bozeman to reach the gold fields of Montana, this road and the Army posts constructed to defend it were a clear violation of the treaty of Fort Laramie. Jim Bridger knew there would be trouble and said so. In an effort to locate a saner route he succeeded in taking wagons for the first time through the wild Owl Creek range to the west, but the way was rough. Travelers preferred the Bozeman Trail and, aided by the threat of the forts, used it with comparative impunity until Sand Creek made all the West unsafe.

In December 1866, a wood train started out from Fort Phil Kearney to forage for fuel in the nearby mountains. One of its scouts sighted some Indians, sent word back to the post. Out galloped Colonel Fetterman, seventy-nine soldiers, and two civilians. The cold air tingled; their half-trained horses pranced; the men were spoiling for a fight. When they spotted a few Sioux they chased them merrily up a gulch. Shortly thereafter the fort heard brisk firing, then silence. More troops went forth to investigate, found every last one of Fetterman's command lying dead on the frozen ground.

Panic swept the undermanned post. Cooks and even prisoners were armed; civilian scout Portugee Phillips rode two hundred miles through a howling blizzard to fetch reinforcements. But Red Cloud, wily leader of the ambush, failed to press his advantage and the war dwindled off to a series of skirmishes—fifty-one of them in the next six months, during which 154 whites were killed and more than 800 head of stock were lost. Then came the climax. On July 31, 1867, Red Cloud ambushed another wood crew. But this time the handful of soldiers had an opportunity to fort up behind the tough frames of their wagon boxes; and when Red Cloud's thousand cocksure savages came howling down the hill, they met a hideous surprise. These soldiers were armed with brand-new repeater rifles, and the carnage they dealt has been called by some excited commentators the most magnificent defensive stand in all Indian history. Red Cloud fought the whites no more. But he brooded as only an Indian can brood. Before he would let himself be confined to a reservation he conducted one last face-saving raid. Across the Big Horns his warriors went, struck viciously at their hereditary enemy, the Shoshone. Thirty of Washakie's tribesmen died; quantities of horses were stolen.

The incident brought Washakie's troubles to a head. After the crushing of the Bannocks, the harassed Federal Government had given the Shoshone a huge hunk of land in central Wyoming, but no definite boundaries had been fixed and hence there could be no definite protection from encroaching whites or Indians. Passionately the chief pleaded for the government to demarcate and defend his land, as it was under obligation to do.

"I cannot go for a buffalo hunt," he mourned, "or my people will be unprotected. I cannot farm, for my crops will be destroyed."

Cry the wind. Whites kept pouring onto Shoshone land, attracted by the fertile valley of the Popo Agie. Then Red Cloud struck. Despairing of government support, Washakie withdrew his band to old stamping grounds around Henrys Fork of the Green, spent his time visiting between Fort Bridger and Salt Lake Valley. But again expansionism, this time in the form of the Union Pacific Railroad, doomed their home. To remove the Shoshone from the right of way the government granted them the 2,774,400-acre Wind River reservation, including the valley of the Popo Agie, and built Fort Brown (renamed Fort Washakie in 1878).

Younger bucks rankled under the humiliation of being shifted around and guarded at the whim of the whites. Their chief's seventy years sat heavy on his shoulders, they grumbled; he was no longer fit to lead them. Hearing the talk, Washakie vanished. For two months, legend says, no Shoshone saw him. Then suddenly the gray-haired warrior reappeared with seven enemy scalps taken in individual combat and flung the trophies at the feet of his detractors. When they could match that, they could talk of deposing him. No one moved.

Still his reservation troubles were not ended. In 1872 the Bannocks petitioned for removal to Idaho. To whites coveting the Popo Agie this presented a logical argument: fewer Shoshone would need fewer lands. Pressure increased. Seeing the handwriting on the wall, Washakie sold for twenty-five thousand dollars six hundred thousand acres of fertile ground he had no chance of hanging onto anyhow.

He had passed seventy now, but war hadn't finished with him yet. When Arapaho raided the South Pass mining towns in 1874, Captain Bates called on Washakie for help. He responded with 166 Shoshone warriors, and in a wild melee the enemy was completely defeated. Opportunity now to avenge a thousand wrongs. But Washakie stood on a hillside, "white hair blowing in the wind as he roared, 'Don't kill 'em any more! We have whipped 'em! Don't kill 'em any more!'"

Nearly eighty years old, and his greatest service to his white allies lay ahead. After the Red Cloud wars the government had abandoned its illegal forts along the Bozeman Trail and had turned the country back to the Sioux. Futile gesture. Gold was discovered in the Black Hills, and the stampede was on. For a time Federal troops tried to keep trespassers off the land of the Sioux, Arapaho, and Cheyennes; but angry prospectors and settlers sneaked by, were attacked by Indians, and set up a yowl for help that all America echoed. Caught in the dilemma, General Sheridan warned the Indians that the whites would be protected. In the war that followed Custer was annihilated and General Crook probably would have been—save for Washakie.

Eight days before the Custer battle and only eight miles distant from its site, Crook was driving against Crazy Horse's alliance of Sioux, Cheyennes, and Arapaho. With the famous Indian fighter were several Crow scouts and 213 Shoshone warriors, "resplendent in all the fantastic adornment of feathers, beads, brass buttons, bells, scarlet cloth and flashing lances." Commanding them was Washakie, naked to the waist and wearing a gorgeous headdress that swept the ground behind his horse's tail. Pomp—plus ability. When Crazy Horse tried to close his pincers in almost exactly the same maneuver that trapped Custer, the Shoshone helped forestall him, and after a sharp skirmish Crook withdrew to lick his wounds.

For these services President Grant later sent Washakie a saddle studded with silver ornaments and splashed with the reds, blues, and yellows so dear to an Indian's color-loving eye. In silence the chief accepted it.

The Indian agent who made the presentation prompted him. "What shall I say to General Grant?"

"Nothing."

Horrified, the agent expostulated.

Washakie looked at him, then made the reply so often quoted in Wyoming annals: "When a favor is shown a Frenchman, he feels it in his head, and his tongue speaks. When a kindness is shown an Indian, he feels it in his heart, and the heart has no tongue."

For services rendered, one silver-mounted saddle. And then this:

Among the Indians whom Washakie had fought at the Bates Battle and later with Crook on the Rosebud were his lifelong enemies, the Arapaho. Crushed finally, this turbulent tribe agreed to a reservation in the Dakotas but quarreled with the Sioux over hunting rights and headed south for new lands in what is now Oklahoma. In eastern Wyoming a thousand or so of them stopped, sent emissaries to Washington to dicker for space along the Platte. Meanwhile it was winter, the tribe was starving, and the government did not know what to do with it. The agents turned to Washakie. Would the Shoshone "temporarily" harbor on their land these enemy people?

Reluctantly the chief called a council. Afterward Agent Patten reported to Washington: "Washakie and his headmen, though they dislike bitterly to divide their property with other bands, have too great hearts to say no. . . . [They] should receive reasonable compensation." But after all they were only Indians. The "temporary" arrangement has never ended, and compensation waited until 1937, when a belatedly appreciative government allowed the Shoshone to file suit and awarded them nearly five million dollars, in return for which the unwilling hosts confirmed their guests' ownership of the lands the Arapaho occupied.

Neither tribe ever liked the expedient. From the beginning each looked down on the other, several disgusted Shoshone moved to Utah and became Mormons, and both groups were mutually mortified when a son of Washakie married an Arapaho girl—one of the only four intertribal unions ever consummated in more than half a century of side-by-side living.

Washakie was an old, old man now, and it is to his old age that many familiar stories attach: the blue blanket he wound tight about his trunk and the tall-crowned black cowboy hat decorated with a silver coffin plate reading OUR BABY, which he had obtained in Evanston; his quirk, after a meal at some white man's house, of putting leftover food in his coat pocket and carrying it to his children or grandchildren; his persistent fears of the Sioux when he was too old to fight again—fears which made him resist vigorously every proposal to abandon the fort which bore his name. It is gratifying to note that in this, at least, the government respected him; although danger had passed, the fort was maintained until 1909, nine years after Washakie's death.

In 1897 he fell ill. He was a hundred years old, more or less (the date of his birth, remember, is uncertain), and now he asked for baptism. It was administered—and he recovered. Powerful medicine this! Ailing Shoshone flocked from far and near to get some for themselves, and missionary John Roberts was beside himself trying to convince them that the value of the ceremony was spiritual, not physical.

Finally the stout heart wore out, and on February 2, 1900, Washakie, chief of the Shoshone, died. His last fear, in a life filled with many fears, was that he might go to white man's heaven and be lost to his people.

CHAPTER VI

AS LEAVES WHEN WINTER COMES

SHORTLY after the close of the Civil War there drifted into southern Colorado's San Luis Valley a twenty-five-year-old veteran who would do more than any other man to break the Utes and open western Colorado for mining. His name was Otto Mears. He looked colorless: undersized, scraggly-bearded, dark of complexion. But life had honed him down, both physically and mentally, until he was as sharp and as resilient as the stub end of a piece of baling wire.

Born in Russia on May 3, 1841, of a Jewish mother and an English father, Otto Mears had been orphaned by the time he was four. For the next five years he was just one more mouth to feed among a maternal uncle's twelve unfriendly children. By the time he was nine his welcome had worn out; alone, he was shipped aboard a lumber vessel to a relative of his father in England. He wasn't wanted there either. Onto another boat he went and off to one more of his multitudinous uncles, this time in New York. Same story—no place for the scrawny, pinch-faced boy who could speak scarcely a word of English. After a few months he was sent off to still another uncle who had joined the California gold rush. Over the Isthmus of Panama by dugout and horseback the lad went—a dreadful trip in the early fifties—and up the coast to the then raw city of San Francisco. There even his supply of uncles ran out. No one in the bay city had heard of the man he wanted. Forlorn and penniless, Otto Mears, just turned eleven, stood literally at the ends of the earth.

A woman he had met on the boat took him to the rooms she occupied with her husband. "Finally the boardinghouse thought the best thing for me was to sell newspapers." Gold-crazy California in the fifties. No one has told us what it looked like to a homeless child. Otto Mears does not. In the laconic autobiography he dictated nearly seventy-five years later to Arthur Ridgway, chief engineer of the Denver and Rio Grande, he covers the period in fifteen sentences. He sold papers, learned tinsmithing, worked for a storekeeper. "I had to get up early in the morning and take a team and go ten miles and load a car with merchandise, but first I had to milk the cows. In lifting the large bundles up so early in the morning, I hurt my back." He never entered a classroom after he was ten, and very seldom before that.

Growing older, he tramped from gold field to gold field, took out naturalization papers, and, at the age of twenty, when the War between the States broke out, enlisted in the First Regiment of California volunteers. "It was hard to tell in the army, when walking, where you are." But he got to New Mexico, fought the Confederates at Val Verde and Pigeon's Ranch, the only major Civil War engagements on Rocky Mountain soil, was shunted off under Kit Carson's command, and dragged his shivering bones through the bleak winter campaign that broke the Navajos.

Finally, in 1864, he was discharged, drifted up to Santa Fe, and got a job in a store. He was a good trader—so good that a rival firm hired him away and set him up in a business of his own. At least the store carried his name, but the backers held the reins, and at the ripe old age of twenty-four Otto Mears was through heeding other men's beck and call. Within a year he was drifting again, this time into Colorado, where his shrewd eyes fell on Fort Garland, which the government had built some years earlier as a damper on the Ute Indians of the San Luis Valley.

At Fort Garland the Army was paying eighty dollars per thousand for lumber, twenty dollars per hundred for flour. Promptly Otto built a gristmill with lava for grindstones, and a sawmill that was held together by wooden pegs and strips of rawhide. To supply the gristmill he homesteaded a farm in the upper part of the valley. It was a long haul from his mill, but the soil was good: his two hundred acres of wheat, primitively sown and primitively reaped, yielded sixty bushels to the acre.

By the time the grain was grown, however, Fort Garland was no longer a market. Undaunted, Mears rounded up some wagons, loaded on the wheat, and headed overland for the gold camps near California Gulch, as the Leadville district was then known. No roads existed. To get over Poncha Pass he had to hack his way with axes and shovels. While he was at it, along came the part owner of San Luis Valley's huge Baca Grant, William Gilpin, ex-governor of Colorado Territory, soldier, explorer, statesman, and, above all, a geopolitician born at least a century ahead of his time.

To this dignitary the sweating young freighter delivered what was perhaps Colorado's first diatribe on the subject of good highways. Gilpin grinned it off, inspected Mears's work, and suggested that the builder charter the finished product as a toll road.

"And while you're at it," Gilpin went on, "why not make the grade sufficiently gradual for a railway?"

Otto blinked at that one, for there wasn't a locomotive within a thousand miles. Nonetheless, Gilpin's words hung in his mind. After he had wrestled his wagons over the pass and had sold his wheat to Charles Nachtrieb in the Arkansas Valley, he went on to Denver and paid the legislature five dollars for a toll-road charter. It was the first sprout in the Rockies' most fabulous transportation system—a system that in due course would branch out to include some of the zaniest railroads ever built.

Other seeds were also taking root. Though only a handful of Americans resided in the upper San Luis Valley, they thought they would benefit from having governmental headquarters of their own. By various intricacies they secured passage of a bill creating a new county, and now began a tug of war for its seat. Otto favored Saguache.[1] It wasn't a town—nothing but a mud-floored store which Otto had built on his homestead by Saguache Creek—but it could be a town if voted as such. Legend says that Otto offered one John Lawrence five hundred dollars to deliver the ballots of the local Mexicans. Lawrence held out for seven hundred dollars. Turned down, he indicted Mears for trying to buy votes, whereupon Otto indicted Lawrence for selling them. The matter ended in a draw and Saguache became the county seat. (The Circuit Court, when trying to sit there, had to spend a day poring over maps to locate the place. First case: the trial of Rocky Mountain Hank for cutting a bartender's hand with a butcher knife. Verdict: not guilty.) Otto, twenty-seven years old now, was elected county treasurer. He collected taxes in hides, furs, and other produce, hauled the stuff to Denver, and converted it into cash. No one in the territorial capital paid much attention to him—yet. But the day was coming when Otto Mears's solid block of southern counties could elect whatever governor or senator he nodded toward.

Of more immediate concern to the settlers of Colorado's western slope, however, were the sawed-off little immigrant's dealings with the Ute Indians. These Utes were a queer, fragmentated tribe. Although compelled by geography to roam the mountain valleys in isolated groups, they had played their small part in history: harrying Spanish colonists,

[1] Concerning the sound of Saguache, one early newspaper said, "It was past the power of pronouncing in the beginning. Probably it was a war-whoop used by the Indians, though it is said to mean something like 'blue earth'—but later it was modified until it may now be safely attempted by people in good health, the usual result being 'si-watch'."

helping spread horse culture, using stone forts to fight off raiding Arapaho and Cheyennes (a defensive wrinkle almost unprecedented among American Indians), putting a sudden end to Robidoux's trading forts in Utah and on the Gunnison River, and, in 1854, wiping out a sordid collection of mud huts on the Arkansas where seventeen Americans and a few Mexicans were celebrating the Christmas holidays with a keg of Taos Lightning. (Six years later the modern city of Pueblo would be founded on those supposedly ghost-haunted ruins.)

These attacks, however, were pretty much hit or miss. The Utes had almost no tribal organization, which was a fortunate thing for the miners who swarmed through the hills after the discovery of gold. Not only did many of the prospectors go forth in small groups, poorly armed, but some of them even used Arapaho Indians as guides, in spite of warnings from Kit Carson, then agent for the Utes, that such an association with the Utes' mortal enemies was an invitation to trouble. Several parties paid for their temerity—in the early sixties horrified travelers found at Dead Man's Gulch in the Gunnison country the mutilated bodies of six Americans and their Indian guide (an Arapaho?)—but luckily there was no general uprising. And when a handful of young bucks, excited by the warlike preparations of the plains Indians, did try a few forays in 1863, they were promptly chased over half the mountains in the state by Major Wynkoop's energetic cavalry. This so discouraged the entire tribe that its multitudinous bands—White River Utes, Tabeguache Utes, Mouache Utes, Capote Utes, Weeminuche Utes, Uintah Utes, and what not—agreed to sit down with the government at a council in the San Luis Valley.

The purpose of the talk was to induce the Indians to leave the valley. They demurred, and for once made their point stick. In 1863 Colorado was too busy with the plains Indians to risk a wrathful attack on her flanks, and today the fruitless powwow would be forgotten save for one thing: the accidental emergence of an Indian leader almost as renowned as Washakie.

White arbiters, realizing the hopelessness of trying to deal individually with each of the bands, insisted that all talks be carried on through a single supreme chief. The Utes' choice for the job was old Nevava, head of the comparatively powerful White River group. The Americans rejected him, choosing instead (perhaps at Kit Carson's suggestion) a squat, murderous, physically powerful, thirty-year-old leader of the inoffensive Tabeguaches. His name was Ouray, and although his standards tended to be strictly utilitarian, he was able to see beyond his own nose. (Carl Schurz, when Secretary of the Interior, called him "the brightest Indian I have ever met.") By way of additional qualifications Ouray was fluent in Spanish and could talk bits of English, having been a sheepherder, during his youth, near Kit Carson's home at Taos.

There was another factor which made the council's choice luckier than the choosers realized: the boundless compassion of Chipeta, Ouray's lovely squaw. Local mythology, impatient of such imponderables as a winsome personality, has had her actively save more scalps than cold facts admit; she did not gallop over bloodied trails with warnings and rescuings, but she did live with a man completely devoted to her, and though the touch of her hand on the workings of his savage mind was perhaps too gentle to be weighed, it cannot be ignored.

Ouray's stewardship is a story of tragedy, and his awareness of the tragedy has touched him with the same dignity that makes Washakie so appealing a figure. Economically the Utes, like all Indians, were doomed. Less than ten thousand of them found bare sustenance in the mountain parks which now support a million whites, and that waste alone became intolerable as the demand for land increased. Meanwhile the enemy was conveniently supplying them with the means for race suicide. As far back as 1835, Lieutenant Gaines P. Kingsbury, a member of Colonel Henry Dodge's far-flung mission to the tribes west of the Mississippi, had noted that the piedmont Indians rated the best things of life, in order of descending importance, as liquor, tobacco, guns, horses, and women. "They are very fond of whiskey, and will sell their horses, blankets, and everything else"—more explicitly, the virtue of their wives —"for a drink of it." The Utes were particularly susceptible (hence added significance to Ouray's lifelong abstinence from both alcohol and tobacco) and by 1886 were so debased that a discouraged agency clerk described them as "blanket Indians . . . lazy, shiftless, vicious, and densely ignorant."

Even their bravery was turned into buffoonery. For example, there existed in Denver, toward the close of the sixties, an agency where "Indian parents might become wise unto salvation and gradually be brought under the refining influence of civilization." To this center of uplift a band of Utes came one day bearing several Arapaho scalps. Sniffing opportunity, Curtis, the agency interpreter, and Dave Cook, Denver's sheriff, put their heads together with a visiting animal trainer named Bartholomew. Why not cash in on Denver's animosity toward the Arapaho by placing the victorious Utes on exhibition in Bartholo-mew's circus tent?

The Utes, who probably were first rendered howling drunk, acceded, but their agent, Major James Thompson, wired the Indian commissioner

in Washington. The show was forbidden, not because it might impair
the dignity of the participants but because the Arapaho might be shocked
into reprisals. However, no law officer in Denver would enforce the re-
straining order, whereupon the Utes, decked out in full war paint,
paraded down Fifteenth Street in a noisy preview to the main show.
Behind them, smirking under tall plug hats, came the impresarios.

Left to his own resources, Major Thompson loaded a brace of pistols
and secreted himself in a strategic doorway. As the paraders drew
abreast, he leaped forth, brandishing his weapons and thundering:

"Vamoose pronto!"

Pronto is no word for it. Executing a lightning about-face, the Utes
bowled over their would-be promoters, trampled the plug hats in the
dirt, and hied themselves to the suburbs, where they sat down around a
keg and reconsidered the charms of a showman's life.

Meanwhile, the wars on the plains having simmered down, the government marshaled its biggest guns, including Kit Carson, long-time friend
of Ouray's, and in 1868 persuaded the Utes to move west of the Continental Divide—or thought it persuaded them. But when the day for the
migration came the Indians refused to budge. Confusion and uncertainty.
Kit Carson had just died at Fort Lyon, Colorado. Who was to reason
with these recalcitrant savages now?

Otto Mears, twenty-eight years old and resident of the territory for
less than three years, was suggested. Little, whiskery, and smelling perhaps of his store and of his mules, he must have looked unprepossessing
enough in that assemblage of gold braid. But he had an ability which the
generals and the politicians lacked, one which had all but disappeared
with the passing of the fur traders. He could squat down in a filthy, lice-
infested tepee and chatter to its occupants without the least show of
repugnance or superiority, attributes which completely tainted the average white man's contact with his red brethren.

Just talking to Ouray's headmen was no mean accomplishment. Ute,
unlike Navajo, was so tongue-twisting a medium that not many Americans essayed it. To the Indians this looked like one more proof of hau-
teur. Accordingly Ouray retaliated in kind. Although he knew English,
he belittled would-be white suppliants, at least in the eyes of his tribesmen, by forcing them to approach him through the medium of an interpreter. But not Otto Mears. Though perhaps the trader spoke Ute
as he did English, with a thick Russian accent, the Indians understood
him. He came as an equal and they listened. From now on his history
and theirs would be inextricably linked.

Scarcely had the Utes moved across the Divide to their new 26,000-

square-mile reservation before the treaty was violated. It should not be assumed, however, that Mears or any other white treaty maker of the mid-nineteenth century had negotiated in bad faith. He could not have foreseen how rapidly the empty land would fill. It was circumstance, not men, which tricked the Utes. In 1871 silver was discovered in the San Juans, and a new horde of prospectors swarmed across the hitherto almost untouched mountains of southwestern Colorado.

The government tried to keep faith. A company of troops was ordered to drive the trespassers off the reservation, but it soon became evident that a small-scale civil war would attend the effort. Next the government endeavored, through Commissioner Felix Brunot, to buy the San Juan mineral lands. The Utes refused to dicker; once again soldiers marched against the infuriated miners. In despair Brunot turned to Otto Mears, now post trader at the agency on the Gunnison River.

How honest was Mears? Did he react principally to this: the certain knowledge that an influx of miners into Indian-free country would enhance the profits of his embryo toll roads and freight outfits? Or to the equally sure realization that nothing in God's world could long stop the miners and that the Utes had best make what they could of a hopeless situation? In his harsh accent he said to Brunot:

"I think I can get them to sign if you let me offer them a perpetual annuity of twenty-five thousand dollars a year. And for Ouray, one thousand dollars a year for the next ten years."

A private payment to one Indian? Brunot scowled. "The United States Government does not tender bribes!"

"It's a salary. He'll earn it, keeping his chiefs in line."

Ouray pocketed the thousand dollars, talked to his people. Did he feel only the smooth, cool touch of the money? Or was the handwriting plain upon the wall? "I realize the destiny of my people," he once told Governor Elbert of Colorado Territory. "We shall fall as the leaves of the trees when winter comes, and the lands we have roamed for countless generations will be given up to the miner and the plowshare . . . and we shall be buried out of sight. My part is to protect my people and yours, as far as I can, from violence and bloodshed . . . and bring them into friendly relations."

In September 1873 enough Utes signed their X's to make the sale valid. Delighted by his success, Brunot proposed to take the Ute agent, General Charles Adams, Otto Mears, Ouray, and several lesser chiefs back to Washington. The fifteen-thousand-dollar three-month excursion was broached to the Indians as a gesture of friendship; actually, as in the case of many another Indian junket, it was designed so to impress the restive chiefs with white men's power that they would be more inclined to heed the terms of their treaties.

East they went. And there, at a reception in the White House, the once unwanted urchin of San Francisco's alleyways shook hands with the President of the United States, introduced Grant to Ouray as the Indians' "great father." Ouray, nothing if not logical, thereupon embraced Mrs. Grant as his great mother, Nelly Grant as his great sister.

Uneasy peace had been bought for an annual twenty-five-thousand-dollar mess of pottage. On annuity day every Ute who could draw breath swarmed into the agencies, collected his allotment of cash and goods—then sat on the ground in front of the store and gambled it all away at Spanish monte. The old curse of improvidence. Broke and either unable or unwilling to find hides on their hunting grounds, they could not clothe themselves. The agencies issued store trousers. These offered certain impediments; promptly the bucks cut out the seats. The dainty beaded (and dirty) buckskin skirts of the squaws failing, the agency issued cloth. Baffled by it, the women cut head holes in the middle and bunched the material around their waists with rope.

They could not even feed themselves. The southern Ute agency talked up farming, brought in mowing machines. The Indians removed the cutting bars and raced each other across the meadows until the improvised gigs fell apart. Once Mears, despite his protests, was ordered to haul in several wagonloads of potatoes. The entire consignment rotted because the Indians refused to touch the unfamiliar food. Indeed, the Ute palate was completely unpredictable. They mixed flour with water and drank it, poured bacon grease in their coffee, and saved the sugar for dessert.

Meat was what they wanted. Each agency maintained a cattle herd. (In the late seventies, when feed was short in San Luis Valley, Mears bought some four thousand head from pinched ranchers, drove the animals to Ute territory, and resold them to the government at a thumping profit.) Every Saturday several fat steers were driven into the agency compound. While howling Indians perched on the corral fence and roofs of the nearby buildings, a rifleman selected by the chief rode forth to do the killing. As excitement mounted and the leaping watchers shrieked approval or disapproval of each shot, the affair turned into a shambles. Finally the last steer was down. Yelling like fiends, the squaws swarmed over the fence, knife in one hand, hatchet in the other. First they split open the skulls and scooped out the brains, valued for tanning. After a furious squabble had settled ownership of the brains, the butchery began. Out came the pancreas, to be gulped down raw, sometimes with roots of camass or of Canadian thistle as relish. Fat was discarded: "He not good, pretty soon heap stink." The rest of the beef was hacked into thin strips and hung on a square rack of willow poles under which a fire burned. As soon as the meat was glazed enough so that flies wouldn't bother it, the fire was allowed to go out and the meat simply hung until dry. Then it was stuffed into containers, the squaws loaded the travois, and the family wandered off into the hills until lack of provisions once again brought them back.

A discontented people. Ouray had his troubles. Chiefs who had never fully accepted his authority and who were jealous of his thousand-dollar salary accused him of misappropriating annuity funds to pay his sheepherders. Plots were made against his life, which the agency was on the *qui vive* to forestall, well realizing that his death might result in an uprising. Wasted worry. The old devil had spies everywhere, knew his enemies. Evidence indicates that he personally murdered at least five of the principal challengers to his power, and only the split-second intervention of his wife Chipeta saved the life of her brother Sapinero.

This worthy and a handful of others, it seems, had decided to assassinate their chief. To bolster courage, they loaded up on whisky, and the plan leaked out. When Ouray rode up to the blacksmith shop at the Cochetopa agency the blacksmith whispered a warning. As Sapinero charged, swinging an ax, Ouray was able to duck behind his horse. The blow missed; the ax handle splintered on a fence post. As Sapinero hesitated, Ouray darted in, flung the man into an irrigation ditch, jumped knees-down on his chest. Chipeta screamed; the blacksmith whooped for help. Sapinero's cohorts, seeing their leader's predicament, took to their heels. Ouray fumbled for the knife at his belt, but before he could free it Chipeta tore it from its sheath and begged for her brother's life. The husband relented and Sapinero scuttled for safety.

Interpret all this as you like: a bloodthirsty man avaricious for power—or an unhappy chief forced into a position he did not want, yet believing he must maintain his policies for the sake of his short-sighted people. Whichever motive is granted, certainly Ouray went his way with a singleness of purpose quite uncharacteristic of the ordinary Indian and as remarkable, in its fashion, as Washakie's more persuasive leadership of the Shoshone.

In spite of him, the explosion came. It hit in the north, and that it didn't spread south was due in part to a mail carrier's warped sense of humor.

This is what happened. At the sale of the mineral lands in 1873 the Utes had reserved for themselves the hot springs at the head of the

Uncompahgre River. Surveys, however, were incomplete, miners poured into the lovely mountain amphitheater, and the settlement of Ouray took form. To keep an eye on the angry Utes, the southern agency moved, along about 1875, from its original site on the Gunnison to the Uncompahgre, with Otto Mears doing the hauling and building the roads.

Among the tenders of the agency's beef herd was Sidney Jocknick, a cowboy who indulged his literary yearnings by serving as agency correspondent for Otto Mears's Saguache *Chronicle*. The drab news items that came Sid's way did not give free rein to his fancy, so occasionally he amused himself by writing up bloodcurdling wars that never happened, robberies that never occurred.

One such flight of imagination described the dreadful slaughter by the Utes of two ne'er-do-wells known as Oregon Bill and Happy Jack. This yarn, like others of similar vein, Sid filed in the wastebasket. Now enters the mail carrier, one Scotty, who fished the story from the basket, read it with a whoop of delight, and sent it to the *Chronicle*. His purpose was to alarm Happy Jack's girl, who worked in the newspaper office, and, should the article be printed, to injure Oregon Bill's intermittent trade of piloting dudes, a business Scotty hoped to acquire for himself.

By weird chance the yarn *was* printed. The Pueblo *Chieftain* picked it up, added an even more warlike tone. From there the story went to Denver, Kansas City, Washington. The War Department ordered an investigation. Out from Fort Garland in the San Luis Valley rode Lieutenant John Conline and a small detachment of cavalry. Happy Jack and Oregon Bill soon proved the falsity of their demise (Jocknick had called it "just desserts"), but Conline kept poking around and discovered what local residents knew anyhow—the Utes were restless. (Later it was learned that some of them, like their brothers to the north, were secretly buying arms and ammunition from unscrupulous traders.) As a result of Conline's report Fort Crawford was established in the Uncompahgre Valley and without doubt helped Ouray keep the southern Utes quiet when, a year later, horror swept the north.

Up there, at the White River agency, the fuse was burning bright enough for anyone to see—though no one did. Annuities were sixty-five thousand dollars in arrears, and because of the failure of certain freighters to fulfill their contracts, agency goods were piling up and spoiling in the Union Pacific's warehouses at Rawlins, Wyoming. The dissatisfied Indians persistently roamed outside the reservation to hunt—and also to bluster and beg around the homesteads of the settlers and, occasionally, to run off a few head of stock. They set fires to the forests.

An old Ute custom, this supposedly made grass grow better in burned areas, drove game within range of the hunters, and left behind, for use during the winter, a supply of dry wood. Unfortunately the haphazard blazes sometimes burned a settler's home or fields; and this irritation, plus the desire of the northern counties for more land on the tax rolls, burgeoned into a vociferous sentiment: "The Utes must go!"

Into the ticklish situation stepped a new agent, Nathan Meeker, erstwhile founder of Greeley, Colorado. Now, an agent's position was anomalous at best. Among innumerable other chores he was supposed to carry out government directives concerning the Indians and at the same time represent the savages when they protested against those directives. Some diplomats managed to handle both reins. But Meeker, though completely honest in a profession where dishonesty was the fashion, was no diplomat. Monumentally self-assured, he believed he could, almost singlehanded, carry out the vague injunction that the Utes be "civilized."

One part of his civilizing process was to turn warriors into farmers. Farming being squaws' work, the bucks objected and were not soothed when Meeker said flatly, "I shall cut every Indian to the starvation point if he will not work." A delegation went to Denver and begged Governor Pitkin to remove the agent. Pitkin not only refused but ordered a detachment of Negro cavalrymen into Middle Park, an undiplomatic gesture, since the Utes detested colored troops, whom they called "buffalo soldiers."

The fuse hissed and spat. Two settlers were killed; stock was stolen. Suddenly, from the San Juans on the south to the Little Snake River on the Wyoming border, dozens of forest fires leaped out of control. In Silverton smoke was so stifling that Mrs. Gus Ambolt had to fan her babies to prevent their suffocating. Two hundred miles to the north a mining-camp superintendent wrote Washington, "The fire is so hot and the smoke so dense we can't reach our flumes to discover how many are destroyed."

None of this fazed Meeker. Stubbornly he ordered his plows to turn up the sod of the Indians' beloved race track. Someone took a potshot at the plowboy, missed; when Meeker rushed out to remonstrate he was chucked bodily over a hitching rail. Finally he wrote for troops, and late in September 1879, Major Thornburg and three companies of cavalry marched for the White River.

At Milk Creek, twenty-five miles from the agency, the powder exploded. In the ambush and in the battle which followed Thornburg and twelve soldiers died. Raked by fire from above, the survivors, including forty-seven wounded, huddled behind their overturned wagons in seventeen shallow, hastily dug pits. More than two hundred and fifty horses, picketed around the bivouac, were methodically shot down by the Indians. Many of them, screaming with pain, broke their tethers, stampeded among the soldiers, and fell dead. Their carcasses were added to the breastworks, loopholes for rifles in some cases being carved right through their bodies.

In an effort to smoke out the enemy the Indians fired the tall dead grass. With wet blankets the soldiers managed to turn the flames, and now the Utes, to coin an old phrase, settled down to a siege. It wasn't tight enough. Scouts slipped through. One of them, John Rankin, by changing horses at ranches along the way, rode one hundred and fifty miles to Fort Steele, near Rawlins, in twenty-seven and one half hours. Other couriers left a note on a sagebrush beside a Middle Park trail. There Captain Dodge's Negro troops found it and, with more enthusiasm than judgment, rushed through a hail of Indian bullets to the impromptu stockade—thus adding themselves to the number of the beleaguered.

For six days, while rations shortened and the stench of dead bodies grew overpowering, the siege endured. Then General Wesley Merritt, after a stirring series of forced marches, charged up from Rawlins. While the Utes were considering what to do about this, a courier arrived from Ouray, who had known nothing of the uprising until apprised of it by messenger. Peremptorily his emissary ordered the warriors to lay down their arms. This command on top of Merritt's cavalry tipped the scales, and soon White River Utes were scattering away through every handy ravine.

What of Meeker? As soon as Thornburg had been ambushed, Indian messengers had rushed the news to their fellows at the agency. There, while the post's three white women were washing dishes, a few bucks slipped into the storeroom and stole several rifles. In a few moments all but one of the twelve male employees were dead, three of them picked off as they were spreading dirt on the roof of a new building. Meeker was scalped, stripped, mutilated, and left lying on the ground with a barrel stave driven through his mouth.

His lame, sixty-eight-year-old wife, their twenty-year-old daughter Josie, Mrs. Price, buxom wife of the blacksmith, the Prices' two infant children, and a man named Dresser took refuge in the agency's new milk-house. The Indians tried to fire the building, but the green cottonwood logs would not burn. That night the occupants made a break for free-dom. Dresser was killed, the women were captured. For twenty-three days they were held prisoner, threatened, mocked, starved, forced to drudge for their captors.

Legend says that Chipeta herself tucked up her buckskin skirts, rode night and day to the enemy camp, and freed the women. Touching but untrue. Merritt's column was now moving southward, and with that club strengthening their hands, General Charles Adams, Otto Mears, and some of Ouray's representatives entered the camp, obtained the release of the prisoners, and took them to the Uncompahgre agency. There Chipeta wept over them, gave them food and clothing, and in such undramatic but heartfelt ways tried to redress the wrong done by her tribesmen.

As word of the massacre spread, every scalp in Colorado tingled. Of this palsied state of mind various advantages were taken. At Alma, in South Park, a drunk shot holes in his own coat and galloped through the town roaring, "The Indians are coming!" Instantly the village evacuated itself, women, sometimes two on a horse, skittering down the road, "not particular if both feet weren't on one side" of their mounts. Into the courthouse at Fairplay the mob panted, deemed the stone walls insufficient, and laid plans for a fort of cottonwood—there being at the time not an armed Ute within seventy-five miles.

Farther south, in the San Juans, a man named McCann galloped wildly up to Jimmy Soward's saloon in Howardsville, where judges were tabulating the results of a county election. "Git up an' git out!" gasped McCann. "The Indians have massacred everybody in Animas City and are marching on Silverton! I got dispatches for the governor! Jimmy, give me a drink!"

He gulped the drink—two or three of them—and clattered on. A small citizens' army rushed to the relief of Silverton, learned the whole thing was a hoax. Some local residents say it had been engineered by merchants in Animas City who hoped for a business boom. If so, the merchants succeeded; troops were rushed in from Pagosa Springs, Fort Lewis was built on La Plata River, and (until the founding of Durango copped the play) Animas City flourished.

To soberer heads nothing about the affair was funny. The demand that the murderers of the agency men be brought to trial swelled to deafening proportions. But who were the actual murderers? Only the Meeker women had any idea, and testimony by squaws was contrary to all Ute tradition. Furiously the tribe refused to accept it. In a stormy council with investigators Ouray suddenly flashed to his feet, hand on his knife. Indians could expect no fairness in Colorado now, he said. He would not surrender the accused unless they could be tried in Washington.

Finally eleven Utes were taken East, but matters bogged down. When it became evident no legal action would result, a curious reaction took place among the Meeker women. At first they had denied being raped by their captors; now, however, Josie and Mrs. Price intimated they had been molested. A belated admission of shame for the sake of justice? Or a spurious effort at vengeance? Probably the truth will never be known.

A year passed, full of sound and fury. Sentiment against the White River Utes, perpetrators of the massacre, crystallized into a demand that they be ejected from Colorado and relocated on a reservation somewhere in the desolate wastes of eastern Utah. The animosity also included the less guilty Utes of the Gunnison and upper Uncompahgre valleys, where large amounts of desirable land added vigor to white arguments. These Indians, too, it was said, must withdraw to more compact holdings and learn to support themselves by agriculture rather than by wasteful hunting over large tracts of ground. By way of compensation, each Ute family would be given private ownership of 160 acres of farming land plus a share in a tribal annuity of $50,000. This sum was to be raised, at least in part, by the government's selling the pre-empted hunting grounds to white settlers and depositing the money to the Utes' account in the United States Treasury.

From the whites' standpoint the plan looked fair. Otto Mears, who favored it, and four other commissioners were appointed to treat with the Indians—and straightway trouble developed. Two of the commissioners, Messrs. Meachem and Manypenny, the latter a man of considerable experience in Indian affairs, did not like the idea of giving the Utes land in severalty, feeling that the Indians weren't ready to support themselves by farming and would be bamboozled out of their holdings by unscrupulous traders. The Uncompahgre Utes also disliked the idea, partly because they were constitutionally opposed to agriculture, but more specifically because they didn't know where the new lands were to be located. The proposed treaty said merely "an adjacent territory" to their old homelands by the Gunnison and Uncompahgre rivers. The difficult situation was not made any easier by the fact that Otto Mears could scarcely bear the sight of his fellow commissioners, a revulsion which Meachem and Manypenny returned in full measure.

Mears won the first round. Together with Ouray, Shavano, and seven other chiefs he went to Washington to talk with Carl Schurz, Secretary of the Interior. Sadly Ouray recognized the alternatives—

treaty or bloodshed. In March 1880 he and the chiefs signed a pro-
visional draft which would become binding as soon as a majority of
the Uncompahgre Utes voiced their approval. October 15, 1880, was
set as the deadline, but back in Colorado a council of Indians rejected
the treaty on the grounds that "adjacent territory" wasn't definite
enough.

At this juncture, while on a good-will trip to explain the treaty to
bands in the extreme southern part of the state, Ouray died. Confusion
mounted. And then, almost on the anniversary of the Meeker massacre
and with the October deadline drawing starkly near, an event occurred
which threatened to strangle negotiations beyond hope of recovery. A
young freighter named A. D. Jackson, firing through the dark at some
drunken Indians who were making a nuisance of themselves around his
wagon, had the abysmal misfortune to kill the son of War Chief Shavano.

Arrested, Jackson was remanded to the court at Gunnison for trial.
The way led through Indian country, and although three hundred idle
soldiers lolled about the district he was turned over to an escort of four
civilians. Utes stopped the cavalcade. Jackson was taken from his guards,
spirited into the mountains, killed, and his body thrown into a gulch.

Fresh panic, fresh fury swept Colorado's western slope. Was this the
first move of a new outbreak? Why didn't the commission do something?

The Indians braced themselves. What now?

Desperate, Otto Mears chucked protocol to the winds, toured the
reservation with a satchelful of cash. Two dollars for a signature. He
paid out twenty-eight hundred dollars of his own money, came back
with fourteen hundred X's duly witnessed for the treaty. "Bribery!"
squealed Meachem and Manypenny, and reported him to the Secretary
of the Interior. Mears was ordered to Washington for trial. Flanked by
Colorado's millionaire senators, Teller and Hill, he strode into the office
of Samuel Kirkwood, Schurz's successor. Yes, he had paid the Indians.
And why not? There had to be a treaty before all hell broke loose, and
to the pragmatic eyes of the Utes two dollars in hand was worth more
than a pack of vague promises. Senators Teller and Hill chugarummed
agreement.

Mmmm, said Kirkwood. Under the circumstances . . . if Mr. Mears
would make out a voucher, the money would be repaid. Then he asked:

"You are sure you can move the Indians?"

"If I'm given enough troops. And," Mears added sourly, "if Meachem
and Manypenny are kept out of the way."

This agreement reached, the next step was to locate the new reservation. There seems no doubt that the Indians had signed their two-dollar X's under the impression that they would be settled at the junction of the Gunnison and Grand (now Colorado) rivers in the extreme western part of the state. But when Mears saw that choice valley he shook his head.

How honest was he? By now he was neck-deep in politics and he certainly realized that since the murder of Jackson no measure short of the Utes' removal from Colorado would satisfy the electorate. On the other hand, he also knew that impatient settlers were stacking up outside the boundaries of the old reservation, waiting for the land to be declared open. What permanent gain was there for the Utes in being moved to fertile fields only a short distance away from their former grounds? Would not the same pressures, the same animosities soon overhaul them again? Why not finish the job once and for all in one drastic relocation?

The proposal split the new commissioners asunder. During a quarrel one of them knocked another flat, but in the end Mears's views prevailed, and it was decided that the Uncompahgre Utes must join the White River Utes on the barren grounds that border Utah's Duchesne River. It is Mormon land, but in those days the Mormons were fair game.

Back in Washington, Meachem and Manypenny shrilled, "Double cross!" Adjacent territory meant land adjoining the old reservation. Utah, retorted Mears, was a territory adjacent to Colorado; thus the terms of the treaty had been fulfilled. Secretary Kirkwood, weighing Western sentiment, decided Mears's sophistry was right and in the summer of 1881 ordered General MacKenzie, with nine companies of cavalry and nine of infantry, to prepare the Utes for exodus. Mears himself was directed to go to Utah, haul in supplies, and supervise, out in the middle of wastelands more than a hundred miles distant from any other habitation, the building of the agency's new structures.

Slowly the outraged Utes were gathered together into a camp on the Uncompahgre River. Day after day was set for the start of the migration. Day after day the Indians stalled: they had to round up their stock; they wanted to go on one last hunt; they needed more supplies for their long trek. General MacKenzie was patient—and careful. By means of an ingenious system of relays, heliographs, and messengers he kept tab on every Ute who stepped outside his tepee. It was well he did. Impatient settlers were edging onto the reservation ahead of schedule, and to cap the tension profit-hungry traders smuggled in packloads of whisky to the Indians.

Inflamed by it, several hundred of Sub-chief Colorow's band decided on rebellion. They broke out of the village, charged down the valley, screaming like demons. MacKenzie's signals functioned to perfection. Cavalrymen swung in ahead of the Utes. Up on the cliffs artillerymen sighted their guns. Alcoholic courage dampened by the swift counter-action, Colorow's men trooped sullenly back to the village, but war drums still throbbed, and all up and down the Uncompahgre settlers who had jumped the gun quaked in their boots.

MacKenzie's patience was gone. At two o'clock in the morning he sent for McNorris and Mears, who was just back from Utah. If the commissioners would sign the necessary orders he would move the Utes at once.

The commissioners signed. Bugles *ta-taed;* messengers delivered the ultimatum; in two hours the Utes had to hit the trail. Up on the bluffs blood-red bonfires showed the loaded cannon.

By dawn the confused and wailing camp was on the move. The Indians were neither harried nor maltreated. Government wagons and drivers hauled their goods, government rations fed them, government ferries transported them across the Grand, and at the new reservation a better agency than their old one stood ready to receive them. All they lacked was happiness. When Mears showed up a few weeks later to inspect conditions and to pay Chipeta in one-dollar bills the seven-hundred dollars allotted her by the treaty, a chief named Cojoe tried to murder him for being the cause of their removal. It was Otto Mears's last contact with the tribe, for he returned to Colorado and his toll roads. Today it seems a sordid end to a long and often useful association. Yet whatever his motives, his vision had been true. Twenty-six days after the last Ute crossed the river, the town of Grand Junction, western Colorado's largest city, was founded on the ground which Otto Mears had predicted the Indians could not hold.

Not quite all the Utes were driven from Colorado in that sad hegira. In the extreme southern part of the state, cut off from the rest of the tribe by the block of mineral lands ceded in 1873, was a band which had played no part in the warlike scenes accompanying the Meeker massacre. As a reward, and to the disgust of neighboring whites, these Indians were allowed to remain in Colorado on the most cockeyed reservation in America's cockeyed Indian history—a ribbon of land one hundred and ten miles long and fifteen miles wide, slashed transversely by seven river canyons, so that it was almost impossible to ride its length. This strip lay smack-dab across cattle driveways used by white ranchers traveling from winter range in New Mexico to summer range in Colorado, and since it was unfenced, Indian stock could not be kept on nor settlers' stock off. Stray chasers from both sides of the line encroached on one another's territory and frequently retrieved animals to which they had no more title than a long rope. Lonely cowboys and lonely Indians, in the course of the years, died beside the lonely trails. And when the Denver and Rio Grande built into Durango, it wandered back and forth across the strip without a by-your-leave from anyone; the Utes, trying to stop one of the first locomotives by lassoing its smokestack, were considerably mortified to have their ponies dragged, their ropes broken, and their efforts vociferously haw-hawed by the trainmen.

Eventually, in 1899, the impossible situation was rectified by a readjustment in boundaries. The opening of the vacated Indian lands to settlement was accompanied, according to the Denver *Republican* for May 4, by "a race that equalled the mad scramble for the broad lands of Oklahoma. . . . Hundreds of horsemen . . . hurdled over the sagebrush and careened over the rough ground in the endeavor to be first on the chosen sites. Behind the cavalcade of rough riders rattled prairie schooners, carriages, and lumber wagons, while dozens of bicycle riders risked life and limb . . ." But perhaps the account was exaggerated or the land not so choice. At least, there are not many people living in the area today.

Belated justice is now coming to the Utes who were expelled from the state. As previously noted, the Indians were to be paid whatever sums accrued from the "cash-entry" sale of their former lands to settlers. But land laws change (in too involved a pattern to be traced fully here), and on June 26, 1934, the last underpinnings of the repayment clause were destroyed by the passage of the Taylor Grazing Act. This bill removed all semi-arid and arid public lands from further homestead entry. It was designed, of course, as a range-conservation measure, and at first no one noticed that some 4,500,000 undisposed former Ute acres were included in the sweeping withdrawal. No one, that is, except the Utes. Quickly enough they saw that an end to homesteading on their old lands meant an end to a large part of their income. Consequently, in 1941 they instituted suit for compensation.

In 1943 the Court of Claims decided that the government was liable for the value of these lands "as for a taking under the power of eminent domain." But what is the value of four and one half million acres sprawled over every conceivable sort of country? Factors undreamed of a few decades ago complicate the picture: the discovery of the Rangely oil fields in northwestern Colorado; oil-shale deposits along the Grand; potential reservoir and resort sites; inflated livestock and agricultural values; even emergency airfields built by the government and dump areas used by the Army for disposing of dud ammunition. For more than a year statisticians, tax appraisers, real estate experts, cattlemen, dry farmers, and what not have droned out figures from witness chairs in Grand Junction. What the eventual total will be no one at this writing can guess; certainly it will run into many millions of dollars.

Probably, too, the huge sum will be a mixed blessing. In general, Indian policy states that anyone who leaves his reservation is not entitled to share in tribal allotments. Prospects of a juicy dividend will tend to confirm many a buck in laziness and improvidence. At the same time, throughout the mountains, younger Indian men and women are chafing. They have been educated somewhat. The war—like all American males, the Indians were subject to service—has been a tremendous eye opener. Employment (as sheepherders, tie cutters, highway and railroad workers, etc.) is easy to find, and no longer must they obtain passes in order to leave the reservation. Automobiles let them travel; jobs enable them, for the first time in generations, to hold up their heads as once their ancestors did, independent, self-sufficient. Ever so slowly, but apparently surely, the decimated tribes of the Rockies are beginning to scatter, perhaps to disappear forever, and once again Ouray's words sound with poignant freshness:

"I realize the destiny of my people. We shall fall as the leaves of the trees . . ."

CHAPTER VII

THE SILVER STAMPEDES

T WO Cornish miners, so the story goes, were sitting beside their mine dump near Central City, Colorado, when along came a stranger with a geologist's hammer in one hand and a blowpipe in the other. After poking through the discarded rocks the outlander asked the Cousin Jacks, as Cornishmen were known, whether they would sell the debris.

The pair gasped. "Dammy, help yourself and willcum. We'd give the whole blasted brock pile to the de'il—it's that no good, old son."

But the stranger, who signed his name Richard Pearce, insisted that they take a check for two thousand dollars. The Cousin Jacks pinched themselves a time or two, raced for Joe Chaffee's bank, and within a week had consumed the windfall on a rousing binge. A little later hindsight came. Pearce and his boss, Nathaniel Hill, hauled the whole blasted brock pile to the latter's Boston & Colorado Smelter in Central City, where the disdained waste netted fourteen thousand dollars. The Cousin Jacks, with real headaches now, railed to their friends, and the story went around that Nathaniel P. Hill was amassing a fortune by swindling defenseless workers.

Actually Hill was saving the life of Colorado's infant mining industry —though not, to be sure, through motives of undiluted philanthropy.

A one-time chemistry professor at Rhode Island's Brown University, Hill had been approached by a woeful Eastern capitalist who had bought a high-assaying property in Central City and then had been unable to extract the gold from its ores. Could the professor devise a solution? Hill went to Colorado and was baffled by what he found. At this point other chemists had given up. But not Nathaniel Hill; the potential rewards for success were too bright. He transported seventy-two tons of ore to Swansea, Wales, and there watched experienced hands smelt it after a fashion. Seeking improvements on their process, he next studied metallurgy for a few months at Freiburg, Germany, hired Pearce as an assistant, and with him worked out a secret method which in 1868 they put into effect in Colorado.

Their process was no great shakes. They charged sixty dollars a ton to handle ore assaying one hundred and twenty dollars, and the matte of gold, silver, and copper their Boston & Colorado Smelter produced had to be sent clear to Wales for ultimate refining. Nonetheless, the fumbling start made investors take a fresh look at the refractory ores which abounded in the Clear Creek districts, and imitators washed a flood of new "patented processes" over the Rockies. Most of these devices were fit only for extracting already minted gold from the pockets of gullible speculators, but out of the disappointments, chicanery, and triumphs came techniques which would bring a brand-new metal to the foreground.

Silver!

Its presence had been detected as early as the first rush of 1859. But silver ore was as hard to mine and mill as gold ore and was worth by the coinage laws of the land only one sixteenth as much—unless, of course, the ore contained sixteen times as much silver as gold. Such ores existed, but prospectors, like most people, were not adept at seeing things they were not looking for. Between 1859 and 1864 several hundred men left the crowded Gregory diggings to tramp up and down the neighboring South Fork of Clear Creek, an almost futile goose chase stimulated by George Griffith's accidental discovery of the single gold-bearing lode in the region.

After five years of this floundering, certain ores from the towering mountains west of George Griffith's town were scientifically assayed. The result was the opening of the Belmont Lode, first paying silver mine in the Rockies (discounting the ancient Spanish diggings). Grab your hats, boys! In 1864 George's town had embraced four log cabins. Three years later, on November 29, 1867, two thousand miners packed the street, stood in ore wagons, perched on roofs and in trees as they roared out a demand that the territorial legislature grant a charter to the city of Georgetown. Within another six months the new metropolis had voted the county seat away from Idaho Springs, standing forlornly on the site of Jackson's first gold strike.

The king was dead, long live the king! In 1868 Colorado's gold production was valued at two million dollars; the silver, worth $1.326 an ounce, at a mere quarter of a million. Twenty-four years later annual gold production had climbed to $5,300,000. Meanwhile silver, though shrunken in value to 87 cents an ounce, had shot up to an annual $20,-880,000. Even lowly lead, ignored in '68 and worth only four cents a pound in 1892, was giving gold a run for its money, with a production record, during that prosperous year, of $4,800,000. The status of the fallen favorite was epitomized in a disdainful jingle by the editor of the Georgetown paper:

Gold, gold, gold!
Bright and yellow—
Hard and cold!

Another ex-miner wrote a dismally long novel through whose pages Gold leers as a ruinous strumpet, while Silver, though sometimes languishing during her lover's trial of the fleshpots, eventually triumphs in the classic manner of all pure virgins. Various aspects of the symbolism are readily guessed; our hero, for example, is maimed while working in a gold mine but labors with abundant health and cheer in an apparently identical silver prospect.

Often unnoticed under all this glitter is a pertinent mechanical factor: in 1869 at the Burleigh Tunnel, a silver property near the new Clear Creek camp of Silver Plume, power drills made their first appearance in a United States mine.

The first silver excitement, though intense, was largely local. Meanwhile far across the divide in Utah another fever was being kindled by a crusty old soldier who reasoned that a mining rush was just the thing to soften up the intransigent Mormons.

The Saints knew that mineral existed in their territory. During the "Mormon War," when Albert Sidney Johnston's column was marching on Salt Lake City, Brigham Young had sent Jim Rollins scooting to a lead deposit in western Utah, where a foundry was established to mold bullets for the besieged Mormons. Later a contiguous district mothered the spectacular Horn Silver Mine, which in ten years produced $54,-000,000 and helped put financier Jay Cooke back on his feet after he had gone broke with the Northern Pacific during the panic of 1873. But the Mormon hierarchy wanted none of that kind of money. Brigham Young had set the pattern when Sanford and Tom Bingham turned up ores during the late fifties in the desolate Oquirrh Mountains, due south of the Salt Lake. "Instead of hunting gold," thundered the Lion of the Lord, "let every man go to work at raising wheat, oats, barley, corn and vegetables and fruit in abundance that there may be plenty in the land."

When the War between the States erupted, Albert Johnston's mantle as occupier of Utah Territory fell on the shoulders of red-whiskered, energetic, violently prejudiced General Patrick Connor. He did not relish the job. Neither did his 750 California volunteers, who offered the War Department $30,000 to let them march on through Mormon land to the battlefields in the East. No sale. The disgruntled troops were ordered into camp on a bench above Salt Lake City, which circumspect hamlet Connor declared to be "a community of traitors, murderers, fanatics, and whores," whose treason he determined to water down by promoting an influx of good American settlers.

How stimulate the immigration? Farmers would not come, for the Saints held an unbreakable grip on the basin's agricultural land. But what about a mining stampede? Having been in California during the gold rush, Connor knew at first hand how that tidal wave had obliterated the sleepy civilization of the Spaniards. Moreover, his men were Californians and understood prospecting. In between Indian battles along the Overland Trail, he turned them loose and awaited developments.

The first strike of importance came in 1863, when a man named George Oglivie sent Connor a sample of ore from the Bingham brothers' old find in the Oquirrh Mountains. History repeated: a frenetic stripping of placer bars, the gradual opening of lode mines, refractory ores, the building of smelters (including Connor's own Pioneer Smelting Works), and then the appearance of lead and silver sulphides. Almost everyone knew that copper was also present in Bingham's narrow canyon, but who cared about copper?

There were other finds, many of them west of this book's arbitrary bounds: at Mercur, where Indians had long ago picked up gold and silver nuggets and where white prospectors gave their mines such titles as The Wild Delirium; and at Tintic, named for a Ute chief who tried without avail to keep settlers away from his favorite valley. The prospecting mania even engulfed the islands of the lake, but none of these finds at first matched the dazzling silver strikes at Alta and Park City, in the Wasatch Range that towered over Brigham Young's mineral-scorning capital.

Both discoveries were made by Connor's ex-soldiers, though they seem not to have profited greatly. At Park City the ores ran deep, water flooded the workings, and not until the multitudinous claim owners joined resources to dig a drainage tunnel did the camp put on its seven-league boots. By then mining was big business; and eventually most of the property wound up in the hands of two gigantic combines, the Park Utah Consolidated and the Silver King Coalition.

At Alta, tucked into the forbidding head of Little Cottonwood Canyon, the main drawback was not water but transportation. For a long time wagons could not get there. The original owners of the Emma Mine dragged their ore down the canyon in "boats" of untanned cowhide, shipped it to San Francisco, sent it by steamer around Cape Horn to Wales, paid outrageous smelter charges—and still netted $180 a ton!

Five thousand eager miners stampeded into the district, and the goings on at the Bucket of Blood saloon curled the hair of the staid Mormons at the foot of the hill. Unfortunately—or fortunately, depending on one's point of view—the Emma's opulent vein pinched out at approximately the same time that the "Crime of '73" demonetized silver and started the white metal on its long decline. As a result, though several Alta mines kept producing until 1885 or so, not even the Rockies' ubiquitous narrow-gauge railroads braved the canyon. For years the camp's sole passenger conveyance was the body of a three-seated sleigh mounted on a handcar and tugged up a pair of slender rails by two black mules hitched in tandem, a slow creep past the enormous white boulders which furnished building stone for the Mormon temple at Salt Lake City and on through seven dank miles of snowsheds. Motive power on the descent, for both ore and passenger cars, was gravity, governed by a set of erratic hand brakes.

The Mormons reacted to all this in typical pragmatic fashion. They mocked the dirty grubbers in the hills, raised crops, fostered home industries behind the protective wall of isolation, and for a thumping profit sold the fruit of their toil to their enemies. Their great freight teams hauled hay and salt and apples to the gold fields in Idaho and Montana; their grocers and farmers hawked food in the Wasatch towns. It was a good thing—too good to remain unchallenged by gentiles, who set up rival firms and engaged in economic warfare made doubly bitter by religious fulminations. Then came the Union Pacific and after it feeder railroads, unexpected allies to Connor's deliberate destructiveness. Cheap goods poured in from the East; ores poured out. Home industries toppled. In every field the boom grew, and Brigham Young's once ironclad hegemony was shattered forever, although many years passed before the Saints would admit the fact.

Following its demonetization, the value of silver dropped one to four cents an ounce nearly every year. For most Rocky Mountain mines this steady sag was more than offset by an accompanying decline in labor and material costs, brought about by the advent of farmers in the valleys and of railroads along Colorado's Front Range. For example, in 1865 at Central City unskilled labor cost from four to five dollars a day; skilled labor, as much as twelve dollars. Nails sold for twenty cents a pound, flour brought from twelve to nineteen dollars a hundredweight, and hay reached seventy dollars a ton. By 1879 miners could be hired in the same town for two dollars to two-fifty a day and head masons for four-fifty. Nails had dropped to five cents a pound, flour to two-fifty per hundredweight, and hay to twenty-five dollars a ton.

Denver Library Western Collection

Chief Ouray and Otto Mears, about 1870, when the Utes had just retreated west of the Continental Divide and trader Mears was barely started on his career as kingpin of the Rockies' most fabulous transportation system.

Cripple Creek prospectors and their burros, shortly after the discovery of the Rockies' richest and most violent gold camp. Unsung hero of the mountains, the donkey enabled his peripatetic master to explore the craggiest recesses of the

A new strike in a remote locality might be accompanied for a few months by fantastic prices, but the indefatigable toll road and railroad builders soon brought a leveling off, and only in the most inaccessible ranges did a mine have to be an all but unbelievable Golconda before its owners could make it pay. In other words, the Rockies were economically ripe for the wild rush of exploitation set off by silver strikes in the lead carbonate ores which gave their name to Leadville, Colorado, in the latter part of the seventies.

Fairyland. For twenty years Leadville very nearly equaled the claims present-day romancers make for it, which is a climax in superlatives for sure. The district had already enjoyed one boom during the early sixties, when California Gulch had been the Rockies' richest gold-placer diggings. But the bars had been quickly exhausted and the miners straggled away, among them Oro City's stolid postmaster and storekeeper, H. A. W. Tabor, and his wife Augusta. The Tabors' flagging energy kept them from traveling any farther than the crumbling towns of South Park, and after a few dreary years news of a new lode-mine discovery in California Gulch brought them shuffling back. Disappointment again. The lode was strictly small-scale, but there was a little activity reworking abandoned dumps, and in 1875 someone built a dinky smelter downstream at Malta. Once more Tabor set up his movable store and post office, and Augusta took in boarders. Perhaps, at times, she remembered the day many years before when she had first seen that fateful gulch. Then, after a desolating trip up from Colorado City, during which she had cried her despair into the fuzzy neck of a burro, she had been the first woman in the camp and the boys had turned to with a will to build her and her husband a log cabin. It had been exciting. A person was able to hope, even after failures on Clear Creek and in Colorado City. But thirteen or fourteen years can use up a lot of hope. Augusta didn't have much left.

Among the Tabors' new neighbors were Uncle Billy Stevens and A. B. Wood. The pair's plan was to set up a hydraulic operation, but the same heavy boulders and black-red sands that had plagued the original prospectors kept fouling up their sluice boxes. Curious, they tested various specimens, found traces of silver float, and followed it back to its source. The vein nearly knocked out their eyes and for a time they tried to keep it secret, but when Wood sold his interest in the claim to a Chicagoan for forty thousand dollars, the news was out. Then the three Gallagher brothers made a similar strike and the rush was on. But not for Haw Tabor; his fruitless attempts at prospecting had crushed interest in mining right out of him. He stuck to his store, weighing beans and playing poker, and because he had time to kill, eighteen miners meeting in a blacksmith shop in January 1878 elected him mayor of the new camp of Leadville.

Even though the season was the dead of winter, a growing trickle of men struggled up the Arkansas River or over the frozen passes of the Mosquito Range. Destitute scores of them begged Leadville's morose storekeeper for a grubstake. To most of them Tabor gave short shrift. But in February two old acquaintances from South Park, German shoe-makers named George Hook and August Rische, pestered him so that he told them to take what they needed and get out of his sight.

Among the items the pair borrowed was an unauthorized jug of whisky. A mile or so out of town they halted to refresh themselves, decided mellowly that the spot they were on was as good as anything else, and commenced to dig. A few yards away in any direction they would have encountered barren country rock. But squarely under their shovels the fabulous Little Pittsburgh Lode crowned close to the surface. Within a year, by pyramiding his grubstaker's one-third interest in the Little Pittsburgh and then selling out for cash and stock just when times were ripest, Haw Tabor became the Rockies' first multi-millionaire.

After that he could not miss. He bought a salted mine, sank the shaft a few feet deeper, and opened the Crysolite, which paid dividends of $100,000 a month. He gave $117,000 for the reputedly worthless Matchless Mine and took out more millions. He founded life and fire-insurance companies, real estate, water and illuminating-gas firms. He built a bank. If one scheme failed, like the street railway company whose cars were too heavy for the horses to pull, it did not matter; there were a dozen other irons in the fire. Augusta, however, was afraid. She had seen luck come and go before. The only difference now was that stakes were bigger. Though finally she consented to turn out her boarders, a little six-room cottage on Carbonate Avenue was as luxurious a home as she wanted. Nor would she act the grand lady to please her now bediamonded husband. Less and less frequently were they seen together. Tabor was a busy man. A deal here, another there, including poker games in private upstairs apartments at the Texas Club, where a thousand dollars often fell with the turn of a card. Also there was an Indian-club virtuoso named Alice Morgan at one of the variety theaters. Tabor never knew that buxom Alice once confided to her actress friend, Erba Robeson, who sometimes held Tabor's head when he was sick in his private box at the Grand Central Theater, that she,

Alice Morgan, could endure his silver touch only when she was dead drunk.

Ten thousand, twenty thousand, forty thousand—no one knows how many people poured into Leadville during 1878–79. Rail and wagon roads had brought population centers comparatively close, and the suddenness of the stampede has no equal in mountain history. They came too fast for the camp to house them, for surveyors to mark their claims, for law to organize, for standards to solidify.

The result was chaos. This potentially wealthiest of municipalities was flat broke. When one mine or real estate owner refused to pay his taxes, all refused. Assessments against gambling houses were ignored; poll taxes were shouted down as bearing harder on the poor than on the rich; licenses for stores and peddlers were declared unjust so long as brothels flourished without fee. The impecunious city could not remove filth or sprinkle summer's ankle-deep dust. Smelters spewed unchecked, stripping whole forests from the mountainsides. The police force was small, underpaid, corrupt. Well-heeled vultures jumped so many claims that poor prospectors formed the Miners' Mutual Protective Association; armed battles for possession were fought aboveground and, on at least one occasion, belowground. Frightened, the wealthier of the Carbonate kings, Tabor included, formed their own militia companies and decked them out in gaudy uniforms. The excuse was to guard the city from the then restive Utes; actually, however, these feudal troops were designed to protect the sponsors' private property. In 1880, when miners laid down their tools in the Rockies' first labor upheaval, the owners' rifle companies were used to battle the strikers. The situation grew so out of hand that Tabor, risen in less than one breathless year from mayor of Leadville to lieutenant governor of Colorado, called in the state militia and broke the power of the infant union for years to come.

Real estate speculation exploded into frenzy. Values doubled, quadrupled, soared almost beyond estimation. Lot jumpers openly marched the streets. Armed ruffians seized and held the tract of the Presbyterian Church. Other gangs twice tried to tear down St. Vincent's Hospital, which finally was guarded by a hundred armed volunteers who were grimly instructed by Catholic Father Robinson to shoot dead anyone attempting to invade the grounds. On the strength of a dubious placermine patent the Starr Company laid claim to most of Leadville and then brazenly offered to sell the citizens their own homes at staggering sums. Some protestors were ejected at rifle point, their houses torn down before their eyes, and the land sold to eager speculators. A "vigilance committee" sent the company a notice "to leaf this town in 10 days or less or come to terms if you do not we will hang you in spite of hell ... you are a dam dirty stink try to monopolize this town but we will wait on you to sure as Christ." Yet in spite of this and similar threats the Starr Company for months kept Leadville in an uproar with what the local newspaper characterized as a "long series of outrages such as would disgrace the wildest Zulu camp of savages."

Living at the town's 10,152-foot altitude was a tax on unacclimated systems. Sixty-odd years later, during World War II, mountain troops stationed at Camp Hale, at nearby Pando, would notice the same effects. The rarefied air lacked oxygen. A man had to breathe fast to keep going, and during winters, when thermometers often registered thirty degrees below zero, the rapid inhalations prevented the air from being warmed before it reached the lungs, a factor further complicated by the way in which the arid atmosphere dried out the entire respiratory system. Inside Camp Hale's barracks, as in Leadville's earlier buildings, stoves were kept red-hot. When a trooper stepped outside, temperatures plummeted a staggering hundred degrees, and his inevitable gasp filled his lungs not only with frost but with the smoke which hung densely in the windless hollows. The result was a chronic cough notorious among soldiers as "the Pando hack." Shivering, homesick Southerners wrote querulous letters back to the cotton fields, and their angry parents instigated a congressional investigation which ended, some rumors clamor, in a complete whitewash while once healthy boys were being carried out of the mountains on shutters. Army doctors and Colorado skiers hoot the whole story. Hale, they say, was no more unhealthful than lower camps, and the "hack" was a chimera magnified out of all proportion by typical Army griping.

Be that as it may, the unprepared Leadville stampeders certainly suffered. Hordes of them did not have and could not get proper food, clothing, or shelter. During the first two winters the town's diminutive hotels could not accommodate even those who were able to meet the astronomical rates. Flophouses flourished. Men paid fifty cents for the privilege of climbing into tiered wooden bunks with an unknown companion and an unwashed blanket, to shiver through an eight-hour shift before being routed out to make room for someone else. Throngs clustered around every bar, drinking all night long both for numbness and for shelter. Exhausted men slept on the floors of saloons, gambling halls, bawdyhouses. Ejected, they crawled into stables, warehouses, ore wagons, packing boxes, even outdoor toilets. The destitute went into restaurants, ordered huge meals, and on presentation of the check begged to be sent to jail; but since the disorganized police force seldom reacted with efficiency, a beating at the hands of the waiters was generally the outcome. Pneumonia, scourge of every mining town, swept the filthy byways. It is easy to exaggerate such situations, yet it seems well established that Leadville authorities buried dozens of victims during the dead of night, lest the toll, becoming known, frighten away stampeders and slow down the boom.

Death in a strange town far from home was always the most depressing occurrence in the silver camps. Morning in Telluride. Through the knife-sharp air rolled the slow bong of a bell announcing that someone killed in a bordello brawl was about to be buried. The sporting fraternity always turned out on such occasions. There, but for the grace of God . . . Valiantly they whooped things up to still the dread in the bottom of their hearts. A dance-hall band paraded in front of the black-plumed, glass-sided hearse. Bass drums reverberated against the cliffs. Behind the entourage straggled a squad of girls from the honky-tonks, clutching their long tight skirts as they waded through the hoof-churned, manure-stained slush of the streets. Rhinestones sparkled on high-heeled slippers. The throngs on the sidewalks fell momentarily still, each man bleak with his own secret thoughts. Ed Pierce, who ran away to Telluride before he was twenty and who described the funerals to me, saw them week after week, yet after each one he would flee into his cheerless boardinghouse room, bolt the door, and all but burst into tears.

Leadville taught prospectors new facts about geology. With the almost simultaneous removal of the Utes from Colorado, miners fanned up and over timber line to re-examine old prospects. A baker's dozen of towns, with Aspen as their raucous center, roared into being amid the majestic peaks of the Elk Mountains. Southward in the even more rugged San Juans a feverish stimulation gripped the tiny settlements that had been founded earlier in the seventies. Inevitably the new searches revealed not only silver and lead but also new deposits of gold, though none of them, until the exotic epoch of Cripple Creek and of Tom Walsh's Camp Bird at Ouray, rivaled in robustness their pale-metal cousins. Railroad-born smelting and supply towns, such as Durango and Gunnison, were scarcely less rowdy.

It is almost impossible to recapture the mood in a piece of a chapter. Random excerpts from newspapers of the time, written in a style as indigenous to the mountains as a slouch hat, may help.

Minor bits of violence and ribaldry were always staple items, as witness various notes in the Aspen *Times* during the spring of 1885.

May 14:

> Night before last, about the time ghosts usually walk, Eva Clark got her little hide full of Aspen sour mash. She then started out to do the town. She indulged her playful disposition a little too much and pushed a poor helpless man off the crossing into the gutter and then called him some pet names. Officer Gavitt came along and tried to induce the fair, frail Eva to go home, this she declined to do and gave the peeler a back hander. This, together with the fact of her being drunk and using profane and obscene language, caused the officer to arrest her. Yesterday she was taken before Judge Sampson to explain her unladylike conduct, which she did not succeed in doing . . . and was informed . . . in his honor's blandest manner that she would be required to pay $23.90 or go to jail.

June 9, under title MIKE SHAY MASTICATES OPPONENT'S AURICULAR ORGAN:

> Sunday morning about six o'clock, a rough and tumble fight took place in Ben Dixon's dance hall. There were no rules or regulations of any kind governing the mill. . . . Biting, scratching, gouging and kicking were allowed ad libitum. The result was that a fellow named Mike Shay bit off the lower portion of his opponent's ear. Shay then made a break to escape. He mounted a horse which he found hitched outside, but the owner happened to be near and with a club induced Shay to get down. Officer Gavitt came along and arrested the biter. . . .

June 13:

> The census taker says the sporting women of the town are averse to telling their real names, or where they were born. . . . This is not strange, as the relations of many of them are under the impression that they are governesses, or milliners, or dressmakers, or music teachers, and that they occupy way-up positions in the society of the Rocky Mountains.

June 18:

> Yesterday morning between 2 and 3 o'clock, just after the Aspen Theater had finished its regular program . . . an additional scene was enacted savoring of tragedy. Julius Benner

was the piano player. Maud Lamb, one of Leadville's estrayed citizens, was his solid girl and was jerking beer in the parquette of the theater. Maud had complained that Julius spent his money and more of hers than was proper. When the theater closed, they had a racket among the chairs, which served Maud as instruments of warfare. Soon after, Julius was standing by the bar in the front room taking a drink, when . . . Maud entered with an open jack-knife partly concealed in her hand . . . and stabbed him in the stomach, and as she was making other strokes at him he knocked her down, when the deputy marshall arrested them. Benner said, "Hold on till I show you something," and backing up against the wall he pulled up his shirt, showing blood flowing freely from a savage wound in his abdomen clear to the bowels. . . . As Benner declined to prosecute, the officer preferred a charge of drunk and disorderly. She pleaded guilty and was fined $5 and costs.

From Durango, where the *Record* was edited by Mrs. Romney, a plump, pretty widow who had left Leadville to try fresher fields, come somewhat homier touches. Thus the birth of the town's first baby was reported on February 5, 1881, as follows:

Miss Una C. Pearson, infant daughter of John and Ella Pearson, bears her honors gracefully, of being the first child born in Durango. . . . We have noticed an unusual number of people going in the direction of the young lady's domicile—frontiersmen who have probably not seen an infant for twenty years; old miners . . . prominent businessmen, teamsters, doctors, lawyers, and women all wended their way to see the new arrival.

One old miner from Silverton presented the little curiosity with a bag of gold dust; McFadden & Son gave a deed for a town lot on Third Street; Mr. Creek sent over four tons of coal; Newman, Chestnut & Stevens gave a dozen bottles of soothing syrup, and John Taylor, Jr., followed with a soft hairbrush, while Griffin & Carpenter sent in a rubber ring and a box of safety pins. Mr. and Mrs. Diamond gave the baby their little "cross dog" Prince to play with when she gets old enough. Robertson and Rawley as soon as they heard the news, went to work making a baby-carriage. Ed Schiffer wanted to give away his baby steam-engine but it makes such a big racket that it would keep the little one awake, so instead, he presented a receipt for a post-office box. The *Record* publisher put her name down for a year's subscription to the *Daily* and *Weekly* gratis. Finch of the Nose Paint Saloon thought his goods were too strong, so he brought a powder-box. Doctor Cowen of the Windsor gave a box of tooth-picks—that's about as much as a bachelor knows about babies. . . . Myers (another bach.) brought up a pony with a sidesaddle on for the young lady to take a horse-back ride.

Apparently the *Record* thought more babies would be a desirable civic asset, for a few weeks later, on March 12, 1881, the paper editorialized under a heading WANTED IN DURANGO:

> We want girls! Girls who can get themselves up in good shape to go to a dance . . . girls who will go to church and to Bible-class on Sunday . . . and who will take a buggy ride after the lesson is over. They will help the livery business, and will also hasten the sale of residence lots, for buggies are the vehicles where homes are first thought of by many people. . . .
>
> We want girls for sweethearts, so that when we get an arm shot off, or are kicked by a mule, or thrown from a bucking horse and are laid away for repairs, we may hear a gentle voice and see the glitter of a crystal tear. . . .
>
> We want fat and funny girls to make us smile all over, and lean and fragile ones to hang upon our arms, and petite blondes who show themselves on sunny days; and stately brunettes, so beautiful in the twilight.
>
> We have mineral enough, and plenty of coal, and oxide of iron. The only lack of our resources is those potent civilizers of their pioneer brothers—the girls!

In spite of the wistful appeal, it would appear that there were at least a few potent civilizers in Durango, for a month later, on April 9, the *Record* announced a grand ball to celebrate the opening of the West End Hotel:

> The opening dinner will be spread in the mammoth dining hall from seven to nine pm when an elegant menu . . . will be raided by Durango's elite. After the royal gorge has taken place, the large force of attendants will spirit away the china and broken-hearted champagne bottles, and Professor Delius and his True Fissure Orchestra will take possession of one end of the room. Then sweet perfumes will greet grateful nostrils, and exquisite strains of Terpsichorean musical messages will be telephoned through auricular drums, past palpitating hearts, to agile feet which will not rest till morn.

Unfortunately a bunch of feuding cowboys shot up the hotel and the grand opening had to be postponed. However, there were other diversions. A vigilante committee lynched one of the brawlers and a week later, on April 16, the editor found solace in wielding her pen over this:

> And a ghastly sight it was . . . A slight wind swayed the body to and fro. The pale moonlight glimmering through the rifted clouds clothed the ghastly face with a ghastlier pallor. The somber shadows of the massive foliage seemed blacker than the weeds of mourning; and the shuffling of hurrying feet in the dusty road, mingling with the weird whistling of the breeze through the pine boughs broke upon the ear with a sepulchral tone . . . Thus the Powers that Be . . . have proclaimed to the world that good order, peace, quietude and safety must and shall prevail in Durango.

Advertisements, then as now, were the financial backbone of the papers. One in the Park City, Utah, *Record* cried, "You can find a large stock of the celebrated Switz Condie non-shrinking wool underwear at Lawrence & Co's. Buy a suit and fool your Chinaman; he cannot shrink them." The Aspen *Times* advised, "Professor Burkhardt has the only bath house in Aspen, and don't you forget it when you need a wash." And, "Oh, what a race of people is it that does not adore saurkraut? Get it at Cowenhaven's." From one end of the Rockies to the other nearly every issue of every paper carried a picture of a woman in a harem costume gazing thoughtfully at a tumbler from which she had just quaffed "Prickly Ash Bitters for Dyspepsia, General Debility, Etc." Electric belts and galvanic batteries were available to cure all ailments of the flesh, and to plug any chance loopholes there was "Dr. Wood's brain and nerve treatment, a guaranteed specific for hysteria, dizziness, fits, and convulsions caused by use of tobacco and alcohol. Also mental depression, softening of the brain, etc., caused by over-exertion of the brain."

Fire was the common enemy of the first jerry-built villages. This led to the formation of resplendent hose and engine companies with eye-searing uniforms and ironclad social standards. Intensely jealous of one another, they sponsored parades, parties, and political clambakes. Once a year the best of them vied at state-wide tournaments in "wet" and "dry" hose-laying runs. But they seldom put out a large fire. The failure was not always their fault. High winds or frozen creeks could and often did defy the most ambitious pumpers. When

Central City's great conflagration broke out in May 1874, firemen belatedly discovered that the deepening of the mines had run the wells dry. Dynamite, not water, was used to save the remnants of the village; during the excitement a hundred thousand dollars in currency was stuffed into a lard pail and entrusted to the bank's Negro porter, who returned every bill of it intact.

Such guttings periodically left many people foodless and shelterless in the dead of a mountain winter, but the disasters had their recompense. The worst of the filth was carted away with the ashes, and the towns rebuilt with brick. Even brick, however, has not proved impervious. Scores of buildings have had their interiors burned up and their exteriors torn down by provident neighbors for hen coops, outhouses, and charcoal kilns. Beams and joists have disappeared as shoring into the ever-ravenous maws of the mines. This slow, steady razing helps explain why present-day visitors find the old metropolises so much smaller than expected.

Away from the main towns, in spruce-log cabins beside some singing stream or by the yellow prospect dumps that freckle the high, gray basins, life was not so hectic. But it had its problems. Shortages of all kinds developed, and improvisation was the order of the day. Four Middle Park prospectors killed an antelope, ate it, and patched their pants with its hide all within twelve hours. Knit socks being rare in Silverton, substitutes were contrived by winding strips torn from flour sacks around the foot and leg. In Telluride wrapping paper was so scarce that butcher-shop patrons carried home their meat and butter impaled on sharpened sticks. When flour was not available whole grain was hauled in from the nearest ranch and ground by hand in old-fashioned coffee grinders. Small children could be transported by bundling them into panniers on either side of a burro. Housewives and bachelors alike struggled with the problems of high-altitude cookery, where standard recipes fail and unreasonable amounts of time and wood are consumed in boiling beans or potatoes. String was priceless, since it was used for wicks in dipping candles, though some lazy rascals were content with the light furnished by a twist of rag floating in a tin full of bear oil. A copper kettle big enough for boiling the family wash, making soap, or scalding hogs was not only a prize but even a mark of social distinction. A favorite legend, which attaches to innumerable crop-eared, bobtailed mules and donkeys, says that the missing appendages fed various starving prospectors. And up at Grand Lake, "Judge" Wescott ate his own chair seat—it was woven from strips of untanned deer hide.

This same "Judge" Wescott obtained his title as the result of a bit of romantic improvisation. Grand Lake's inevitable first single maiden had appeared, had been wooed and won, and a wedding had been scheduled when someone pointed out that the camp possessed no preacher. The inhabitants, not to be deprived of a long-anticipated celebration, thereupon organized a town and elected Wescott justice of the peace. Next no one could find a Bible, so a volunteer rode twenty-four miles to borrow one from old lady Kinney at Hot Sulphur Springs. At the reception following the wedding the bridegroom got in a fight with a man named Galliger and was soundly trounced. Wescott fined Galliger five dollars on the spot, and the new court's first proceeds were by unanimous consent used to buy drinks for the crowd.

Being justice of the peace did not hamper Wescott's private war with Bill Avery, known as the Pirate, who had appropriated as dwelling quarters a dugout which once housed the justice's donkeys. When in his cups, Avery would load up his .50-caliber needle gun and blow the chinking out of Wescott's cabin. The nearsighted justice retaliated by ramming a fistful of black powder, nails, and bolts into Jezebel, his muzzle-loading 8-gauge shotgun, and belching scrap iron all over the Pirate's dugout. Aside from bruises to Wescott, who was knocked flat by each of Jezebel's recoils, the only casualty in the intermittent feud resulted when a piece of stove bolt pinned the seat of Avery's trousers to his hide and had to be removed with an old bullet mold which local settlers used for pulling porcupine quills from their dogs' noses.

Accidents could be gruesome—explosions, cave-ins, and falling rocks inside the mines; rebellious stock, fire, and, most dreaded of all, avalanches on the outside. Most of these snowslides ran regular courses, were spotted, named, and avoided. But at times a long-dormant slope would peel off its white blanket with a horrifying sweep; and even though the slide itself did not strike a building, the concussion sometimes exploded nearby structures into kindling wood, and mules a considerable distance away are known to have been totally deafened. A reputed 140 people died in the workings above Alta, Utah, during the seventies. After a 1906 slide at the Shenandoah-Dives Mine north of Silverton, twenty-two grotesquely twisted bodies were stacked like cordwood in the morgue until they could be thawed, straightened, and claimed. At 7:30 A.M. on February 28, 1902, an avalanche swept away a large part of the Liberty Bell above Telluride. When a rescue party rushed to the scene, a second slide hit them! In all, nineteen men died, including the writer's great-uncle, and my stepfather escaped only by seizing a tree as he was hurled past and clinging on for dear life.

The story of Billy Maher epitomizes the innumerable tragedies that stalked the lonely cabins. Billy and an Italian partner were working a prospect above the Terrible Mine, near Ouray. It was cold (they had to take their potatoes to bed to keep them from freezing) and the snow was deep, but they decided to wolf the winter through. Then one morning some dynamite Billy was thawing in the oven blew up, demolished the cabin, blinded and mutilated the miner. His partner, less severely injured, wrapped Billy in a blanket and started downhill to the Terrible for help. There were skis at the cabin, but the Italian could not use them. It took him seven hours to flounder one mile. Only four men were at the Terrible. Fearing they could not pack Billy down the hill unaided, they sent the Italian on to the nearby Virginius Mine with instructions for a relief party to come to the Terrible and wait for them.

In time the rescuers reached Billy, loaded him on a sled improvised from skis, and toward midnight staggered wearily back to the Terrible. No relief was there. On the exhausted quartet went, to the livery barn at Porter's, where they bundled the now unconscious Billy aboard a sleigh for Ouray. After catching some sleep they returned to the Virginius. They were sore.

"Why the hell didn't you send us help?"

"We did. Four men left as soon as we got word."

"Where are they?"

"We'd better look."

The whole force went up the trail. Sure enough, they saw a fresh avalanche track and at its base a hat. Near the hat a frozen hand protruded from the waste. The four rescuers were dead. And so, too, in the hospital at Ouray, was Billy Maher.

A grisly humor—if humor is the word—attends some of these frozen deaths. A sexton at Leadville, digging a grave, struck a vein of silver and chucked his corpse into a snowbank, where it stayed until spring while the cemetery was staked off into mining claims. At Ohio Creek in the Gunnison country, Louis Ahern's partner died. The ground was frozen too hard for Louis to dig a grave, yet he could not keep the body in his warm cabin, and he did not want to heave it out where coyotes would devour it. So he compromised by laying it on a top shelf in his milkhouse, where he stored the butter he sold to neighboring miners. Along came Frank Lightley. As Frank's order was being wrapped his eyes wandered along the shelves. Abruptly he changed his mind about his purchase, and for months afterward the bewildered Louis had more unsold butter on his hands than he knew what to do with.

It is no wonder the people played hard when they could. But it was not all wild. Cabin raisings and the accompanying all-night hoe-down dances were perennial favorites. During winter, sledding was popular, though not entirely harmless. One evening's sport at Central City ended when a huge wood sleigh loaded with merrymakers jumped the road, hurled one man through a startled resident's window, broke a boy's jaw, and shredded a "$40.00 overcoat." At the Tomboy Mine, above timber line in Telluride's Savage Basin, miners even tried putting great wings on their toboggans, but the disastrous wrecks accompanying these primitive attempts at gliding soon discouraged the practice.

Celebrations in the towns, principally on the Fourth of July, featured competitions between fire companies and rock-drilling contests, for the latter of which huge blocks of the hardest granite were set up in the middle of the main street. Backed by enormous wagers and weeks of practice, two-man teams tried to see who could punch out the deepest hole in a prescribed time. One brawny miner, bare to the waist and crouched on his knees, held the steel, giving it adroit turns to keep it from sticking. His hairy-chested partner whammed the drill with a massive sledge. Winded, the striker would trade off with the turner, and it was no phenomenon for a competent pair, inspired by the cheers of a thousand spectators, to drill a two-foot hole in fifteen minutes.

Horse races were popular, too, but no more so than foot races. Every mine had a champion sprinter whom fellow workers supported, with cash, against any and all comers, a bit of home-camp boosterism which led many a nimble barnstormer to disguise himself as a tramp prospector and drift from town to town, trimming the local hopefuls. Notable among these wandering professionals was Harry Bethune, who frequently finished his races running backward and thumbing his nose at his red-faced rivals. Prize fights and wrestling matches of all varieties were likewise favored, challenges often being issued by means of paid advertisements in the local papers, as witness this from the Park City, Utah, *Record*, January 5, 1889: "I hereby challenge any man in Park City for a wrestling contest, collar and elbow style, for $50 to $100 a side. This challenge is open to Thos. Kearns for any or all of the five styles for the same stake. Forfeit money will be covered at this office—J. B. Streder."

More cultural activities were not missing. The increasing complexity of mining and milling brought trained technicians to the Rockies. They in turn brought their wives. To prove that all the women in Leadville were not of the sporting-house ilk, Editor C. C. Davis of the *Democrat* stole photographs of "one hundred of the most beautiful and cultured ladies of the city, grouped them upon a broad page of highly calendered paper, and printed the impression from lithograph stones in the highest style of art." He had to steal the pictures because no respectable woman of that day would consider having her likeness in a public paper (though how Davis managed the thefts he does not say), and when news of the stunt leaked out indignant husbands restrained publication by means of a court injunction.

However, though the ladies might be publicity-shy, they were busy. Churches flourished, temperance societies marched, musicales and lectures were arranged. Sentimental legends attach to the "first" piano in every mountain village. In Rico, after the Marshes' grand piano had been installed in its muslin-lined, four-room home, the town stationed spies to watch for the advent of daughter Helen, "a slim bit of a girl . . . who could not only paw hell out of the ivories, but who also . . . sang like an angel." In time she came. Rain was pouring down when at last she approached the piano. Outside, hidden by a window curtain, a hundred drenched men huddled against the side of the house. She sang "Home, Sweet Home" and "one of the fellows leaning against the window began to swear softly, and the old man heard him and jerked up the shade, and there we were, a hundred of us, looking mighty foolish and mushy as we peered in at her."

As their contribution to culture the more flamboyant of the carbonate kings built opera houses. The mountain towns, shining up their pasts for the benefit of the tourist trade, love to boast of the famous actors who came all the way up the hill to grace their boards. Actually, it would have been more astonishing if the road shows had passed the silver camps by. The opera houses offered quick profits on the way to California, and a certain lack of Broadway manners on the part of the audiences could be overlooked amid the handfuls of gold coins which such magnates as Haw Tabor and William Bush showered on the stage by way of applause.

Occasionally, of course, mountain humor could be annoying. When famed Fanny Buckingham was touring Colorado with *Mazeppa*, her attendants could not lure her special steed into the Denver and Rio

Grande's narrow-gauge boxcars. It was necessary to the act, for it had been trained to bear her, strapped in revealing gossamer to its bare back, up an inclined ramp to a climactic exit amid pasteboard rocks. When Fanny declined to appear without it the manager of the Leadville house wrung his hands. His show was sold out. Could not a gentle local horse be substituted? Miss Buckingham, after toting up the balance sheet, at last nodded agreement, and a docile milk-wagon animal was hired. Unfortunately, a now nameless miner happened to be in the stable when arrangements were consummated. That night, as the audience watched with bated breath and Mazeppa was borne aloft by her fiery charger, the blast of a fish horn rang through the theater. Thinking milk was to be delivered, the horse froze to a halt. Miss Buckingham kicked furiously. Somewhat confused, the horse took a tentative step. Another blast. Another stop. Another kick. The audience bellowed its joy, Miss Buckingham spoke certain unrehearsed lines, and the curtain tumbled hastily down on the most anticlimactic climax in *Mazeppa's* long and spectacular life.[1]

Fine, high days. In 1890 the Sherman Silver Purchase Act, which required the United States Treasury to buy 4,500,000 ounces each and every month, shot the price of the white metal up from $.84 to $1.05 per ounce. Immediately thereafter it resumed its steady decline (back down to $.87 by 1892), but the government's artificial market seemed a certain guarantee against any crippling collapse. Meanwhile technological advances boomed, most significantly the world's first commercial transmission of high-pressure electricity by L. L. Nunn to the Gold King Mine above Ames, near Telluride.

He was a tiny man, this Nunn, a lawyer, not an engineer. Oldtimers say he got his degree in a saloon when someone hit him over the head with a lawbook. But he was canny. My old friend, the late L. G. Dennison, liked to tell how Nunn persuaded him to buy a long garden hose to bring water to their adjoining houses in Telluride. Denny was content just to have water to drink, but Nunn cashed in by

---

[1] First and most famous of the mountain opera houses was Central City's. An exception, it was financed not by an individual but by sale of stock to that always musical town's loyal citizens. Defunct and decaying, it was at length willed to Denver University, as apparently white an elephant as ever existed. But adroit publicity refurbished it in its gay eighties' glory, and in 1932 it was reopened with Robert Edmond Jones's production of *Camille*, starring Lillian Gish. Every summer now big-name shows and big-name actors hit Central City in the Rockies' most diligent cultural exploitation of the good old days, to the tune of gorgeous merrymaking and prices that would choke a gasp from the shades of H. A. W. Tabor himself.

installing a bathtub in his house and charging party-bound miners fifty cents per immersion.

In 1888 the Gold King Mine, twelve thousand feet high, was attached by creditors. Nunn, as lawyer for the owners, obtained a stay in proceedings and found that the situation could be saved if the high cost of fuel for steam power could somehow be reduced. In a canyon far below the mine roared the San Miguel River. Electricity suggested itself, but at that time electric power had never been transmitted over flat land, let alone up 2.6 miles of forest-bristling, cliff-studded precipice. The wise boys told Nunn it could never be done, but, being a lawyer and not an engineer, he lacked sense enough to believe them. Ferreting out a few technicians willing to take a chance, he fought man-killing terrain, ice, avalanches, forty-below-zero temperatures, and furious electric storms to build his line. Then he housed his first crude wooden-based generators in a log hut at the bottom of the hill. Attendants threw control switches with long wooden poles; the six-foot arcs lighted the whole mountainside and had to be broken by a whiff from the operator's hat. Since no one knew what it was all about, workers had to train themselves on the spot. Nunn established a technical library in a two-room log cabin, badgered visiting scientists into giving lectures, and so started one of the first systematic efforts ever made by a United States "corporation" to train its employees for responsible positions. (Out of this grew the Nunn-endowed Telluride Association at Cornell University, and unique Deep Springs in the desolate White Mountains of western Nevada, where carefully screened undergraduates, all expenses paid, learn not only book lore but the practical side of running their own self-sufficient organization far from the "distractions" of the outside world.) Soon the Gold King was humming profitably under sixty thousand volts of electricity, Nunn was building high-tension lines across thirteen-thousand-foot Imogene Pass to other eager mines in the San Juans, and new fields at the feet of the Wasatch Mountains were beckoning frantically to his Utah Power and Light Company.

High, fine days. Every foot of the Rockies had been combed. Surely no new strikes could be made. But they were. In 1891 Nate Creede found the Holy Moses in the southern part of Colorado and the town that bears his name roared to life in a rust-colored canyon so narrow that it can contain only a single street. It was Leadville again. Speculation ran wild. Houses were building all night long; if you were able to drive a nail you were a carpenter; if not, you held a lantern for someone who could. Cabins, tents, and shanties were built as far up the canyon side as it was possible to anchor a six-by-ten hut with the cliff for a back wall. Shacks were built on poles laid across the stream. Soapy Smith ran his con games; Bob Ford, killer of Jesse James, was shot down in turn. Theodore Renniger picked up a stone to throw at his burro, saw it was ore, staked out the Last Chance, and turned around and sold a third interest for $65,000. The Denver and Rio Grande Railroad, racing up from Wagon Wheel Gap, found so many footmen following its tracks that two guards had to be stationed on each engine's cowcatcher to keep someone from being killed. On February 18, 1892, the Creede *Candle*, under the heading O, Ho, A MAYOR!, reported, "Creede now has a council and mayor, with what authority those who desire may solve to their own satisfaction. . . . The first meeting of the council . . . recommended the following scale of assessments: Saloons, $5.00; fancy houses, each girl $2.00 a month and landlady $10.00; other branches of business, $2.50 a month; express wagons, $3.00. It was decided to have bills printed warning of a fine of $10 for committing a nuisance in the street or creek."

Editor Cy Warman, surveying the busy scene, was moved to pen his locally famous jingle, whose best-known stanza goes:

> *Here's a land where all are equal—*
> *Of high or lowly birth—*
> *A land where men make millions*
> *Dug from the dreary earth.*
> *Here the meek and mild-eyed burros*
> *On mineral mountains feed—*
> *It's day all day in the daytime*
> *And there is no night in Creede.*

There are those who declare that Creede, if given a chance, would have surpassed even Leadville. But it never had a chance. In less than two years after the rush started, panic gripped the United States, the Sherman Silver Purchase Act was repealed, mints in India ceased coinage of the white metal, and an epoch ended. Three quotations from the *Candle*, spaced within three weeks' time, tell the story of despair.

June 30, 1893:

> Creede is in the condition of an audience at the theatre when the curtain has just gone down on an act of thrilling interest. . . . A string is pulled in far-off England, a twist by the politicians, and silver drops out of sight—the Heroine in the clutches of the Wicked Villain.

But like all well-behaved audiences, the Creede audience in front of the stage of real life . . . is content to sit awhile, laugh at the grim humor of the comedy part, discuss the beauty of the portion just enacted and wait for the final outcome, conscious that however subtle the villain's arts, the fair Heroine will be rescued.

July 14, 1893:

We can whistle because we know pleasant meadows lie ahead. . . .

July 21, 1893:

Unless relief comes in the only way miners in Colorado will accept as honorable—the reopening of the mines—look out for the inauguration of a bread riot that might result in a second Paris commune.

There were no Paris communes. Actually the drop in silver output was not as abysmal as some mountain histories proclaim. But it was bad enough. From 1893 to 1894 Colorado's production sagged from $20,154,107 to $14,667,281. After that, for two years, it climbed above $15,000,000, then began a slow decline which in 1902 dropped under $10,000,000 for the first time since the Leadville boom. Most of this output, however, came from mines in Leadville, the San Juans, etc., which also carried gold and could weather the storm. Pure silver camps—Alta, Georgetown, Aspen, Creede—never recovered. Haw Tabor, who had cast Augusta aside in order to take unto himself the physical lushness of Baby Doe McCourt at a spectacular Washington wedding attended by President Arthur, lost every dime of his once uncounted millions. Fearfully he accepted a job as Denver's postmaster and not long thereafter dropped dead. Unlovable though he seems from today's perspective, he nonetheless commanded loyalty from his women—Augusta first, then Baby Doe, who took up abode in a decrepit shack at the closed Matchless, clung to it through abject poverty, tried to work it herself in ragged miner's clothes, watched her daughters forsake her for squalid fates, and in March 1936 was found half clad on the floor of her hut, frozen to death.

Hundreds of other men and companies failed. This, together with the general economic stagnation that prevailed during the depression, sent unemployed miners pouring out of the hills to join the march of Coxey's Army on Washington. One contingent actually stole a train, wrecked it, seized another, and progressed as far as central Kansas before being dispersed by Federal deputies. Years later, in 1900, former silver miners in the new gold camp of Cripple Creek were still bitter enough to threaten Theodore Roosevelt with violence when he stumped the district as vice-presidential candidate of the gold-standard Republican party.

The king was dead. But his story is not complete without the saga of the courtiers who served him so lustily—the freighters, the packers, the toll-road builders, and the bustling narrow-gauge railways.

CHAPTER VIII

OVER THE HUMP

ONE disgruntled prospector, answering the questions of a reporter for the Denver *Tribune* concerning the mineral regions of southwestern Colorado, unconsciously summed up the starkest single problem that confronted the entire Rocky Mountain area.

"The San Juan," he said (and the name of almost any mining locality may be substituted), "is the best and worst mining country I ever struck. It has more and better mineral . . . but, you see, it's no good. You can't get at it except over ranges like that" (sticking his arm up at an angle of eighty degrees) "and when you're in, you see, you're corralled by the mountains, so you can't get your ore out."

Materials in, ores out—three quarters of a century ago any donkey packer, wagon driver, toll-road builder, or railway engineer who could guarantee that feat became a regional hero and reaped commensurate financial rewards. It was not the San Luis Valley farmer who received one hundred dollars a ton for hay in Leadville, nor the Mormon fruit-grower who got fifty cents each for bruised peaches in Alder Gulch, Montana. It was the freighter; and although his customers suffered unparalleled indignities, general opinion inclined to the belief that he earned every nickel he charged.

The Colorado rush brought the problem to a head in a hurry. In the two months of May and June 1860, an estimated 11,000 wagons hit the trail from the East, hauling, among innumerable other things, 160 quartz mills, some of which were as ponderous as they were impractical. Now quartz mills could be and have been transported piecemeal on the backs of animals—if one has enough animals. In 1874, for instance, a marshaled herd of sad-eyed burros lugged an entire smelter 250 miles across the Continental Divide to Silverton. Wagons were preferable. But wagons involved roads.

The more resolute of the pioneers chopped and dug their own paths. The result was not a highway, merely an opening. The annals of every mountain town are full of tales of original settlers who descended awesome hills with felled trees tied to the backs of their vehicles for brakes; who doubled up their teams and heaved mightily at wheel

spokes to surmount some summit; who chained logs to the upper sides
of the wagons so they would not tip over while rounding precipitous
corners.

It was a backbreaking way to travel. The first wagon to crawl from
Twin Lakes over what is now Independence Pass and down the Roaring Fork to Aspen spent six weeks on a journey of less than fifty miles.
Traveling the same route today, one wonders how the lone wagon
ever did it at all. One also wonders about two other questions which
the records neglect to answer: Why did the adventurer so tax himself
(mule trains made the trip in a fraction of the time), and what did he
accomplish with his maltreated vehicle after he reached the rugged
and then roadless environs of Aspen? Well, perhaps a semi-immobilized
wagon is, to its owner at least, a satisfying monument to the powers of
persistence.

The great bulk of the wayfarers were not so resolute. They rolled
along as far as roads existed, then camped in tent colonies in some
valley and waited for workers to complete the trace over the next
summit. Their reminiscences tell of trading with Indians, patching
clothes, shoeing horses, playing cards, drumming up dances, and heart-
ily cursing the slowness of the road builders.

Creating passageway for these impatient hordes brought forth various
methods of financing. Occasionally mining camps would levy local
taxes for hiring the necessary labor; at other times community-minded
citizens would, in a burst of enthusiasm, subscribe a day's or a week's
work with their own tools and horses. But the most common method
was for the road builders to charge the traveling public tolls. During
the sixties and seventies there was a spate of such companies in Colorado. Incorporation was simplicity itself. An applicant paid the territorial legislature a modest fee—often as low as five dollars—stated only
what towns were to serve as termini for the road, and then hied himself out to choose his own route by his own devices, generally the
squinting of one eye. His charter authorized him to issue capital stock,
to use such public-land stone and timber as were required, and to
collect tolls based on mileage and on the type of vehicle and stock
using the highway. Persons bound to or from funerals and religious
services were entitled by law to travel free; hence many an impecunious
miner chose Sunday for his journeyings. If possible, the road company located its toll stations in a narrow canyon, so that horsemen,
cattle drovers, and sheepherders could not beat the fare by circling
off through the woods. Free advertising was readily obtained through
the columns of local papers, as evinced by this excerpt from Denver's

Rocky Mountain News, April 1860: "I am happy to inform the people of this vicinity and the travelling public generally, that through the untiring energy and perseverance of Colonel McIntyre and others, as fine a mountain road to Tarryall, by way of Bradford, as I have ever travelled, will soon be completed for their accommodation. . . . A large force of men is at work. . . ." It will be noted that the statement, though enthusiastic, was also ambiguous enough to free the writer from any charges of misrepresentation.

Of these scores of ambitious toll-road companies some never got beyond the paper stage, a few were designed for the sole purpose of bilking investors, and many were completed only in part. Those that were pushed through often impoverished rather than enriched their builders. A typical example is the story of Berthoud Pass, now part of U. S. Highway 40 and probably the most famous all-weather crossing of the Continental Divide in Colorado.

Originally the pass was surveyed by Captain E. L. Berthoud and Jim Bridger in a futile effort to attract first the Overland Mail route and later the Union Pacific. As part of the come-hither attempt, Berthoud and several others started building the road on their own in 1862. Conditions were difficult. Editor W. N. Byers of the *Rocky Mountain News*, who had acquired the mineral waters at "Saratoga West" (now Hot Sulphur Springs) and who was therefore interested in the road as a means of developing tourist trade to his embryo resort, once found a frozen corpse sitting on a stump that, when the snow melted, stood fifteen feet aboveground. Weather, altitude (11,315 feet) and cliff-like grades so discouraged Berthoud and his associates that they sold out to William Cushman, Georgetown banker, who in turn exhausted both his own funds and the money he raised selling stock to the public. Flat broke, Cushman turned over his interests to W. A. Hamill for seven thousand dollars. Not until October 1875, after thirteen years of sporadic effort and bitter disappointment, did the first stage cross the mountain.

From then on Berthoud Pass grew in fame and profit. Indeed, it was too popular for the public to stomach enriching one man; the state bought Hamill out for twenty-five thousand dollars and made Berthoud perhaps the first free crossing of the divide in Colorado. Now new hordes poured over in addition to the usual freighters, miners, and ranchers—hunters bound for Middle Park and tourists headed for Grand Lake. Among the latter were at least two bicyclists, Mrs. Agnes Hatch and her husband, who pedaled and pushed over the hump in 1893, frightening cattle out of their way by opening and closing Mrs.

Hatch's umbrella. On a repeat trip the next year Mr. Hatch, "being liberal-minded," suggested bloomers for his wife. Reluctantly Mrs. Hatch agreed, but "I also made a full skirt I could button on hurriedly." Apparently it was a wise precaution. One huge freight team, spotting the unskirted bloomers, nearly plunged off the road. After that, on hearing horses or people approach, Mrs. Hatch "hurriedly" covered the alarming garment out of sight, and there were no more reports of terrified horses or dumfounded freighters.

One man who did not go broke, although he built about 450 miles of road over fourteen or fifteen passes, some of them as high as Berthoud and many of them far more rugged, was Indian-trading, storekeeping, pint-sized Otto Mears. It was a shoestring start. In 1867, while gouging out his first crude road over Poncha Pass in order to haul his otherwise unsalable wheat out of the San Luis Valley to the Arkansas, Mears was floundering in financial quicksands. His Saguache store owed fifteen hundred dollars' worth of bills, and creditors were growing ugly, when into town swept a flashy carriage owned by one William Laddingham. Who Laddingham was Mears didn't know. Small matter. He gave his patched trousers a hitch, scraped up an acquaintance, and in his heavy Russian accent soon persuaded the spellbound Laddingham to invest in a "horse ranch." The sum—fifteen hundred dollars. Laddingham swept on; Mears paid his debts. Four months later, when Laddingham returned to see his horses, only the intervention of Otto's friends kept him from paying a precipitate visit to the sheriff. However, Mears had saved the store and the Poncha Pass road, ancestor of nearly every major highway in the San Juan district.

Mears's next venture was a road over Cochetopa Pass to his store at the Ute agency on the Gunnison River. This purely local project was given delusions of grandeur by Enos Hotchkiss and various other visionaries, who threw in with Mears and garnered enough funds for him to extend the road on up the Lake Fork of the Gunnison. Their plan evidently was to continue over the lofty pass above Animas Forks and so reach the burgeoning mineral districts around Silverton. They did not make it, however. After ninety-six killing miles of the work had been finished, Hotchkiss accidentally discovered a rich vein of gold near the present site of Lake City. He promptly lost interest in the road and work came to a stop.

A digression is almost unavoidable, because only a mile or two away from the road's end another party of wayfarers had come to a far more hideous halt a few months before. This was the ill-fated Packer party, whose oft-exploited story is the Rockies' only close rival to the cannibalistic horrors of California's Donner tragedy. A not-so-familiar telling of it comes from Sidney Jocknick, a cowboy who happened to be in the vicinity at the time.

In December 1873, Sid Jocknick and Gene Kelley, in charge of the government's Ute agency cattle herd in the Gunnison Valley, cornered a magnificent elk high on a snow-covered bluff. Unable to escape through the deep drifts, the elk charged the mounted pair. It was a furious melee. Kelley's rifle jammed; Jocknick's was empty. But Sid's horse had no intention of being gored. Whirling, it lashed out with both hind feet, delaying the beast until the cowboys' two dogs, Swipes and Snooks, could wallow up and divert the elk's attention. Unfortunately Jocknick dropped his gun in the turmoil. Before he could recover it and reload, the elk broke away and escaped.

The disgruntled pair climbed to the top of the bluff and with field glasses searched for their quarry. They saw it, hopelessly out of reach. They also saw a distant column of smoke, almost invisible against one of the bleakest winter vistas in the Rockies. What on earth had caused that wavering thread? No Indians were abroad. The mining rush to the San Juan had scarcely started, and it seemed incredible that prospectors could be so many hundred miles from the settlements at such a season. Speculating curiously, the cowboys returned to their cabin.

A few days later, just before New Year's, 1874, they had their answer. A feeble knock sounded at their lonesome door, and two specters staggered in. The one whose name they later learned was Burke promptly keeled over in a dead faint. The other, Lot Loutzenhizer, sank in a heap, babbling incoherently.

Bit by bit during succeeding days the story was pieced together. The previous spring in Salt Lake City a group of men had read in the papers an account of a gold strike at Summit, Colorado, on the eastern slope of the divide. Twenty of them banded together to try their luck, but not one of them was familiar with the country. Then they learned that a petty convict, Alfred Packer, working out a fine with a chain gang on the city streets, knew Colorado. On his promise to serve as guide they bailed him out and started their six-hundred-mile journey.

It was a hard-luck trip from the start. They lost most of their goods trying to raft the Green River, and it was late fall before they finally reached Chief Ouray's camp on the Uncompahgre. Fed and rested, they discussed going on. Ouray, all too familiar with the furious winters of the San Juan, endeavored to dissuade them. Half the party accepted his offer of shelter for the winter; the others determined to press ahead.

Burke, Loutzenhizer, and three more left first. Packer and five others promised to follow in a day or two but failed to appear. Meanwhile the Burke party was caught by a fiendish blizzard. Lost, foodless, and half frozen, three of them played out. Then Burke and Loutzenhizer killed a coyote that was feeding on carrion, gave part of the carcass to their companions, and crept on with the remainder, seeking succor. Chance led them to one of the agency's cows. They killed it, drank its blood, plowed helplessly ahead, and at last spotted the cabin—the only building, aside from those at the agency itself, within scores of miles.

Promptly Kelley and Jocknick dragged a sledload of provisions to the three half-dead survivors, one of whom clutched the coyote's skull in his arms and for a long time refused to give it up. Back at the cabin, as their coma of despair wore away, they began to worry about Packer and his five companions. If the group had left the Indian camp, where were they now?

Kelley and Jocknick searched as best they could, found nothing, and decided Packer had stayed on the Uncompahgre. Weeks drifted by. Then members of the party who had wintered with Ouray straggled by. Yes, they said, Packer and five others had departed as scheduled.

Search was redoubled. Then suddenly Packer appeared at the agency. He had hurt his leg, he told the sympathetic agency staff. His companions, annoyed at his slowness, had turned south toward Silverton, leaving him to wolf through the winter on berries and squirrels. But he looked plump enough, and his first request was for whisky, not food. This was remembered a few days later when he flashed a big roll of bills in the gambling halls at Saguache; and on an Indian's finding strips of human flesh along Packer's back trail, the man was arrested.

Intensive search for his companions was begun, but it proved fruitless until J. A. Randolph, a wandering photographer and artist for *Harper's Weekly*, chanced on five corpses in a spruce grove. The skulls of four had been crushed by blows apparently delivered while they slept. Evidence indicated that the fifth had been shot after a fierce struggle. Flesh had been cut from all of them.

Faced with this discovery, Packer said the fifth corpse was of a man named Bell; that Bell had gone insane and had killed the four, and that he, Packer, had killed Bell in self-defense. Yes, he had rifled the men's pockets and had devoured the bodies in order to escape starvation. But he was not guilty of murder.

No one believed him. In lieu of jail he was chained to a rock at the agency but somehow escaped. Several years later he was recaptured in Wyoming, tried, and found guilty. A yarn still widely believed in Colorado states that in pronouncing sentence Judge M. B. Gerry, a stanch Democrat, thundered (there are variations, of course): "Packer, you depraved Republican son of a such-and-such, there were only five Democrats in Hinsdale County, and you ate them all!" Actually Gerry's comments were delivered in periods more rounded: ". . . When the shadows of the mountain fell upon your little party and the night drew her sable curtains around you, your unsuspecting victims lay down on the ground and were soon lost in the sleep of the weary; and then, thus sweetly unconscious of danger from any quarter, and particularly from you, their trusted companion, you cruelly and brutally slew them all. . . . I sentence you to be hanged by the neck until dead, dead, dead . . ."

Granted a new trial on a technicality, Packer received forty years for manslaughter. Of this term he served only a small part. The Denver *Post*, always alert for a circulation-building crusade, decided there was enough doubt of his guilt to warrant turning loose its sob sisters on as lachrymose a campaign as any in that paper's long list of super-sensations. Packer was paroled. And still legend would not leave him alone. The one-time meat eater, so the culminating tale runs, retired to a small ranch and became a confirmed vegetarian.

Mears's road past the fatal spruce grove languished for traffic. Hotch-kiss's mine (it apparently played out, was abandoned, and later reopened as the fabulous Golden Fleece) was by itself no commerce builder. Somehow more prospectors had to be lured to the region. So Otto in 1875 established a newspaper in a tent, the *Silver World*, and appointed Harry Wood editor. Wood's first issue was a eulogy of Lake City's climate, scenery, and mineral resources, come-hither gems which Wood carried on snowshoes across the divide and scattered up and down the San Luis Valley. By spring the rush was on, but Otto wasn't content with one paying road. Another influx of miners was pouring into Ouray, a hundred miles away, to which vicinity the Indian agency also moved in an effort to keep down friction between Utes and prospectors. Promptly Otto drained his already shallow resources to chop out a road for them to use.

To fortify his finances he wheedled from the government in 1876 a contract to carry mail to Ouray. (He was in Washington at the time as one of Colorado's first presidential electors.) The joker in this document was the heavy fine which would accrue should he fail to maintain the once-a-week schedule. Although service was to start in the dead of winter, the undersized promoter rushed back to the mountains in high humor, built relay stations twenty miles apart, and marked the trail with tall willow stakes. On the advice of a former Hudson's Bay Company employee, he decided to use a dog sled and to hire a driver proficient with "Norwegian snowshoes," or skis, as we would call them today.[1]

There was a heavy snowfall that winter—stumps of trees cut along the trail stood ten feet high the next spring—and Otto's dog sled was Ouray's only mobile contact with the outside world. Citizens soon were ordering tobacco, coffee, flour, sugar, boots, and even ladies' hats sent in by mail. Loads grew tremendous; in manhandling them back onto an overturned sled or in sitting on top of them while the sled scooted downhill, the driver occasionally ground tobacco into the sugar or mashed the hats beyond recognition. Irate customers complained by telegraph, but Mears had friends in Washington; the postmaster tartly ordered the citizens to refrain from using the service as a freight vehicle for groceries and haberdashery.

The spring thaw turned the mail road to a sea of slush. Neither wagons nor sleds could navigate, and Otto's hired drivers refused to budge, though the fine for non-delivery would bankrupt their employer. So Otto strapped the heavy sack onto his own tough small shoulders and floundered off through wet, waist-deep snow under which icy waters sucked at his boots. It took a good part of a week to cover the seventy-five miles, but he beat the deadline.[2]

At last luck began to break. In 1877 the lead-carbonate excitement in Leadville lured such piles of edible produce out of the San Luis Valley that in three months Mears's original Poncha Pass road paid

[1] It was not the only use of dogs in Colorado. Another team of them, for example, handled freight in Silverton and at the end of their daily rounds were rewarded with a stiff and eagerly appreciated jolt of whisky.

[2] Mail service in general adds an epic footnote to mountain history. When twenty-six families were snowed in the town of Gothic during the winter of 1880, Louis Berthell not only skied eight miles over the Continental Divide with his sack of mail but on each trip carried to the destitute families a five-gallon can of coal oil and a fifty-pound sack of flour or beans. In 1883, on the first mail run from Steamboat Springs to Hayden in northern Colorado, John Adair and N. W. Brock, pulling three hundred pounds of mail on a hand sled, lost their way—elk had eaten the green willow trail markers. It took them eleven hours to go eleven miles; on reaching shelter Adair plunged his frozen feet into a tub of ice water, wrapped them in burlap, poured kerosene over them, and went on. When one carrier near Ophir failed to appear on schedule he was suspected of absconding; three years later his body was found in the remnants of a snowslide, the mailbag still strapped to his back.

back more than its construction had cost. The next year the rush to Gunnison prompted him to build a highway over 10,856-foot Marshall Pass; for eighteen months he operated it at a profit, then sold it for $40,000 to the Denver and Rio Grande Railroad, which wanted to use it as a roadbed in the frantic race to reach Gunnison's lush markets ahead of the Denver and South Park. This was the first real money Mears had ever made, and to it he soon added fat tolls wrung from the Army while General MacKenzie's soldiers and sutlers were scurrying over the Ouray road pursuant to their duties of kicking the Utes out of Colorado.

At first MacKenzie was reluctant to pay Mears's fees and threatened to smash the toll gates unless they were opened. "You do," Otto said coolly while half a regiment chafed at MacKenzie's back, "and it'll cost you your commission." The general reflected. Somehow or other, he knew, this whiskery little Indian commissioner and road builder had influence. Grudgingly he signed a voucher and continued to sign them until the Utes were gone and Otto Mears had collected from the War Department, according to one estimate, a round $100,000 for the use of his rutted road.

Now he could branch out. His roads spiraled into every mining town in the San Juans. When he collected toll receipts he dashed about in a silver-studded buckboard, changed his high-stepping mules at every relay station, and covered a hundred miles a day. Popeyed citizens borrowed Frémont's shopworn tag and proudly called him the Pathfinder of the San Juan. He was, of course, no more a pathfinder than his famous predecessor, but he was certainly the path builder supreme of the southern Rockies.

Climactic job of all (until he switched to railroad building) was his famed Circle or Rainbow Route, which climbed out of Ouray on a breathless, thousand-foot-high shelf gouged from solid rock, passed the paint-pot grandeur of Red Mountain, and snaked spectacularly down into Silverton. Perhaps this should be his monument. He has others: cindery Mears Junction on the Denver and Rio Grande, near Poncha Pass, lovely but almost unknown Mears Peak near Dallas Divide; and a stained-glass-window portrait in the state capitol in Denver, a building whose construction he supervised and whose dome he covered, in spite of furious objections, with thin gold leaf symbolic of Colorado's economic beginnings. But somehow the spectacular beauty of the Red Mountain road seems more fitting. Yet it was not to be. Though the state, when transforming the road to a free automobile highway, did set a commemorative tablet in the granite where his toll station once stood beside pluming Bear Creek Falls, the road itself was called the Million Dollar Highway, for reasons obscure. (One improbable yarn says it was surfaced with gold-bearing gravel whose million-dollar value was not discovered until after the road had been completed.) Mears Highway, some grizzled old-timers still insist, would have made more sense.

The toll roads, built for profit, were not all that could be desired, as stage passengers soon discovered. There were exceptions; the one over Marshall Pass, before the advent of the Denver and Rio Grande, was graded so excellently that Barlow and Sanderson's ornate stage could whisk twenty-two passengers seventy-five miles in seven hours, with twenty minutes out for lunch. Run-of-the-mill transits, however, were something else. Often enough, wayfarers paid to ride, then were forced to get out and walk up steep pitches or help dig the vehicle from a mudhole. J. J. Gibbons, itinerant Catholic priest, tells of going from Ouray to Silverton "in the usual way without any more serious inconvenience than that of being obliged to shovel snow, open the road, and help drag out the horses from the high drifts." One stage driver who happened to catch Otto Mears as a passenger tried to illustrate the true condition of the Lake City road by careening full tilt over every bump and chuckhole in the highway, but it was too patent a trick to catch the canny Otto. Alighting at the next station, he stretched, yawned, and drawled, "Ah, what a beautiful sleep I had!" Countless reminiscences and newspaper editorials speak of loose log bridges (if bridges existed at all) through whose interstices water boiled alarmingly, of boulders and landslides, of tipping wildly over into icy drifts; and on May 9, 1885, the Aspen *Times* saw fit to grumble, "Three jacks in a jack train coming over the range yesterday, fell in the mud and were trampled out of sight by the rest of the train. . . . What kind of a condition must the roads be in when this is the case?"

The great fear, particularly in Wyoming, was being caught in a blizzard. Results could be disastrous. On January 31, 1883, a northeaster swooped down on two stages, one traveling from the South Pass mining towns to the Union Pacific station at Green River, the other from Green River to the Pass. The lone passenger in the first was eighteen-year-old Maggie Sherlock, bound for school in Salt Lake City; in the other were the driver and two male fares. Night caught and stalled both vehicles. Leaving Maggie bundled in the bottom of the sleigh, driver George Ryder tried on foot to reach the station at Dry Sandy. It was only a mile away, but in the featureless maelstrom of the blizzard Ryder did not

know where he was. All day on February 1 he stumbled in circles, retreated to the sleigh, tried again the following morning. That day he
succeeded, but crawled into the cabin so nearly dead he could only
mumble. The station tender pushed out with a team, found Maggie Sherlock unconscious but alive, and brought her back to Dry Sandy, where
young missionary John Roberts, just arrived on his way to long years of
devoted service among Washakie's Shoshone, nursed her back to life.
He could not do so much for the driver. Ryder died, as did two of the
three occupants of the other sleigh. The sole survivor lost both feet and
most of his fingers. Nor was the toll finished. Another wayfarer came
crawling into Dry Sandy on his hands and knees; he, too, lived, but
minus both hands, several toes, part of his nose and ears.

Passenger service was microscopic compared with the movement of
freight. The high-sided wagons and trailers hogged the roads, and when
they encountered a common citizen at a point too narrow for passing,
it was John Doe's wagon that had its wheels removed and its bed tipped
against the bank so that the Brobdingnags could roll by. John seldom
complained; his livelihood depended on the freighters and he revered
them accordingly. They might be arrogant, profane, and given to
quarrelsomeness, but they could move anything anywhere, and that
meant profit to the entire region. In their heyday, even when competition was most rife, price was a secondary consideration. Speed and bulk
were the criteria; Dave Wood is still remembered because in a single day
his strident roustabouts moved five hundred thousand pounds of merchandise across the fearful roads of the San Juans.

Picture one of the outfits: three or more spans of mules hitched to
each wagon, with a trailer coupled on behind if the way lay downhill.
On the steep upgrades huge numbers of animals might be used; A. E.
Raynolds of the San Luis Valley put twenty to a wagon, hitched five
abreast. The skinner rode the left-wheel mule and controlled the leaders
with a jerk line. Another rope from his saddle ran to the top of a long
brake pole manipulating huge wooden brake blocks which on steeper
roads, such as in the Ouray district, had to be replaced nearly every day!

Loads (excepting ore) were incredibly heterogeneous, ranging from
pipe and wheeled machinery to plate-glass windows, and had to be
stowed with dexterity to prevent shifting or smashing on the rutted
roads. Travel was so rough that double-thick iron tires were used, and
the life of a team or wagon was calculated at no more than three years.
A sedate pace was often impossible even if desired, for in rounding a
curve only the wheel animals could keep the tug chain tight, and the

momentum of the wagon itself had to be used to make the swing. Curves, therefore, were approached at a run—a risky maneuver should another wagon be galloping at the same curve at the same time. To forestall collisions, warning cow or sheep bells were often hung to the necks of the leaders.

A wagon going uphill had little momentum, so telegraph poles were pressed into service as pushers. Holes were bored through these poles, doubletrees affixed, and one to three spans of mules harnessed behind the vehicle. Men rode the pusher animals, an unenviable job, for if the wagon stopped abruptly, the pole bucked so violently that the skinners were apt to be tossed to the ground.

Snow was the indefatigable villain. At the first sign of a freeze, black-smith shops were jammed with fighting stock waiting to be shod with "corks" (calks). Runners replaced wheels, and on steep downgrades were rough-locked with chains; additional braking power was some-times furnished by a dragging, anchorlike claw which contributed no small bit to tearing the roads to pieces. And still there were runaways, as in the case of Ike Stephens, traveling from Ouray over Red Mountain with a big load of eggs, dead pigs, general merchandise, and two hung-over miners. While crossing a tilting slope, the wagon box shot off the runners. The horses pulled Ike free, but the eggs, dead pigs, and slumber-ing miners shot over the cliff, dropped a hundred feet or so to a steep slope, and skidded to a tangled rest in the creek bottom. The eggs were not deemed salvageable, but the two miners were fished out "in an India-rubber condition," though still alive.

Occasionally even the animals wore snowshoes—flat boards bolted to their hoofs and equipped with sharp calks to prevent slipping. In an emergency a man might put his own wool socks on a horse's front feet to enable it to get traction on ice, while butter smeared over the hoofs helped keep snow from balling up in crippling wads.

In the worst of the canyons, crews were everlastingly at work shovel-ing out snowslides, but one winter the Mother Cline avalanche between Ouray and Silverton spilled too much packed snow across the highway for workers to remove it. A temporary road was built over the blockade, but spring thaws softened the surface snow to an impassable slush; ac-cordingly Otto Mears bored through the slide a snow tunnel 580 feet long and high enough to pass a six-horse Concord stage. It lasted well into the following summer, a source of profound civic pride to the natives, who dragged visitors from miles around to see it.

These spring thaws turned all the roads into quagmires which rotted the hoofs of the animals, rendered both sleighs and wagons all but immobile, and reduced the countryside to despair. When the B. C. Wheeler Express and Pack Train made its first crossing of the Continental Divide from Buena Vista to Aspen in the spring of 1881, fifty-two days were required for the short journey, and the skinners both of that train and of others had to jettison a large part of their merchandise, food, and liquor, intending to return for it later. But thieves beat them to the goods, so that the Aspen *Times* warned darkly: "The public must not be aghast if some morning one or more of these night wolves are found dangling to the limbs of trees with these words pinned to the soles of their feet: 'Gone to join their companions in crime.'" Another pack train coming out of Silverton to Del Norte had better luck with jettisoned goods. Caught in a fall blizzard, the skinners chucked the cargo, fled for safety, and returned the next spring to retrieve intact from twenty-foot drifts their merchandise—huge bars of gold and silver bullion.

Obviously the expenses of the freight companies were terrific. But so were profits. In 1879 four youths (A. G. Bowman, A. S. Church, John McDonald, and Will McClain) arrived in Colorado Springs on the top of a Denver and Rio Grande freight car. Inside the car were their ten horses and mules, a couple of knocked-down wagons, a camp outfit, a few sacks of beans and potatoes, and three-hundred-dozen eggs. In the Springs they put their outfit together and headed up Ute Pass for Leadville. The road was jammed so solid with wagons that it took them nine days to go the 135 miles, and when the quartet reached Leadville they could find no place to put up their stock. They turned the animals loose with hundreds of others to graze on the neighboring hills,[3] sold their eggs at a profit of twenty cents a dozen (one wonders how fresh the merchandise was by this time), considered prospecting, saw richer gold along the toll roads, and turned their makeshift outfits to freighting. The first year they did forty-one thousand dollars' worth of business, which does not necessarily imply that they hauled vast quantities of goods. Rates were astronomical. In the early days at Telluride, for example, mine owners could not afford to bother with ore that assayed

---

[3] Such conditions, plus the high mortality rate of plains stock at the ten-thousand-foot altitude, made Leadville a happy hunting ground for horse thieves. Importers of stock were sure of fast sales, few questions, astounding prices. Departing, the thieves often took from the hills varying numbers of untended animals, although this branch of the traffic stirred the horse-short citizenry to vigorous countermeasures. One large but clumsy raid by two amateur bandits resulted in a furious gun battle at Cottonwood Creek. Both raiders were killed—and not until then did the posse learn that one of the thieves was a beautiful girl of about sixteen "with delicate and refined features." The other was a boy of twenty or so. Silently the avengers buried both under the cottonwoods. No one ever learned their names, their backgrounds, or what had prompted their disastrous fling.

The main street of Creede, Colorado, 1892, during its frenetic silver stampede. The boom collapsed a year later, when repeal of the Sherman Act crippled the entire mountain area.

A stagecoach leaves the typically rococo mountain grandeur of an Ouray hotel for a crossing of Mears's Rainbow toll road to Silverton, Colorado. The lone female passenger occupies the seat of honor beside the driver.

less than three hundred dollars a ton; and even after competition forced a leveling off, freighters blandly charged, if cargoes were unwieldy and roads steep, five dollars to move one ton a single mile.

Where mines perched too precariously for roads, pack trains of mules and burros struggled up the zigzag trails. Articles too heavy for a lone mule to carry were lashed to poles slung between two animals in tandem or were dragged by long lines of mules on "go-devils," a sort of iron-shod stoneboat mounted on iron rollers. Ingenuity solved fiendish problems. When Dave Wood was hired to haul three quarters of a mile of steel cable to the Nellie Mine above Telluride without cutting it, he computed the footage a single mule could carry. Then he laid the cable out in two parallel lines down the middle of Telluride's main street, spent two snarled days winding it up in a series of opposing coils four feet in diameter—one coil for each side of a mule, with a carefully calculated amount of slack to extend between each animal. At dawn on the third day he led his mules between the lines, hired every packer in town, lashed the two-block-long necklace aboard, and was gone before most of the business houses had opened for the day.

In time the difficulties and expense of freighting by animals led the more inaccessible mines to institute trams: great cableways leaping from tower to tower, diving over cliffs, hurdling gorges, their endless chains of buckets carrying supplies up, ore down (and still carrying; a few of the trams are yet operating). They also enabled miners to live in town, though commuting by winter was chill enough, especially when a temporary breakdown halted the cramped, jiggling, open-air buckets above some icy gulch. Such experiences help explain why the hard-rock stiffs of the mountains consider those who ride the present-day ski lifts for pleasure as slightly demented.

Another device for transporting men was the self-returning horse. Miners rented the beasts in town, rode them, in local vernacular, "up the hill," tied the reins to the saddle horn, and let them go. That meant the animal's work was done, and the horses knew it. Many a walking miner tried to get a free ride by catching them as they jogged back down the trail toward home, but the wily horses always bolted. If a man wanted to ride, he got aboard at the proper place or not at all.

Sometimes these four-legged taxis developed, either by inclination or training, certain prejudices. In Ouray one hoary plug named Gray Fox was taught to dislike men carrying gunny sacks. He let them mount at the barns because the rules said he must, but as soon as he had transported them beyond the city limits he invariably bucked them off. For the hostlers at the livery stable, this was a handy trait. Whenever a miner showed up bearing a demijohn as solace for his upward journey, he was mounted on Gray Fox, the demijohn meanwhile being solicitously placed in a gunny sack and tied to the saddle horn. Sure enough, Gray Fox would soon amble back minus rider but plus the sack, whose contents the delighted hostlers promptly hid in a manger. When the sputtering miner limped back for another horse, he was told that Gray Fox had also lost the sack somewhere along the trail.

Today the extent of the traffic between the towns and the richer mining districts is difficult to imagine. At loading-up time, from dawn to sunrise, the streets were an indescribable tangle of wagons, oxen, mules, horses, donkeys, men, and goods. Roadways and sidewalks were piled high with cook stoves, baled hay, rails, lumber, blasting powder, coal, food, and what not; and even after the trains had swept it all up the trails, the towns bulged and stank with the appurtenances of the mighty effort: with clanging anvils and gaping barns, with mountains of hay moving in from the farms, with hills of manure—and with black swarms of flies that drove housewives to tears.

It has all vanished now. Until the last war a few freighters and packers in the more isolated sections did hold out against encroaching motor trucks; but the earth-defying bulldozers, the high-centered, four-wheel-drive vehicles, and the trailer-pulling tractors which emerged from the conflict as surplus property have sounded the death knell. Even the highest basins are yielding to the most ubiquitous set of wheels man has yet devised, wheels to which mountain dwellers are flocking with wide-eyed delight. A new legend is growing in the mining towns:

"Joe, didja hear? The first jeep came over Mineral Pass this afternoon. Nothin' to it, except a little pick an' shovel work in a coupla places. Those things can go *anywhere!*"

CHAPTER IX

THE LITTLE GIANTS

I N FEBRUARY 1948, a snowslide roared down the steep cliffs of Toltec Gorge in southwestern Colorado, picked three cars off the end of a laboring Denver and Rio Grande Western train, and hurled them over the lip of the canyon. The fact that the fourteen startled occupants of the coaches escaped the two-hundred-foot fall with their lives was accepted locally as a not untoward incident in the amazing story of narrow-gauge railroading in the Rockies.

Narrow-gauge signifies, of course, a span of three feet between rails, as contrasted to the standard gauge of four feet, eight inches. A dozen or more of these diminutive roads once chuffed grandly into every major Colorado mining camp. Their luxury trainlets boasted curtained dining alcoves, sleepers whose berths were scarcely as wide as a good-sized plank, staterooms housing tiny brass beds, and parlor cars that flaunted red velvet seats, red carpets, and silver-plated kerosene lamps.

Today Colorado's narrow-gauge mileage, though still exceeding that of any other state, has shrunk by two thirds, and only two companies of consequence remain, both operating principally in the eye-dazzling San Juan Mountains in the southwest. One is the Rio Grande Southern, now an unbelievable junk heap of many sorrows, whose passengers clatter over its torn and twisted rails in converted automobiles. The other is the narrow-gauge division of the Denver and Rio Grande Western, over whose tracks in the Animas Canyon avalanches have been known to pile debris eighty-seven feet deep. Such things tend to interrupt service. At times, notably in 1916 and again in 1932, the snowbound residents of Silverton have been able to obtain food for themselves and hay for essential dairy stock only by ordering it wrapped in small bundles and shipped in via parcel post, a stratagem which required the government to substitute mules for the immobilized mail trains and to lose eighty-six dollars per ton of merchandise in keeping the railroad's customers alive. Yet in spite of three quarters of a century of such disaster, the Denver and Rio Grande has somehow managed to stagger groggily back to its feet and keep on punching. In 1948 it even paid a dividend on its common stock, the first one in sixty-seven years!

The little giant comes by its toughness naturally. It was born for warfare in 1870, when the city of Denver faced strangulation because of lack of transport. The Union Pacific, after flirting with the infant capital for years, had suddenly shied off northward to Wyoming's easier terrain, and many of the town's timorous merchants had fled to Cheyenne in pursuit. By means of a desperate flurry of bond issues, financial flip-flops, and legislative legerdemain, Denver did lure in the Kansas Pacific, but the Union Pacific counteracted by having its subsidiaries make eyes at the town of Golden, which in 1868 had lost the state capital to Denver and was eager to help starve her sister city to death. To make matters worse, the Atchison, Topeka and Santa Fe was hopping westward toward New Mexico, grimly bent on draining away Denver's business to the south just as the Union Pacific had to the north.

The obvious countermeasure was for Denver to build a railroad south. However, only investors of the most sanguine disposition could view the prospect without cold shivers. Mining had stagnated following the early rush of exploitation, and the territory was in the doldrums. From 1860 to 1870 Denver had shown a net gain of exactly ten inhabitants. Colorado City and Pueblo, the only two towns of note between the capital and Santa Fe, boasted a combined population of less than fifteen hundred, and the stage to the southern part of the state carried, on an average, less than thirty passengers a week. Yet a railroad *might* develop those empty wastelands, and there was at least one newcomer to Colorado who had no intention of letting the Santa Fe turn the trick unopposed.

He was General William J. Palmer, a redheaded Philadelphian who had cut his railroading teeth first with the Pennsylvania and later with the Kansas Pacific, where he had set various phenomenal construction records during that road's final surge toward Denver. He had also learned mining engineering as a student in England and had mastered the strategy of quick attack on limited supplies as a Northern cavalry commander in the Civil War. To these robust accomplishments General Palmer added an austere aura of "culture," a suspicious word to the Rockies in those times; and even today the stamp of his culture is discernible in at least one of the towns to which his railroad gave synthetic birth; namely, Colorado Springs. His own home caught it too. He modeled the turreted pile after the Duke of Marlborough's castle, searched the countryside for weathered rock that would impart an appearance of age, and secured an antique-looking roof by importing tiles from an old English church. To avoid smoking up this feudal misfit he used as a chimney a long tunnel bored off through the mountain-side. There is no record, however, that his finickiness toward soot ever extended either to the Denver and Rio Grande Railroad or to the iron-and-steel works he built at Pueblo.

That iron foundry (ancestor of the present Colorado Fuel and Iron Company) was typical of the general's sweeping vision. During his days with the Kansas Pacific, when Palmer had been scrambling through the Rockies in a search for suitable passes to the Western ocean, he had looked beyond the crags and gullies to a vast mountain empire of grazing, agriculture, lumbering, mining, and smelting, all tied in with an industrial development which rail transportation alone could bring about. A planned economy—planned by William J. Palmer and associates. Nor did he intend to stop with Colorado. Down the Rio Grande River he would go (hence the name of the railroad), across the inter-national border, and clear to Mexico City. All he had to do was beat the Santa Fe—plus, of course, a few natural obstacles.

Just one cloud darkened this rainbow: finances. Public largess in the form of land grants was going out of fashion. The most the Denver and Rio Grande ever got—and even this was not confirmed until 1872— was a right of way two hundred yards wide, grounds for depots (which had to be spaced at least ten miles apart), and permission to use native materials in construction work. This stinginess of the national govern-ment Palmer partially offset by persuading a few local counties and cities to issue bonds in favor of his railroad, and by the formation of subsidiary land- and town-development companies. The good old West-ern idea behind the latter scheme was, of course, to sell building lots in a proposed village on the theory that if the village prospered the lots would rise in value. As guarantee of prosperity the Denver and Rio Grande's development companies pointed to the still-trackless Denver and Rio Grande. The argument enabled them to sell consider-able property, but it also created animosities which, as we shall see, soon proved costly indeed.

With the aid of William Bell, a wealthy Englishman who had come West to recuperate, Palmer sold $300,000 worth of stock in Philadel-phia and $700,000 in England. A million dollars—not much of a back-log for building a railroad to Mexico City. Palmer and his partners, who had studied narrow-gauge operation in Europe, decided to eschew heavy rails, heavy engines, and heavy cars in favor of the lighter iron and cheaper rolling stock that could be used on a three-foot-wide track. Naturally this motive of economy was soft-pedaled in the road's pub-licity. Instead, the promoters whooped about the advantages of narrow-gauge construction in the mountains, where the need for thin road-beds, tight curves, and steep grades precluded broad-gauge work except at prohibitive cost. At the ceremonies of driving the first stake on July 28, 1871, one orator was so carried away by his thesis that he cried to the world, "The railway men of the nation are learning that they have been building too broad a gauge. In twenty years . . . [wide gauge] will be as much a curiosity as three-foot gauge is today!"

Lightweight the original equipment certainly was. The first engine and tender tipped the scales at a mere twenty tons, half the weight of broad-gauge locomotives of the time. The first cars were thirty-three feet long, six and a half feet wide, and yet somehow crowded in thirty-four passengers, each of whom paid fare at a rate of ten cents per mile. Double seats were placed on one side of the narrow aisle, single seats on the other for half the car's length; in the other half, to prevent dangerous listing, the arrangement was reversed, the resultant jog in the aisle disguised by a transverse partition across the middle of the coach. Unloaded cars were so light that in 1879 a windstorm blew an entire train off the track at Palmer Lake, on the divide between Denver and Colorado Springs.

Track laying was pushed with a vim. Colorado Springs (or rather the then vacant site of Colorado Springs) was reached in three months, and within less than three years the brand-new town boasted a population of twenty-five hundred souls. By 1872 rails had touched Pueblo, whose population promptly doubled. Tourist trade boomed, particularly among water quaffers bound for the mineral springs at La Fort, which someone soon had the good sense to rename after the Ute god, Manitou. Nonetheless, the "baby road," as the Denver and Rio Grande was affectionately known, remained shaky on its financial feet. The panic of 1873 brought work to a stop and left the treasury in such a lugubrious condition that Otto Mears, freighting out of Saguache with two or three wagons, was able to win rate concessions by threatening to establish a rival ox-team line!

As the nation struggled out of the depression the road finally justified its name by leapfrogging the Sangre de Cristo Range into San Luis Valley and touching the Rio Grande River at Alamosa. By now, however, surveys had proved that the easy way into New Mexico was not down the Rio Grande's lava-bristling canyon, but south from Pueblo and through storied Raton Pass.

Known to motorists today as part of Highway 85, the short hop across Raton does not look particularly rugged, yet for a couple of centuries it had been enough to send the creaking wheels of the Spanish and of the Santa Fe traders detouring far to the east and south. During the Mexican War, General Kearny's Army of the West had built a sort of passageway through it, but newly wed Susan Magoffin, following in the Army's footsteps, did not find the results impressive: "Worse and worse the road! They are taking the mules from the carriages this afternoon and half a dozen men by bodily exertions are pulling them down the hills. And it takes a dozen men to steady a wagon with all its wheels locked—and for one who is some distance off to hear the crash it makes over the stones is truly alarming. Till I rode ahead and understood the business, I supposed that every wagon was falling over a precipice. We came to camp about half an hour after dusk, having accomplished the great travel of *six* or *eight* hundred yards during the day."

It remained for an old mountain man, Richard Lacy (Uncle Dick) Wootton, to build the first satisfactory road over the Pass. Weighing more than two hundred hard-muscled pounds, with a wild shock of bristling black hair to match, Dick Wootton had done almost every harebrained thing it was possible to do in the frontier West. Born in Virginia and comparatively well educated for the times, he drifted into Bent's Fort on the Arkansas before he was twenty. During the waning days of the fur trade he roamed far and wide over the mountains with the trappers, returned as a hunter to the fort with Kit Carson and Lucien Maxwell, and served in the Mexican War as a scout. After the war his interests became varied. He fought Indians, hunted grizzlies, chased bandits for the sake of the reward, and raised buffalo for the Eastern market. In the early days of the California gold rush he duplicated Lucien Maxwell's and Kit Carson's feats of driving sheep from Taos to the Sacramento Valley—nine thousand head of them, herded by himself, four assistants, and one dog, plus eight trained goats for luring the huge flock across rivers. Along the way—more than a thousand miles of desert, mountain, and hostile Indian land—Wootton lost a mere hundred head, sold the rest at a thousand-per-cent profit. Financially well heeled, he returned to New Mexico, briefly operated first a freight outfit on the Santa Fe Trail and then one of the West's most rugged stage lines from Santa Fe to Independence, Missouri. The Colorado gold excitement led him, in December 1858, to open infant Denver's first saloon and general store.

The money he made disappeared as fast as it came, and about 1866, when he was fifty, he began to think of security for his old age. A toll road over Raton Pass seemed the answer. From his friend Lucien Maxwell he obtained title to twenty-five hundred acres of strategically located land, giving Maxwell in return a lifetime pass over the road. Next he secured the necessary charters from the Colorado and New Mexico legislatures and set to work blasting boulders, felling trees, bridging and grading the twenty-seven-mile route. Indians he allowed to travel free, since they would not have paid anyhow. Everyone else coughed up—one dollar and a half for a wagon, twenty-five cents for a rider, five cents for loose cattle or sheep, rates sometimes collected at the point of a gun. At the Colorado end of the pass he built a barn and hotel, the latter a crude timber, adobe, and rock cabin decorated with hunting trophies and bearskins thrown over packing boxes. At this stop he fed man and beast and reaped well. Though he kept no records himself, an assistant who operated the toll road during one of Wootton's absences collected $9,193.64 during a fifteen-month period. The silver coins thus garnered Uncle Dick packed to the nearest bank in an old whisky keg lashed to a mule.

Because of his strategic location Uncle Dick naturally became acquainted with the Denver and Rio Grande field crews when they surveyed the pass in 1876. Unfortunately for the Denver and Rio Grande, however, Wootton was much friendlier with a slouching, serape-clad individual who spent the same period grazing a small herd of sheep about the Denver and Rio Grande camp. This apparently harmless Mexican was in fact Raymond Morley, engineer for the Atchison, Topeka and Santa Fe, which had run head on into Palmer's road at Pueblo and was now eying the same outlet to the south.

From a standpoint of finances neither road was ready for the expensive plunge into the mountains. For months there was an unspoken truce while each fiddled around with local matters and secretly tried to marshal its forces for the showdown. The break came in February 1878. Bludgeoned into motion by their new general manager, William Strong, the Santa Fe's directors voted a timorous twenty thousand dollars for location work. It was a ridiculously inadequate sum, but it amounted to a declaration of war. Knowing this and realizing that possession was nine points of the law, Strong ordered engineers Kingman, Robinson, and Morley to get a construction crew into Raton and start grading along the line Morley had jotted down while disguised as a sheepherder.

This the Denver and Rio Grande learned as soon as it happened. Their telegraph line joined the Santa Fe's at Pueblo, and for some time they had been decoding their rival's messages. When Morley and Robinson boarded a Denver and Rio Grande train to ride from Pueblo to El Moro, nearest railhead to the pass, they saw the railroad's two chief engineers also southward bound. Ducking out of sight, the Santa Fe men talked things over. It had been their plan to recruit workers at Trinidad, but if the Denver and Rio Grande was also on the march, there was no time to lose. Staking everything on Uncle Dick Wootton, they hired a buggy in El Moro and dashed through the freezing February night to the tollhouse at the foot of the pass. There they rousted out the old mountain man and explained the situation.

Uncle Dick might have balked. After all, a railroad would put him out of business. But apparently he knew the iron wheels were going to roll him down sooner or later, and, besides, he did not like the Denver and Rio Grande. That money-starved railroad had an annoying habit of ignoring established villages in favor of townsites laid out by its subsidiary development companies and with its low transportation costs luring merchants and shippers away from their former stands. When this had happened at artificially created El Moro, a scant four miles from Trinidad, which was as much a home town as Uncle Dick knew, the enraged citizens of the latter village had promptly flung wide their welcoming arms to the Atchison, Topeka and Santa Fe.

"Sure I'll help," Wootton told Morley and Robinson. Back into the house he went, collared some freighters and Trinidad youngsters who were having a dance, handed them shovels, and hurried them out into the darkness. When the Denver and Rio Grande's crew puffed up the trail half an hour later, they stared in dismay at an odd assortment of graders shoveling like beavers under the light of Wootton's lanterns. Raton Pass belonged to the Santa Fe by right of prior possession, and (aside from construction engines) the first locomotive to thunder through into New Mexico bore the fitting name "Uncle Dick."

Triumphant, the Santa Fe announced, scarcely six weeks later, that it was going to build squarely into the heart of the Denver and Rio Grande's self-selected domain, from Pueblo through the towering Royal Gorge of the Arkansas River to the rich new silver camp of Leadville. General Palmer hit the ceiling. Wires crackled with his secret orders to spirit a grading crew into the two-thousand-foot-deep gorge, which was barely wide enough to admit a single track, and hold it at all costs.

This time it was the Santa Fe's telegraphic decoders who peeped through the transom, and Ray Morley was ordered to get on the ground first.

When Morley reached Pueblo, a Denver and Rio Grande work train was already making up steam for the forty-three-mile run to Cañon City at the mouth of the gorge. Legends of how he beat that train are numerous. One says he hired a two-horse carriage and roared off through the night like a Roman charioteer; another, that he galloped a livery-stable nag to death and finished the race on foot. According to his daughter, Agnes Morley Cleaveland, he secured from a friend a magnificent black stallion, rode it as a thoughtful horseman should, at an alternate walk and lope, and reached Cañon City at dawn with the animal little the worse for wear. Nor was outdistancing a locomotive on horseback as spectacular as it may sound. Morley had a slight head start, and Denver and Rio Grande trainmen, unaware that a rival was riding through the night, took things easy over the new unsettled road-bed.

History repeated. The Denver and Rio Grande had refused to build inside Cañon City's corporate limits, although the town had voted a bond issue to bring the railroad there. Consequently the Denver and Rio Grande-hating merchants promptly helped Morley round up a gang of men, plenty of picks and shovels, and wagons for transporting them. When the Denver and Rio Grande's crew marched onto the scene, they were once again too late.

This time, however, Palmer had no intention of backing down. Charter rights, surveys, the filing of plats, statistics, claims, and counter-claims became the mire of a legal swamp which today is almost intraversable. Out in the field, meanwhile, construction crews of both roads kept furiously at work. Since the Denver and Rio Grande controlled the existing rails and wires from Pueblo to Cañon City, the Santa Fe had to haul in materials by team and dispatch messages by a three-times-a-day pony express. Frantically Palmer's men endeavored to bottle the enemy in the heart of the gorge by putting graders to work at its western end. The Santa Fe leapfrogged past them, and, where the canyon widened, each side angrily graded out parallel routes toward Leadville. Survey stakes were stolen, boulders rolled down the moun-tainside on workers, individuals were beaten up in barroom brawls, and death's-head warnings were nailed to various doors. Each side built stone forts to protect its holdings, each imported hired gunmen. News-papers worked themselves into a froth, and before the uproar was over almost the entire state had split into two camps. Yet the bloodshed which nervous observers daily predicted never quite developed, al-though a perusal of some of the more excited contemporary accounts leaves the reader wondering why.

Then abruptly General Palmer appeared to toss in the sponge. Early court decisions had gone against the Denver and Rio Grande, and its stock was sagging. In October 1878, to the consternation of his supporters, the general leased his entire system to the Santa Fe. The victors, however, rode their triumph into the ground. Trying to meet the cut-throat competition of the Union Pacific and Kansas Pacific, they set up discriminatory freight rates that threatened to squeeze the northern and central parts of the state dry. By April 11, 1879, the *Rocky Mountain News* was groaning, "We are ground down by the most grasping, blood-sucking corporation Colorado has ever known. . . . Give us back the little road. . . . Then we can live again."

At approximately the same time a surprise ruling by the Supreme Court reversed the trend of previous decisions and awarded the Denver and Rio Grande prior rights to the Royal Gorge, though allowing the Santa Fe to use Denver and Rio Grande track over such stretches as were too narrow to admit twin roadbeds. Palmer, who had used the breathing spell to recoup his financial position, now charged the Santa Fe with breaking practically every clause in the lease and demanded the return of the property to the Denver and Rio Grande. Immediately there was a tremendous jockeying in local courts. Armed mobs began to assemble; extraordinary bits of folklore were born. One improbable yarn relates that a bribed conductor, ordered to beat his rivals to Denver with an important message, immobilized the enemy engine by detaching and throwing into Palmer Lake one of its drive rods. This done, so the tale goes, he mounted a handcar, spread his overcoat as a sail, and was wafted merrily down the divide to the capital city!

Finally a Federal court maintained Palmer by declaring the lease invalid and ordering the property returned to the Denver and Rio Grande. The Santa Fe, confident that the sheriffs of the southern counties would not enforce the edict, breathed defiance, whereupon the Denver and Rio Grande made up armored trains and sent them chugging along the contested line. Now came the celebrated battle of the depots and roundhouses. There was a deal of shooting and fisticuffing, particularly at Pueblo and Cañon City. Most of it was noise. Several heads were undoubtedly broken and perhaps a man or two killed, though it is now impossible to determine just who and how many through the acrid fog of contemporary records. Certainly matters might have been worse had not Bat Masterson and his squad of toughs, imported by the Santa Fe from Dodge City to Pueblo, sold out in a secret deal ·with officials of the Rio Grande.

The smoke had scarcely cleared away when a new court order reinstated the lease! But Eastern financiers had had enough. Jay Gould, who was trying to soften Union Pacific stock with the threat of a

rival transcontinental line, bought control of several Western railroads, including the Denver and Rio Grande, and scowled so fero-
ciously at the Santa Fe that it accepted a settlement out of court. In this
compromise of March 1880 the Denver and Rio Grande paid the Santa
Fe $1,400,000 for its construction work in the gorge, notably the fa-
mous Hanging Bridge, and promised not to build into Santa Fe, New
Mexico. In return, the Santa Fe relinquished all claims to the canyon
and agreed to stay away from Leadville.

Thus disentangled, the Rio Grande cast suspicious eyes on a rival
little giant, the narrow-gauge Denver, South Park and Pacific. This
Cinderella road, although flexing an awesome set of muscles in 1880,
had started life as a sickly child indeed. Originally its incorporators
had planned to build up Clear Creek and over Berthoud Pass to Utah,
but W. A. H. Loveland's Colorado Central had beaten them to the
punch. (This man Loveland also had transcontinental dreams, and he
was stubborn. On learning he could not spiral even narrow-gauge rails
over the Big Divide from Clear Creek, he had concocted a fantastic
scheme for whisking his passengers and freight across the hump in
cable buckets. However, the Colorado Central never progressed beyond the Georgetown-Central City district, and the tram died still-
born.) Thwarted by Loveland, the Denver and South Park crawled
from Denver a few miles out to Morrison and gasped through the panic
of '73 by hauling excursions of Sunday-school children, whereupon its
rivals with raucous laughter christened it the Sunday-school line. But
while they were hooting, it managed a reorganization and crept up the
canyon of the South Platte.

There, too, excursions helped keep it alive. The South Platte River
teemed with trout which could be caught literally from ties' end. The
railroad advertised the fact, ran special trains from Denver every day
during the season, dumped each fisherman beside whatever bush he
chose, and picked him up on the return trip.[1] So popular did the idea

[1] This informal sort of service still prevails on Colorado's surviving narrow
gauges. A hunter, fisherman, or mountain climber can get on or off wherever he
waves his hat. And occasionally passengers find a chance to reciprocate. Once on
Embudo Hill in northern New Mexico a Denver and Rio Grande engineer happened
to cough his false teeth out the cab window. He halted the train and backed it up to
the scene of the disaster, where several passengers joind in the search for the missing
plates, which were found by a tourist from Chicago. And more than once the
writer, together with many another traveler on the Montrose–Salida run, has piled
out into the rain to help shovel mud slides from the track. Such informality and
mutual aid help explain the fierce love which so many Coloradoans have for
their decaying little giants.

become that often on week ends No. 75 pulled out of the Denver depot in two or three jam-packed sections.

Finally the Denver and South Park reached its namesake, South Park, and there languished until the Leadville boom snapped it into vigorous life. Freighters jammed the railhead with ore, clamored for goods. Eastern capitalists all but fought for the privilege of lending John Evans money for pushing construction on to the new mining metropolis, but he no longer needed their solicitude. The Denver and South Park achieved the distinction of being perhaps the only railroad in the world to earn what it cost before construction was completed. This trick was turned partly by milling the high-grade mineral it scraped from its own right of way, but mostly by hauling the mountains of ore which freighters piled into each advancing depot.

After the Denver and Rio Grande had won the Royal Gorge fight, Jay Gould, now masterminding both narrow gauges, hooked the Denver and South Park onto the Denver and Rio Grande's rails for the final run up the Arkansas to Leadville. But it was all a side issue to Gould. Having manipulated the pawns to a checkmate of the Union Pacific, he cast them aside. The liberated Rio Grande promptly told the Denver and South Park to go build its own trackage, which the latter, now a protégé of the Union Pacific, proceeded to do with alarming vigor. Although Leadville is on the eastern slope of the corkscrewing Continental Divide, the Denver and South Park hopped over 11,494-foot Boreas Pass to the western slope and then back across 11,-320-foot Fremont Pass to get there. Grades on Boreas, sprinkled with no less than eleven snowsheds, were a terrific 4½ per cent, so that the straining Cook mogul engines could pull no more than three loaded cars at a time. Once when a circus train stalled near the summit, the elephants were unloaded and with their heads against the caboose furnished the impetus necessary to boost the train over the hump.

Operational costs ate up the dazzling revenues which had reached ten thousand dollars a day during the short time when the Denver and South Park had used its reluctant rival's track. To make matters worse, the Denver and Rio Grande opened a rate war which forced the fare of a passenger trip from Denver to Leadville as low as twenty-five cents. On top of this came the race to the new camp of Gunnison. The Denver and Rio Grande got the jump by purchasing Otto Mears's toll road over Marshall Pass and coasted down the Gunnison River while the Denver and South Park was boring through Alpine Tunnel and out onto a breath-catching shelf approach that cost one hundred thousand dollars a mile to build (more than a millon and a quarter dollars per mile at today's prices). This financial load, plus dwindling ore shipments as smelters moved into Leadville, marked the beginning of the end. In 1889 the Denver and South Park was sold at foreclosure, passed through a dreary series of mortgages, and was abandoned hunk by hunk until today only gullied terraces mark the old roadbed that once carried the gaudiest little passenger trains in the gaudy Rockies.

The fate of the Denver and South Park did not make the least warning dent in the overweening optimism which enthralled Western railroad men during the latter part of the 1880s. Among the wild schemes promulgated, the wildest was William Gilpin's round-the-world "Cosmopolitan Railway." Gilpin was a man of many parts. Graduated from West Point at the age of seventeen, he had lost his youthful shirt practicing law and editing newspapers, then had toured the West with one of Frémont's expeditions, had left the Pathfinder to explore much of the Rocky Mountain area on his own, had fought the Navajos with Doniphan in '48, and had predicted the Colorado gold rush some time before it actually developed. As first governor of Colorado Territory, Gilpin equipped eleven companies of soldiers for the Civil War by issuing $375,000 worth of unauthorized drafts against the Federal Government, a move which created local panic and led to Gilpin's ejection from office when the Treasury at first declined to honor the drafts.

Possessing a vast fund of knowledge on almost every subject under the sun, Gilpin next dreamed up the "isothermal axis," a globe-circling band of favorable climatic and temperature conditions, "trunk line of intense and intelligent energy, where civilization has its largest field, its highest development, its inspired form." Though today's geopoliticians recognize him as a pioneer in their field and sort many sound kernels out of his bombastic chaff, Gilpin's contemporaries regarded him as a little bit crazy. It was his wont to seize Denver acquaintances by a coat button, then close his eyes and orate on his pet theories. One yarn says that a desperate captive snipped off the imprisoning button and sneaked away, leaving Gilpin to convert the small piece of horn clutched firmly between his fingers. Burden of his most earnest talk was a railroad to follow his "isothermal axis," crossing the Pacific via a bridge over the Bering Strait, plunging through Siberia, and eventually linking Paris to New York. Denver was to be the hub of the system, and a feeder line was to run from the Colorado city through Mexico to Patagonia at the southern tip of Argentina. The road's main purpose was not to be sordid commercialism but—"Divine task! Immortal mission!"—to carry products, help, and civilization to the Orient.

Although the plan seems fantastic today, it was once seriously discussed by many magazines and newspapers. Blueprints actually were put on paper, talks were held with the Russian Government, and surveyors hit the field in Alaska—not all, of course, at the direct instigation of William Gilpin and not all in connection with one huge, globe-circling company. But in the end it fizzled away, and meanwhile Colorado railroad builders concentrated on local projects which they fondly supposed had more chance of success.

Most ambitious of these concerns was the Colorado Midland, a broad-gauge road which planned to cut in on the Leadville market by blasting a grade up Ute Pass from Colorado Springs. This offered a much shorter route than did the narrow-gauge loops of either the Denver and Rio Grande or the Denver and South Park, but mere distance is no criterion in the mountains. The string of tunnels and wide broad-gauge curves which the Midland had to build heaped up wicked expenses, and the 4-per-cent grade was a perpetual danger to its heavy cars. In the early nineties, for example, a loaded ore train ran out of control down Ute Pass, jumped the rails at Tunnel No. 5, and corked the bore tight with a monstrous wreck which killed engineer and fireman and ended traffic over the line for several days.

Having reached Leadville in 1886, the Midland immediately found itself involved in a race with the Rio Grande for Aspen. The Denver and Rio Grande, which by now knew its way around the mountains, went smoking off north across Tennessee Pass, then south to Glenwood Springs, and east up the Roaring Fork River to Aspen, a wriggly trail that described almost a complete circle. Chuckling wisely, the Midland pushed due west on a route incomparably shorter. But once again mileage did not tell the whole story. The broad-gauge road had to punch a 2064-foot tunnel through Hagerman Pass (11,528 feet in elevation, perhaps the highest standard-gauge tunnel in the world), and by the time it reached the Roaring Fork, the Denver and Rio Grande was ahead of it. Dirt flew furiously, but the narrow-gauge held its lead and crossed the tape amid a frenzy of rejoicing described in the Aspen *Times* of October 28, 1887:

"At noon the public schools . . . marched to the scene in a body, headed by the teachers, and the railroad officials courteously loaded them all on the train. The teachers were invited to ride with the engineer, and each of the ladies presented him with a bouquet gathered as a memento of the occasion. . . . At 3:40 the screaming whistles and the roar of giant powder [from every mine in the vicinity] announced the rails had struck the Roaring Fork bridge. Here the work had to slow down because the mules had to be detached from the rail cars, but at 4:00 sharp the track had pushed across the long trestle and had reached the depot flat. . . . Again came the thunder of giant, while steam whistles on all sides joined the din. . . . A wagon load of beer had been provided and was carried to the men by water boys while they worked."

The celebration wound up with a monstrous barbecue, grand ball, and a parade under two thousand Japanese lanterns. When the Midland came creeping along a little later, its reception from the surfeited towns-folk was something in the nature of an anticlimax. Indeed, all the Midland's thrusts at the Denver and Rio Grande ended anticlimactically. When the two roads indulged in a rate war, the Midland gave away free excursion rides to Glenwood Springs, only to have the Denver and Rio Grande match the move and toss in, for good measure, a free swim in the hot springs at the baby road's Glenwood resort hotel. And although the Midland's competition forced the Denver and Rio Grande to broad-gauge its main line through the Royal Gorge, over Tennessee Pass, and down the Colorado River to Grand Junction, even this redounded to the Midland's embarrassment. For once again the Denver and Rio Grande got on the ground first. Completely humbled, the Midland was forced to rent, at a galling fee, the Rio Grande's new rails for the lower part of its Grand Junction run.

Back on the divide, meanwhile, the furious mountain winters were making the widely ballyhooed Hagerman Tunnel and Midland Loop look more and more like ice-encrusted white elephants. The top seven miles of the climb devoured almost as much in operating expenses as did the rest of the line put together, and to do away with them an affiliated company began drilling the two-mile-long Busk-Ivanhoe Tunnel, some 530 feet lower down the mountain. Drilling it took three years and cost twenty lives, and no sooner was it done than the railroad and the tunnel company fell to squabbling. Turning its back in a pout, the Midland blasted out the solid ice which had accumulated in the Hagerman Tunnel and went back to doing business at its old stand. Rather hopelessly the Busk-Ivanhoe people advertised their property for sale. There were no bids. Who wanted a tunnel going from nowhere to nowhere?

Then on January 27, 1899, a howling blizzard struck the divide. An expensive rotary plow was trapped on the west side of Hagerman. So was a three-engined livestock train of twenty cars, every one of whose animals froze or suffocated in the growing drifts. Frantically the Midland tried to open the line. Each day a mighty rotary "08," pushed by six of the road's biggest locomotives, growled out of the Leadville roundhouse. Behind it came the "Snowbird Special," baggage cars loaded with workers known as snowbirds, their overshoes wrapped in gunny sacks, their eyes shielded by dark glasses, their faces blackened with charcoal. After they had dug trenches for the rotary, the six loco-motives blasted the gargantuan machine against the drifts, backed up and hammered again—day after day for nearly three months. Not un-til April 17 did another train run through Hagerman Tunnel. By that time the Midland was ready to eat crow. Groggily it paid four million dollars for the Busk-Ivanhoe Tunnel and tried to get its finances back in shape. But it was too late. Though Cripple Creek ore discoveries kept the eastern part of the line alive, the western section withered away. In 1918 the last train ran through the Busk-Ivanhoe; a man named Carleton then bought the tunnel and roadbed and turned them into an automobile toll highway, which at present writing also seems destined to join the ghosts of so many other Rocky Mountain trans-portation curiosities.

And still men dreamed of a direct mountain crossing to Utah. So far only the Denver and Rio Grande had got there, and it went clear south to the Royal Gorge to do it. Surely, Denverites thought, someone could find a way to go straight west and really give the Union Pacific a run for its money. The next to try was stodgy David Moffat, who had hit Denver during the rush of '59 as a peddler of stationery, books, and related trinkets. After gaining control of the First National Bank, he served as president of the Denver and Rio Grande from 1883–91 and added to his millions by speculating in Leadville, Creede, and Cripple Creek mines —a dull, patient, acquisitive man with visions of empire in his head.

Toward the turn of the century Moffat and William Evans, president of the Denver Tramway Company, proposed an electric crossing of the divide to the resorts around Grand Lake and Hot Sulphur Springs. At least that seems to have been Evans's idea. But Moffat was not content to toy with glorified streetcars. Suddenly he wired Evans, who was in the East trying to finance the electric line, "I have decided to build a steam railroad from Denver to Salt Lake City. Electric plans too slow."

Moffat meant that personal pronoun. He knew he could not scare up a nickel's worth of outside backing, for the tight-knit financial hierarchy of the East had no desire to see some mountain upstart tweak the nose of the mighty Union Pacific. According to Colorado historians, President Harriman of the Union Pacific even persuaded the Department of the Interior to declare Moffat's proposed route through Gore Canyon an essential reservoir site and to refuse him right of way, whereupon Teddy Roosevelt saved the situation by jumping into the squabble on Moffat's side. Be that as it may, Moffat, now more than sixty years old, was quite prepared to spend his entire personal fortune nurturing his brain child, which he christened on July 18, 1902, the Denver, Northwestern and Pacific. Eleven years later, after its sights had shrunk and a reorganization had been effected, it was renamed the Denver and Salt Lake, but to Coloradoans it was always the "Moffat Road" and will be so termed in this account.

Engineers started out on a conservative but staggeringly expensive 2-per-cent grade, diving in and out of thirty-one small tunnels in a single twenty-mile stretch on their way toward James Peak, where Moffat intended to pierce the divide with a 2.6-mile bore. Such a tunnel, however, was beyond Moffat's unfortified purse. So he ordered curves tightened and the grade increased to 4 per cent on a "temporary" by-pass over the top of Rollins Pass at Corona, 11,660 feet in elevation.

Building a railroad above timber line during the dead of winter was a construction engineer's concept of hell, but Moffat, sitting in his warm office down in Denver, was in a sweat to reach the revenue-producing coal fields at Yampa. Induced by double pay, a handful of workers struggled on through as man-killing conditions as any rail builders have ever encountered. During that dreadful winter they discovered temperatures of forty below, drifts forty feet deep. Obviously Moffat's engines were going to need protection, so crews built a two-mile snowshed, but in spite of it, during succeeding years the line was often blocked for weeks at a time, and maintenance costs turned Dave Moffat's once tight pockets into sieves. Somehow he kept crawling on, however, season after season, until 1911, when, still clutching at the lifesaving straw of a tunnel, he went East on another desperate mission to raise money—and dropped dead. After that the road gave one more spasmodic lurch to Craig, in northwestern Colorado, 232 miles from Denver but less than halfway to its goal at Salt Lake City. There progress stopped and it settled down to a weary career as one of the most hard-luck short lines in America.

Every other mountain railroad in Colorado had been built to tap a mineral region. The Moffat, however, had nothing on which to subsist except a little coal, hay, lumber, and livestock. Old-timers insist that it never really helped the sparsely settled territory it was designed to serve. True, livestock operators benefited, and Craig became, it is claimed, the largest sheep-shipping center in the world. But the ordinary artisan saw his local markets undercut by merchandise from the eastern slope, and farm produce could not compete in Denver with goods raised nearer the metropolitan centers. Nonetheless, the people loved their train. No matter how late on a bitter winter night it pulled into Granby or Hot

Sulphur Springs, sleigh bells jingled frostily as the inhabitants poured down to the station to greet it. Though it might not run for weeks at a time, it was their one link with the outside world. Until it arrived, store shelves were empty. Until housewives saw what was unloaded from the baggage cars, they could not plan their meals.

Snow! Every frigid yarn spun in every stationhouse in the land can be outmatched by those told of the Moffat. My aunt, Helen McGrew, relates how once very window in the train was blown out by a blizzard, while at the conductor's orders she stood clutching the icy bell rope, ready to signal the engine should the rear car leave the rails while the crew put the train in reverse and fought their way back to shelter at the nearest depot. On another occasion, when she was taking her two babies out to Denver, one of them desperately ill, a storm caught the train as it was starting down the divide. Supposedly operating on a daylight schedule, it carried neither sleepers nor dining car; and when the clogged wheels bumped to a stop in the white, howling maelstrom, the passengers felt somewhat uneasy. However, they leaped out with the crew, commenced digging—and kept digging. By battering the engine into the drifts, backing up, digging some more, and whamming ahead again, they managed to force their way onward at a rate of approximately one mile per day. When the precious fuel for the coach's stove gave out, the male passengers (Mrs. McGrew was the only woman aboard) made a bed out of their overcoats for the children. All food gone, the conductor struggled on foot back to a deserted depot and returned with three cans of condensed milk.[2] Then as matters for the sick baby were becoming desperate a lone woman appeared through the drifts, bundled to the ears and wearing the usual mountain mukluks—gunny sacks wrapped around overshoes. For some days, she said, she had been watching the smoke of the train from her farmhouse deep in the canyon, and it had occurred to her that there might be a child aboard. Finally she had wallowed up through the drifts to see, carrying with her in a sack a gallon jug of milk and a loaf of bread. Steadfastly she refused to accept payment for the lifesaving gift, until at last, giving way before Mrs. McGrew's insistence, she said:

[2] Solicitude of trainmen for their passengers is often a heart-warming note in the icy tale of winter travel. Once when the heaters in the day coach of a snowbound Colorado Midland train gave out and the sleeping-car conductor refused to admit the shivering wayfarers to his warm domain, the train conductor snowshoed back to Granite, bought a fifteen-mile Pullman ticket for each day-coach passenger, and so enabled them to pass the next four motionless days in comparative comfort.

"If you wouldn't mind writing me a letter once in a while, I'd appreciate it. The winters do get lonesome up here."

Snow! The Moffat had to have a tunnel or die. Cold-blooded rail economics, if left to itself, would have passed the sentence without a twinge. But the city of Denver had meanwhile grown to the point where it was pinched for water, and water could be brought from the western slope via a tunnel. Why not combine the two projects? In 1922, after nearly ten years of internecine bickering, a bond issue for the purpose was passed, and within a matter of months miners were at work at the heading under James Peak. Considerably lower and longer than Dave Moffat's original brain baby, the six-mile bore ate up six lives, nearly five years of time, and eighteen million dollars. Only twenty-three miles' running distance and half a mile in elevation were saved. But what miles! Once four huge Mallets had been needed to haul twenty-two freight cars over the top—if they could move at all. Now a single ordinary consolidated engine could whisk the same number of cars through the tunnel in twelve minutes, as contrasted to the former running time of seven hours!

It was a monumental accomplishment—too monumental, some people thought. Why should a stub line that ran to a dead end out in the middle of a wilderness have the second largest railroad tunnel in America? But the Denver and Rio Grande, which for fifteen years or so had been watching the tunnel struggle with a coolly calculating eye, saw how to make the big hole serve as more than a gateway to nowhere. At one point on the Colorado River the Moffat came within thirty-four miles of the Rio Grande's looping main-line rails to Salt Lake City. Closing this gap would reduce the Denver and Rio Grande's run from Denver to the Utah metropolis by an enormous 175 miles. A deal was arranged allowing the Denver and Rio Grande to use the Moffat Tunnel. Ignoring the anguished howls from Pueblo, which would lose its position as a division center on the main line, and the fact that the depression of the thirties had once again broke it flat, the one-time baby road next wangled a $3,850,000 loan from the Reconstruction Finance Corporation, sent its rail layers beavering down the flaming red canyon of the upper Colorado River, and in 1935 finished the Dotsero Cutoff, which has been called the last major piece of the new railroad construction in the United States.

A few of the old mountain high jinks were left to spice the ceremony. Though the directors who had arranged the deal in paneled board rooms might be impersonal, the Moffat railroaders weren't. They knew well enough that Colorado's favorite little giant was now controlled by "foreigners" (the Missouri Pacific and Western Pacific, with Burlington and heaven knows how many other interlocking financial fingers giving the pot an occasional stir). Moreover, Moffat men loved their back-breaking line with that fervor which railroading seems to breathe into its followers; they shared a never-quite-extinguished hope that someday Dave Moffat's heirs would push on from Craig to Salt Lake City. The Dotsero Cutoff apparently doused that flicker forever. Well, so be it. The overlords of finance had spoken. But until the last second of the last minute of the contract had arrived, no Denver and Rio Grande wheel would turn on Moffat steel. To make sure of it, they chained ties across the switches. Nor would any outsider muscle in on Moffat terri-tory. Streamliners might purr sleekly through the tunnel, Diesel horns might blat in the towns of Middle Park, but no fancy foreign trains would stop there under penalty of a stiff monetary fine. The contracts said so in plain black and white. This was Moffat domain.

Came the day of the cutoff's formal dedication. Gleaming special trains were loaded with governors, a gross or two of railroad presidents and top industrialists, plus herds of run-of-the-mill bigwigs from throughout Colorado and Utah, all bound for the junction of the rails, where there was to be a massive outdoor barbecue and a round of speeches broadcast over a nationwide radio hookup. And now the Moffat's refusal to let a Denver and Rio Grande locomotive tour its rails until the formal opening ballooned suddenly into an unexpected contretemps. The engineers on the special trains had not the faintest idea what the unfamiliar Moffat track was like, nor had the Moffat pilots assigned to them the least notion of how to run either the brand-new steam behemoths or the even stranger Diesels. Confusion mounted; the specials and their chafing passengers ran later and later.

Meanwhile at the rail junction an unpredicted storm toppled the bar-becue tables and scattered paper plates all over the landscape. As rain drenched the alarmed masters of the ceremony, the radio engineer hauled out his watch, frowned, and began to shake his head. But the little giant had long since grown wise in the ways of extemporizing. Leaping to the empty microphone, a Denver and Rio Grande publicity official sono-rously ad-libbed to the nation speeches purporting to be out of the mouths of the governor of Colorado and the president of the Rio Grande. When delighted reporters edged toward the telegraph station with what they supposed was a scoop for their papers, an alert Denver and Rio Grande henchman cut the wires and the instruments clicked their humor into unhearing space. Before the ruse was discovered the belated specials pulled in. The barbecue was transferred inside some construction sheds, the sodden ceremony went on with no more confusion than might be reasonably expected, and the wined-and-dined reporters were persuaded to reconsider the irreverent tone of their dispatches.

Moffat men smiled behind their hands, but if they hoped the fiasco was an omen of the future, they were badly mistaken. Without this additional transcontinental link, the lines to the north and south might well have bogged down under the glut of traffic occasioned by World War II. Moreover, Denver was able to leap to new prominence as a manufacturing center. Naval LCTs made there were shipped unassembled through the tunnel and cutoff to the Pacific; each craft required thirty cars, and their superstructures, rising eighteen feet three inches above rail level, caused trainmen to hold their breath in tight tunnels. Even after hostilities ended, the tonnage remained gratifyingly huge, but it could have been greater had not the Moffat been hauling the materials needed for the vast new irrigation projects below Grand Lake. Moreover, increasing numbers of skiers, sportsmen, and tourists would welcome better service to the Middle Park resorts. In short, the stub line was a thorn in the Denver and Rio Grande's fattening flesh. On April 11, 1947, they plucked it out by absorbing the entire system, including the branch line to Craig. Now Dave Moffat's ghost was dead.

Or was it?

Some years before, oil had been discovered at Rangely in the northwestern part of the state, a dreary desert section of the dreary Uinta Basin, which sprawls between Utah's Uinta Mountains and the main spine of the Continental Divide in Colorado. For a time the Rangely field languished for want of a market, but the petroleum shortage created by the war brought it booming into prominence amid cries by excited geologists and speculators that Rangely in particular and the whole Uinta Basin in general constitute the greatest undeveloped oil reservoir in America. The section is also uncommonly hard to get at. Businessmen, fuming over the difficulties of trucking supplies on tortuous dirt roads, are frenziedly agitating for the Denver and Rio Grande to fulfill "Dave Moffat's dream" by pushing its rails on from Craig through the basin to Salt Lake City. Such a line, they trumpet, would be even shorter than the Dotsero Cutoff, and think of the business along the way!

An answering howl, made resonant by the horrid fear of losing their pay rolls, is of course coming from the division towns along the Denver and Rio Grande's present main line. Tugged at from both sides, Wilson

McCarthy, the Rio Grande's new president, is playing coy. Maybe there would be a lot of business at Rangely—and maybe not. For one thing, what about pipe lines? Those are fighting words to any railroad, and McCarthy would like assurance that his tank cars and not pipe will carry all this liquid gold, guarantees which the oil companies quite naturally refuse to give. Very well, then. The Denver and Rio Grande, say its stockholders, has a perfectly good main line to Salt Lake City without wasting money on a new one. After going through five bankruptcies in the course of its hectic career, the road is at last earning dividends almost as whopping as General Palmer had hoped for. It has given Denver her long-desired direct-line connection with the Pacific, and has a biting slogan to flaunt in the faces of its old enemies, the Union Pacific and Santa Fe—"Through the Rockies, Not Around Them." Why get in a lather about an oil field?

Somewhat to its astonishment, the Denver and Rio Grande is also discovering that even its history has commercial value. Every summer hundreds of starry-eyed rail fans pour into the southwestern part of the state to goggle at the last of its unique little narrow gauges. To care for these unexpected pilgrims, in 1947 the road added a glass-topped observation car, the Silver Vista, to the daily San Juan, plying from Alamosa to Durango through avalanche-shattered Toltec Gorge, the last "varnish" trainlet left in the land. The Vista is also employed twice each summer week on the startling Animas Canyon run from Durango to the once bawdy mineral metropolis of Silverton, an excursion so popular that the Vista's reserved seats are regularly sold out days in advance. Through the glass car's gleaming windows tourists can crane their necks at some of the wildest scenery in America, meanwhile recalling, if they are of nostalgic turn of mind, the heroic legends of the past. For, to borrow a phrase, giants used to walk this land. Little giants.

And that brings us back to Otto Mears and the littlest giant of them all, the incredible Rio Grande Southern.

CHAPTER X

THE LITTLEST GIANT

E VERY railroad fan in the United States knows the name Rio Grande Southern, partly because of the lush press-agentry of Lucius Beebe. To most short lines this would be an enviable distinction. But not to the Rio Grande Southern, which trundles wearily around the western flank of the San Juan Mountains in southwestern Colorado and at times wishes desperately that Mr. Beebe had gone somewhere else with his cameras and his jocund prose. It does not want its picture taken, its history romanticized, excursionists swarming in. Its most ardent wish is just to die in peace.

For years it has been trying to ease out of existence, but each time it starts sinking happily into its coffin something comes along to jerk it out again. The depression of the thirties seemed a golden opportunity—until farmers fleeing from the dust bowls of the Great Plains poured into once empty Dove Creek and there raised such quantities of wheat and pinto beans that the Interstate Commerce Commission, heeding their clamor, refused to let the rusty wheels find rest. Another apparent knell was the war, with its demand for scrap iron and for narrow-gauge engines to be used in Alaska. But just when the requisition orders preluding the funeral had been signed, up popped that ultra-modern bit of scientific fiendishness, the atom bomb, and the only suitable means for transporting the bomb's uranium ores was the most anachronistic of trains, the Rio Grande Southern.

Sole railroad touching some four thousand square miles of convulsed territory (an area larger than Rhode Island and Delaware combined), this unhappy heap of essential junk owns 162.5 miles of mortgaged track, 112 trestles, and practically no level stretches whatsoever. Its wavering rails connect termini a scant sixty air-line miles apart; and, as nearly as such a construction feat can be the work of one man, it resulted from the singlehanded efforts of Russian-born Otto Mears. The stubborn Mr. Mears spent nine million dollars building it in 1890–91 and was moved to the task, in part, because another short-line railroad he was trying to create could not hurdle a meager eight-mile gap between Ironton, near Red Mountain, and Ouray.

A mention of geography is essential here. The San Juan Mountains, which split southwestern Colorado into innumerable, almost isolated pockets, are said, possibly with exaggeration, to contain "more vertical topography than any other section of comparable size in the United States." In the northern part of this rugged area is the famed San Juan mineral triangle, with the town of Silverton at its apex to the south, Telluride at the western point, Lake City at the east, and, midway between the latter two on the northern base of the triangle, the lovely mountain village of Ouray. From these camps and their satellites have poured hundreds of millions of dollars in gold, silver, lead, zinc, copper, and iron ore. As in all mining regions, a greater total value of merchandise has gone back into the ground than ever came out as mineral.

Driving at the San Juan triangle from the south, east, and north, the narrow-gauge Denver and Rio Grande Western Railroad hooked its iron tentacles into Silverton, Lake City, and Ouray during the 1880s, thus providing the periphery of the region with transportation to and from the outside. Inside the triangle, however, there were no locomotives. Residents grumbled. Although Silverton and Lake City were only twenty-six air-line miles apart, a train trip between them dragged out to 305 uncomfortable miles. Silverton to Ouray (twenty-three miles by today's automobile highway) was worse—approximately four hundred locomotive miles. Also because of intervening peaks, Telluride, though only ten direct miles from Ouray and thirteen from Silverton, had no rail connections whatsoever.

The local grumbling was, to be sure, partly a matter of principle. There was no need to travel by train. A vast meshwork of burro trails and toll roads interlaced the region, all of them swarming with pack animals and wagons of every description. Some of these toll roads and freight outfits were owned by that diminutive one-time Indian trader, Otto Mears. By 1888 he was doing very well indeed, but it occurred to him that he might do even better with a railroad.[1]

Mears at first had no delusions of grandeur: all he wanted was a twenty-odd-mile line from Silverton past Red Mountain to Ouray. He knew the ground, could use part of his Rainbow toll highway for a roadbed, and ran no danger of having his knuckles rapped by the jealous Denver and Rio Grande, which, for once, had no desire to break its

---

[1] The only thoroughgoing research into the Mears railroads is that by Mrs. Josie Moore Crum of Durango, Colorado, who has salvaged most of these facts from oblivion. Other bits of flotsam and jetsam derive from my own experiences, beginning with the time I was first transported on the Rio Grande Southern in a wicker basket, to eventual graduation as a cow valet riding in the green caboose of its bone-shaking stock trains.

neck in a competitive race for *those* passes. The field thus clear, Otto incorporated the Silverton Railroad Company, produced singlehanded $725,000, and sent his tracklayers to corkscrewing light thirty-pound narrow-gauge rails up 5-per-cent grades and around thirty-degree curves to Sheridan Pass, 11,235 feet high.

Here trouble developed. The north side of Sheridan Pass was too rugged for even thirty-degree curves. As a solution, a turntable was set in the junction of two arms of a wye, so located that each arm dropped downgrade onto the table. On reaching the table the engine was uncoupled, spun around, and headed up the other arm. The cars were next coasted by gravity onto the stem of the wye; then the little ten-wheeled Baldwin locomotive hooked onto what a moment before had been the end of the train and, with the once forward-looking passengers now peering in the other direction, chuffed merrily on its way.

By the winter of 1888 the road had reached a flourishing mine with the piquant name of Joker Tunnel and was such a howling success that it was running two full trains a day each way, its parlor cars handsomely beplushed and bepaneled for the benefit of the crowds of nail-booted miners who rode them. (One tall tale of the period says that experienced passengers rode in the front of the car on the way up the divide, then, on crossing the summit, hurried to the rear, thus avoiding the pools of tobacco juice which collected in the lower end.) Passenger rates were twenty cents a mile, with no reduction for round trips. Freight tariffs, likewise based on mileage, were commensurate.

Beyond Joker Tunnel, Otto was handed disquieting news. He had leaped over Red Mountain without looking, and now his engineers told him he could not spiral track on down Uncompahgre Canyon to Ouray. The toll road for a bed? Impossible. It twisted like a dog's hind leg, hit grades of 19 per cent. No steam engine built could negotiate the stretch.

Mears worried his whiskers. Blocked now—with only eight miles to go! If steam wouldn't do it, how about those new-fangled electric locomotives he had heard about? There was water power aplenty in the canyon.

The surveyors scuttled back, sighted, platted, scratched their heads, and returned despondent. Seven-per-cent grades would tax electric locomotives, and to achieve even that they would have to blast several long tunnels, build gigantic trestles, heap up mountainous fills. The eight miles of territory thus tapped could never repay the expense.

Well, Mears thought, if he could not push iron through the San Juans, he might perhaps circle around them to the west. Such was the genesis of the Rio Grande Southern. Romanticists like to say it was motivated purely by bullheadedness; and beyond doubt Otto Mears did derive a certain aesthetic satisfaction from tying the loose ends together. But the railroad bug had bitten him hard, and of late he had been pondering about the untapped resources west of the mountains: coal fields beyond Durango, lumber near Dolores, cattle on Dove Creek, mineral at the huge mines of Rico, Ophir, and Telluride. The blockade north of Red Mountain was simply the prod which sent him into motion.

From Ouray he backed twelve miles down the Uncompahgre to Ridgway; from Silverton he backed south fifty-odd miles to Durango. Denver and Rio Grande rails served these points, and it would have been dangerously brash to have attempted paralleling even a single foot of the little giant's right of way. Then he incorporated the Rio Grande Southern, sold nine million dollars' worth of stocks and bonds by merely mentioning the offer, and told his roustabouts, eagerly waiting at both termini, to start hustling. On the southern, or Durango, end of the job, construction sailed along at the satisfying rate of half a mile a day. Hopping over Dallas Divide from Ridgway was comparatively easy too; there Otto used still another of his toll roads for a bed. But stepladdering a way out of the canyon of the San Miguel at Ophir was something else. Six months were spent zigzagging the short four-mile Ophir Loop up the towering cliffs, and legend says that Otto was so terrified on his first locomotive ride over those dizzy tracks that he wanted to get out and finish the journey by carriage. If so, it was a feeling shared by many a later traveler.

Even before construction was finished in 1891, the Rio Grande Southern paid a $1.25 dividend on its forty-five thousand shares of stock. The Silverton road was also flourishing, and in the rosy glow of success Otto sent his surveyors down into New Mexico. A fever that had wasted other Coloradoans was singing through his veins—an outlet to the Pacific. Meanwhile, to please his friends and clients, he issued special sets of passes for free rides on his trains. The first issue was handsomely tooled out of soft white buckskin, unusual enough, but by no means up to Otto's dramatic taste. To more intimate friends he handed out silver watch fobs and then solid silver plates about the size of a calling card, engraved with the recipient's name, and surrounded by a delicate silver filigree. So far, so good. But for really impressive use were plates of solid gold, likewise engraved and filigreed.

Then came the depression of '93 and the abysmal collapse of silver prices. While Otto was still blinking, mines closed left and right, panic spread, stocks plummeted. One year and seven months after the Rio

Grande Southern had opened for business, a receiver of the Denver and Rio Grande stepped coldly into Otto Mears's shoes.

Spectacularly broke, Otto folded his tent and stole quietly East to Washington, D.C., where his political weight in Colorado made him welcome. From the nation's capital he hacked the old Chesapeake Beach Line through Maryland to the bay, sold out, and looked for fresh fields. Significantly, the world's newest form of transportation caught his eye: he joined the Mack brothers as first president of their truck company. But he was not happy turning wheels from an office, and his tiny, restless feet yearned for the old trails.

Back in Colorado was a dinky four-mile line, the Silverton Northern, which he had built in 1889 up the Animas Canyon from Silverton in order to tap the prolific mines of Cunningham and Arastra gulches. This alone of all his ambitious roads still remained in his control, and it was again reaping well. In 1902 its single locomotive, lone passenger coach, and ten boxcars had earned a dividend of 10 per cent. Otto's dollar-sharp ears pricked up. Why not use the Silverton Northern as the beginning of a new rail empire? As a first step, why not extend its narrow-gauge tracks over the towering divide at Animas Forks to his old stamping grounds at Lake City?

In 1903 he hurried back from New York City to try, although his surveyors told him the best grade they could work out, even with the aid of another of the old Mears toll roads, was a killing 7 per cent. Among the laborers he imported were a hundred Navajo Indians. Otto could speak Ute well enough, but he had never learned Navajo, and at the age of sixty-two he didn't figure to start. Valiantly he endeavored to direct the bucks by windmilling his arms. Amused, they windmilled back until his whiskers bristled with rage. Another thing that irritated him was the way they would drop their work to throw stones at ground hogs; as a countermeasure he purchased twenty-five rifles and hired a delighted squad of small boys to slaughter all marmots in the vicinity, so that the Indians would have no distractions.

Perhaps these petty annoyances were symbolic. The Silverton Northern never crossed the divide but halted beside the mines at Animas Forks, at the top of a grade so steep that a locomotive could struggle up with only one loaded and one empty car at a time. Coming down, it never dared haul more than three full cars at once, and then the sweating brakeman had to keep the hand brakes clubbed all the way to the bottom of the hill. Still, the passenger train made a brave show over its nineteen miles of track, pulling a combined sleeper-and-dining car, with four upper and four lower berths to a side, and snowy-white tables that served as exotic meals as could be had on any railroad in Colorado. In the course of the years, however, the varnished little car turned over so many times that its sole remains finally ended up as a porch swing in Durango.

In 1904, Otto regained control of his turntabled Silverton Railroad to Red Mountain, left New York permanently in 1907 to manage his Silverton roads and mines, and in 1915 added to his system by purchasing the Silverton, Gladstone and Northerly, which during its heyday ran two full trains a day over its seven and a half miles of track. Unsatisfactory echoes. He never managed to recover his real love, the Rio Grande Southern; and the dream which had once reached to the Pacific was shrunken now to a couple of canyons.

Yet the old vitality still burned at the core of the man. In 1909 floodwaters tore hideous gaps into the Rio Grande Southern's tracks below Ophir. Its managers, perhaps secretly relieved, wagged their heads. Nothing could be done. Then in came Otto, plug hat askew on his white head and fire in his eyes. Let his child lie there and bleed to death, would they? No, sir! Swiftly he sized up the grievous wounds, hired a few hundred laborers, and hovered by the bedside until he had set matters back to rights for the bungling stepfathers.

Later he performed comparable surgery for the Denver and Rio Grande in Animas Canyon below Silverton, clearing in thirteen days a stretch of mangled track which dismayed company officials had predicted could not be opened for six weeks. But the big fight, the fight that endeared Otto Mears to the entire San Juans, came in 1911, during his seventieth year. Another flood ripped the Denver and Rio Grande's Animas Canyon tracks to shreds, and this time the disaster struck in October, just before the paralyzing fist of winter closed on the San Juans. Fear rippled through Silverton. Mines, merchants, and housewives had not yet laid in their winter supplies, and if blizzards struck before the rails were cleared, the town would be destitute.

By telegraph desperate Denver and Rio Grande officials in Denver beseeched Otto Mears to do what he could. By nightfall he had hired two hundred and fifty men, had brought down rolling stock and equipment from his own railroads. But there was one thing which neither his own depleted yards nor those of the Denver and Rio Grande could furnish. That was coal to keep the work trains running. Silverton's unreplenished bins were all but empty.

Mears toured the town, appealing to mills, to stores, to homeowners. "Give us your coal!" The people shivered. Emptying the bins at the mines meant stopping production; at home, the threat of freezing. And suppose the tracks weren't rebuilt in time? Suppose their last bits of fuel were burned to no avail? Suppose . . .

But Silverton had faith in Otto Mears. The mines opened their doors; storekeepers sent hoarded coal in drayloads; children lugged it to the depot in sacks. White whiskers, frock coat, and all, Otto climbed into the cab of the lead locomotive and roared down the canyon. For nine weeks his crew and another pushing up from Durango raced the weather. And they won. Supplies poured into Silverton in the nick of time, and winter became not a specter of terror but just one more season of deep snow and cold.

Those deep snows were hard now for Otto Mears's tiny body to endure. In 1917 he moved to Pasadena, California, and there, in 1931, aged ninety, he died. His last request was that his ashes and those of Mary Kampfshulte, the red-haired German girl he had married in 1870 when he was a two-bit Indian trader peddling goods out of an adobe store in Saguache, be scattered over the divide between Lake City and Silverton, high in the mountains he had fought and conquered and loved.

Mile by mile his Silverton railways dwindled to nothingness, and repeatedly it has seemed that the Rio Grande Southern must suffer the same sour fate of gradual abandonment. The orphaned child pays low wages, no dividends, and since 1928 has paid no general property taxes. Its ties rot; its thin little rails sag and dip. Ancient engines are wrecked, patched, rusted. Often, in crawling up one of the passes, the gasping locomotives, running out of water, must leave their cars behind, pant on to the nearest tank, drink deep, and then wheeze backward to retrieve the patient load. High water, huge mud slides, and shattering avalanches, born in peaks that receive the greatest precipitation in Colorado, deal it annual haymakers. Yet year after year the Rio Grande Southern creaks on, full of cinders, smells, and misery, a railroad of old, old men, for no youngster will tie his fortunes to such a hopeless cripple.

Railroading on the Southern requires patience and perseverance. In 1920, while escorting fifteen cars of cattle and six of apples over a rain-softened roadbed, head shack J. H. Crum and his crew, using camel-back frogs and vitriolic language, overcame twenty-five separate derailments during a single trip, twenty-two of them within one six-mile stretch. On another occasion, when a cattle car tipped over in a cut, the crew released the animals by chopping a hole in the roof. Brand Inspector Seth Etheridge, who happened to be along, walked to a nearby ranch, borrowed a horse, and drove the steers to Mancos, four miles distant. Meanwhile the trainmen somehow hauled the errant car back on the track, chugged into town, borrowed a less damaged vehicle, reloaded the steers, and steamed ahead, all within two hours.

Some of the wrecks were weird indeed. Once in a snowstorm an engine ran into a wagonload of dynamite, showered itself with miraculously unexploded sticks of giant powder, and came to a stop with one wheel of the wagon draped around its smokestack. Another time a rail fell off a flatcar, rammed against the inside bank, was thrust through the flimsy side of the caboose, and then gouged and hammered the cab to pieces—meanwhile injuring not a single one of the cowering crew inside. In February 1925 a narrow snowslide cannonaded down a mountain and began picking cars out of the middle of a twenty-five-car train. Brakeman Horrell, on top of a car that lay directly in the path of the avalanche, ran wildly for the rear of the train. The slide plucked the car almost from under his heels and hurled it into the canyon. Meanwhile the train's momentum carried Horrell's new haven into the white torrent. Again he jumped, was carried backward as he ran, jumped, and ran again. All told, his stationary sprint carried him across seven doomed freight cars before the broken segment of the train groaned to a halt and let him catch his breath.

By the early thirties the Southern's affairs had reached so parlous a state that death seemed inevitable. Revenue had fallen off by 85 per cent, creditors were suing for $5,566,793.53, and the road was put into the hands of still another receiver, Victor A. Miller, a man of considerable imagination. Aided by his superintendent, Forest White, Miller talked the government into doubling the Rio Grande Southern's mail subsidy, made new labor contracts, effected heroic economies in operation and maintenance, and, above all, instituted the now nationally famous Galloping Geese.

A wondrous hybrid is a Rio Grande Southern Goose, a huge motor truck adapted to running on rails. In front are seats for seven passengers (more often squeeze in); behind is a freight compartment built like a boxcar. Six of these fugitives from the highways take care of daily needs, ore and cattle shipments being handled by regular freight trains, and they have saved the reluctant life of the Rio Grande Southern. A narrow-gauge locomotive, for example, packs one hundred tons of non-revenue-producing weight, whereas a Goose tips the scales at a mere seven and a half tons—no small factor on those decrepit rails. Furthermore, a train must travel with engineer, fireman, conductor, and brakeman working at hourly wages, plus the overtime which is almost a certainty on that run. The Goose is driven by a lone motorman who is paid by the month.

A whirring, clanking, grinding run it is, over dizzy shelves, swaying curves, and sagging trestles that scare unacclimated passengers half out of their skins. Occasional runaways have sent occupants diving for their lives into neighboring snowbanks—whereupon, on at least two occasions, the Goose has zoomed unattended to an upgrade and stopped while its irate cargo tramped after it afoot. One such escapee even brought itself to a halt smack dab in front of the Ridgway depot. Just the same, it is safer to jump. Runaway Geese have also left the rails and have piled themselves up with as much violence as did their iron predecessors, whose rusty remains for years lay scattered along the base of the cliffs, disquieting omens in the eyes of more timorous tourists. Finally, during the war those unhallowed bones were removed for scrap.

Gone also is the brief atom-bomb stimulus which the war brought to the Rio Grande Southern. Shipments of lead, zinc, and uranium ores have fallen off, and perhaps the weary littlest giant will be allowed to die. But one should not be too sure. Though the Southern may deem suicide acceptable, its patrons do not. They live in a formidable land where truck highways, especially during winter, are atrocious to the point of impassability, and under such conditions a crippled railroad is better than no railroad at all. Mines are no longer the main economic base of the countryside. There are growing numbers of dry farms in Dove Creek, beef and dairy herds in Montezuma Basin, swelling flocks of sheep near Lizard Head, undeveloped resources of coal and lumber sprinkled everywhere. The orphan may be roused once again.

If so, it may need a new engine.

An 1898 mule train takes off with a load of timbers for one of the mines perched on the dizzy cliffs above Telluride, in the San Juan Mountains of Colorado.

A mountain climber ropes down from one of the spires of the Big Divide. Although all major peaks have been climbed, many lesser pinnacles challenge the addict with the lure of a first ascent.

CHAPTER XI

VIOLENCE

FORTUNATELY for Colorado, the Rockies' greatest gold camp waited for its bloody development until after the collapse of silver in 1893. One is tempted to descry the hand of Providence. The bonanza might have been found in '59, when Pikes Peak was the rallying call for the first stampede to the mountains. But the rush veered off to the Clear Creek diggings; and although prospectors continued to sniff sporadically around Pikes' western flanks, only twenty-five airline miles from the bustling resort of Colorado Springs, they never guessed that nearly half a billion dollars lay beneath their feet.

To cap the paradox, certain promoters in 1884 did their unwitting best to reveal the treasure. Rumors trickled out that one Chicken Bill, prospector, had made a strike on the slopes of Mountain Pisgah, a small volcanic cone west of Pikes Peak. In rushed a small army of hopeful, only to scowl in bewilderment when they found neither familiar granites nor sparkling quartz. Indeed, Pisgah's cheerless environs were pierced by very few outcroppings a man could explore, and the sylvanite ores which did reveal themselves looked mighty unprepossessing. Still, for lack of something better to do, the boys might have stuck around for a more thorough investigation had not someone discovered a bottle of gold chloride, frequently used for salting claims, in the possession of one of Pisgah's promoters. Convinced they had been hoaxed, the angry stampeders gathered up ropes and guns and went looking for Chicken Bill. He had vanished. After consoling themselves with a mass drunk, the frustrated lynchers went home.

Perhaps it was just as well. Silver-happy Colorado did not need gold in 1884. Ten years later she would. The delay, however, proved costly to some of the men of '84. When fresh rumors reported in 1891 that a cow hand named Robert Womack had found gold at Pisgah, of all places, they snorted to themselves and stayed where they were.

Womack, too, was unlucky. Known to his fellow cowpunchers as Crazy Bob because of a penchant for digging holes in the barren ground, he had discovered ore at the bottom of a painfully burrowed forty-foot shaft, had taken it to an assayer in Colorado Springs, and had learned that it was worth $140 a ton. Tremendously elated, he went on a stem-winding toot—and woke up to discover he had sold his holdings for $500.

The news got around and people began straggling in. By October 1891, some nine or ten months after Womack's discovery, there were enough of them shivering out the high-altitude fall in brush huts and tents that George Carr, foreman of the ranch which grazed stock in the district, wired his employers. The cattle were being boogered. Should he make these squatters jump? The Denver real estate firm of Bennett & Meyers, which owned the small ranch near Pisgah where Womack had once worked, sent young Bennett down to investigate. Being a real estate salesman, Bennett decided on a course that might not have occurred to plain cow hands. He platted a town and sold three or four hundred building lots. His company tried to call the place Fremont, but the miners were used to referring to the district by the name of the stream which watered it—Cripple Creek. They transferred the title to their ragged settlement of shanties. It certainly did not sound—or look—very golden.

One example will be enough. Early in the spring of 1891 a Colorado Springs carpenter named Winfield Scott Stratton followed Womack's tracks up to Pisgah. Stratton knew something of mining. In fact, his prospecting trips irked his wife, and when he left home on this latest goose chase she divorced him for non-support. Undismayed, he puttered around through the boulders and briar patches and on July 4, 1891, staked out the Independence and Washington lodes. In less than ten years he was worth more than twenty million dollars and possessed eccentricities to match. Once the manager of the Brown Palace Hotel in Denver insulted him. Some say that Stratton and a female companion were refused a room; others that he was scolded for throwing champagne bottles down the huge central well into the lobby. Anyhow, he was annoyed. So he stalked out, bought the property for a million spot cash, stalked back, and fired the offender. But in his own way he had a heart as enormous as his fortune. Every panhandler in the state could touch him. One winter he bought coal for all the poor in Victor and on another occasion gave every laundress in Colorado Springs a bicycle to ride to work. When he died he left the bulk of his fortune to the Myron Stratton Home in the Springs, an institution to care for anyone incapable of earning a living.

Many another man has shared the golden flood which Cripple Creek poured out. Some were the veriest greenhorns, like a poor druggist named Jones, who threw his hat in the air, dug where it fell, and became a millionaire. But a far greater number had difficulty earning enough to eat. A backwash of '93's panic flooded the slopes of Mount Pisgah. In the East, which was only a three- or four-day train ride from Pikes Peak, banks and factories had closed, coal and Pullman strikes racked the shattered economy. In Colorado and Utah thousands of silver miners were jobless. From all sides the destitute came swarming. Inside the treeless, hole-pitted, dump-warted six-mile square of treasured earth which constituted the working limits of the field, no less than ten towns took form: Cripple Creek itself, then Victor, rough-tough Altman, Goldfield, Independence, Gillett, Anaconda, Elkton, Ariqua, Mound City.

Wages, when there were wages, were three dollars a day—bare subsistence, because transportation difficulties involved in circling Pikes Peak kept food and clothing prices sky-high. The meanest of unpainted shacks rented for fifteen dollars a month, firewood cost four-fifty a cord, and water was five cents a bucket. And even this sort of subsistence was denied to many, for the embryo mines could not absorb the glut of labor. Thousands found nothing to do, among them certain men who began to preach that "wealth belongs to those who produce the wealth." That was one reason, though only one, why hate bloomed so bitterly when the explosion came.

It was not long. Although wages were uniform, working hours were not. Some mines operated eight-hour shifts, some nine, some ten. This obvious sore spot was probed in August 1893, when H. E. Locke, superintendent of the Isabella Mine, ordered his men to go from an eight- to a ten-hour shift with no increase in pay.

Now these miners did not consider themselves ordinary laborers; they were hiring out at wages, so they thought, only until they could grubstake themselves for a fortune hunt of their own. Here, then, was a personal affront, to be met with personal means. The Isabella miners surrounded Locke outside the workings and gave him such a piece of their minds that the order was rescinded. But the spark had been struck. Fearing that other mines might make a similar move, workers from all over the district formed a union with headquarters at Altman. To strengthen themselves still further, they affiliated with the Western Federation of Miners, born two scant years before at Butte, Montana. From this infant prodigy soon would grow the infamous Industrial Workers of the World, to spread through all America the lessons of terror learned so well in Colorado.

The workers had reasoned accurately. In January 1894 a loose-knit organization of mine owners ordered the ten-hour shift with no increase in pay. They felt justified. Expenses were mounting as they dug deeper, other Colorado mines maintained the long shift, and working conditions in the dry, well-ventilated Cripple Creek diggings were better than in most localities. Furthermore, the market was oversupplied with labor willing to work on any terms—or so management believed.

Promptly the baby union of Altman declared a strike. Superintendent Locke of the Isabella, whom the workers blamed for dreaming up the nefarious move, was captured with his bodyguard, disarmed, and told to make tracks down the hill. He did, and several owners who not long ago had been penniless prospectors themselves decided to reinstate the eight-hour shift.

Others were bullheaded. Their mines were water-free and would not be injured by a shutdown. Two railroads were rapidly building toward the district, and a wait until cars arrived would save three dollars a ton in the cost of freighting ore. Let the strikers stew!

The Altman union proved unexpectedly stew-proof. Free boarding-houses for the strikers were instituted, manned by volunteer cooks and financed by a tax on union members working the "fair" mines and by donations from other locals in Colorado and Montana. Unhappily these outside contributions were accompanied by unwanted and unofficial gangs of toughs, principally from the Coeur d'Alene region in Idaho.

Gradually minor bits of violence began to appear. Unionists broke into stores and warehouses, stole arms and provisions. Non-unionists were beaten; a deputy sheriff was shot. Down in Colorado Springs, which was the seat of El Paso County and headquarters of most of the mine owners, Sheriff Bowers was called into consultation by the operators. Could he furnish protection for a large force of strike-breakers?

Bowers said no. El Paso County was too poor to equip the army of police which such a move would require.

"We'll equip them," the operators said, and Bowers agreed. If he detected any incongruity in letting a supposedly impartial law-enforcement agency be financed by one of the parties to the brawl, he kept it to himself.

Late in May 1894, 125 deputies disembarked from the Florence and Cripple Creek Railroad and marched toward Altman. The miners were ready, entrenched in a regular military camp atop Bull Hill, a high, steep-sided bluff overlooking the town. To warn the deputies back, they seized the shaft house of the Strong Mine and with a massive charge of dynamite blew it to flinders, a move which incidentally trapped three mine officials inside the shaft.

As debris flew through the air the deputies retreated. Out of sight of town, they set up camp beside the railroad. Meanwhile, back in Altman, the explosion had uncorked pandemonium, gaily abetted by a large group of drunk railroad construction workers who had just received their pay checks. Into this chaos stepped the outside toughs. Some of them loaded a freight car with dynamite, planning to coast it into the deputies' camp and touch it off. Others surged through the streets, howling for a wholesale bombing of every mine in the district. Fortunately President Calderwood of the union and other cool heads managed to forestall these early moves, but that night a mob seized a construction train and with a miner at the throttle roared down the track to attack the enemy stronghold.

It was a disorganized, unled, every-man-for-himself battle, fought in pitch darkness from behind stumps and rocks. Finally the attackers were beaten off. One dead deputy and one dead striker lay on the field. Five more miners were captured by the deputies and held as hostages. In retaliation the union fished the three Strong officials out of the ruined shaft and incarcerated them. Eventually all eight captives were released through a formal prisoner-of-war exchange unprecedented in United States labor strife.

Exaggerated news of the imbroglio created intense excitement in Colorado Springs, where sympathy inclined toward the side of the mine owners. An additional thousand deputies were gathered from all over the state and marched toward Cripple Creek under command of Sheriff Bowers. In Denver, Governor Waite issued a proclamation ordering the miners to lay down their arms and commanding the illegal army of police to disband. The deputies refused, so naturally the miners maintained their fortifications on Bull Hill. However, President Calderwood did manage to close all saloons in the district and appointed a committee of fifty to run out the toughs in the union, a move not attended with success.

Soberer owners, notably railroad builder Dave Moffat and J. J. Hagerman, now professed willingness to arbitrate. After a good deal of geeing and hawing these two, together with Governor Waite, President Calderwood of the union, and various civic leaders, met at a Colorado College hall in Colorado Springs. Proceedings were interrupted when a mob invaded the campus, bent on lynching both the union president and the governor. Hurrying to the front door, Judge Lunt pointed out to the mob what a disgrace such a proceeding would be to the fair name of the town. His listeners were not impressed, but under cover of the distraction Calderwood and Waite sneaked out a side entrance and boarded a train for Denver. There, two days later, a compromise was effected. The union, whose case had looked hopeless at the outset of the strike, won its demand for an eight-hour day but lost a stipulation that union men be given preference in all hirings.

News of the settlement touched off a wild ringing of bells and street dancing in Colorado Springs, but the celebration was premature. The army of deputies declined to disband on the grounds that they held warrants for the arrest of several strikers who were taking refuge on Bull Hill. When General Brooks of the militia endeavored to place himself between the adversaries, Sheriff Bowers snapped that state troopers had no authority over county officials, and on June 8 the deputies advanced against Bull Hill.

Considerable carnage loomed. The besieged workers had mined the slopes and had rigged up a cannon capable of shooting beer bottles loaded with dynamite. However, Brooks threw his troops into double-quick and again intercepted the deputies. There was a deal of furious talk, the soldiers threatened to open fire, and the deputies withdrew. The union then allowed the militia to occupy Bull Hill and peacefully dispersed.

To console themselves the deputies marched into Cripple Creek the next day, arrested numerous persons, clubbed others, and forced many a reluctant citizen to join their parade. It was a final spasm. Once more Brooks intercepted the column, and this time the deputies withdrew to Colorado Springs, where they at last disbanded. Slowly order returned, punctuated by brutal, secret attacks on various individuals who in one way or another had been prominent during the fracas. And the seeds of trouble remained: class lines drawn knife-sharp, new prejudices and precedents for violence, and a lawless element of opportunists ready to feast on disorder.

Now the canker spread to Leadville. Living was hard there. Sixty-five per cent of Leadville's miners were married; their average grocery bill was thirty-three dollars a month, while rent, fuel, water, and clothing ate up at least thirty dollars more. These corners the workers (who did not labor and were not paid on Sundays, holidays, or during layoffs) had to shave on a wage of two-fifty per day, which the owners in that depression-haunted silver camp thought was high enough. When the union struck for three dollars, "scabs" were imported and the melee was on. The sheriff, friendly to the union, neglected to protect strikebreakers, many of whom were soundly gun-whipped and run out of town by union "regulators."

When the exasperated owners of the Coronado and Emmet mines

built protective board fences around their surface workings, the regulators heaved a dynamite bomb over the Coronado barrier one midnight, set the place afire, and killed one of the town firemen who had the temerity to try putting out the blaze. Inside the fence the "scabs," seventeen men and one boy, cut loose with a fusillade that killed three of the attackers. Their ardor now somewhat dampened, the regulators shifted to the Emmet, where they blew a hole through the fence with a cannon contrived from a piece of steam pipe. But here, too, they were met with such a hail of buckshot and rifle bullets that they hastily withdrew, leaving still another corpse behind. The only fruit of their violence was a hurry-up call for the militia; and after a long period of bitter negotiating the strikers capitulated, going back to work in February 1897 on the owners' terms.

Four years later came Telluride's turn. There in 1901 strikers closed the Smuggler-Union Mine, perched precariously atop one of the gigantic bluffs that gird the canyoned headwaters of the San Miguel River. With an extraordinary thumb-to-the-nose gesture the Smuggler operators hired strikebreakers on exactly the terms the union had asked for and had been denied. Infuriated, at daybreak on July 3 the strikers ambushed the armed night shift of strikebreakers as they came from work. In the ensuing battle among the gray boulders and dark spruce trees three men were killed. The scabs then retreated inside the mine buildings, bearing with them five wounded brethren.

Now the strikers took possession of the one hair-raising trail leading to the mine and warned would-be reinforcements from the agitated town at the bottom of the hill to keep away. However, the writer's stepfather, who was then packing mail to the mines with a mule train, decided to investigate and bring back to Telluride definite word of the situation. Unfurling a small American flag, he spurred up the trail, calling in effect, "Make way for the United States mail!" The bluff worked, and he gained the buildings where the scabs were holed up beyond range of the attackers' desultory firing. There he found one of the wounded men in desperate need of immediate medical attention.

What followed may be apocryphal. However, legend says that my stepfather (dead these fifteen years and hence not available for verification) cut leg holes in a long striped canvas mail sack, inserted the wounded man, weighed, stamped, and addressed him parcel post to the hospital. Then he told the glowering strikers they had better not monkey with government mail and led his cargo down the hill. Meanwhile, the beleaguered scabs ran out of ammunition and surrendered on condition that they not be molested. As soon as they were disarmed several were ruthlessly beaten, one was shot, and all were marched not toward town, where many had families, but over bleak thirteen-thousand-foot Imogene Pass and told to make themselves scarce. Shortly thereafter a settlement was reached in which the union regretted "the recent outrages" but won its wage demands. Ill will still rankled, however. A year later an unknown assailant killed Arthur Collins, manager of the Smuggler, as he sat reading by his fireside.

Mere entr'actes. Cripple Creek, which had rung up the curtain on the drama, was now ready with a climax featuring as double-dyed a villain, by his own account, as the Rockies have ever seen.

Following the 1894 strikes the town had boomed incredibly. Fifty thousand people lived in the six-mile-square district whose ten towns were laced together with an elaborate system of trolleys and fed by no less than three separate railroads. Scientific mining developments enabled the mines to sink shafts fifteen hundred feet or more deep; new cyanide milling processes made profitable the handling of low-grade ores. Gold production rose until it hovered in the neighborhood of twenty million dollars per year. By 1897 a total of 3057 mining companies had been incorporated with an average capitalization of a million dollars each. Many of them, located outside the golden six-mile square, were sucker bait, but enough reaped with such fantastic success that some Colorado historians have declared their production pulled the entire nation out of the panic of '93—which, of course, is mere civic pride on the loose. However, Cripple Creek, South Africa, and Klondike mines did help check a world-wide decline in prices, fortified the arguments of the gold-standard advocates in Congress, defeated William Jennings Bryan, and wrecked forever any future large-scale silver agitation.

Living was high, wide, and handsome. The town of Gillett put on bullfights (until state authorities intervened), and out of the massed brothels of Cripple Creek came an unofficial national anthem. Here, where prostitutes were segregated by nationalities and cribs bore the names of their occupants rather than street numbers, thrived a tumultuous Negro singer named Amanda Green. Amanda had a temper. When her swain of the moment deserted her one winter night to visit a high-yaller girl in Old Town, Amanda raised such a ruckus with a carving knife that six policemen had their hands full hauling her off through the snow to the lockup. Now Amanda's music fitted her temperament. She composed several ditties, one of which a traveling actor named Ernest Hogan set down on paper. Necessarily he changed its words somewhat and then passed the song on to a Colorado regiment in the

Spanish-American War. From there it circled the globe. Its name: "There'll Be a Hot Time in the Old Town Tonight."

In 1899, Teller County was created out of the western end of El Paso County. This meant that county business was no longer centered in the mine owners' conservative seat at Colorado Springs but was shifted to Cripple Creek. The result was an economic and political anomaly—an entire county absolutely geared to a single industry, gold mining. Such an opportunity the Western Federation of Miners (whose headquarters had been moved from Butte to Denver) was too vigilant to overlook. Union men were voted into nearly every one of the county's executive, administrative, and judicial posts. Union sheriffs seldom arrested union men, and union juries even more rarely returned decisions against them.

This extreme power the Federation decided to use in a strike against the smelters at Colorado City (just west of Colorado Springs), where most Cripple Creek ores were refined. The quarrel started early in 1903, was apparently settled in March, but exploded again on July 3. Immediate cause of the new flare-up was a charge that Manager Mac-Neil of one of the smelters was discriminating against a grand total of nine union men who had participated in the first strike. Breathing fire, the Federation ordered a fresh walkout and, to make it doubly effective, asked the Cripple Creek mines to ship no ore to the smelters. Indignantly most of the owners refused, as the union must have known they would. Calmly, then, the Federation ordered thirty-five hundred men out of fifty mines. (Some workings which smelted their own ores or which complied with the edict were allowed to continue operations.) There seems no doubt that the union hoped by this display of strength to frighten the Colorado legislature into passing an eight-hour-day labor law—a grievance of no direct concern to Cripple Creek, where an eight-hour-day had prevailed since the 1894 walkouts.

This strike was not submitted to a vote of the miners. During good times the conservative majority had ceased attending meetings, thus enabling a radical minority to pass a resolution allowing the union's executive council to call strikes on its own authority. Now the rank and file paid for their indifference. They had scant interest in a smelter quarrel involving nine men who lived in a town forty miles or more away. Yet loyally they laid down their tools in a protest which soon would cost a score of lives.

In September a few strikebreakers were beaten and a shaft house was burned, whereupon the owners, through the extraordinary compliance of a *union* sheriff, armed deputies of their own choosing and wired Governor Peabody for militia. An ex-banker and an ultra-conservative Republican (Teller County was solidly Democratic), Peabody dispatched a thousand soldiers—without bothering to ask either county officials or union leaders whether the situation warranted the move. In other words, the mine owners were very successfully stacking the deck.

However, state-wide sympathy favored them, for they were deemed, not unreasonably, to be the victims of an unfair, essentially political strike. Moreover, the Western Federation of Miners was suspect. It had officially espoused Socialism, and at that time Socialists were identified in the popular mind with bewhiskered revolutionists tiptoeing through alleyways with round black bombs. Although most of the Federation's members probably were not in full accord with either Socialism or with violence as a political philosophy, there was justice for the popular view. The union's president, after pointing to the United States Constitution's guarantee of the right to carry arms, had exhorted his locals, "I strongly advise you to provide every member with the latest improved rifle . . . so that in two years we can hear the inspiring music of the martial tread of 25,000 armed men in the ranks of labor."

Foolishly the militia invaded Cripple Creek with a highhanded arrogance that solidified the union's hold on members who once had been opposed to the strike. A stockade known as the "bull pen" was erected at Goldfield; into it active Federationists were chucked without trial or even preferment of charges. The staff of the union's local organ, the Victor *Record*, which had not been particularly inflammatory, were imprisoned for criminal libel. General Brooks, commander of the militia, stated flatly, "I came to do up this damned anarchistic federation," and when civil authorities freed several prisoners, he promptly rearrested them.

Strengthened by Brooks's show of force, the owners redoubled their importation of strikebreakers. Fury swept the miners. And now enters our villain, whose blood-wallowings, if his own word is credible, make Billy the Kid look like a missionary.

His name was Albert Horsley, but when he blew up the governor of Idaho he was traveling under the alias "Harry Orchard," and it is by that cognomen that he has gone down in infamy.

Born in Canada, Harry Orchard married in the United States, acquired a small cheese factory, fell into bad company, dissipated his savings, burned down the factory for its insurance, and ran off to British Columbia with another man's wife. His paramour deserting him, he drifted into the Coeur d'Alene mining district of Idaho, where he ran a milk route and obtained a one-tenth interest in a prospect hole which later developed into the multimillion-dollar Hercules Mine. Unfortunately Harry Orchard did not retain his interest in the mine. Having once again drunk and gambled himself into bankruptcy, he joined the Western Federation of Miners and on April 29, 1899, helped dynamite a gold mill at Wardner, Idaho. This bit of union violence led to Governor Steunenberg's sending in the Idaho militia. With the law breathing hot on his neck, Orchard sold his interest in the yet unproved mine and floundered over snowy passes to refuge in Montana. When later he realized what he had lost, his bitterness against militia in general and Steunenberg in particular would have far-reaching repercussions.

For the next three years Orchard was a typical tramp miner, wandering from camp to camp all over the West. In July 1902 he landed in Cripple Creek, where he supplemented his wages by stealing highgrade ore and peddling it to crooked assayers.

When the heavy hand of Brooks's troops clamped down on the Colorado district, President Charles Moyer and Secretary W. D. (Big Bill) Haywood of the Federation decided, so Orchard says, on a reign of terror calculated to frighten the strikebreakers and to bring wavering union members back into line. The first step was to be the destruction of the Vindicator Mine. Broke, restless, and hating all troops, Orchard volunteered to do the job for two hundred dollars, knowing full well that he might kill every scab in the workings.

His first clumsy attempt nearly ended in his capture, but he crawled back into the Vindicator through an unguarded side tunnel and set a booby trap which exploded on November 21, 1903, killing the mine superintendent and the foreman. The Federation, of course, denied complicity and charged that the dead officials had been caught in a blast they were rigging up in an effort to discredit the union. The Mine Owners Association, on the other hand, leveled an accusing finger at the Federation and offered a five-thousand-dollar reward for evidence leading to the conviction of the perpetrators. There were no takers. Later on in Denver, Orchard says, Big Bill Haywood congratulated him. "You got two good ones; a few more and we'll have everything our way."

As a result of the explosion and of a barely frustrated attempt to wreck a train loaded with strikebreakers, Governor Peabody proclaimed Teller County "to be in a state of insurrection and rebellion"—though these two outrages, obviously the work of no more than half a dozen men, were the only evidences of upheaval. Promptly militia officers superseded civil government, ordered all newspapers censored, all arms confiscated, assemblages of people in the streets forbidden, and declared that "any person able to work . . . who shall be found loitering or strolling about, frequenting places where liquor is sold, begging or leading an idle, immoral, or profligate life, or not having any visible means of support, shall be deemed a vagrant," subject to arrest.

Under this elastic law scores of men were imprisoned. Drunk with power, many officers and soldiers strutted the streets in petty tyranny, insulting women, forcibly invading some homes, and occasionally roughing up individuals who dared murmur against them. Concurrently the Mine Owners Association issued a statement declaring: "The avowed purpose of this association is to drive the disturbing and dangerous element of the Western Federation of Miners from the district and from the state," and adopted a card-check system which prevented any union member from obtaining employment in the mines or mills of the district.

Meanwhile the strike had spread to Telluride. There during the winter of 1903–04 a mob of Citizens Alliance members (an organization of non-mining employers that worked in close accord with the Mine Owners Association) forcibly deported as vagrants several batches of union workers. President Moyer and Secretary Haywood of the Federation promptly rushed down to Ouray, just across the range from Telluride, to devise countermeasures. With them they took the ubiquitous Mr. Orchard, who had spent the winter developing certain lethal devices: dynamite disguised by pitch to resemble lumps of coal so it could be planted in mill-fuel piles; "greek fire," a liquid that would burst into flames when its container broke; and a mixture of chloride potash and sugar which could be set ablaze with a drop of sulphuric acid.

The union heads leased an old mine at Red Mountain, within striking distance of Telluride, gathered together several of the deported miners, armed them, and kept them busy with military drill. They also debated whether to poison Telluride's water supply with potassium cyanide or to roll barrels of dynamite down the mountainside into the town, which was under militia rule. These cheerful discussions were given a new turn on March 5, 1904, when militia in Telluride arrested five Federation members as vagrants and chained one of them, Henry Maki, to a telephone pole. An alert unionist snapped a photograph of Maki and took it to Moyer. Gleefully the president made up a placard headed, "Is Colorado in America?" and bearing, along with Maki's picture, an

American flag on whose stripes were printed such sentiments as "Soldiers Defy Courts in Colorado! Union Men Exiled from Homes and Families in Colorado! Wholesale Arrests without Warrant in Colorado!", etc.

Arrested in Ouray and taken to Telluride on a charge of desecrating the flag, Moyer's release on a writ of habeas corpus was refused by General Bell and Captain Bulkeley Wells of the militia (the latter of whom was also manager of the Smuggler-Union Mine). Ordered to pay Moyer five hundred dollars each for false imprisonment, the pair declined as military personnel to submit to civil jurisdiction but at last obeyed a command of the state Supreme Court to take their prisoner to Denver. Secretary Haywood, going to the depot to meet Moyer, was severely beaten by soldiers and turned over to civil authorities. The Supreme Court then declared Moyer legally held by the militia, but events were zooming to a climax in which these minor matters would be forgotten and the charges dropped.

After Moyer's arrest, which the union blamed on Governor Peabody, Harry Orchard was summoned back to Denver to do away with that despised head of the state. Ill luck frustrated the murder attempt, but he did manage to while away the time with a squalid back-alley slaying of a deputy detective named Lyte Gregory. Meanwhile the strike in Cripple Creek was going badly. The troop-protected mines were operating successfully with scab labor, factional quarrels were splitting the local unions, and the discouraged workers were about ready to give up. At this juncture, so Orchard says, Haywood decided to annihilate a gross lot of scabs by bombing the depot at Independence, where the night-shift men waited to catch the 2 A.M. train home after work. Such action, the secretary thought, would prove the aggressiveness of the union, awe its enemies, and bolster the morale of backsliding members.

Orchard and a colleague named Steve Adams were chosen to do the work. It was Orchard alone, however, who on the night of June 6, 1904, wriggled under the depot platform with two boxes of dynamite and a tricky detonator of sulphuric acid. He was nervous. "I might have blown myself up." But he planted the charge without accident, ran a wire a couple of hundred feet out to an old ore house, and hunkered down to wait.

The locomotive's headlight split the darkness. On the platform tired workers yawned and gossiped. Others, released from their jobs a moment or two late, came racing down the dark hillside. They were lucky. Before they reached the station a thunderous explosion shook the night. Bodies were hurled 150 feet up the mountain, some so mutilated that at noon the next day sheriff's men were still picking up hunks of flesh in tin pails.

With debris raining around him, Orchard lit out for a tent where he was camped with a pal named Johnny Neville. Neville did not know what Orchard was up to. A few days before, the pair had burned down Neville's saloon to collect its fire insurance, and Johnny supposed they were going to use the proceeds on an innocent hunting trip in Wyoming. To Wyoming they went. Orchard was never quite sure how many casualties his blast had inflicted. Neither, apparently, were Independence authorities. Thirteen had died and perhaps as many as twenty-seven had been wounded (figures disagree), six of whom had to have one or more of their mangled limbs amputated. For this job, according to Orchard, he received three hundred dollars from the union—$23.08 per life, with injuries tossed in free.

If Haywood had really thought to strengthen the union by this blast, he made a hideous miscalculation. Armed mobs poured into Victor, where the militia was gathering in the armory. Suddenly a street riot swept the town. During it two more men died and three were wounded. Unionists fled into their hall and barricaded it. When they refused to surrender, the militia riddled the brick building with volley after volley. Four members wounded, the strikers asked for a truce and were herded into hastily improvised bull pens. Behind them enraged citizens rushed through their hall and smashed its furniture to bits.

In vain the Federation charged the Mine Owners Association with loosing the blast to bring down popular wrath on the union and offered a ten-thousand-dollar reward for capture of the culprits. Cripple Creek refused to believe these cries of innocence. Even the union-supporting Victor *Record* editorialized, "Call Off the Strike!" (Shortly thereafter its plant was demolished by parties unknown.) Mobs vandalized every union hall, store, and warehouse in the district. The Mine Owners Association and the Citizens Alliance, often using threats of death, drove union judges, mayors, councilmen, and sheriffs out of office, replacing them with appointees of their own. This was mob rule, yet the militia, supposedly on hand to maintain orderly government, abetted the upheaval in every way. Under their watchful eyes seventy-three union men were loaded aboard a train on June 10, taken to the Kansas line, kicked off, and told to get out of Colorado. Thirty-three more were driven into New Mexico, and all during July smaller groups were deported to other towns in Colorado. There is no telling how many hundreds fled of their own volition, while less notorious workers quietly dropped union membership and took out Association cards. Although the Federation refused to call off the strike, its back was broken.

Colorado being deemed temporarily unhealthy for Harry Orchard, he was sent to California to assassinate Fred Bradley, a prominent anti-union man in that state. The lead-pipe bomb which Orchard says he connected to Bradley's doorknob succeeded only in permanently disabling its victim, and since the cause of the explosion was deemed to be a leaky gas main, Bradley collected ten thousand dollars in damages from the gas company. The disappointed Federation then recalled Orchard to Denver, where he spent the winter in fruitless stalkings of a Supreme Court judge, an official of the Colorado Fuel and Iron Company, and Governor Peabody. During the course of these activities a booby trap laid in a vacant lot for Judge Gabbert caught, instead, an inoffensive citizen, Merrit W. Walley, and blew him to bits, to the great mystification of the neighborhood.

According to Orchard's story, Moyer and Haywood now sent him to Boise, Idaho, to kill ex-Governor Steunenberg, still hated by the Federation and by Orchard for the Coeur d'Alene affair. The assassin hooked one of his favorite devices to Steunenberg's gate, ran down the street, heard a boom, and said to himself, "There he goes!" Back in his hotel, he put a vial containing a few drops of sulphuric acid into his coat pocket. This careless move exploded a forgotten detonator cap in the pocket and so rattled Orchard that he neglected to cover bits of incriminating evidence. Soon he found himself under arrest.

In jail Orchard "got religion," so he says, and to James McPartland of the Pinkerton Detective Agency dictated a full confession, implicating Moyer, Haywood, and a stanch union sympathizer named George Pettibone in the Steunenberg murder. Back in Denver this trio fought extradition but were forcibly kidnaped and taken to Boise for trial. The United States Supreme Court admitted the illegality of the kidnaping but said that since the men were now in Idaho they could be tried without the court's inquiring into how they reached that jurisdiction!

The case was a national sensation. President Theodore Roosevelt publicly branded the union officials as "undesirable citizens," while the Socialist party nominated Haywood for governor of Colorado.[1] A rising young prosecutor named William Borah conducted the trial for the state of Idaho. Opposing him in the first of their titanic legal battles was Clarence Darrow.

Haywood was tried first. There is no need to follow the complex pyrotechnics of the case. Crux of the matter was Orchard's "confession," upon which Borah depended for conviction. Darrow's attack was to make Orchard look like a complete liar and thus discredit his unsupported statement that the Federation officials had hired him to kill Steunenberg. The defense lawyer succeeded. He made Orchard's "religion" look like a private dispensation from the Pinkerton Agency's McPartland; as a motive for murder he brought forth Orchard's loss of the Hercules Mine. Haywood was acquitted; so was Pettibone in a later trial, and the case against Moyer was then dismissed.

All through the mining states labor pranced in jubilation; at Park City, Utah, 650 silver miners paraded the streets under a huge banner reading "Undesirable Citizens." Triumphantly Moyer and Haywood went East, where they had been instrumental in founding the notorious Industrial Workers of the World. Haywood in particular was an evil genie in the IWW's long series of bloody strikes. When the Russian Revolution broke out he scurried to Moscow to give the Bolsheviks the benefit of his experience in planned terrorism. But perhaps they decided they could do without him. At least he has never been heard of since.

As a reward for turning state's evidence, Orchard was granted life imprisonment instead of execution for the Steunenberg murder. How many other deaths rest at his door? Did he tell the truth about the Independence depot and all the rest? Or was he a capitalists' tool, trying to swear away by infamous perjury the lives of the Federation leaders? Darrow privately admitted to Ben Rastall, who has made the most thorough investigation of the Cripple Creek strikes, "I don't know. Nobody knows. Probably no one ever will know."

Cripple Creek's golden incubator hatched far more than blood or currency inflation; and at least one of its foster children, the Utah

---

[1] From the Boise prison Haywood wired the convention: "While sitting with my lately widowed, gray-haired mother, in the shadow of this jail, surrounded by guards, I received your message. . . . After a brief reflection on the duties of a member of the party, I said to Mother, 'I will accept the nomination.' The maternal love in her eyes was partly veiled with a mist gathered from the lake of tears, while, like a benediction, she spoke these words: 'It is well, my son.' Thus your notification was received and accepted."

Copper Company, grew into a lustier rooster than even its loud-crowing stepparent.

Like the rest of Utah's lead-and-silver camps, Bingham Canyon, south of the Great Salt Lake, had been flattened by the panic of '93. The tottering frame houses sagged dispiritedly along the slope-girt streets. Rheumy-eyed old-timers, dreaming of precious metals no longer precious, had only wan smiles of derision for Colonel Enos Wall's strange notions that Bingham's low-grade copper ores could be turned into a profit. Wall, however, piddled along, relocating abandoned claims and finally importing two young engineers named Gemmell and Jackling to wrestle with his apparently unconquerable technical problems.

In 1899, Gemmell and Jackling issued a report that was destined to revolutionize mining throughout the world, although at the time the august *Engineering and Mining Journal* gently tut-tutted the whole business and warned investors to beware of "Jackling's Wildcat." This was an unpropitious start. Jackling's scheme (by now he had bought into the infant copper company) depended on prodigious amounts of heavy equipment, which in turn required extensive financing. No one would listen until finally he approached flamboyant Spencer Penrose and Charles MacNeil in Colorado Springs.

These two men had already dipped joyously into the flood of Cripple Creek gold washing through their smelters at Colorado City and were not averse to wading even deeper. In 1903 they gave Jackling the backing he needed. The result was the Utah Copper Company, the Rocky Mountain area's most potent single industrial asset.

During the past forty-five years more than six billion pounds of copper have been gouged from Bingham's eye-staggering open-cut pits. Mere gold, silver, and molybdenum, mined in princely quantities, are regarded as by-products, and the total value of its yield approaches a billion and a half dollars—double the output of Leadville and Cripple Creek combined! So perhaps gold and silver were not the *sine qua non* of the mining frontier. Indeed, down in New Mexico, where the fable of precious metals first began, copper (save for periodic slumps) is about the only non-ferrous mineral that amounts to a hill of beans, and it is a rare year when either gold or silver production touches a paltry million dollars. Copper, too, occasioned Wyoming's only real, though short-lived, mining boom, when in the early 1900s the Encampment fields in the Sierra Madre Mountains briefly accounted for more traffic on the Union Pacific Railroad than did any other source. And coal, of course, tops even copper. But coal, in the popular mind, is neither a

typical Rocky Mountain mineral nor shot with the glamour of its
brighter rivals—though it has stirred up some dime-novel brews of its
own: the Ludlow "massacre" in Colorado, for instance, and Chinese
race riots at Rock Springs, Wyoming.

At times various rare metals have shouldered into prominence—
tungsten, which spiraled dizzily during World War I, only to fall flat
on its face under pressure of Chinese competition; and radium, which
suffered a similar collapse with the discovery of pitchblende deposits
in the Belgian Congo. At that period radium (worth something like
150,000 times as much as gold) was laboriously refined from the
uranium oxides present in western Colorado's carnotite ore, a soft yellow substance Indians had used for face paint and cowboys for
scribbling their names on cliffs. Later, during World War II, uranium
was discovered to have other potentialities and the workings were
feverishly revitalized, although at the time the heavily guarded miners
had no idea of the world-wide dismay they would help precipitate at
Hiroshima.

The same war zoomed another rare-metal workings into Colorado's
hugest mine. This was Climax Molybdenum, its great white dump,
tangled trestles, cavernous mills, and sweeping rows of workers' houses
sprawled 11,300 feet high squarely on top of the Continental Divide
at Fremont Pass, sixteen miles from Leadville. Here is a Cinderella
story even more glittering than Utah Copper's. Long years ago miners
found those ores and thought, from their grayish appearance, that they
might contain low-grade lead. Indifferent, they passed on. But finally
the true identity of the mineral was determined, and a small group of
men began fiddling with the old prospects. It was a shoestring struggle.
Time and again they lost heart—and almost lost their holdings. Among
other things, they had to set up experimental laboratories and devise not
only methods for refining but even for using their product. Eventually
special steel alloys were developed. Business flourished during World
War I but slacked off so much after the armistice that the mine closed,
then caught on again; and by World War II Climax was ready to break
production records nearly every month. It is a wondrous monopoly.
Bartlett Mountain, at whose fat flanks the mine chews happily away,
contains more than two thirds of the world's known supply of the
metal. Had you been able to buy some of the original Climax stock
(which you could not have, the corporation being jealously sealed),
you would already have realized a profit of more than 116,000 per
cent on your investment! A nice figure. People reading it often become
starry-eyed over the possibilities of mining ventures; and by judicious

references to this and similar dividend miracles, promoters of worthless holes in the ground annually dupe thousands of otherwise rational citizens.

Meanwhile silver and gold have gone their own erratic ways. During the doldrums of the 1930s Franklin Roosevelt arbitrarily upped the value of gold by two thirds, silver received a corresponding shot in the arm, and a minor boom was on, not so much in the development of new properties as in the reworking of old ones. If these mines happened also to contain lead and zinc, they were lucky, because during the war such armament-necessary metals brought to the operators priorities for machinery and labor. Gold and silver which were unavoidably dug out at the same time were retained as incidental by-products.

Straight gold mines, however, fared ill. Gold tips no bullets, sheathes no tanks. At once-mighty Cripple Creek, where a huge tunnel was being dug to unwater the old shafts, a WPB order on October 15, 1942, closed the workings tight. Hopelessly the local newspaper intoned, "We, the 3000 people of the Cripple Creek district who are about to die, salute the bureaucrats who have seen fit to annihilate us." Miners broke all precedents by working the last Sunday allowed to blast loose every possible pound of ore. Grudgingly the WPB granted a sixty-day cleanup period. And then the stillness which miners hate beyond all else settled dismally over the barren hills.

Now the war is over. But labor and material costs have skyrocketed, while the price of gold stays fixed. Except for the footsteps of tourists, very few echoes sound among Cripple Creek's ragged bones. But, faint though the echoes are, old-timers listen with a smile. Hear that? There's still life. Many things—bloodshed, hatred, fire, pinched veins, flooded tunnels, the insane gyrations of a manipulated national economy—many things have staggered the camp. But nothing ever quite killed it in the past; nothing will now. So they say, a high, bright flush in their wasted cheeks. And maybe they are right.

CHAPTER XII

MOO!

EVEN before Cortez had finished subjugating Mexico in 1521, along came Gregorio de Villalobos with a boatload of sharp-horned Andalusian cattle. It was inevitable. Every colonist necessarily has his cow; and although the Spanish ravaged mercilessly with one hand, they tried with equal industry to create with the other. Northward went the padres with their cattle, on the theory that the animals would help Christianize the Indians. But the favorable climate beyond the lower Rio Grande carried the experiment out of bounds. Southern Texas soon swarmed with long-legged, snake-lean, massive-horned creatures that no stretch of the imagination could call domestic.

At the tip of the Rockies a comparable spawning was checked by New Mexico's more rugged terrain and more biting winters. In fact, Oñate's colonists and their descendants preferred sheep and goats to cattle, a predilection still discernible among the Southwest's Spanish Americans and Indians. Nonetheless, numerous longhorns existed, tended by herders as unkempt and unlovely as their charges. These solitary, leather-clad men lived summer and winter in lean-to huts that were nothing more than a sloping surface covered by cowhide, with open sides and a small fire burning in front when weather was bad. For food the herders depended on mush and on game they hunted with bows and arrows. True cowboys, they never walked but were always astride wicked mustang ponies coveted by the lurking Indians; and although they wore no shoes, they somehow strapped enormous spurs to their callused heels. Except possibly for the *vaqueros* of Spanish California, the world has seen no other group of riders so dexterous with the ropes they called *lazos*.

It was these New Mexicans and not Texans who furnished enterprising Americans with cattle for the first great trail herds. Destination of the drives was the California gold fields. The way led, with variations, out of Taos into Colorado, over Cochetopa Pass, north through Brown's Hole to the Overland Trail in southwestern Wyoming, and along this to the Sacramento. In general the route had been blazed and was principally used by sheep, whose herders were such illustrious men as Uncle Dick Wootton, Kit Carson, Lucien Maxwell, and Francis Xavier Aubry, a bull-strong Santa Fe trader who in 1853 rode a relay of horses from Santa Fe to Independence, Missouri, in five days and thirteen hours, thus planting in the minds of Senator Gwinn of California and a superintendent of Russell, Majors & Waddell the notion that later grew into the pony express.

One wonders why cattle should have been taken to California at all. The coast region was so full of the animals that in the 1830s hides and tallow alone had value, and then only when Yankee ships from shoe-making New England sailed around the Horn to dicker. However, in 1853 McClanahan and Ross went overland with several hundred cattle and two thousand sheep. At approximately the same time W. H. Snyder and W. A. Peril set forth with straight cattle on an almost unrecorded journey that ate up two years and a wintering at Brown's Hole, in northern Colorado, long before subsequent "pioneer" mountain ranchers would dare risk so dangerous an experiment with the weather. Mormons, too, drove westward the cattle which they raised, among other places, on islands in the Great Salt Lake.

The New Mexicans themselves were less venturesome, but their fly-by-night traders did take cattle to the disreputable posts they maintained around the toes of the Rockies. One such "fort" was the unsavory Pueblo on the Arkansas, which Indian Agent Tom Fitzpatrick scowled on as "the resort of all idlers and loafers . . . depot for the smuggling of liquor," and which Francis Parkman described as "a wretched species of fort . . . miserably cracked and dilapidated." Yet both men mentioned with relish the fact that the dingy spot possessed a vegetable garden as well as "a tolerable supply of cattle, horses, and mules."

These cattle Uncle Dick Wootton found useful, in the early 1840s, for another of his long list of ingenious commercial ventures. Having captured forty-four buffalo calves, the burly mountain man took them to the Pueblo and with consummate chicanery foisted them off on as many reluctant cows. Even after reaching adulthood, the ponderous beasts continued grazing with the post's animals, and Uncle Dick had only to show them to a popeyed visitor to sell them at a handsome price. Delivery presented no problem. Uncle Dick simply threw the bison in with a few domestic cattle and drove the bizarre herd seven hundred miles across the plains to Kansas City, where their purchaser consigned them to divers showmen and "zoological gardens."[1]

---

[1] The story, told by Wootton to one of his credulous biographers, has been doubted. But it could have happened. Many a pioneer Frankenstein tamed a buffalo calf, then wondered what to do with his shaggy monster. When the Abner Lumans, parents of my aunt's husband, were married, one of their wedding gifts was a pair of buffalo. Nonplused by this prodigality, even in the boundless Green

When Americans began to penetrate the mountains, they, too, drove cattle with them—a better grade of stock, in general, than the Mexicans possessed. Before the 1830s were well under way Bill Sublette and Robert Campbell had hazed stock west across South Pass and north to Yellowstone River. In '43 Frémont jotted in his diary that Lancaster Lupton's Colorado trading post "was beginning to assume the appearance of a comfortable farm: stock, horses, and cattle were ranging about on the plains." Bent's Fort was comparable. Indeed, its pastoral qualities so impressed Chief Yellow Wolf of the Cheyennes that in 1846 he proposed, without success, to instruct the Indians in cultivating ground and raising cattle, so that the Cheyennes need not pass away with the buffalo. By 1852 Seth Ward, partner of fur-trading Robert Campbell and post sutler at Wyoming's Fort Laramie, was wintering his work oxen on the Chugwater with such success that soon herders for Russell, Majors and Waddell began to duplicate the money-saving feat. And in 1859 indefatigable Horace Greeley, when passing through Fort Bridger, noted "several old mountaineers who have herds of cattle which they were rapidly increasing by a lucrative traffic with the emigrants, who are compelled to exchange their tired, gaunt oxen and steers for fresh ones on almost any terms. . . . J. R. [probably mountain man Jack Robertson] . . . has quietly accumulated some fifty horses, three or four hundred head of neat cattle . . . and is said to be worth $75,000."

In short, the Great American Desert was no desert at all. Thousands of men—Kearny's Army of the West, driving its own beef herd into New Mexico; farmers plodding to Oregon, to California, to Utah—saw with amazement how avidly their animals gobbled this seared-looking vegetation which did not break down under freezing but cured on the stalk as nutritiously as Midwestern hay. But what good was all that green-brown gold? Livestock markets were microscopic, and the tide of emigration rolled on with no presentiment of the changes which during the next two decades would send the frontier hurtling hundreds of miles beyond the Missouri to embrace an industry worth hundreds of millions of dollars.

Two principal factors—Texas and the railroads—are rightly credited with being the Aladdin's lamp which produced this transformation. In fact, a few Texans beat the railroads to the mountains by several years. Who was first is uncertain. Perhaps it was John Dawson, who is sup-

River country of Wyoming, the newlyweds shipped the beasts to San Francisco's Golden Gate Zoo, where they became the foundation stock of that organization's bison herd.

posed to have rushed a herd northward in '59, when hungry argonauts were scuttling toward Pikes Peak. Certainly Oliver Loving, a significant name to mountain ranching, was in the vicinity of Pueblo in 1860, peddling his trail-gaunt longhorns in small batches to local butchers and settlers. But the Civil War stopped the experiment in a hurry, and the Rockies were compelled to obtain beefsteak from other sources.

Freighters brought the first surplus livestock to the Big Divide and incidentally created a myth which apparently cannot be downed. Late in the fall of 1858 enterprising "Colonel" Jack Henderson braved the early blizzards of the plains to haul a badly needed load of supplies to the Cherry Creek settlements. Unable to shelter or sell his oxen, he turned them loose to die. They did not. While hunting buffalo the next spring Henderson discovered the creatures in better flesh than before, drove them back to Denver, and buttonholed the stampeders with his revolutionary news about grazing possibilities near the mountains. The belated "discovery" would have drawn a yawn from cow-raising fur traders, but legend persists in ascribing the Rocky Mountain livestock industry to Henderson. (Or to some other freighter; the same yarn, with different heroes, is current throughout Colorado and Wyoming.)

At first the gold rushers were not interested in gold on the hoof. But after other freighters had had experiences similar to Henderson's and after nuggets had proved unexpectedly hard to find, a few of the boys reconsidered. One was John Iliff, who drifted disconsolately up to the Oregon Trail and there laid the foundation for a million-dollar fortune by purchasing discarded oxen from cross-country emigrants, fattening them, and selling them to L. Butterick's Denver abattoir for five and a half cents a pound live weight. Another was Sam Hartsel, who threw away his unprofitable shovel and spent the last of his savings buying footsore dray stock from his South Park neighbors for ten to twenty dollars a head. After herding the creatures through the hills for a time he passed them on to a butcher in the now vanished town of Hamilton for one hundred dollars each.

Fortunately, Hartsel's vision reached beyond immediate profits. Realizing that the market for anybody's tough old work ox could not stay strong forever, he went to Clay County, Missouri, and bought 148 high-grade shorthorn cows and several registered bulls. Businesslike ranching was at last on its way to the Rockies, but it took a while to get there. Indian uprisings kept Sam Hartsel fidgeting nervously along the Santa Fe Trail for two years before he could push his historic herd onto the high, lush plains of South Park.

Meanwhile the Civil War had ended. In Texas poverty-stricken ranchers eyed their worthless longhorns and pictured the markets in the North. The resultant surge to the shipping towns along the westward-pushing railroads is a story of the plains, not of the mountains. There were, however, a few rugged individualists who disdained the common trails for the high country beyond track's end.

Nelson Story was one. He had wandered into Denver as a freighter, then in 1863 had joined the stampede to Alder Gulch, Montana. There he prospered, digging out thirty thousand dollars' worth of dust. But as he shoveled, Story noticed something more permanent than placer bars—fine grass. Early in '66 he sewed ten thousand dollars in greenbacks in his clothes, told his partners Bill Petty and Tom Allen to hit the saddle, and rode south to Fort Worth. His eye on the future, he purchased not steers but a thousand cows with their calves thrown in. Twenty-seven men strong, the drive started north.

It was a hard-luck trip. By the time the saddle-sore cowboys reached Wyoming's Bozeman Trail and saw the cool peaks of the Big Horns ahead, frost was in the air. And Red Cloud's Sioux were spoiling for trouble. Story was warned to turn back. Instead, he armed his men with brand-new rapid-fire rifles and pushed brazenly on. Up at Fort Phil Kearney, Colonel Carrington hit the roof. No fool cattle drover was going to start an uprising in *his* bailiwick. Out clattered troopers with orders to bring the herd to the fort and keep it there.

For three weeks Nelson Story glared at the November skies and pictured the blizzards that were on the way. Finally he gained permission to move the herd to new grazing grounds on the other side of the fort. When darkness fell he kept right on going. Twice, during succeeding days, Indians struck. Twice the cowboys fought them off, losing only one man and very few cattle in the desperate running battles which cost the lives of thirty Indians. On December 9 the herd limped triumphantly into Virginia City, Montana. A few days later Red Cloud wiped out every man of Colonel Fetterman's command in the Big Horns, and not for four more bloody years would another Texas longhorn reach Montana.

About the same time Story started his epic drive Charles Goodnight learned that government buyers at Fort Sumner in eastern New Mexico were crying for beef to feed the Navajos whom Kit Carson had broken at Cañon de Chelly and had exiled to Bosque Redondo. This Goodnight, six feet tall and weighing an iron-muscled 225 pounds, was a pariah in Texas. He had fought with the North, his clipped beard gave him an unpleasant resemblance to General Grant, and his disgruntled

Rebel neighbors figured it was quite ethical to steal him blind. To salvage what he could, Goodnight decided to risk his cattle on the Horsehead Trail across the Staked Plains to the Pecos River in New Mexico, a dreadful route short on water and long on Comanches. Building the West's first chuck wagon, an ark so ponderous ten oxen strained to pull it over the broken land, and recruiting the assistance of the veteran Oliver Loving, Goodnight pointed toward the mountains with a motley bunch of steers, cows, and calves.

The partners were lucky. They parched themselves, their men, and their frantic animals almost beyond endurance, but they met no Indians. And at Fort Sumner they sold most of their herd for the unparalleled price of eight cents a pound live weight, all paid in mellow gold coin.

Remembering the hungry miners in the Colorado foothills, Loving drove the Army-rejected culls over Raton Pass (where, to the outrage of his free Texas soul, he had to pay Uncle Dick Wootton a ten-cent toll on every creature) and in unfastidious Denver found a market for his long-suffering beef. Meanwhile Goodnight rushed back to Texas for another herd, driving ahead of him a pack train loaded with government gold. Along the way several of the mules stampeded, and Goodnight had to ride like a fiend to corral six thousand dollars' worth of vanishing profits. But he made it, rounded up more cattle, and pushed them across the Horsehead in a month. This time he was paid in silver, including sackfuls of dimes and quarters so bulky that he had to haul them home in a wagon.

Fortune like that could not last. The next year, in the spring of 1867, the partners, in company with a one-armed cowman named Bill Wilson, were hit hard by Comanches, who made off with thirteen hundred precious head. When at last the remnants of the herd gained the Pecos, Loving and Wilson were sent racing ahead to Fort Sumner for the awarding of the beef contracts. Indians ambushed them. Though their horses were killed, the two managed to crawl to temporary safety among thick cane brakes along the sandy river. Loving, shot twice, was nearly unconscious. Leaving him alone, one-armed Bill Wilson floated past the waiting Comanches by night on a raft of weeds and trudged nearly a hundred miles to where Goodnight and his men were following with the slow-moving cattle.

Immediately a rescue party set forth, but Loving was not to be found. Somehow, living without food for a solid week, he dragged his wounded body past Comanche scouts to a traveled trail where Mexicans picked him up and carried him to Fort Sumner. When the distraught Goodnight arrived he managed to get on his feet, but blood poisoning did what the Comanches could not, and a few days later Oliver Loving was dead.

Following the trail his partner had blazed into Colorado, Goodnight began pushing successive trail herds along the base of the Rockies, avoiding Wootton's all-embracing toll gate by forging a new crossing of the mountains north of Raton. Among the purchasers of his wares was John Iliff, who in 1868 paid forty-five thousand dollars for a herd he drove on to Cheyenne and fed to construction workers of the Union Pacific, the first Texas longhorns to reach trail's end in Wyoming. Using profits from the Iliff and other sales, Goodnight established a couple of ranches near Trinidad, Colorado, and settled down to what looked like a prosperous career. But rustlers and the panic of '73 broke him. Destitute, he moved into the uninhabited wilderness of the Staked Plains and there in lonely Palo Duro Canyon wrested from the Indians and the buffalo his world-famous JA Ranch.

Pioneer Coloradoans looked askance at these Texans. Thanks to men like Sam Hartsel, they had a flourishing little livestock industry of their own. They did not want their ranges overgrazed, nor their blooded Durham and shorthorn cattle polluted by these ugly, fever-bearing longhorns. Accordingly the Colorado legislature in 1867 thundered, "It shall be unlawful for any person or persons to import . . . any bull, cow, ox, steer or cattle of whatever description known as 'Texas cattle' for the purpose of small stock raising, growing, herding, feeding, or for any purpose whatsoever."

Never did so sweeping an edict prove so futile. There was money to be made in "Texas cattle," and the foothill ranchers who wanted them excluded had personally to give the law what few teeth it possessed. One night in 1869, for example, riders attacked a Texas herd, killed four animals, wounded thirty more, and stampeded the rest. Useless violence. The Union Pacific had already crossed Wyoming, in 1870 the Kansas Pacific pounded into Denver, and soon the Santa Fe would burst across the Colorado line on its way to New Mexico. In Chicago, Philip Armour and Gustavus Swift were revolutionizing the meat-packing industry, and before long refrigeration would open the markets of Europe. "Send us meat!" In the face of that insatiable cry Colorado's feeble little exclusion law expired unmourned. Later, when competition and dwindling grass supplies forced ranchers to improve and protect their herds, it would be reborn throughout the West in a flurry of quarantine measures. But by that time the longhorns had shown the way to new fields of gold and could retire with honor.

So picturesque were the Texas cowboys and so firmly has their lore become rooted in the nation's consciousness that Oregon's share in stocking the mountain states has largely been forgotten. It was a strange close to a long circle. During the 1840s a steady trickle of Durhams and shorthorns had limped across South Pass to the new farms of the Northwest. There they had multiplied far beyond the ability of local markets to absorb them, and now, thirty years later, their descendants limped back across the same pass by the hundreds of thousands.

At first the Oregonians made the eastward drive primarily to reach railroad connections with Eastern slaughterhouses. The closest loading point, of course, was the Union Pacific in Utah, but by grazing the animals across southern Wyoming and into western Nebraska, the ranchers lessened both freight bills and the serious shrinkage involved in a longer haul. So over South Pass they came, and along the way they found their herds making a profound impression on embryo mountain ranchers. The chunky Oregon steers obviously furnished more and better beef per animal than did the gaunt longhorns. Moreover, they spread no fever. Only one thing stood in the way of spreading them across Wyoming's grassy hills—the Sioux Indians. When these were crushed after the Custer massacre, the rush for Oregon cattle as foundation stock was on.

Every spring during the late seventies and early eighties, scores of Wyoming ranchers and their men boarded the train at Cheyenne and rode to Kelton, Utah. This was the jumping-off place for the Northwest—a raw, dismal town largely built of railroad ties and jammed with freighters, wagons, and bewildered emigrants. The stage trip from Kelton to Baker, Oregon, was hell on wheels: scorched sagebrush and lava beds, the petrified passengers equipped by the stage company, according to the weather, with slickers, buffalo robes, or long linen dusters. But the goal at the end was enough to hoist a cowman happily back into his saddle: fat Oregon cattle and husky Oregon horses which could be resold profitably to buyers for the street-railway companies in Eastern cities.

Except that the cattle were, on the average, more tractable than longhorns, the drives were much like those from Texas—grueling hours, eye-searing dust, choking stretches without water, and numbing monotony broken now and then by a stampede or a brush with renegade Indians. For lead steers the outfits used work oxen discarded by the freight companies. These gentle creatures could be caught with salt, haltered, and dragged through roaring stream fords as an inspiration to the more timorous range cattle behind them. Newborn calves were a nuisance. Sometimes an effort was made to haul them in a wagon, but they seldom survived and it was more expedient to kill them at once. Since the bereaved mother tried to go back to the spot where last she had seen her offspring, she had to be restrained by neck-yoking her to another animal who would drag her willy-nilly along with the herd.

The Lander Cutoff was the popular route. Lying north of the old Oregon Trail, this shorter but rougher road had been built during the "Mormon War" so that emigrants could avoid chance conflicts with the angry Saints in northern Utah. At the western edge of Wyoming the cutoff dropped into a timber-bordered, grassy-bottomed mountain valley that looked like heaven after the bleak wastes of southern Idaho. Years before, on seeing its teeming game and icy, trout-filled streams, its Mormon locators had described it as the star of all valleys. And so it had got its name—Star Valley—though the first half-frozen colonists had briefly added a cynical syllable to make it Starved Valley. The Edmonds Anti-Polygamy Act of 1882 helped fill it up, because Wyoming, wanting population enough to become a state, would not aid Federal authorities in enforcing the law. When zealous Idaho process servers went after polygamists in Star Valley's borderline towns of Alpine and Freedom, the Mormons simply stepped across the street to Wyoming and impunity. Economically, too, the earliest Saints found a windfall—great deposits of pure salt which they dug up and sold in Idaho and Montana mining camps for as much as sixty cents a pound.

After a delicious rest in Star Valley the Oregon herds pushed on over South Pass and down the well-worn trails beside Sweetwater Creek, already a famous ranching section. There the rope raveled out, some strands going into Colorado, some into the Dakotas, some into the Big Horns, where they met other Oregon herds that had come through Montana and had swung south along the Bozeman Trail. Thus from all sides the numberless herds rushed in to fill the vacuum left by Indians and bison.

Like another vacuum filler, the thunderclap, the result was uproarious, involving the cattlemen in bloody vendettas with thieves and Indians, with sheepmen and farmers, with each other, even with state and Federal law. Echoes of the complicated struggles, most of which arose from the need for elbow room on acres once deemed overabundant, still reverberate in the nation's press and legislative halls; and it is difficult, considering the stock raisers' relatively small numbers, to name another group around whose pummeled but unbowed head so much controversy has raged for so long.

Unchecked rustling first forced the cattlemen to consolidate their power. Rancher preyed on rancher, foremen on their bosses, freelancers on everyone. Operations were as grandiose or as petty as human nature. With the advent of the railroads (and before systematic inspection had begun) whole trainloads were stolen and shipped to the East before the owner suspected his loss. At other times a single calf was enough to supply a temporary need. Up on Wyoming's Sweetwater Creek, Jim Averill and Ella Watson, better known as Cattle Kate, built a roadhouse near their impoverished homesteads. Here cowboys could obtain drinks from Jim and more intimate favors from Ella in return for an animal or two. When the homesteads began running more cattle than their foundation stock could account for, suspicious ranchers ordered the pair to move. They refused, and one dark night they were lynched. Although six men were investigated in connection with the incident, no one was tried.

Most vicious of the rancher-versus-rancher feuds was New Mexico's involved Lincoln County War, which turned the police and political functions of the entire territory upside down and spawned the coldest little killer ever to be overglamorized in folklore—Billy the Kid. One offshoot of the unhappy fracas was the Stockton-Eskridge gang, who typify the grubby sort of outlawry that at various times terrified the mountain hamlets. After fleeing from New Mexico, the Stockton-Eskridge boys established themselves at the infant railroad town of Durango in southern Colorado. Here they capped a career of general rowdiness by crashing a dance across the line at Farmington, New Mexico, and killing an inoffensive cowboy named George Brown. The upshot, after considerable sound and fury, was a retaliatory raid by Farmington cowboys and a wild gun battle in the center of town, during the course of which a frightened Durango baker stuffed his children in a brick oven for safekeeping and the grand opening of the West End Hotel was precipitously postponed. Enough was enough. The local Committee of Safety, which had just cut its teeth by lynching a barroom killer named Moorman, rose in wrath and persuaded Stockton, Eskridge, and company to move elsewhere.

Not all communities were so self-reliant. In that same year of 1881 the sheriff of Conejos County, east across the divide from Durango, wired in despair to Colorado's Governor Pitkin, "The county is powerless against armed desperadoes." Not until the state stepped in with a one-thousand-dollar reward and a shipment of arms for extra deputies was the situation brought under uneasy control.

Long before this the stockmen had banded together for mutual protection. Quickly their local groups were knit into state-wide federations; the Colorado Stockgrowers Association, started in 1867, was reorganized in 1871, the same year that saw the founding of a similar body in Wyoming. Although both groups hired private detectives who were not averse to shooting rustlers in the best style of wild-West fiction, their main efforts were devoted to a legislative plugging of the holes through which thieves operated. Brands, sanctified as private property, were systematically recorded with state officials. No man was allowed to use a mark even vaguely similar to his neighbor's, an obvious deterrent to easy, across-the-fence alterations. However, no brand has yet been devised which some light-fingered artist could not rework—or at least try to rework.

As a further check on alterations, the associations stationed brand inspectors at all major shipping and receiving points, even as far away as Kansas City, Chicago, and St. Paul. These sharp-eyed individuals developed an uncanny ability of spotting tampered brands. In cases of doubt they clipped the hair off a suspected creature for a better look at its hide, or even killed and skinned it, since fresh burns show up more strongly on the underside than do old ones. If discrepancies were found, the shipper had to explain in a hurry.

It was one of these gimlet-visioned inspectors who in 1919 looked with suspicion on thirty-two head of cattle which Anna Richey, "thirty and purty," drove by herself to the Union Pacific's loading pens and shipped as her very own. Vaunted Western chivalry did not extend to thievery. Anna Richey, respected daughter of a cattleman and widow of a Kemmerer, Wyoming, schoolteacher, was icily accused of rustling. On her way to be tried she was ambushed and shot, for fear, local folk whispered, that she might talk too much. Recovering, she was sentenced to six years in prison, the only woman in Wyoming to be convicted legally of rustling. But she never served the sentence. Released on bond to wind up her affairs, she died under mysterious circumstances. Poison at the hands of whoever feared her tongue was suspected but never proved.

The establishment of roundup districts which were worked on specified dates and along specified routes was another bar to rustling. Roundup foremen were hired and paid not by the participating ranchers but by county commissioners, state auditors, or association treasurers, as the law might provide. Mavericks (grown cattle without brands) were sold by the foreman at auction and the money turned by him to a designated repository—the county school fund in Colorado, after 1901. No man, however honest, could go onto the open range, gather cattle, and "gin them around" at his own will. If he did he was instantly suspect; even ranchers working their own land generally found it wise to send advance notice or their intention throughout the neighborhood.

Various other restrictions were imposed on the freedom-jealous cattle barons, but measure piled on measure never proved sufficient. To-day's rustler plies his trade in mobile butchershops hidden in trucks, kills by guns equipped with silencers, and vanishes on trackless rubber wheels. So serious did his depredations become that Congress in 1941 made interstate stock thievery a Federal offense, but high prices attendant on wartime meat shortages boomed the illegal trade as never before.

The fight against rustlers gave the stockmen a cohesion unknown among other Western settlers. Quite naturally the associations used this power for political ends, often to set their own houses in order. Legislatures were prevailed upon to pass all sorts of regulatory measures: quarantine laws, rules for the condemnation of diseased cattle, regulations concerning the number and quality of bulls that could be turned onto the open range. State bounties for predatory animals were instituted (though Governor Grant of Colorado grumped, "The state is under no more obligation to protect the herdsman's flocks from wolves and lions than it is to pump water from silver and lead mines"), and rewards were paid for grubbing out locoweed, until it was discovered that farmers were raising the stuff and netting more in bounties than they could from a comparable acreage of potatoes. Railroads felt the heavy hand in a law that made them responsible for every animal killed by a train. The number was considerable—2242 head in Colorado in the depression year of 1886, leading to suspicions that some ranchers deliberately drove poor stock onto the tracks. But poor-stock prices were never paid. It was amazing, one official sighed, how "a Texas cow crossed with a locomotive invariably produced a thoroughbred," and soon the railroads found it cheaper to fence every mile of their right of ways.

But woe to the outsider who tried to regulate cattle. In April 1874, the Denver *Mirror* complained bitterly, "That a city of 20,000 inhabitants should permit bovines to straggle about its streets at all times of day or night, to frighten timid pedestrians, impede traffic, scare horses, and occasionally indulge in the diversion of tossing a small boy or a purblind old lady into the air—is one of those strange anomalies it is impossible to apologize for." The Denver council, however, seemed to feel no need for apology; blandly it voted down an ordinance that would have restrained the straggling bovines. Its progressive neighbor, Greeley, did have a pound law, but violators were fined a mere ten cents and costs. Alamosa, in the San Luis Valley, was completely re- signed: noting that cattle were killing young trees in the residential section, the paper advised irate property owners to plant larger, hardier shoots. And in Wyoming in 1884 the territorial legislature made the Stockgrowers Association a quasi-governmental arm by handing over to it the enforcement of all laws dealing with the cattle business!

The wielders of this enormous power were no pampered plutocrats. Though their brief sojourns in Denver or at the ornate Cheyenne Club were cushioned in luxury, life on the range was hard. The first ranch houses were seldom more than dugouts roofed with earth, their doors consisting of hides stretched on pole frames. The presence of a woman (many a matrimonial-agency bride and many a soiled dove from the railroad towns made loyal mates for the early cowmen) perhaps re- sulted in a log cabin or in a shanty of raw yellow lumber hauled scores of miles from the nearest sawmill, but fancy trimmings were eschewed in favor of such necessities as barns, tool sheds, smithies, corrals, and the like. During the flush times of the eighties a few resplendent man- sions began to appear, but these in the main were the playthings of foreign investors.

Injury from a falling horse or charging cow was a daily expecta- tion. The confining of Indians to reservations by no means ended danger from that source—partly because, in the early days, they re- fused to stay confined. Sometimes they went through the formality of obtaining government permission to cross the lines for grazing their horses or for hunting. Sometimes they just went. In neither case were they prone to conduct themselves as visitors at suffrance on the land which once had been theirs. In 1882, when cowboys asked a large group of them to move their tepees off grazing grounds along Buffalo Creek in western Wyoming, and then aggravated the insult by defeat- ing the Indians in a horse race, the red men gave vent to their spleen in characteristic fashion. "They took willows," Norris Griggs, one of the cowboys, recalls, "set them afire, and riding their horses, they dragged the burning willows back and forth through the deep grass until they had set the whole country afire. It burned to Green River, and in places it burned over the [Hoback] Rim," toward Jackson Hole. It burned for a week, destroying tens of thousands of acres of feed, and "this was Indian vengeance."

In northwestern Colorado fat old Colorow's wandering Utes became so unruly that a combined force of government troops and cattlemen met them in outright battle, killed several, and herded the rest under military escort back to their Uinta reservation. Southward, in San Juan County, an unrecorded number of cowboys died in various hit-and-run battles with the Southern Utes, a livestock company sued the Federal Government for $68,000 damages caused by its restless wards, and the Durango *Idea* bleated, "There must be bloodshed!"—to which the Ouray *Solid Muldoon* added an angry P.S.: "Shoot low!"[2]

Meanwhile Eastern and foreign capital had discovered the livestock industry. It was Romance with a capital *R*—adventure and sport while making a fortune without effort. To the mountains flocked staid Scottish and British capitalists, the younger sons of titled nobility, and job lots of Eastern collegians to whom a working vacation on a Colorado or Wyoming ranch was a social must.

Enormous swindles were perpetrated. Government land was sold as a part of a ranch's "holdings," and cattle were transferred on the basis of a foreman's "book count," which all too often bore scant relationship to the number of steers actually on the range. Some property was even paid for and the promoter gone before the purchaser bought a land map and began a frantic hunt for a ranch which had never existed. And those new owners who did come into possession often had not the foggiest notion how to run their playthings. Ranch houses, particularly in Wyoming, were used mainly as hunting lodges, and foremen were frequently selected from the ranks of the owner's impecunious friends. Practical ranching suffered. One Scottish foreman, his sensibilities wounded by the unaesthetic practice of branding, undertook to mark his animals with paint, but had to report in chagrin to his employer that the paint was "not sufficiently adhesive or permanent." All Wyoming laughed, but some of these imported foremen, like Scotsmen John Clay and Murdo McKenzie, grew to stature with the livestock industry, became political and economic powers in the mountain states.

The most inept of ranchers could hardly help making money during the early 1880s. The price of a Texas steer delivered in Wyoming rose from eight dollars to twenty, then to forty and even fifty on some feed lots. Incredible success stories fired the imagination of the world: how Alex Swan of Wyoming in five years gained control of two hundred thousand cattle; how the Scotch-financed Prairie Cattle Company was

[2] The stockman-Indian story is not entirely one of unfriendliness, however. In 1879, when drought was killing Judge Carter's cattle near Fort Bridger, Chief Washakie let him drive twenty-eight hundred head through the Shoshone reservation to virgin territory in Big Horn Basin. A few years later a similar favor was extended to a sheepman named Woodruff.

founded in 1881 and within two years was paying dividends of 20 per cent from 125,000 animals grazing five million acres of land in Colorado, New Mexico, Oklahoma, and Texas.

A frenetic boom was inevitable. Pioneer cattlemen as well as foreign investors scrambled to increase their holdings. Small settlers flocked out of the Midwest with more "barnyard animals" than is generally remembered today—one hundred thousand such cattle, far better than the longhorns in quality, rattled westward over a single railroad in 1883 alone. The result was a ferocious competition for land. Water was the key. By controlling a choice stream site, a man also controlled the grazing land as far back as a cow could walk. One person, however, could legally homestead no more than 160 acres. Accordingly ranch hands were hired to file in their own names, then turn the land over to their employer; other quarter sections were taken up in the name of a man's wife, cousins, and nephews, some of whom never saw the land they supposedly used as home. Purchase from bona fide settlers filled out the gaps, and if a homesteader proved stubborn about selling he was "persuaded." One device was to take up land completely around him, then deny him access to his property. Colorado's John Iliff, though not as ruthless as some, did acquire fifteen thousand acres of patented land along the South Platte, which in turn gave him absolute dominion over forty times that much range.

When a man called such open country "my range," he meant it. Contrary to popular mythology, it was the cattle baron and not the agriculturist who first made extensive use of barbed wire, fencing off such huge tracts of the public domain that the barriers actually blocked the building of roads to new settlements and forced stagecoaches to take long detours to reach the next town.

Occasionally this highhanded usurpation troubled the stockmen's consciences, and they discussed means of obtaining legal title to the land they were using. One proposal was for the Federal Government to turn the public domain over to the states. Another, advocated by such men as Silas Bent and Uncle Dick Wootton (who had turned to ranching after selling his toll road to the Santa Fe), was for outright sale, at prices ranging from five to ten cents an acre. A more popular idea was that of long-term leases, while still other men plumped for pastoral homesteads of from three thousand to twenty thousand acres. Eastern legislators, however, held to the philosophy of a nation of small freeholds, and all the proposals died.[3]

[3] In 1916 the pastoral homestead was revived when Congress finally allowed stock-raising homesteads of 640 acres. Nothing could have been more injudicious.

Meanwhile cattlemen went right on fencing the open range, arguing that it was the only way by which they could protect their grass and animals from the low-grade stock that was crowding in on them. By 1885 protests against 193 illegal enclosures were on file in Washington. Almost all Laramie County, Wyoming, had become a private preserve, and in Colorado three dozen "best citizens" had wired 2,640,450 acres for their own use. Angry homesteaders raised such an outcry that the Secretary of the Interior, Henry Teller of Colorado, incautiously suggested that settlers cut any illegal fence that denied them access to land on which they wished to locate. Unfortunately, the nesters did not always discriminate. Plier-happy homesteaders in Colorado's San Luis Valley slashed every panel along a two-mile stretch of the Baca Grant, then discovered that the land was deeded and the barrier legitimate.

Finally, in August 1885, President Cleveland ordered ranchers to remove every unauthorized fence from the public domain and dispatched Negro troops to Cheyenne to see that the order was obeyed. The soldiers were not needed. Catastrophe had arrived with the edict, and during the next two years ranchers were so stunned by successive blows from both nature and economics that there was little fight left in them.

The boom of the early eighties had collapsed; prices were falling as fast as they had once soared. Drought seared the land. Skin-and-bones cattle cropped the overgrazed grass to the roots. Almost no winter range was left, and never was a healthy winter range so desperately needed. On November 17, 1886, blizzards began to shriek across Wyoming and Montana just as tens of thousands of gaunt cattle were being trailed toward the Union and Northern Pacific railroads. When at last the numbed cowboys pushed the herds up to the loading pens, they learned that low prices had plummeted still lower. Many a despairing rancher, unwilling to pay more for freight than the animals would net him in the East, simply abandoned his herds beside the tracks, where so many died that bone gatherers for fertilizer factories reaped handsomely the next spring.

Temperatures skidded to unprecedented depths—forty-six degrees below zero in Lander, Wyoming—and stayed there. A brief chinook during February only compounded the disaster, because the thawing

---

A family needs about one hundred head of beef cattle to support it, and 640 acres of average mountain grazing land will carry at most thirty head. A lot of people were ruined finding this out. By 1923 more than seven million acres had been appropriated in Colorado alone. Then the awakening came, and droves of once hopeful occupants either let their land go for taxes or sold it at a pittance to small-time speculators. The scars—bits of rotted fence or collapsed shacks—can still be seen all over Colorado's western slope.

snowbanks promptly refroze as hard as iron, and the cattle could no longer paw through them for what grass remained. Trying to drift before the continual blizzards, animals piled up against the illegal fences and froze to death in heaps. Others sought out the cottonwood groves along the streams, to strip bark from the trees. In many cases this poor provender was denied them, for Indians were cutting the timber to feed their ponies. In final desperation, once-wild cows flocked into the shivering towns, as if man, who had terrorized them so long, could offer salvation now. But all they found to eat was the tar paper on the shacks. When a frantic Eastern owner wrote his employee, Charles M. Russell, for a report on conditions, the then unknown cowboy artist replied with a desolate drawing which launched him to fame—a dying steer surrounded by starved coyotes and succinctly titled, "Last of Five Thousand."

So ended an era. As one rancher put it, "The water wasn't squeezed out of the cattle business; it was frozen out." Overcapitalized, shoddily managed companies disappeared so utterly that mortgage holders often did not bother going through the motions of foreclosure. The outfits that survived reorganized their methods completely. Hay raising for winter feed became an integral part of operations, reserve pastures were provided for emergencies, and the picturesque but uneconomical longhorn gave way to white-faced Herefords that ate no more grass but provided far more beef per animal. This Hereford was a valuable creature. As a result, the white-faces were run in comparatively small, closely supervised numbers, and the day of the gargantuan outfit which turned loose tens of thousands of longhorns to fend for themselves was gone.

Though the numbers of cattle suffered sharp reduction (by two thirds in Wyoming between 1886 and 1895, after which time it climbed again as the number of small ranches increased), the competition for land did not end. Homestead laws being what they were, the public domain necessarily remained the stockman's chief source of grass. But the public domain was shrinking. Agriculturists were crowding in and chopping up the range with their picayune fences. During the late eighties dry farming went through another of its popular fads, sending armies of destructive plowmen onto benches which once had supported only cattle, while the slowly broadening scope of irrigation laced the range with ditches that were as effective barriers as was wire.

In places drought and unscientific farming of unadapted crops ruined both the homesteaders and the land as thoroughly as the cattlemen predicted. But in choicer regions at the foot of the mountains or in the valleys, the nesters clung on. Violence flared, augmented by animosities between small and large cattle operators. The little fellows, many of whom were old-time cattlemen trying to regain their feet after the disaster of the eighties, claimed with justice that the big companies were hogging the range; and their anger was not mollified by the fact that many of the large outfits were foreign-owned. Quite humanly the little operators began to look on these soulless corporations as fair game, to be plundered as a matter of civic duty. Thus, though they resented the name thief that was hurled at them, they soon found themselves making common cause with professional rustlers on one hand and with "sodbusters" on the other—a weird combination whose endless strings have been endlessly harped by the writers of fiction.

The beef barons roared in wrath. Depredations were serious, and legal help was not forthcoming. Although their detectives, often extraordinarly bold and able men, made arrest after arrest, it was almost impossible to secure convictions in counties inhabited chiefly by small ranchers and farmers. Quite humanly, therefore, the big boys retaliated by taking the law into their own hands. Widespread murders, which of course called for vengeance, became the source of monotonously similar folk tales all over the West. Of all these bloodlettings, the so-called Johnson County War of 1892, in Wyoming's Big Horns, is the most notorious.

Actually it was not a war—only two men died—but it might have been. Wyoming stock growers hired a couple of dozen gunmen in Denver and reinforced them with thirty or so cowboys. At the KC Ranch below Buffalo this army, after a dramatic all-day siege, managed to kill Nick Ray and Nate Champion, leaders of the Johnson County small ranchers. Word of the fracas reaching Buffalo, County Sheriff Red Angus swore in a hundred or so small-rancher "deputies," drove the enemy into shelter at the TA ranch, and launched an attack from behind hay bales and a movable shield built of logs. Results might have been disastrous—the attackers were armed with dynamite—but saner citizens had alerted Governor Barber. He appealed for Federal troops. Cavalry from Sheridan stopped the war in the nick of time and hauled the invaders back to Cheyenne, stronghold of the Wyoming Stockgrowers Association. There the gunmen were imprisoned—in a private hall to which their families had free access and from which the men themselves could take brief vacations whenever fancy moved them. Expenses of the incarceration—one hundred dollars a day for food, guards, and rent—were charged against Johnson County. But Johnson County was broke. Finally Cheyenne's Judge Scott huffed, "Inasmuch as . . . the county of Laramie could no longer finance the bankrupt county of Johnson . . . he was forced to release each and all of the aforesaid prisoners on their individual recognizances." No trial was ever held.

Still the range dwindled, and cowmen were forced to seek rough, wild ranges where plows could not follow: tawny, rimrocked mesas and the high, flower-jeweled basins between the snowy peaks. Transhumance—the seasonal migration of herds from summer to winter range and back again—became the rule rather than the exception, but even this brought no relief. For a new competitor was already there.

Sheep.

Like longhorn cattle and mustang ponies, sheep were a Spanish importation, particularly favored by the padres since the animals could be tended by Indian converts. They were poor, runted stock. Wool was their chief reason for being,[4] yet their light, silky fleece clipped no more than a pound or so per head. Numbers, however, made up for other lacks. Hundreds of thousands of them ranged in New Mexico alone, and from there they followed the gold rushers and settlers all over the West.

From the beginning they were hated. Texas cowboys associated them with Mexicans, whom they had never loved, and the dislike was increased by the instinctive contempt which men on horseback have always felt for men who work afoot. But the greatest fury arose over the way a close-packed herd would clip the grass right down to the earth and then tramp out its roots with their razorlike hoofs. Given ample room, sheep, of course, graze harmlessly. But in the early West they were not given room. A ewe is the most helpless of creatures. Weather, predatory animals, deep water, mudholes—almost any mountain hazard—can kill one. Man and his dogs constantly have to furnish protection, and to make that protection effective for the greatest number possible, the woollies were jammed together in bands almost as evil-smelling and destructive as their enemies claimed.

At first there was little conflict. Sheep were weed eaters. They preferred the broad-leafed foliage of the mountains to grass, and larkspur, so deadly to cattle when it is in bloom, harmed them not at all. So during the summer the flocks tended to keep high among the rocks and timber where riding after cattle was difficult, and the only tiffs that occurred came when shepherds and cowboys chanced to meet on the winter range.

[4] Raising lambs for food did not become important until the beginning of the twentieth century, when irrigation produced vast quantities of alfalfa and sugar-beet tops, on which sheep fattened to unsuspected succulence.

Then, late in the seventies, speculators discovered that it was possible to buy sheep in Oregon and California for a dollar and a half a head, spend another fifty cents each trailing them to the Rockies, and sell them there for three dollars. Sheep poured toward the mountains, incredible trail herds led by goats and driven by dogs. The dogs were faithful, but the goats sometimes balked, especially at stream crossings. When this happened the herder seized the bearded recalcitrant, threshed him soundly with a stick, and turned him loose to try again. Convinced now that water was preferable to manhandling, the chastened goat obediently waded or swam across. The bolder sheep followed, then the more timid—except when the leaders heard the drags bleating behind them, lost their heads, and stampeded back again. When this occurred there was nothing to do but pen the herd against the riverbank for two or three days and starve it into crossing. Such perplexities, faced amid solitude, smell, and continual bleating, help explain the sheepherder's habitual look of melancholy.

By 1886 there were two million sheep in Colorado alone (up from 110,000 head in 1880), and they were flooding into Wyoming at the rate of two hundred thousand a year. The disastrous winter of 1886 accelerated the trend, for many bankrupt cattlemen turned to this new business where a start could be made on a shoestring. Quality was slowly improving, thanks to men like Utah's John Seely, who never owned a pair of shoes until he was sixteen and who as a boy traveled along fence rails to keep his bare feet out of the snow. Along with other Mormon sheep raisers in the Wasatch Mountains, Seely concentrated on raising blooded Rambouillet and Merino rams which they sold at tremendous prices, for an infusion of good blood increased wool clips from two or three pounds per animal to as much as thirty pounds, under favorable circumstances.

No pursuit was a greater gamble than sheep raising. Profits were huge; risks were desperate. The epics of courage, resourcefulness, and perseverance are as stirring as any connected with the cattle industry. Lucy Morrison, for instance . . . In 1882, Lucy, her invalid husband John, and their three infant daughters moved out of Idaho into Wyoming with two lumber wagons and two thousand head of sheep, intending to winter near South Pass. By spring they had only two hundred head left, and John Morrison was ready to quit. But not Lucy. She sold one wagon for garden seed and set about making a home for her family in a tent one hundred and fifty miles from the nearest doctor. When she was off herding she tied her children to the sagebrush to keep them from getting lost. She pulled herself through a nearly fatal

attack of dysentery by living on ewe's milk, went first two years
and then four without seeing another woman. Threatening Indians she
frightened off by sprinkling camphor around the tent and telling the
savages the children had smallpox, and, weaponless, she killed a marauding mountain lion by putting ground glass in a sheep's carcass. Cattlemen burned her wagons and scattered her flocks. But she sent her girls
through normal school, gained control of seven thousand acres of
deeded land, ran sixteen bands of sheep on the public domain. After
John Morrison died she married a sheepman named Curtis Moore but
ran her business independently of his. Toward the end of her life,
known now as the Sheep Queen of Wyoming, she took to wintering
in California, where she bought a comfortable home—then rented it
and lived in the garage in her old spartan fashion.

Lucy Morrison Moore and scores of other mountain sheep owners
at least established home ranches, paid taxes, and otherwise met the
duties of citizenship. But many were complete itinerants, ranging
wherever there was grass, grubbing it out, and moving on. These ir-
responsible peripatetics infuriated the cowmen beyond all else and
by natural transference increased the odium in which all sheep were
held. Throughout the West vicious feuds exploded as rivals fought for
land to which neither had title.

Circumstances seemed to favor the cattlemen. It was no trick for a
group of riders masked by hoods of gunny sacks to surprise a sheep
camp, tie up the one or two herders, burn the wagons, shoot or club
part of the animals, and scatter the rest for the coyotes. Retaliation
by the sheepmen was less spectacular: a dead horse or dead cow here
and there, a poisoned spring, the driving of cattle from water holes with
willing dogs. Yet sheer weight of numbers spread the woollies farther
and farther.

Next the cattlemen established "deadlines" and ordered sheepmen
not to cross them. The cowboys meant business. In 1895, when Jack
Edwards hired professional gunmen as herders and forded the Little
Snake River on the Colorado-Wyoming border, three hundred men
moved up Fortification Creek to drive him back. He did not resist.
Others did. In 1902 Wyoming sheepmen defiantly moved ten thousand
animals across a Bridger Mountain deadline to the slopes of Green
River. Out from Pinedale came the cattlemen, overpowered the herders, clubbed thousands of helpless animals to death (it was cheaper and
quicker than shooting), and left behind great heaps of bones that for
years served as one of the world's most eloquent keep-off-the-grass
signs.

Instance could be piled on instance. To counteract an impression that Wyoming was running blood, the Board of Sheep Commissioners in 1903 toted up the state's known casualties and announced that during the range wars of the preceding ten years "only" fifty men had been murdered, "only" twenty-five thousand sheep had been killed.

Two things helped restore order. One was the 1909 Tensleep raid under the shadow of the huge maroon cliffs of the Big Horns. There masked cattlemen killed sheep owner Joe Emge, his camp mover, and a herder named Jules Lazier. This involved the Federal Government, for Lazier was a French citizen, and in the end the United States had to pay a twenty-five-thousand-dollar idemnity for his death. Moreover, the National Wool Growers Association was now strong enough to make its weight felt. Twenty thousand dollars were produced to solve the case. Appropriately awed, Sheriff Felix Alston stirred his stumps as no previous Wyoming sheriff ever had in a sheep fracas. One key witness committed suicide, leaving a note implicating several neighbors. This resulted in a rush to turn state's evidence and arrange deals for lighter sentences. Although no one was executed, three men were imprisoned for life, others received shorter terms, and the entire Rocky Mountain West indulged in a bit of unwonted reflection on the wages of those who live by the sword.

The other damper was Uncle Sam himself, working through the Forest Service. This had been started in 1891, but the number of reserves increased slowly and stockmen did not pay much attention until 1898 or so, when rangers began informing them that animals could be grazed on forest land only by permit and under such procedures as the service laid down. Reaction varied between incredulous bellows and outright resistance. Feeling over the Yellowstone Reserve in Wyoming was so intense that Buffalo Bill Cody warned A. A. Anderson, the new superintendent (who happened also to be a well-known artist in the effete East), not to return to his Wyoming summer home. Anderson returned. Arsonists tried to burn down his ranch house. He held meetings to explain and pacify. Typical of the response was the Meeteetse *News's* caustic comment, "Mr. Anderson can, by a single stroke of his diamond-bedecked hand, put out of existence that noble animal [the sheep] that clothes his unclean body."

Breathing defiance, forty armed men came up from Utah with sixty thousand sheep. Promptly Anderson mobilized sixty-five rangers and met the invaders amid the stupendous scenery of Jackson Hole—though presumably no one at the time found the beauties of nature softening his soul. After serving a gross lot of injunctions the rangers squeezed the herds back against the Green River country, where touchy cattle-men killed eight hundred animals and beat up a herder. While the invaders were licking these wounds Anderson slapped on staggering fines for trespass and made them stick in court. Pummeled thus from all sides, the sheepmen decided that they had better take out permits after all. Since then the Forest Service's edicts have been listened to with respect, if not always with approval. Moreover, the rangers have spread the doctrine of brotherly love among their antagonistic wards. In the Forest Service's half-century control of the high places, there has been only one case of violence between sheepmen and cattlemen—a 1918 raid in the Gunnison Forest of Colorado, where cowboys tied up a herder beside a stream with the momentarily incongruous name of Oh-Be-Joyful Creek and drove five hundred of his sheep over a cliff.

In 1934 the Taylor Grazing Act extended restrictions on the use of public lands by private individuals from the forests to all the rest of the open range. Homesteading, except in special cases, was ended, rigid regulations were clamped down—and vociferous quarrels were born whose fury has been carried throughout the nation (and often magnified) by newspapers, magazines, women's clubs, electioneering congressmen, and related crusaders. Far more than grass is involved, for a tremendous intertwining of not-always-reconcilable policies has enmeshed the mountains under catchwords first popularized by Teddy Roosevelt—conservation and reclamation.

CHAPTER XIII

THE GOOSE'S GOLDEN EGGS

THE truth? What is the truth?

From one viewpoint the rape of the West is a horror story without equal. Figures do not exist to express its enormity. Who kept records on the beaver ripped from the streams, the minerals gouged from the earth through unhealable scars, the forests slashed and burned? How estimate the meadows forever destroyed, the tons of topsoil washed from denuded hills, underground water tables turned to dust, rivers poisoned by mill tailings, herds of game animals putrefying where they fell?

After perusing the wanton lines the average American is apt to exclaim that protection for what is left can never be exercised too vigilantly.

Others, however, are beginning to say that there can be too much of any good thing. Without denying the historic need for conservation, they feel that in overenthusiastic hands it becomes a blind sentimentality and that the Rockies are in danger of being conserved from everything, including legitimate use. The quarrel that has thus been engendered is violent, full of ill-tempered denunciations, contradictory statistics, and wild skirmishes up blind alleys.

Wild animals were, of course, the first native treasure to melt away before the onslaught of exploitation. Indians, mountain men, and early pioneers killed, in part, because their business or their stomachs demanded it. But they also killed for sheer excitement. The utilitarian value of a grizzly bear, for example, was largely limited to the oil which could be rendered from its carcass, yet an Indian found as high honor in wearing the claws of slain grizzlies as in counting coup on a fallen enemy.

So extravagant was the red man's awe of the huge beasts that Lewis and Clark were amused by it—until various members of their expedition ran afoul of the nine-foot, half-ton monsters, pumped them full of lead, and still had to climb trees, jump over cliffs, or leap into the Missouri to escape. As the fur trade swept westward, one invariable goal of its neophytes was to kill one of these "white" or "yellow" bears. Superior Nimrods became folk heroes. Joe Meek was renowned throughout the Rockies for his bear-slaying feats, just as Buffalo Bill Cody later became a household name by slaughtering in eighteen months 4280 bison for the construction crews of the Kansas Pacific Railroad. Legend piled on legend, the most famous being that of old Hugh Glass, Ashley hunter, who was mangled by a grizzly, left for dead, regained consciousness, and dragged his broken leg on a hundred-mile crawl to Fort Atkinson. But none of these tales of ursine fury is quite as astounding as Peno's yarn of ursine benevolence.

In the 1840s, Peno, a French-Canadian trapper, was gored by a wounded buffalo in Wyoming's Powder River country. His gun lost and his leg shattered, he crawled along like Hugh Glass, eating berries and sleeping when exhaustion felled him. Once he awoke to see a huge grizzly nearby. Scared stiff, the man played dead for as long as his nerves could endure, then peeked again. The bear was still there. Now Peno noticed that it was lame; in fact, it seemed to be asking for help. Since the man could not flee, he took a chance, crawled up to the huge beast, and pulled a splinter from its pus-swollen paw. Its pain eased, the bear slept. Frantically Peno crawled away. Along came the bear—not to molest him but gratefully to stand guard until they spied an Indian camp where the man could receive succor. And that is how Peno Creek got its name. . . . Well, maybe. Such things perhaps happened sometime or other, because similar myths have been current since the tale of Androcles and the lion's paw.

Bears were not the only targets, nor calloused trappers the only hunters. Apparently no one could resist the fever engendered by the teeming plains. Even that staid missionary, Dr. Samuel Parker, traveling West with Marcus Whitman in 1834, felt his trigger finger itch, battled his conscience—and grabbed a gun. Soon the Santa Fe traders were augmenting their incomes by guiding hunting parties along with their caravans. Bent's Fort became a favorite resort, and by the mid-1830s the first of a long series of foreign noblemen had reached the crest of the continent.

He was Sir William Drummond Stewart, seventh baronet of Grandtully, and his conceits were wondrous. He packed with him over thousands of tortuous miles fine brandies, cheeses, olives, potted meats, candies; he dragged artist Albert Jacob Miller from one end of the Rockies to the other, preparing sketches for the huge oil paintings that later graced the Stewart castle in Scotland; in 1837 he lugged out to the fur rendezvous a set of medieval armor—casque, cuirass, greaves, and all—into which Jim Bridger squeezed his frame, mounted his startled horse, and curvetted about to the delight of Indians and trappers. Yet Stewart was no pampered tenderfoot. He could, and did, hold his own on storm-swept trails, in rendezvous drinking bouts, during Indian fracases. When he left the Rockies to assume his title it was with real regret. And the mountain men missed him. As a token Bill Sublette shipped to him in Scotland live grizzlies, buffalo, and deer. But neither these nor Miller's paintings were adequate substitutes. In 1843 Stewart came back to the Rockies. With him he brought a magnificent retinue, financed in part by rich Americans who traveled along as paying guests on what was perhaps the Rockies' first de luxe sportsmen's tour.

Some of the men who followed Stewart were less attractive. One was Sir George Gore, Irish peer for whom Colorado's Gore Mountains were named. In 1855 His Lordship hit the Rockies with forty servants, a score of dogs, bundles of fishing rods, an arsenal of small arms, six wagons, and twenty-one carts. A special corps of ax- and shovelmen prepared roads for the wagons, and Old Gabe himself, Jim Bridger, was hired to guide the way to the lushest hunting grounds in Colorado, Wyoming, Montana, Idaho, and Oregon. Statistically Gore lived up to his name, slaughtering forty grizzlies, nearly three thousand buffalo, and more elk, deer, and antelope than he bothered to count. At that, he had his principles. When the American Fur Company asked an unreasonable fee for freighting his trophies and hides to St. Louis he burned the entire outfit rather than be imposed on. Nor did he tolerate diversions. Legend attests that a member of his party discovered gold on a now unidentifiable stream in Colorado, whereupon Gore promptly moved camp for fear desertions by his men would inconvenience his hunting.

But Gore was an amateur. Professionals entered the field about 1870, when the railroads approached the Rockies and Eastern dealers began offering from $1.75 to $3.00 for a buffalo hide, depending on its quality. The toll almost passes estimation. One lone individual, Brick Bond, is reputed to have killed six thousand buffalo in sixty days. For a dozen years the plains swarmed with parties who carried their lead with them by the ton and melted it down in frying pans to make bullets. Huge wagons and trailers built like hayricks hauled the hides back to the railroad towns, where acres of ground were covered with skins stretched out to dry. Except for a few tender humps and tongues which were shipped East in barrels, most of the meat was left to spoil where it lay; and in 1874 homesteaders near Granada, Colorado, gathered up and sold to Eastern fertilizer factories a pile of bones twelve feet high,

twelve feet wide, and half a mile long! By the time the incredible blood-
letting was over the Indian had been reduced from self-sufficiency to
a sullen dependence for his food on whatever the white man saw fit
to give him, and the vast plains lay empty before the onrush of homesteaders and longhorns.

Even before this the new territory of Wyoming had become alarmed
by the decrease in her wild life, and in 1868 the legislature passed the
first game laws in America. In Wyoming, too, came another first of
even more import to conservation in general—the establishment of
Yellowstone National Park.

One of the earliest of the West's scenic marvels to be known, Yellowstone was the last to be believed. For sixty-odd years after John Colter
had first wandered through its chill forests during the winter of
1807–08, a string of trappers—Joe Meek, Jim Bridger, Warren Ferris,
and even that indomitable Catholic missionary, Father de Smet—had
tried in vain to tell the world about its boiling mudholes, geysers, water-
falls, and canyons. All they got were laughs, and Yellowstone came to
epitomize the West's penchant for tall yarns.

Finally, in 1859, the government ordered Captain W. F. Raynolds
to lead an exploring expedition up the Yellowstone River and its tributaries. Opportunity lay at Raynolds's finger tips. As geologist he employed one Ferdinand Vandeveer Hayden, a then unknown ex-school-
teacher and ex-doctor whose restless curiosity led the Sioux Indians
to name him Man Who Picks Up Stones Running. And as guide the
expedition possessed Old Gabe. Bridger, however, had a bad time of it.
Reputedly he discovered gold on this trip but at Raynolds's command
discarded his specimens to avoid stampeding the soldiers. On another
occasion, after he had engineered a crossing of the swollen Big Horn,
Raynolds rendered his thanks not to Jim but to Providence. And although Bridger was about the only man alive who could have led the
way to Yellowstone's fantastic heart, the expedition bogged down and
turned back before it reached the park's present boundaries.

During the next decade Montana's gold boom brought towns and
ranches within less than a hundred miles of Yellowstone's steaming
basins, and still nothing but rumor was known of them. Then, in
1869, a trio of ranchers—Folsom, Cook, and Peterson—wandered past
Yellowstone Lake into Lower Geyser Basin. They could hardly believe their eyes. Indeed, so the story runs, Dave Folsom respected his
reputation for truthfulness so much that he would tell his adventures
to no more than a handful of sympathetic friends in the frontier town
of Helena. He could not have picked better listeners: Cornelius Hedges,

a Helena lawyer, Walter Trumbull, son of the United States senator from Illinois, and two territorial bigwigs, Henry Washburn, the surveyor general, and Nathaniel P. Langford, Montana's collector of internal revenue. This quartet, plus four more adventurous local citizens, decided to scout the region for themselves; and although the trip was unofficial, they possessed influence enough to secure from nearby Fort Ellis an escort of five cavalrymen commanded by Lieutenant Gustavus Doane.

The rest has been told often enough to be household history. As the group sat around one of their last campfires they discussed the commercial advantages of homesteading the region's more spectacular sites. But Cornelius Hedges said no. The entire district, he argued, should be set aside and protected by the government as a national park for the use of everyone. There was grumbling, but Hedges was eloquent enough to convert the party, particularly Nathaniel Langford, who lay awake all night turning Hedges's idea over in his mind.

After that, with active help from the others, Langford was a man with a mission—so much so that people said even his initials, N. P., stood for National Park. He lectured in the East, wrote articles for *Scribner's Magazine*, heard himself denounced on all sides as "the champion liar of the Northwest." But one of the men who heard him talk was Captain Raynolds's former geologist, Ferdinand V. Hayden.

After surviving the War between the States as a surgeon in the Union Army, Hayden had returned to his true love in double capacity, as professor of geology at the University of Pennsylvania and director of the government's new "Geological and Geographical Survey of the Territories," renowned today simply as the Hayden Surveys.

Among his revolutionary ideas was that of employing a photographer to record the look of the land, although at the time picturemaking was more of a magician's stunt than a science or an art. Outdoor "snapshots" involved unpacking a muleload of equipment, setting up a lightproof tent, flooding a glass plate with collodion, immersing it in a bath of silver nitrate, and then rushing out to the camera, meanwhile keeping the plate moist with wet blotting paper or a towel. The picture taken, the photographer bolted back to the tent, flooded the plate with developer, rinsed it, fixed it with cyanide, varnished it, and prepared it for transportation. One drop of perspiration would ruin a picture— and so would the fall of a mule carrying the plates. But Hayden located a pioneer Omaha photographer who thought he could do the trick, a man whose deft touch with those primitive cameras has in some cases not been surpassed even today and whose file of negatives is a priceless record of the vanished West—William H. Jackson.

Additionally fortified by artist Thomas Moran, the survey forged into Yellowstone in 1871, Professor Hayden, as usual, wearing a weather-beaten frock coat. When the group returned, all the famed "liars" of the West—Colter and Bridger, Folsom and Langford—were vindicated. Hayden himself lobbied in Congress for the bill, introduced by Montana's delegate, which would create Yellowstone National Park. It was a remarkable piece of legislation, because this was an era when the government was exerting every effort to push public land into private hands, and support was lukewarm. Then, with just the right touch of showmanship, Hayden laid a gold-stamped, leather-bound portfolio of Jackson's photographs on each congressman's desk, and in January 1872 the bill was passed.

As a reward for his services, Nathaniel Langford was made the park's first superintendent—but given no money and almost no legal authority with which to work. For five years he drained his own pockets to pay his expenses and his assistants'. Persuasion and education were his only weapons. Sometimes they were not enough. Despite the park's remoteness, tourists began piling in to see this new public-owned wonder. Since many of them had the notion that the place was "theirs," they killed any animal they wished, packed off any specimen that struck their fancy. Finally, frustrated at every turn, Langford gave up and quit.

So notorious did the situation become that in 1886 troops were called on to protect the park, and Fort Yellowstone was built at Mammoth Hot Springs not so much to ward off Indians as to keep white savages at a respectful distance. But even this was a kind of governmental schizophrenia. The park superintendent was responsible to the Department of the Interior; the troop commander and the Army engineers who built roads and trails, to the Department of War. Co-operation was not always notable. Moreover, laws were inadequate. Poachers could be chased out of the park but not punished; yet innocent tourists were subject to continual harassment for petty rule infractions because the fines thus extracted were the supervisor's main source of income.

Profoundly shocked by the wanton destruction of wild life in the park, writer Emerson Hough and George Bird Grinnell, editor of *Forest and Stream,* launched a strenuous campaign not only for the guarding of Yellowstone's animals but for game conservation on a nationwide scale. Finally, in 1894, Congress passed legislation for the protection of game in all national parks, but not until 1916 was administrative sanity provided by the establishment of a workable National Park Service with clear-cut channels of responsibility.

Meanwhile the idea of conservation had spread to the states. Colorado ruled against public hawking of wild meat and fish, which for years had been a staple element in the diet of the mining camps. Wyoming, on becoming a state in 1890, went so far as to forbid any non-resident's killing big game within her borders, then realized she was overlooking a sure-fire source of revenue and in 1895 instituted the selling of non-resident shooting licenses for a thumping fee.

Various problems of enforcement arose. By an 1869 treaty with the United States the Bannock Indians had been given the right to hunt on public lands. As a new-fledged state Wyoming declared that this right was subject to normal game regulations, and in 1895 dispatched forty deputies to arrest Chief Racehorse's band for killing seven elk out of season in Jackson Hole. "Season," of course, meant nothing to the Indians. Resentful and bewildered, they broke away from their captors while passing through a clump of trees. One was shot and a two-year-old papoose was seized as hostage. Hearing the sound of distant gunfire, the village of Jackson shivered in its boots, and excited newspapers outside Wyoming headlined the massacre of its inhabitants. But by now the Bannocks knew the folly of a resort to arms. Racehorse gave himself up for trial in the district court, which reread the 1869 treaty and declared him innocent.

Promptly Wyoming appealed the case to the United States Supreme Court. Here the decision was reversed and the doctrine firmly established that all states own the game within their borders and can control it as they see fit. This meant, of course, that animals in national forests were subject to state law and that Federal rangers had to work with state authorities in matters of enforcement—a sometimes discouraging experience in early days. A. A. Anderson once arrested a poacher in the Yellowstone Reserve (not to be confused with the national park), only to have a jury of the man's friends decide, "He did it all right, but we won't find him guilty this time."

From game protection to game propagation was but a step. Here, too, Yellowstone led the way. In 1901, after poachers had reduced the park's buffalo to twenty-two, Congress appropriated fifteen thousand dollars for the creation of a new herd. Fortunately, two small bunches of privately owned bison remained alive in the United States, the so-called Goodnight Herd in Texas and the Pablo-Allard Herd in Montana. Eighteen cows were bought from the latter, three bulls from the former. By 1923, thanks to careful protection and such arduous chores as rounding up the ton-sized beasts for annual vaccination, Yellowstone's famed Thundering Herd numbered more than nine hundred head and was gulping down a thousand-odd tons of hay each and every winter. In short, the elephant was growing a little bit white, and Congress hastily authorized the Park Service to give away bison to any public or private concern that had facilities for handling them. One pair went to Florenz Ziegfeld, others to a movie company, and still more to zoos in practically every state of the Union. Meanwhile a curious reversion in taste had taken place. Once Indians, trappers, and pioneers by the tens of thousands had lunched with relish on buffalo steaks. But when the bison-rich government offered surplus stock to butchers and to the dining-car commissary of a transcontinental railroad, an indignant public refused to touch it!

What was done with Yellowstone's buffalo was repeated throughout the Rockies with elk, deer, antelope, mountain sheep, and game fish. The huge Jackson Hole elk herd, which suffered periodic decimation with every hard winter, received its first helping hand in 1907, when private subscriptions were undertaken to buy feed. In the same year, outraged by the way in which elk were killed for their teeth alone (indeed, the beasts were—and are—sometimes trapped while floundering in heavy snow, deprived of their two large teeth, and then left to starve without those essential masticators), the Wyoming legislature made tusk hunting a felony and memorialized the BPOE to discourage the use of real elk teeth as a watch-chain emblem.

The Elks co-operated, but private subscriptions to buy hay fell short. Accordingly, in 1909, Wyoming appropriated five thousand dollars for the purpose and asked Congress to establish a game refuge, an appeal made eloquent by S. N. Leek's poignant photographs of the starving beasts. From then on the idea snowballed. Feeding stations and state and Federal game refuges were established throughout the Rockies. The Biological Survey went all out to trap or poison predatory animals that prey on game herds and on domestic livestock. Fish hatcheries kept step, pouring billions of fingerlings into streams whose pollution has been more and more jealously watched. So firmly have recreational policies become fixed in mountain thinking that surveys for irrigation projects must today include solemn studies on the effect, good or bad, which the invasion will have on wild life in the area concerned.

So far no one has objected to the principle of the thing. But there have been objections to its all-inclusive extent. Deer in particular increase fantastically under protection. Locomotives of the Moffat road were killing so many of them in Colorado's Middle Park and service was so disrupted that in 1938–39 the State Game and Fish Department had to hire men to drive the creatures off the tracks as trains approached. Ever since 1933 the same department has had to employ an official herder to chase deer out of the gardens of irate homeowners in populous Canon City, at the eastern foot of the Sangre de Cristos. Ranchers are even more beset. One forthright lady cattle owner of my acquaintance recently appealed again and again to the Forest Service in western Colorado for help against elk that were ruining her fences and gorging on her hay. Not receiving what she considered adequate response, she slew several of the marauders and telephoned the rangers to come up and get their goddamn critters. Local sportsmen were outraged, but to the lady concerned (and to many property owners like her) it was a matter of livelihood; she would not, she feels, have been condemned for shooting a rustler in lieu of the sheriff's failure to act, so why all this furor over some thieving elk?

The problem is not an isolated one. An estimated 40 per cent of all national forest land is devoted to the grazing of game. In 1917 the deer population of Utah's national forests was estimated at 8105. Today there are 200,000. Sportsmen are delighted, as are the towns, resorts, filling stations, dude ranches, professional guides, manufacturers, and what not who thrive on the Rockies' multimillion-dollar recreation industry. And yet . . . Utah's ranges, where these 200,000 deer graze, are already overstocked with cattle and sheep. The world, some ranchers mutter, perhaps selfishly, is hungry. While men starve, three hundred to five hundred deer per day are winter-fed on a hoof-bared slope above the Mountain Dell Reservoir in the Wasatch Mountains, where fecal matter and putrefaction from corpses drain into Salt Lake City's chief source of drinking water. So far little more than contour trenching has been done about it. The sight of three hundred deer happily munching hay packs a tremendous aesthetic wallop. Furthermore, as all legislators know, far more people hunt and fish than run livestock; and sportsmen's organizations are among the most vocal pressure groups in the land. Popular sympathy is on their side—with reason. Except for conservation, there would be no deer in Utah at all.

Moreover, as conservationists are quick to point out, the threat to game is greater than ever, owing to increased population and to three new mechanical horrors: the jeep, the horse trailer, and the airplane. The cross-country advantages of a jeep to a hunter interested simply in traveling till he finds something to shoot are obvious, and where a jeep can't go, a horse can. All a man needs to do is load a nag and a bale of hay into a trailer, drive a couple of hundred miles out from the city to an elk range he has previously spotted, ride a little distance off the highway, make his kill, and be home before the week end is over. Airplanes have been used to flush geese from Wyoming lakes toward waiting hunters, and although I know of no case where game animals actually were shot from one, the possibilities are self-evident. During a recent two-month period a pair of Montana Nimrods bagged two hundred and fifty coyotes from the air, one piloting and the other strafing with a twelve-gauge shotgun. Why not antelope? And the plane is handy for scouting. Eastern sportsmen fly over the mountains, spot their game, land at the nearest airport, and arrange for horses. An overnight trip is often enough—sometimes more than enough—for light planes that can land on a mountain lake or meadow.

Old-time outfitters do not like it. "Getting into the wilderness used to be the main part of hunting," James Moore of Dubois, Wyoming, reminisced. "We ranchers would round up cooks and wranglers and pack stock, and take a small party out for two or three weeks. They wanted to rough it, and it's a good thing they did. Nights were cold. Sometimes we'd be snowed in; maybe we'd lose our horses and have to walk out. But it gave you something real to remember. Now . . ." He looked up at the timbered ridges of the Wind Rivers. "Well, maybe this is sport. But it seems like just a case of getting meat."

Because of the huge increase in the number of these mechanized meat gatherers, protectionists argue, the conservation program must be stepped up still more: stricter laws, more feeding stations, broader game preserves. As for the ranchers who would like to use that grass and hay for livestock, and food alarmists who believe every available square foot of land should be put to productive use . . .

The truth? What is the truth?

About two and a half centuries passed before most Americans ceased regarding trees as something to get rid of. In the East dense forests had long impeded travel, had made the clearing of farmlands a grueling labor. Accordingly, when the first miners reached the forests of the Great Divide, no twinges of conscience stayed their axes. After riding through the Georgetown mining district in the early 1870s, Isabella Bird was shocked into declaring, "Mining destroys and devastates, turning the earth inside out, making it hideous, blighting every green thing as it usually blights man's heart and soul."

The miners had company—tie cutters for the railroads. Right-of-way grants allowed the early companies to appropriate whatever timber they needed "adjacent to the line of the road." Since there were no trees on the plains, Henry Teller of Colorado, while Secretary of the Interior, stretched the word "adjacent" to mean anything within fifty miles of the proposed track, and thereafter billions of ties floated down the mountain streams to waiting construction crews.

This wholesale hewing left behind great piles of slash which a careless spark would turn into an inferno. So would a deliberate spark, should the stuff happen to inconvenience anyone. If the resultant blaze also burned standing timber, why worry? Forests were being consumed right and left anyhow. Sheepherders fired them to make herding easier; fuel purveyors, in order to provide a supply of dry poles; Indians, to scare game or just out of pique; casual tourists, to see the spectacle. And in summer there was always the hazard of lightning. No means existed for checking the conflagrations, even if some rare soul had wanted to try, and they raged until they burned themselves out. Early journals are filled with references to haze caused by forest-fire smoke. Many a late-summer night was pinpricked with the angry glow of "death-fires [that] gleamed," said Dr. E. E. Edwards, president of Colorado State Agricultural College, in 1880, "like the camp fires of an avenging enemy."

True, there was some agitation against this waste. When Colorado became a state in 1876 (the same year in which the American Forestry Association was founded in the East) there were written into her constitution two short sections paying lip service to the ideal of forest preservation. In a sense the articles were milestones; although completely unimplemented, they were the first such provisions ever to be drafted in a state constitution. However, another nine years passed before the legislature gave them a very feeble set of teeth, and this belated inspiration was due, in part, to the growing need for irrigation water.

The West is semi-arid. The rich farming regions where American irrigation first developed—Santa Fe, Salt Lake City, and Greeley, Colorado—receive, for example, an annual average precipitation of about fifteen inches, which is not enough to support most crops. But in sight of each locality are cloud-capturing peaks where the annual moisture harvest soars toward fifty inches. Most of this falls as snow, which as early as 1880 Dr. Edwards had recognized as a treasure richer than the Rockies' vaunted store of minerals: without it "the land would be as desolate as a field of death. . . . It holds the golden harvests that are to wave on the plains below. And the trees are the protectors, the guardian spirits of the snow. Therefore . . . protect the trees." At about the same time another early conservationist, Elwood Meade, was warning Colorado farmers with less poetry but more dollars-and-cents bluntness that self-preservation demanded a check on fires, sawmills, tie cutters; that in all common sense it was cheaper to preserve natural reservoirs than to build artificial ones.

Finally, in 1885, the state roused itself enough to appoint Colonel Edgar Ensign the first forest commissioner in the Rocky Mountains. But it neglected to give him a salary. For two years Ensign, like Nathaniel Langford in Yellowstone Park, supported himself and his office out of his own pocket.

Perhaps this experience helped persuade him and his backers that the Western territories were not capable of guarding their own interests. Anyhow, whatever his motives, one of the first things he and the infant Colorado Forestry Association advocated, in January 1886, was the withdrawal from private acquisition of all timberlands on the headwaters of the principal streams in the Rocky Mountain region.

Other men had advanced similar proposals for other sections of the country, and instantly all were attacked as socialistic and un-American. Governmental philosophy had long declared that public lands were being held in trust for future settlers, but now the situation seemed to merit review. Homesteaders were not interested in the winter-frigid, steep-sloped, untillable lands of the high country. Nor were timber claims being filed; it was easier simply to steal lumber from the public domain, and, besides, the wood of the Rockies is not as valuable commercially as Eastern and Northern hardwoods or the giant stands of the Pacific coast. In short, nearly everyone was ready to despoil the forests of the divide, but very few were willing to assume responsibility for them. Something had to be done, and as the states neglected to act, popular sentiment swung toward Federal intervention.

Finally, five years after the Colorado proposal, President Harrison in 1891 withdrew from public entry the Yellowstone Reserve in Wyoming and the White River Reserve in northwestern Colorado. Once again, however, that curious lag between governmental words and governmental practice manifested itself: no money was provided for administration until 1897. This time there were no Langfords, no Ensigns to fill the gap, and as a result few people paid attention to the new setup. Moreover, Washington was advancing with what seemed lamentable caution to eager conservationists. After a dozen years less than one quarter of Colorado's forests were embraced by the reserves; and in 1903 impatient chambers of commerce, granges, colleges, teachers, civic organizations, commercial firms, and private individuals signed gigantic petitions urging Congress to get moving—an interesting point to remember on hearing, as one occasionally does, that the Forest Service muscled into the West unwanted.

By the time the delayed administrative arm of the reserves began to work, not timber but water conservation (together with related problems of erosion control) was recognized as the prime need of the intermountain area. This in turn depended on maintaining adequate covers both of trees and of humus kept porous enough by roots, earthworms, larvae, fungi, etc., that it can absorb up to 50 per cent of its own volume in moisture. Within thirty years after logging, humus will shrink to as little as half its former depth, from which state it will not build back for another eighty to a hundred years; the earth packs and water rushes off in soil-robbing sweeps.

Fire, of course, intensifies the disaster. One example will suffice. On a hot August day in 1944 a boy playing with matches started a fire that burned over somewhat less than six hundred acres on a hill above Salt Lake City. Unfortunately three small ravines headed on that crucial ground. The next year, on August 19, 1945, a cloudburst hit the mountains back of the city. The only canyons dangerously affected were those three small ravines. Down them into the city poured a wall of water, mud, and boulders. Luckily most of its energy was spent on a cemetery, where coffins were exhumed and gravestones piled in grotesque heaps. But the flash flood also filled basements with debris, washed out roads, and buckled walls to the tune of $346,000 worth of damages—a ten-minute toll of roughly $575 per burned acre. Certainly no one would have supposed from looking at the brown little hill that it was worth so much.

To fire, flood, and logging control few people objected. But improper grazing can also harm ground cover, and here the infant Forest Service ran into yeasty opposition. Always an errant and touchy individualist, the stockman instantly suspected his new overlord of every hidebound evil of bureaucracy: arbitrary rulings, deafness to appeals, blatant inefficiency.

Many administrators of the early forest reserves did little to dispel those suspicions. Rangers, who had to furnish their own horses out of a salary of fifty dollars a month, were often political appointees of indifferent caliber. Yet they were expected to check trespass over wide areas, enforce game laws, supervise lumbering and grazing, fight fires. Since they could not possibly do it all, most of them, with a few notable exceptions, did nothing beyond plague handy neighbors over minor infractions. To make matters worse, the government itself seemed to have lost all common sense. Under the Forest Lieu Act of 1897 a citizen owning land within a reserve could swap it for equal acreage outside. Sniffing opportunity, these high-minded owners despoiled their holdings, then blandly exchanged them for lands of infinitely greater value. Within eight years the government had been left holding an odorous bagful of three million worthless acres, and shocked mountain dwellers were beginning to roar.

Meanwhile the king conservationist of all, Theodore Roosevelt, had become President. Under his crackling eye, the once slow-moving reserves put on seven-league boots, until finally, in 1907, further acquisitions in Colorado were prohibited by congressional law. Two years before that the controversial service was switched from the Department of the Interior to that of Agriculture. The name of its tracts was changed from forest reserves to national forests, and in a complete organizational shakeup, which put the administrators under civil service, Gifford Pinchot became chief forester.

As Pinchot realized but most ranchers did not, conservation problems are world-wide. This review of them, which necessarily limits itself to a portion of one mountain chain, is, in a sense, inaccurate through its very superficiality. However, the narrow view is the one which concerned the settlers of the Rockies. When "Pinchotism" descended upon them, when politically appointed rangers found themselves displaced, when professional land locaters and newspapers carrying land-office advertising were frozen out of business, and above all when stockmen were told they must henceforth pay for using public grass, a mass howl rent the heavens.

As is usual in such controversies, side issues became the targets of bristling sarcasm. For example: in straddling the mountains the forests embraced millions of acres of grassy, above-timber-line basins, to say nothing of a multitude of solid-rock peaks. No one but a governmental fathead—so said the sheepmen who had to buy permits for grazing the basins—would call such places "forests." Bureaucracy, too, came in for its normal sledge-hammering: "a vast army of carpetbaggers and aliens," bellowed *Ranch and Range*, September 1909, "whose principal duty seems to be the collection of revenue from the unfortunate pioneers who are trying to hew a home out of the wilderness." States' rights advocates leaped into the fray by crying that the government's huge land grab (each side consistently calls the other land grabbers) was removing valuable acres from state tax rolls. This argument the Forest Service tried to still by allocating 25 per cent of its revenues from grazing and lumbering permits to state roads and school funds, another 10 per cent to the building of local fences, bridges, trails, etc. However, the charge remains unsilenced. Tax proponents still say their form of land revenue would exceed the forests' 35-per-cent remittance. The truth? Who knows? Statistics for an adequate comparison are non-existent.[1]

All over the West grazing land is at a premium, but for years the Forest Service has steadily cut down the number of cattle and sheep it allows in the high country. In Colorado, between 1924 and 1945, the total number of permits dropped from 4265 to 2814; the total number of stock was forcibly reduced by 210,248 head. More telling than the reduction in numbers, however, has been the sharp curtailment in the time animals are allowed to remain in the forests. The over-all time drop, for both cattle and sheep, has been about 33 per cent. This means that somehow the individual rancher must find 33 per cent more feed, by buying or leasing private land which often has to have its carrying capacity increased by irrigation and seeding. The investment is heavy. Suppose the stock grower takes the plunge, develops spring, fall, and winter pastures—then finds his summer permits cut overnight, as has happened. By that much his investment has been rendered worthless. Naturally he squeals. Naturally he wonders what sort of stability he can expect from this bureaucracy whose decision cannot be readily appealed and whose long-range policy seems, at least so far as individual cases are concerned, impossible to predict.

The Forest Service just as naturally retorts that it must be governed by broad and not isolated considerations. For example, ranges which seem lush in wet years will be overgrazed during droughts, and this fact, which the individual rancher forgets when eying an individual section, must be borne in mind by the planning boards. Nor are domestic animals the only claimants for consideration; increasing pressure is being exerted by matters of water, game, lumbering, recreation.

[1] The tax argument, incidentally, reveals inconsistencies in human nature. Today many conservationists are objecting to Jackson Hole National Monument, created in 1943 and bordering Grand Teton National Park. The park, they say, includes the true scenic attractions of the region; the adjacent hole is nothing but a glacial outwash full of nasty commercial developments, and, what's more, its elevation to a monument removes land from the tax rolls of counties who have no revenue sources to spare. Yet for years other conservationists have been dismissing the stockman's national-forest-tax protest as a red herring!

There are other dissonances. The conservationists' key argument in favor of the Forest Service is water protection. Yet one prime cause of objection to Jackson Hole as a monument is the reclamation dam at Jackson Lake! Indeed, the mere mention of a dam in a national park or primitive area sends some conservationists into furies. Parks, monuments, and primitive areas, they point out, are the only spots where future generations will be able to see the wilderness which once bulked so magnificently in American history. Hence the areas must be kept unspoiled. It is an appealing argument. But it does conflict with other appealing arguments. The truth? . . .

The rancher, so says the Forest Service, is hardly the one to determine his fair share in respect to these other interests.

These rumblings, however, are mere coos compared with the din which recently has broken forth over the so-called Taylor Grazing Lands. Until 1934 the open range still embraced several hundred million acres which no one felt were worth claiming under the only methods available—a 160-acre agricultural homestead, a 640-acre pastoral homestead, etc. Since the land was unoccupied, the stockmen went on using it as they had for the past three quarters of a century. Then, under the aegis of another conservation-minded President named Roosevelt, the Taylor Grazing Act was passed and a system of permits instituted for the erstwhile free range.

The weather gave the new administrators a rousing welcome. An unprecedented drought in 1934 had left the mountain states shaggier than an old horse brush. But shortly after the government started it rehabilitation program rains fell and grass grew. Some exuberant administrators were inclined to credit the blossoming to the New Deal, which caused *Cow Country*, official organ of the Wyoming Stockgrowers Association, to chide gently that such jokes were "making a good laugh for the boys." A louder laugh resulted from the revelation that an ill-advised administration publicity photographer was lugging around with him a prop cow skull to lend a grisly touch to his pictures of "depleted" range in the Dakotas.

However, the government did try to improve the public domain. The Civilian Conservation Corps dug wells, put check dams in eroding arroyos, built ponds, drift fences, bridges, etc. Some stockmen did not like even that. They said (whether rightly or wrongly is beyond the ken of this commentator) that the efforts cost more than they were worth. They railed bitterly over the fact that by now fifty-nine different Federal agencies had a thumb in the land-management pie. And finally, after the war, they decided to end the "intolerable" setup by successfully lobbying in Congress for the cutting off of the appropriations of the Grazing Service and by recommending bills which would allow ranchers to purchase from the government such lands as they might desire.

Reaction in the nation's press was, and continues to be, violent. Its frequent ill temper has made proponents of the sale plan intemperate in turn, and they are crying out that the public is being misinformed.

One thing that rouses their wrath is the charge that the sale of the public domain is being advocated by no more than a handful of "big" operators. Now it is quite true that the proposal is not favored by a clear-cut majority of stockmen; however, from my own talks to a sprinkling of ranchers in four Rocky Mountain states, it does not appear that numbers are limited to a handful or that opinion is determined by size. Perhaps the largest sheep operator in the Colorado Plateau area is dead set against the proposal. So is a slightly bigger than average cattleman on the eastern slope of the Wasatch Mountains in Utah; he fears the sale will touch off such a competitive scramble among *little* applicants that all land values will be upset for years. Perhaps he is right. One Wyoming farmer-rancher running less than fifty head of beef cattle vehemently favors the sale as the only economical means by which he and others like him can expand. On the other hand, small operators of the North Fork Valley stockmen's associations, meeting at Paonia, Colorado, unanimously denounced the proposal as a program which "would establish grazing empires at the expense of . . . small stockgrowers." The truth? . . .

Big or little, those who favor the sale resent implications that they waited until the end of the war, when the whole nation was sick of controls, and then tried to slip through this brand-new piece of devilment on the sly. The proposal, they point out, is not new. Mountain man Uncle Dick Wootton went to Washington to plump for it in 1877; the National Livestock Association recommended it at its Forth Worth convention in 1900; and when the Taylor Act was inaugurated in 1934 the Wyoming Stockgrowers Association protested with a resolution favoring ultimate disposal of the lands to private owners.

As a matter of fact, say the sale proponents, their detractors are the ones who are being sly, for they are trying to create an impression that the sale of Taylor lands will also result in the sale of forest lands, and that no-trespassing signs will then appear beside favorite fishing streams, hunting grounds, and camping sites.[2] Actually, they point out, no association has officially advocated the demise of the Forest Service. However, the Forest Service's biggest guns are stumping the West as if life depended on the success of their defense. Is their fear justified? Or is it a mere sympathetic quivering of bureaucratic nerves over the troubles of its brother bureau, the Grazing Administration? That truth is hereby willed to someone else for determination.

There are other causes of contention, but none so bitter as the broad one over national policy. Conservationists fear that if these millions of acres of public domain are turned over to private individuals, the land will be ravaged, game will be crowded out, eroding silt will choke

[2] "Won't privately owned Taylor lands be posted?" demanded sportsmen. "Immaterial," say stockmen. Taylor lands lie mostly in semi-arid winter-range country where recreationists seldom go.

reclamation projects, and the eventual bill to the public will be in-estimable. In support of their contentions they point to the two sections of the Rockies longest used by white settlers, northern New Mexico and central Utah.

In both states are century-old rural cemeteries. A casual glance inside and outside their fences is enough to show what grazing can do to vegeta-tion. Stockmen, however, resist the argument; the graveyards, they say, lie in areas intensely grazed by overcrowded stock from small farms and households. Away from the towns—for instance, along the rights of way of the Union Pacific in Wyoming and the Santa Fe in New Mexico, both fenced for nearly half a century—no such contrast is discernible.

Next the conservationists read from early Mormon records which describe waving grass where now only sagebrush and junipers thrive. Utah towns, they say, are paying a high price for the exploitation which killed that grass. Since 1893 the hamlet of Mount Pleasant has suffered twelve disastrous floods originating on the overgrazed hills above town. The last one, on July 24, 1946, cost the community $106,000. Other floods between Bountiful and Farmington in 1923 and 1930 took several lives and $1,000,000 in property. Investigation by the Forest Service and the Utah Agricultural College showed the washouts arose "in the heads of canyons which . . . have been depleted of vegetation and de-nuded of plant litter, chiefly by overgrazing but to some extent by fire." This overgrazed land, some 18,500 acres, was privately owned. From 1850–1930 it had produced an estimated cash income of $148,000. For $39,000, Davis County and the United States Government bought 13,120 acres of it, spent another $300,000 on flood control and reseed-ing measures. What, ask the conservationists, is the profit in that kind of private ownership?

Along the Rio Puerco in the Jemez Mountains of northern New Mexico they find another example. Seventy-five years ago those grassy meadows supported 12,000 sheep, half a dozen villages, and several ditches irrigating 3600 acres. Then 240,000 sheep and 9000 cattle were crowded in. Now a chasm one hundred feet wide and twenty feet deep slashes the no-longer-grassy valley. Twelve ditches have been de-stroyed, only five hundred acres are left in production, half of the sole remaining town of La Ventana has fallen into the arroyo, and the rail-road, perpetually undermined by floods, has been abandoned. But the big bill is going to come from the 18,000 acre-feet of silt discharged annually by the Rio Puerco into the Rio Grande, which in turn dumps it into the vital Elephant Butte Dam.

These, the stockmen retort, are isolated cases caused by a few short-sighted individuals such as are found in any industry. And they produce statistics of their own. A thirty-year study by the University of Wyoming reveals that, although a steadily increasing number of sheep have been wintering on the Red Desert in the southern part of that state, ranchers have nonetheless shown consistent gains in the size of their animals, the fatness of the lambs, and the amount of wool—all without harm to the forage. Then, for a clincher, the sale advocates point to Texas, whose land is almost entirely owned by private individuals. Has lack of Federal supervision, they ask, led stockmen of the world's greatest ranching district to ravage their land and thus graze themselves out of business?

The truth? What is the truth?

CHAPTER XIV

JONATHAN CARVER'S CRYSTALS

CAPTAIN JONATHAN CARVER, zigzagging in 1767 through the Mississippi Basin on an abortive attempt to reach the Pacific Ocean, listened wide-eyed to the Indians. Far to the west, so they assured him, was a marvelous range "called the Shining Mountains from an infinite number of crystal stones of an amazing size, with which they are covered, and which, when the sun shines full upon them, sparkle so as to be seen at a very great distance."

Later wayfarers, pushing West for furs, for gold, for Oregon's fertile fields or the lush trade of Santa Fe, were less naïve. As their wagons rolled over the spring-green prairies and they caught that far-off sheen against the sky, they knew it for what it was. Mere snow, in summer a curiosity, in winter a death-bearer more implacable, more unpredictable than Sioux or Navajo. Crystals, indeed! Don't let it catch you in the passes, that's all. On they went.

On July 24, 1847, one of the last carriages of a train of seventy-odd vehicles pulled up on a bench overlooking the Great Salt Lake Valley. In it was a sick man, who now leaned forward and stared intently. He was thick-handed, thick-bodied, strong, but lately racked by a now unidentifiable disease called mountain fever. Today, however, he was feeling better. His small eyes held steady; we may imagine that for a moment his iron jaw relaxed under its austere fringe of beard.

Well it might have. The view that met him was, and is, a lovely one: long sweep of land to shimmering lake; soft, sun-warmed air, brooks tumbling brightly from the canyons. Over his left shoulder the Wasatch Mountains speared upward into the Cottonwood Peaks, and, blue across the lake and to the south, more mountains ruffled the horizon. For a long moment he looked, then nodded satisfaction.[1] The carriage jounced on, and at two o'clock in the afternoon, where City Creek

---

[1] Thirty-three years later at a Mormon jubilee, the driver of the carriage, Wilford Woodruff, belatedly recalled the exact words his passenger had spoken that memorable day, words which in 1947, the year of Utah's centennial, all America heard again: "It is enough. This is the right place, drive on."

broke from its canyon and split into twin sparkling forks, Brigham Young, Lion of the Lord, rejoined his people.

There were 158 of them, including nine women and two children. Three months before they had been sent out as an advance party to blaze a way and plant crops for the thousand and a half Saints who soon would follow them from Winter Quarters, near the present site of Omaha. It had been a long trail, an anxious one. But if the men cried "Hosannah!" when they reached the Promised Land, those nine women probably did not. The plains were huge and empty; dust puffed, clung to their skirts. There were no trees, and in places great swarms of crickets as large as their thumbs crawled across the iron ground.

Straightway the menfolk set to work planting potatoes and marking out more plots for corn, beans, and peas. It was high time. The season was late and there had to be food for the multitudes who were coming. But the baked dirt was recalcitrant. Plows splintered. In despair the workers threw a brush-and-earth dam across the creek and softened the ground by "conducting" water over it.

Do what those Mormons of 1847 could not. Call the roll of the rivers born where the snow shines on the high peaks: the turgid Missouri, the glittering Snake Fork of the Columbia, the Green arm of the canyon-carving Colorado, all of them heading on a glacial hogback far above timber line in the Wind River Mountains of Wyoming, where a man can, if he possesses that particular bump of curiosity, visit three great ocean sheds in as many minutes. Now turn south, ignoring a galaxy of tributaries until you come to the Arkansas; though it rises within rifle-shot of the South Platte branch of the Missouri, it joins the Mississippi many miles below. And south again. Here the Rio Grande and the Pecos burst from the rolling uplands and wind sandily toward the Mexican border. Finally, a big hop west where more streams sing down the Wasatch Range to lose themselves in the lakes of Utah's Great Basin.

Water everywhere, racing willy-nilly. How many barrels? How many miles?

Ask the statisticians. They are making hay, those mathematical-minded gentlemen of the Bureau of Reclamation, the Federal Power Commission, the Forest Service, the Department of Agriculture, the Bureau of Mines, the Grazing Service, the Geological Survey, the Office of Indian Affairs. They map and measure every trickle, thrust yardsticks into snowbanks, set rain gauges on hilltops, stream gauges in the valleys. And it is only the beginning. Other men are evaluating soil, classifying grasses, picking dam sites, estimating timber stands, correlating it all with a life-and-death factor known as runoff. Back and forth they go, counting acres already irrigated and acres that can be irrigated. One million three hundred and fifty thousand are already under ditch in the Upper Colorado River Basin alone. Now put a new dam here, another there, a third on this site, a fourth, a fifth—and the acreage is doubled— on paper.

Why double it? Here comes the economist with his charts. Hay at so much a ton, potatoes at so much a bushel. Grain elevators bulging, fat lambs feeding on sugar-beet tops, mines of copper, gold, lead, vanadium, coal. Wealth created—and wealth saved by controlling the wild rush of the waters. Fewer basements filled with mud, half as many bloated cattle bobbing dead on the floodwaters, less wreckage tangled around the remains of a railroad bridge.

And it is only the beginning. Falling water is energy; the mystery of a cascade can be turned into the mystery of a copper wire. Power . . . Silent giant strength swinging stork-legged across gorge and desert. Great wheels turning, housewives reaching into a deep-freeze unit or fingering nylon stockings in an air-conditioned store, kids yelling under floodlights at a ball game. This we have and more, and still the horizon reaches. Look. In Colorado alone there are whole mountains of oil shale containing more petroleum than all our known underground pools; if and when normal reservoirs are exhausted, only power can unlock that reserve. And the railroads. Plagued by the coal situation, they have been eying more closely the Milwaukee's clean, swift electrical crossing of the Rockies in Montana.

And the incidentals: so many tons of concrete and steel; so many man-hours of work for heaping up earth for dams or scooping it out for canals; plus more man-hours spent in distant cities to build steam shovels and insulators, and to provide food, clothes, shelter for those who do build them—it can be run out to infinity, even to absurdity. Now toss in the imponderables: the catch in your throat as a speedboat roars where once was only a dry sage flat. White sails dipping, cameras clicking. Dry flies and barbecue pits. Water. The great peaks smiling . . .

And it is only the beginning. This is not just the Rockies. It is a third of all America. It is Spokane and St. Louis. It is Omaha, Little Rock, and El Paso; Los Angeles and San Diego. It is ten thousand communities in between—towns where often there were no towns before the rivers yielded. It is a neon sign on a movie marquee, a tenderloin

A. L. Fellows, photographed by Will Torrence during their exploration of the Black Canyon of the Gunnison River, Colorado. The six-mile-long irrigation tunnel that resulted from their survey was an early-day reclamation epic.

Homer Reid

The snow of the high peaks is the Big Divide's most priceless asset. Conserved by the natural reservoirs of the forests, it provides pasturage for flocks, irrigation for farms, power for the cities, recreation for sportsmen. (Wilson Peak, near Telluride, Colorado.)

steak in an electric oven, a water sprinkler flashing over a bed of golden zinnias.

There is also the matter of footing the bill.

Add and then add again until your brain, recoiling, can only sum it up in one dry pedestrian sentence, as Herbert Hoover did in 1929: "Every drop of water that runs into the sea without rendering a commercial return is a public waste."

Or perhaps you would rather stand in the Colorado State Capitol Building at Denver and there among murals of Indians, miners, and cowboys read these lines by Thomas Hornsby Ferril:

> *Here is a land where life is written in water.*
> *The West is where the water was and is*
> *Father and son of an old mother and daughter,*
> *Following rivers up immensities*
> *Of range and desert, thirsting the sundown ever,*
> *Crossing a hill to climb a hill still drier,*
> *Naming tonight a city by some river*
> *A different name from last night's camping fire.*

Such are Jonathan Carver's crystals.

If the Mormons of Brigham Young's advance party realized in 1847 that they were making history on the banks of City Creek, their records do not reveal it. It was the old story of necessity mothering the future. —there lay the broken plows, helpless in the dry earth; a few feet away water gurgled. The solution was obvious (Osborne Russell, who had helped build Fort Hall in 1834 and who delighted in hunting trips to the Salt Lake Valley, had noted in his journal as early as 1841 how these very benchlands could be watered), and it calls forth a question often squabbled over: Were the Mormons the original irrigators of America?

Of course not. Even the Mormons make no such sweeping claims. Archaeologists have discovered a multitude of traces throughout the Southwest to show that prehistoric Indians had built dams, canals, and stone terraces before Columbus discovered these shores. When the Spaniards pushed north out of Mexico they found the primitive systems, adopted some, abandoned others (which had not previously been abandoned during the severe drought of 1276–98), and added new ones of their own. By 1807, when Zebulon Pike was being escorted past Albuquerque as a semi-prisoner for armed trespass on the lands of His Catholic Majesty, he noted that "the citizens were beginning to open the canals. . . . We saw men, women, and children of all ages and both sexes at the joyful labor, which was to crown with rich abundance their future harvest and ensure them plenty for the ensuing year."

Well, then, what about the widely accepted Mormon claim of being the first *Anglo-Saxons* to irrigate?

From the barren standpoint of "firsts" this, too, must edge back. To start with conjecture, irrigation was coming into common usage in California between 1830 and 1840; during the same period many Anglos were acquiring land there either by marriage or by taking out Mexican citizenship, and it is unreasonable to suppose that not a single one of them thought of aping his neighbor's ditches. To this supposition add the written word of early travelers in the Rocky Mountain region. Farnham *(Travels in the Great Western Prairies)* recorded that in 1839 a group of Mexican and American trappers were raising grain and vegetables above Fort Bent on the Arkansas, and remarked that the river "can be turned from its course over large tracts of rich land." Frémont in '43 mentioned a vegetable garden at Fort Lupton, and in '47 Francis Parkman obtained green corn and vegetables at the Pueblo where Fountain Creek runs into the Arkansas. Not proof of irrigation? True. Still, one who has seen that ground wonders how else gardens could have been made to mature during the arid summer season.

Anyhow, there are more definite records. Marcus Whitman, stalwart missionary, was irrigating in Oregon at least as early as 1841. In 1846, a year before Brigham's pioneers took the trail, one James Hatcher, ex-mountain man, broke a ditch a mile long out of the Purgatoire east of present Trinidad, Colorado, and watered therefrom a sizable corn patch—precious good it did him, too, for Indians came whooping down the draw, tore up his greening shoots, and persuaded him and his family to go elsewhere in a hurry. Finally, in the same summer of '47 when the Saints were damming City Creek, that marvelous word painter, George Ruxton, after seeing irrigation at San Carlos and detecting the trend in Western economics, wrote *(Life in the Far West),* "The depreciation in the value of beaver skins has thrown the great body of trappers out of employment and there is a general tendency amongst the mountain men to settle in the fruitful valleys of the Rocky Mountains. Already the plow has turned up soil within sight of Pike's Peak"—and elsewhere, too, one might add, for when the Mormons arrived in Salt Lake Valley, Miles Goodyear, to Brigham's great interest, was already growing corn on the nearby Weber, though whether or not he was irrigating no one bothered to mention, so far as I can discover.

But this is a bootless controversy and overlooks the essential nature of the Mormon contribution. Whatever scattered efforts at water diversion may or may not have been made before their advent were just that—scattered, the unco-ordinated scratchings of isolated men who wanted to eat. To be sure, self-preservation prompted the Mormons also. But it was more than the preservation of one man or one family; it was a hardheaded, foresighted clinging to an entire way of life.

Most of the Saints had come from comparatively humid lands and were used to comparatively high levels of living. Now they stood on the edges of a desert. Either they must adapt themselves, or they must adapt the land. The former course they refused to take. Their predecessors, the mountain men, had done that and in the process had become little better than white Indians. Therefore, it was the land which had to change, and the streams chuckling down from the snow crystals of the Shining Mountains furnished the only tool. This is the Mormon triumph—not mere water diversion, which the Spanish, at least, had done en masse before—but the transference of their Anglo-Saxon mores to a land not suited for them; the defeat of desolation without sacrifice of social, economic, or spiritual standards; the transplanting, in short, of a civilization.

By the fall of 1848 five thousand Saints had poured into the valley. In an economy where every family meant a farm, this flood burst the dikes of the embryo settlement; and Brigham Young, his eye on an empire that he hoped would reach from the Rockies to the Sierra Nevada, took steps to channel the flow. An amazing institution, the "call," was developed: any Saint, no matter how prosperous or contented he might be on a self-chosen homestead, was henceforth subject to being sent to any spot the church hierarchy might select. Harsh the system may have been—but scores of hamlets throughout the Rocky Mountain region bear witness to its efficacy.

Wherever they went the Saints took with them the knowledge of co-operative irrigation learned on the benchlands above the saline lake. Note the word co-operative, for it was to sink or swim as a group that these colonists breasted the unknown, and every man jack of them knew the feel of a shovel in a ditch. We can still read old community balance sheets, scrupulously toted up, where such labor is credited against assessments for the community's water. We can still see, high on the side of the lime-rock cliffs, such breathless ditches as the Logan-Hyde Park-Smithfield Canal, which was chipped out and trestled up in 1861 with no better tools than ox-drawn scrapers and the unmachinelike arms of men, women, and children—a hand-hewn ditch, incidentally, which nearly ninety years later is yet delivering water.

Not all the efforts were successful. Often the only survey was an eye squinted over a glass of water, and occasional disaster attended the discovery that the end of the ditch was higher than its mouth. Still, within eighteen years some 65,000 people were finding sustenance on 150,000 acres watered by one thousand miles of canal. Nor was all this effort confined to Utah. As early as 1854 a group of Mormon settlers had reached Fort Supply in the southwestern corner of Wyoming and was hacking a ditch out of the Green, the first scratch in the Colorado River Basin, where larger scratches were destined eventually to defy geography and leap clear to the Pacific and a cluster of mud houses just beginning, in '54, to shorten its name to Los Angeles.

Northward the trickle ran and soon the omnipresent ditch was siphoning water from Salt River into that loveliest of mountain vales, Star Valley on the Idaho-Wyoming line, where devotees insist the gamiest trout in the West are still to be found. Eastward, too, the tide was spreading, into lands already settled, and new frictions appeared. For example, in July 1878, Brigham's successor, John Taylor, ordered five families experienced in high-altitude farming and irrigation to explore the headwaters of the Rio Grande in Colorado. Reaching the San Luis Valley, they found several Mexicans and gentiles trying to grow wheat in the moist bottom lands. The Mormons sniffed contemptuously. In such spots grain kept green and growing until, bang, the September frosts nipped it unheaded. But up on the sandy loam of the benches it would have a chance to mature, and a ditch would water the benches. Laying their plans, the scouts sent word back to Utah and wolfed through the winter by freighting hay to Leadville and cutting ties for the Denver and Rio Grande.

The next spring, 1879, more Utah colonists arrived and a shiver of alarm rippled through the older settlers of the valley. The Mormons, local gossip buzzed, intended to establish a belt of towns twenty-five miles apart from Utah through Colorado to Nebraska and introduce polygamy. Wrathfully a valley paper thundered, "Must the Utes go is no longer as much a question as shall we allow the Mormons to settle?"

Undeterred, the Saints dug their canal. But on the morning scheduled for the ditch's inauguration they found a crude dam thrown across the river channel in such a way as to keep water from their head gates. And on the bank of the stream stood a group of grim-faced gentiles, waiting to see what the outnumbered Mormons would do.

It was an ugly moment. If the Saints retreated, where would the rout end? On the other hand, if they accepted the challenge . . . At a nod from their leader they jumped into the stream, floundered to the obstruction, tore it out. Perhaps sheer boldness carried the day. Perhaps the gentiles felt a secret admiration for these men who had pointed a way to better farming. Or perhaps it was just the sleepy influence of the Spanish Americans watching from under the shade trees on the bank. Anyhow, though there were catcalls and threats and a stone or two was chucked, no violent opposition developed. Within a year the Mormon communities of Sanford, Bountiful, and Manassa were taking root in the lower San Luis Valley. (From the last-named place came a youngster so handy with his fists that sports writers called him the Manassa Mauler; his name, of course, is Jack Dempsey.) In 1880 a reporter from the Denver *Tribune* went down to examine the supposedly ticklish situation, found instead peace and prosperity, attended a Mormon dance, and reported to his readers, "Had not the laws of Colorado been somewhat stringent as regards the number of wives a man should have at once, we should have embraced that faith—and all those pretty little divinities. We left this enticing little place and its charming Mormonesses with regret."

Farther and farther the tide rippled, not always with church sanction. In 1893 a wildcat company penetrated the dry sage flats of the Big Horn Basin in northern Wyoming, established a settlement at Burlington, and began gouging out canals to water the Burlington Flats, Byron and Germania benches. Progress was slow, action disjointed. There was no strong leader; '94 was a harsh, dry year; the church frowned on the project. Discouraged settlers drifted away. But the stalwart hung on, rallying to the old song:

> *Come, come ye Saints! No toil nor labor fear,*
> *But with joy wend your way;*
> *Though hard to you this journey may appear,*
> *Grace shall be as your day.*
> *'Tis better far for us to strive,*
> *Our useless cares from us to drive.*
> *Do this and joy your hearts will swell.*
> *All is well! All is well!*

Then came one of those strokes of pure luck which so often brighten the hard-luck pages of Mormon history. The Burlington railroad decided to extend its lines to Cody. The Mormons secured a contract to do the grade work, whereupon the church council changed its mind, approved the project, and even advertised it. Settlers flocked to the grading camps, plows bit into the brown earth, and when the work was done the Saints toted up their earnings—ninety thousand dollars. Now the canals could be finished. Townsites sprang up at Byron, Cowley, and Lovell; experimenters tried their hand with that curious commodity which was beginning to revolutionize agriculture and livestock feeding in the West—the sugar beet. And the historians wrote dryly, "Thus began a movement which left a deep imprint on the Big Horn Basin. Mormons have been connected with many irrigation projects since."

Meanwhile the gentiles in Colorado were undertaking their own struggles with water. Although a few agricultural communities had been established in the lower San Luis Valley prior to the gold rush (the 1851 decree for the San Luis ditch is the state's oldest, and the Guadalupe ditch, built in 1854, is still functioning), the main effort along the eastern rampart of the Rockies was originally expended in obtaining water for placer claims. Gold was more exciting than potatoes, and, besides, Zebulon Pike's and Major Long's legend that the country was unsuited to agriculture took a long time dying. This in spite of ample evidence to the contrary. David K. Wall, for example, having helped grubstake and encourage John Gregory's development of the latter's epochal placer strike, himself stayed prudently behind at Golden, planted a garden, irrigated it from Clear Creek (a trick he had learned from Californians, not Mormons), and raised vegetables that netted him two thousand dollars the first year, eight thousand dollars the next. At the same time William Kroenig was doing the same thing with equal success farther south on the Huerfano.

As if these weren't portents enough, some passer-by accidentally dropped a few grains of wheat in the dooryard of W. H. Parkinson's cabin at Denver; the next spring up they came, untended, attracting considerable comment but evidently pointing no moral. For the pioneers, had they wished, could have obtained from the office of W. N. Byers's *Rocky Mountain News* several packets of vegetable seeds which had been left there for free distribution. Indeed, Byers continually and everlastingly editorialized about the possibilities of Colorado agriculture, pointing out, among other things, that a Mrs. Lundstrom at Empire, elevation nine thousand feet, had grown truck where loggers and prospectors said it could not be done—and then, the next winter, had charged the scoffers five dollars for a cabbage and one dollar for a single large onion. But it was no use. The siren voice of the mines was sweet, and when a laggard start at farming finally was under way in 1864, nature, as if to punish such dilatory tactics, sent in swarms of grasshoppers. What with the ravages of these pests and the harassing of freight outfits by the Indians, corn that winter sold for ten dollars a bushel; hay reached one hundred dollars a ton. Sadly General John Pope, in command of the Department of Missouri, reported in 1867 to his superiors that "the region was beyond the reach of agriculture . . . utterly unproductive and uninhabitable by civilized man."

The railroads changed the picture. The Denver Pacific was completed from Cheyenne to Denver in June 1870; the Kansas Pacific reached the capital city a few weeks later. No longer was it necessary to trail across the plains in a covered wagon at the uncertain mercy of the Indians. Moreover, both railroads were land-grant companies, anxious to convert dead holdings into solvent real estate, and immediately they began furious advertising and promotion campaigns to dispel the desert myth. A typical excerpt: "Cabbages weighing 50 pounds were [at the Denver Fair] too common for especial mention; and we could easily credit the story of the prudent house-keeper who sent her child to market for the smallest head he could find, and he came home bending under the weight of a fourteen-pounder, having searched vainly for one of less weight."

Visionaries, too, were at work. Lean, stern-faced Nathan Cook Meeker, one-time agricultural editor of Horace Greeley's New York *Tribune* and destined, as we have seen, for martyrdom at the hands of the Utes, took a trip through Colorado in 1869, felt the hot touch of inspiration, and rushed back to New York to talk to his old boss. The result was a prominent announcement signed by Meeker and endorsed by Greeley: "I propose to unite with PROPER persons in establishing a colony in Colorado Territory. The persons with whom I would be willing to associate must be temperance men. . . . Moral and religious sentiments must prevail."

Thousands of replies poured in. Assured that the Union Colony would succeed, Meeker and two associates scuttled back to Colorado, selected a godforsaken-looking site near the junction of the South Platte and Cache La Poudre rivers, plunked down sixty thousand dollars for twelve thousand acres of Denver Pacific and privately owned lands, secured another sixty thousand acres of government ground, named the town to be Greeley, and commenced their surveys. In early May 1870, fifty-odd families arrived, looked around, saw that "Greeley is . . . part and parcel of the Great American Desert, midway between a poverty-stricken ranch and a prairie dog town . . . bounded by prickly pears," and began to cuss Meeker, Colorado, and anything else that was handy. The first train that chugged back East took several of them with it. But the majority stayed, partly because they had hog-tied themselves by sinking everything they owned in the venture, and more kept arriving. Within a year the population numbered 1155, centering around a village that contained no saloons (it never has had a legal one), a newspaper, a bank, hotels, several stores, and boundless civic pride—though when Isabella Bird passed through on her extra-ordinary trip to Estes Park, later to culminate in a six-hundred-mile solo horseback ride through the mountains, she found Greeley hot, dusty, treeless, and teeming with flies.

To their astonishment the colonists learned what the Mormons had already discovered elsewhere, that the sandy uplands were more fertile than the river bottoms. This meant ditches—longer, wider, deeper ditches than any the Mormons had yet attempted—and the placid net-work of canals which they learned through trial and error to construct served as a pattern for later colonies and later irrigators. In fact, seeing Greeley's prosperity, all Colorado, particularly the northeastern sec-tion, went ditch-crazy. Towns were born; some, like Fort Collins and Longmont, living into prosperity; others, like Colfax, dying back to dust. Speculation ran rife, with capital pouring in from all over the United States. The Grand Valley Ditch, in western Colorado, borrowed $200,000 from the Travelers Insurance Company of Hartford, Con-necticut; four years later the ditch's tangible assets were sold at fore-closure for one fifth the original investment. More recently a promoter lured a handful of homesteaders onto the adobe flats of San Miguel County, failed to deliver adequate water, and hied himself off to a career as a temperance lecturer in Grand Junction. "He'll dry up the town all right," the bitter joke ran. "He's had enough practice here."

Of all the dizzy schemes, perhaps the dizziest was the one proposed by Professor Cyrus Thomas, entomologist with the Hayden Survey. "My plan," he wrote, venturing away from his chosen field, "is to throw up an embankment running north and south from the Arkansas to the North Platte rivers, then by throwing dams across these streams, to turn water into this reservoir. A wall 30–40 feet in height . . . [will] form a lake six to eight miles wide and 200 miles long, enough to ir-rigate 12–14,000 square miles." As his boss, Dr. Hayden, dryly pointed out, the Platte and Arkansas at the most discharged 73,873,000 cubic feet per annum, enough to fill Professor Thomas's reservoir two feet deep. Since the evaporation rate was five feet per annum, the professor would have experienced trouble in keeping his reservoir moist.

Not until 1888, when the Supreme Court of Colorado declared that ditches were common carriers and could make only reasonable charges for transporting water, did the fever of overoptimism and stock speculation taper off. By this time there were more acres under irrigation in Colorado than in any other state, a lead held until 1919, when California spurted ahead largely on the basis of farms watered not by ditches but by wells. Had Nathan Meeker not been murdered by the Utes, he might have lived to see one of his predictions knocked into a cocked hat. Within fifty years, he had boldly said back in the seventies while listeners guffawed, there might be as many as two hundred thousand Colorado acres under water. Well, in less than twenty years there were a million and a quarter; today the figure is inching toward three and a half million.

So long as ditches were comparatively simple, the building of them was not beyond the means of private or co-operative companies. But ditches alone weren't enough. The late-summer months were those when water was most urgently needed, and they were also the months when streams were lowest. Soon it became obvious that reservoirs for storing the spring runoff were necessary, and starting with the Mormons' old Newton Dam in Utah in 1871, dozens upon dozens were built. They were devilishly expensive, however, and as later canals had to go farther back into the mountains for water and build larger lakes for storing what they managed to secure, agriculturists began crying for financial help from the states or from the Federal Government.

The railroad grants set the pattern for the earliest proposals. Said the planners, let irrigation companies, either public or private, be given grants of land on the basis of which they could issue bonds, then later redeem the bonds from sales of reclaimed land. It was an alluring idea. As early as 1873 a convention of delegates, assembled in Denver for the nation's first "Irrigation Congress," formally plumped for it; in December of the same year, needled by Governor Elbert of Colorado Territory, President Ulysses Grant recommended the plan to Congress as a means of implementing a canal hundreds of miles long from the Rocky Mountains to the Missouri River.

Nothing came of the dream beyond a flamboyant stock company which died in the prospectus stage. For one thing, the Western states and territories, dominated by the amount of government-owned land within their borders and hostilely suspicious of anything which might open the door to more Federal meddling, had caught up from the South the baton of "states' rights." Politically sensitive to such cries, Congress moved warily. First, under the Desert Land Acts of 1877 and 1891, it tried to foster individual reclamation by selling would-be farmers as much as 640 acres of land for a mere $1.25 an acre, provided the patentee made certain efforts at irrigation. All very well—except where was the individual to get water? Results being predictably negligible, the reclamationists set up a howl nearly as loud as that of the states-righters, and a compromise was evolved, the Carey Act of 1894. This provided that, upon application, a state or territory might be given one million acres of government land if it reclaimed this land within ten years. The state could turn the holdings over to private companies for development.

Again enthusiasm was lukewarm. However, one project completed under the Carey Act is interesting because of the persons involved, notably Buffalo Bill. After his wild-West circus closed for the season, it was the custom of the goateed showman to go back to Wyoming and relax with a few cronies on a hunting trip. According to A. A. Anderson, that amazing combination of forest ranger and painter in Paris salons, this is what happened one evening after dinner as a group of the boys were sitting on the banks of the Shoshone River. Said one, "Let's found a town here and name it after Cody." Agreed. George Beck, delegated to pick a site, rode onto a wind-swept bluff overlooking the stream, gave his hat a toss, noted where it fell, jogged back, and reported, "Gentlemen, the city of Cody is founded."

Buffalo Bill, it would seem, took the matter to heart. Utilizing the provisions of the Carey Act, he and Nate Salisbury secured a tract of land, erected a hotel and other buildings, acquired a coal mine, and, again according to Anderson, persuaded the Burlington to put in the same branch line whose contract for grading work saved the goose of the Mormons who were treading the edges of ruin not many miles away. Cody also built a canal of sorts and development went limping along.

Meanwhile the states' rights advocates had been snowed under by proponents of Federal aid to irrigation. Yielding to the massed demands of Western farmers, Eastern manufacturers seeking larger markets, labor unions, newspapers, and the big stick of Theodore Roosevelt, Congress on July 17, 1902, passed the Reclamation Act. This gave Buffalo Bill food for thought. His private reclamation project was growing too big to handle, and he decided to turn over to the government all his land and water rights. Within two years the Reclamation Service (today the Bureau of Reclamation) had started construction of the 328-foot-high Shoshone or Buffalo Bill Dam, for a long time the nation's loftiest.

As might be expected, the Reclamation Service fumbled some of its early projects, occasionally chilled its backers with icy financial losses—and now and then came through with heart-warming stories of human triumph. Most spectacular of all, perhaps, is the tale of the Uncompahgre, or Gunnison, Tunnel, project of southwestern Colorado.

The settlers who had swarmed into the Uncompahgre after the ejection of the Utes in 1880 had, with the fine frenzy of optimism prevalent in those days, taken up some one hundred thousand acres of farmlands, then had discovered that there was ample water for thirty thousand acres, and had fallen, some of them, into an era of sounding quarrels and expensive litigation, none of which moistened dead crops or prevented "tremendous loss and hardship." Meanwhile, a few miles distant, the Gunnison River pounded its majestic way northwestward toward the Grand (now the Colorado). Life itself—except that the water was locked in the bottom of a titanic granite gorge more than two thousand feet deep and, in the trough at the Narrows, only forty feet wide. The Utes with wonderful understatement called it the "place of high rocks and much water," and Captain John Gunnison, sniffing through the region in 1853 for a feasible coast-to-coast railroad path, had taken one quick look and had gone the other way. No man had ever penetrated to its gloomy heart.[2]

Then in 1890 a one-time miner named F. C. Lauson had a dream—no metaphor; he actually went to bed, so he says, and there envisioned conquering the ridge between the Uncompahgre and the Gunnison with a tunnel. Trouble was, it was quite a ridge. It took Lauson four years to tongue-whip the dubious citizens of Montrose into financing a survey which beat around the edges of the canyon and so determined that the levels of the Gunnison and of the valley were such that a bore would be physically possible—and horribly expensive. However, by dint of adroit log rolling, the Colorado legislature was induced to appropriate twenty-five thousand dollars for starting the work. Popguns to hunt elephants! A few miners slithered down into the canyon, exhausted the funds gophering out a thousand or so feet of granite, and climbed back out again.

This might have ended the story had not the newborn Reclamation Service come along. One glance showed the government men that the project would cost millions, not thousands, of dollars, and they refused to risk the expenditure on the basis of an incomplete survey. Engineer

[2] In 1933 the most spectacular part of this eye-filling region was set aside as the Black Canyon of the Gunnison National Monument. Because of mediocre roads it is still not widely visited.

Abraham Lincoln Fellows was told to traverse the canyon and get its story.

Here was a poser. The few parties who had tried wintertime exploration over a supposed highway of river ice had failed dismally. Whitewater exploration had ended in wrecked boats and near drownings; the only man ever to reach the head of the Narrows, a trapper called Moccasin Bill, told Fellows no one could go farther and live.

Orders were orders, however. Fellows went down to the Montrose newspaper office and advertised for an assistant—"a strong swimmer, unmarried, temperate, and obedient." In answer came William W. Torrence, who had been with a party that had lost its boats in 1900. Knowing from his experience that boats were impracticable, the pair decided to pack their equipment through on their own backs, reinforcing themselves along the way with supplies brought down from the rim. Weeks were spent finding three tiny breaks in the walls where such a descent might be possible, and the job of relief agent was entrusted to a man named Dillon.

Equipped with light instruments, a minimum of food, and pneumatic mattresses to use as rafts for emergency crossings of the river, the pair shoved off from the railroad siding of Cimarron. Fifty miles to go. At first it was just a slow slog through brush and over talus, with an occasional swim where great ribs of rock crowded the pathway into the water. But by the third day the rapids had grown tumultuous, the pine-clad slopes had tilted into an almost unbroken line of bare brown cliffs banded with startling veins of pink pegmatite. No longer was it possible to skirt an obstructing wall by swimming the white-capped river. Up the cliffs the pair would climb, hunkering in fright when an occasional boulder crashed down from the heights above, find a narrow ledge and wriggle along it until the barrier was passed and they could drop again to the river's noisy edge.

Finally, after Fellows had bruised and otherwise maltreated himself by falling twenty feet into a gooseberry bush, they dragged into Trail Gulch, first of the three refitting points. Two nights and a day they rested, told Dillon to bring them new shoes to replace those already shredded by the rocks, and pushed on again. Progress became so slow that at night they built huge fires of driftwood to let Dillon, watching from above, know they weren't dead but merely delayed.

Now the Narrows, forty feet wide, a third of a mile deep. Here Moccasin Bill had turned back. Fellows looked at Torrence.

"Will, this is your last chance to go out."

Torrence peeled off his clothes, put them with the instruments on the rubber mattress. Pushing the raft ahead of him into the snow-born water, he called back, "Here goes nothing."

Fellows followed. The pinching jaws slipped behind, the canyon bed widened enough to make room for an indescribable tangle of boulders which had fallen from the cliffs above. And there, sitting on one of the hugest of the rocks, was the faithful Dillon.

The next half dozen miles are the worst. The walls soar higher, nearly half a mile now, leaving a slit into which the sun can shine only at midday. In places incredible boulder falls have collapsed from the cliffs, burying the channel so that the river must gurgle blackly underneath, hunting whatever interstices it can find. Legend, trying to make that first trip even more dramatic than it was, says that at one point the two explorers hurled themselves into the howling stream and let it sweep them underneath an obstruction they could not climb. At that, Fellows almost managed it, though not deliberately. A whirlpool sucked him in, and only by frantic effort—he was a magnificent swimmer—did he escape doing what later was ascribed to him as solemn fact.

So they struggled on, climbing over each other's shoulders, plunging into the water, hauling themselves out. Six hours were spent negotiating one four-hundred-yard stretch. They lost their rafts, their food, but not their precious instruments. The days passed, hunger pinched. As they staggered along half-starved, they saw, another legend relates, a young mountain goat, ran it into a crevice, dispatched it with a butcher knife. Fellows's account is somewhat different: "While climbing 30 to 40 feet above the stream, I stepped out to a spot where there were some small bushes. . . . Up sprang two mountain sheep which had been apparently lying asleep. One was so dazed it sprang over the cliff and broke its shoulder on the rocks below." Less exciting, perhaps, than the butcher-knife story, but a meal from that sheep's hindquarters rebuilt their dwindling strength.

Now came the greatest of their discomforts, an icy drizzle of rain which gave them no chance to dry out when they climbed from the stream after still another fording. It was a gaunt, shivering, ragged pair who, fourteen miles from the rendezvous at the Narrows, finally reached Red Rock Canyon and once again found Dillon waiting, a hot meal ready.

One more stretch and the fifty-mile journey would be over. They tried. But they were ill from overexertion, loss of sleep, wet food, and too little of it. For ten days they had lost flesh at the rate of two pounds a day, though they were physically toughened men. They had climbed more cliffs than they had remembered to count, had swum the river

seventy-six times, were bruised and lacerated from head to foot. And
in a sense their job was complete; they had learned where the tunnel
would have to be. After pushing another eight miles or so down the
relaxing canyon, over easier ground than they had previously covered,
they gave up, turned back to Red Rock, and climbed into the sunshine
of the dry piñon-and-sagebrush mesa.

On the basis of their report the Reclamation Service went to work
on both ends of an 11-by-11½-foot bore located in the gentler upper
stretches of the canyon, where the river construction camp would not
be so desperately hard to supply. And still the gorge would not relent.
In December 1906, drillers broke into a fault which poured onto their
heads (or would have, if they'd stayed) a million gallons of scalding
water an hour. The carbon dioxide gas which accompanied the flow
caused several months' delay while a 700-foot ventilating shaft was
driven from the surface.

This devilish fault extended nearly half a mile. Heat rose to a humid,
dripping ninety degrees; gushes of mud periodically buried tracks and
tools and frightened timid workers into quitting in the middle of the
shift. But year after year work plugged along until in 1909 nearly six
miles of tunnel had been blasted out and President Taft was able to
drive across the sandy desert to the western portal, place a silver bell
on a golden plate, and so declare the project officially opened.

It is anticlimax to have to add that, although the work was authorized
under the Bureau of Reclamation's repayment plan, the Uncompahgre
district has never managed to keep far enough ahead of maintenance
expenses to meet the nearly seven-million-dollar cost of the bore and
its attendant 489 miles of ditch. It did, however, save the Uncompahgre
Valley and raise the value of an acre of land from two dollars to nearly
eight hundred dollars on a fruit-producing farm; and though reclamation
men wince when you say Uncompahgre, their not illogical defense is
that there are bound to be some sour spots in any trial-and-error process.

Cost amortization was the bureau's earliest and biggest headache.
They thought they had a sure thing. Operations were begun in the
rosy era when irrigation was still deemed to be the West's Midas touch,
and it was supposed all they had to do was throw open the reclaimed
lands on the basis of first come, first served, and send in the check whenever it's handy, please. No effort was made to screen out incompetent
farmers, and such a highfalutin creature as an irrigation engineer to
help newcomers select desirable sites and lay out workable water
systems was considered a silly luxury. A prospect, often greener than

the advertised-to-be greenness, simply wandered into the shanty of some local old-timer who had set himself up in business as a "guide," was loaded into a spring wagon drawn by a span of mules, and bumped off across the roadless sage to pick his future home by guess and by golly. Credit was almost non-existent, building materials were things read about in catalogues, and scientific studies concerning the adaptation of crops to the type of soil and the amount of water available were undreamed of. Not until the plains began to sprout almost as many deserted houses as corn shoots did thoughtful agronomists pause to figure the profit in a carrot when annual water charges reach, say, thirty-three dollars an acre; and those sturdy twentieth-century pioneers who somehow managed to live through this period deserve a monument as tall as any ever built to Oregon trailer or Indian fighter.

Today things are managed differently. First, the repayment period was extended from ten to twenty and finally to forty years, and such red-ink spots as the Uncompahgre are now few and far between. Power developments, while adding enormously to the bill for the vast systems, also help enormously in underwriting the expense, to say nothing of the economic and living-standard potentials thus added to the region. Credit strings have been untied, qualified agriculturists help the settler examine his site, and irrigation experts render advice from masses of information gained through forty-five years of experiment. More important, perhaps, applicants are screened (by local boards, not by the government) on the basis of experience, financial reliability, and character soundness, with preference going to veterans.

It has brought a new and stable race to the land, trained farmers and those who work for the farmers on the irrigation systems—the maintenance crew, the watermaster, and that cowboy of the canals, the ditch rider. Every mountain settler knows the last mentioned. Perhaps he is a youngster just out of college and driving a jeep; perhaps, deeper in the hills, he is a grizzled veteran on a splay-footed old nag that will stand patiently by while he gets off and works. Probably he is employed by a private or co-operative organization rather than by the government. (The Bureau of Reclamation is the giant of the Western water scene, but don't forget the little fellows. In Colorado alone there are nearly six thousand individual and partnership affairs, more than five hundred co-ops.) But whoever pays the ditch rider, the silhouette of him against the sky line is now as familiar as the sagebrush. Day after summer day he makes his rounds, scraping weeds from the head gates, tamping gopher holes, dragging the bloated carcass of a ewe up the slippery banks, draining the ditch the heart-stilling night when the

Johnsons' youngest fails to appear. When the sun is hot and water short, he mediates quarrels, allays bitterness. He delivers messages, runs errands, relays gossip, yet never tells the families on the lower ditch what those on the upper really think of them. Never too busy to show how he works or to retell his accumulated lore, he is the hero of the kids who come racing barefooted across the stubble when they see him approach. . . . One recalls a mountain ditch high where dappled aspen shadows lay. A brown pine-board cabin set on stilts. A square, brown man, everlastingly patient. "Now do it this-a-way . . ." Or, "That gives me to mind the day I was moseyin' by an' . . ." Long rides on the slow-curving banks, the man-feel of adventure when one was allowed to jump waist-deep in the frigid water and help wrestle a crib log into place, the awesome glint of a steel trap sliding into the runway of a bank-perforating beaver, the jerk of a hand-trimmed willow pole above a secret eddy where big trout lurked on their way up from the reservoir. And with it all, through it all, the blood and sinew of it all, the sound of water flowing endlessly to the farms far below.

Early pioneers, struggling in the springtime with the flooded Platte, the Green, the Arkansas, the Rio Grande, thought that here was water without end. They were wrong. The flow was limited, and out of the struggle to allocate it grew a brand-new conception of property rights.

The idea took root almost unnoticed. The miner whose flume first cajoled water from its natural bed around a hill point to a dry gulch had no idea that he was thumbing his nose in the august face of English common law. Neither had the first Mormon emigrant nor the first of Meeker's Union colonists. Nonetheless, their picks and shovels were busily digging the way for the now famous "Colorado doctrine," a legal concept which would have shocked Lord Coke right out from under his powdered wig.

The question finally shaped up for the courts one hot summer day in 1879 when a Colorado farmer named George W. Coffin found the ditch leading to his fields dust-dry. St. Vrain Creek, which supplied him, had been dammed by an organization with the intriguing name of the Left Hand Ditch Company. Moreover, this presumptuous company was taking the water out of its natural channel and ditching it over a ridge to another creek. Wrathfully Mr. Coffin demolished their obstruction. The company, instead of shooting matters out like gentlemen, promptly sued him.

Coffin's attorneys offered in his defense a multitude of English common-law pronouncements on the subject of riparian rights, pronouncements which clearly state that no one, even though he owns lands bordering a stream, may prevent its natural flow to the owners of the soil below. But the Colorado Supreme Court pooh-poohed the contention. "Shall we deprive one of benefits after he has by large expenditure of time and money carried water from one stream over an intervening watershed and cultivated land in another valley?" So here were the seeds, already recognized by Congress in 1866, of water rights according to prior beneficial use or, as it is sometimes called, the doctrine of appropriation as opposed to the doctrine of riparian rights. Because of it everyone west of the Mississippi is living a different sort of life today.

On the basis of this doctrine, the Larimer County Ditch of Colorado toward the turn of the century crossed not just a ridge but the lofty Never-Summer Range and whisked the headwaters of the Laramie River (a tributary of the North Platte) back through the Green Mountain Tunnel. No one paid much attention to this brazen mountain hop nor to the Uncompaghre Tunnel. Then ditches began crossing the Continental Divide itself. The Skyline Ditch Company tapped the headwaters of the Colorado River above Grand Lake and sold the acquisition on the eastern slope of the Rockies. In 1906 the Reclamation Service added to Provo's supply by knocking a hole under the Wasatch Mountains and appropriating still more flow from the Colorado River's watershed. Nobody squawked. Southern California, Los Angeles in particular, had not yet begun to experience her desperate thirst.

In 1911 things changed. The Larimer Ditch decided to drill a new tunnel under the Never-Summer Range and take additional water from the Laramie River. This time the diversion hurt, and Wyoming reared up with an agonized yowl. She owned that water, she said; residents way down on the Laramie had been using it for years. Nonsense, retorted Colorado. The water was hers by right of being deposited within her borders by God's own clouds and she could do with it as she chose.

Thus the battle was joined and continued almost endlessly. Finally, however, in 1922 the United States Supreme Court decided Wyoming owned the water by right of prior beneficial use, no matter how far down the river it had been appropriated. But the court also ruled that a Colorado user could seize any unappropriated flow and take it wherever he wished—clear out of the basin of its birth and on to Timbuktu if he liked.

Los Angeles, the Imperial Valley, Phoenix, Salt Lake City, El Paso, Santa Fe, and way stations cocked their ears. Prior beneficial use, eh? And whatever wasn't already claimed could be taken anywhere, could it? Well, now. Suppose the boys in the upper basins—look at Denver, already snatching up Colorado River rights for diversion through the proposed Moffat Tunnel—suppose they grabbed it all. We'd better get in while the getting's good.

The result might have been, in the words of one arbitrator, "a wild scramble in a contest of speed for first development"—except for another precedent. Kansas and Colorado, after a protracted and still undetermined legal suit over the waters of the Arkansas, had at length quit the courts in disgust, had sat down around a table, and had drawn up a treaty, called a compact, outlining their respective rights. (All very good, Congress said, sticking its nose in, provided the Federal Government is party to such goings on.) The idea worked. Other controversies resulted in similar agreements with Nebraska and New Mexico, and the way was opened for that most famous of all interstate compacts, the seven-way agreement between the states of the Colorado River Basin,[3] which in turn gave the go-ahead to that most famous of reservoirs, Lake Mead and the Hoover Dam. It has not all been sweetness and light, however. Arizona stayed out in a huff until 1944. New demands all up and down the stream have led Provo and Greeley, Pueblo and Salt Lake City, Los Angeles and Denver to eye one another with mutters of "Robber"—though interestingly enough not one of the major cities pre-empting Colorado River water is located within its drainage shed. So who is stealing from whom?

To make sure each claimant would eventually get the last pint he was entitled to, an intensive study was begun of every snowflake which falls on the Shining Mountains. A devastating fact soon emerged. Beneficent Nature, who once had seemed so prodigal with the West, is no longer beneficent enough. There is not—ponder it, ye Chambers of Commerce—there simply is not sufficient water in the Rockies ever to allow the full and unlimited development of all the arable land lying between the hundredth meridian and the Sierra Nevada.

Meanwhile, how solve the desperate problems already facing the West? The east slope of the Rockies and the Salt Lake Valley, to take two acute examples, had by the middle 1920s touched their economic ceilings. It was a case of too many people trying to live off too restricted an area—restricted not by size but by lack of available water. Fifty-seven per cent of Colorado's population was jammed within seventy-five miles of the capitol building. At the foot of the Wasatch Mountains the situation is even more pressing. According to R. C. Johnson

[3] Wyoming, Colorado, Utah, Nevada, New Mexico, Arizona, California, plus additional treaties between the United States and Mexico.

of the Bureau of Reclamation's Salt Lake City office, there is an agricultural concentration approaching that of Japan, the average farm being only fifteen acres in size and those fifteen acres panting on the hot edge of drought.

How had such an impasse come about in the supposedly sparsely settled West? It was inevitable. An original settler found a good piece of land and enough water for one family's needs. He fared well, died, passed the holdings on, say, to four sons, who soon were trying to support four families on ground that previously had taken care of one. To be sure, there was plenty of unoccupied land they might have moved onto, but there was no more moisture within reach of the community's resources. The only answer was more intensive agriculture on smaller plots, but intensive farming is greedy for water, and so this solution did not work either. Many young people gave up in despair; during the decades 1920–40 more people left Utah than came in, although the state's birth rate, highest in the United States, enabled her to show a small net gain in the census tables.

The war checked the drift and brought an unnatural influx of population and industry, another notorious water gulper, into both Colorado and Utah. Thus an already worrisome problem was rendered doubly acute. What to do?

The answer has been a series of reclamation projects which stagger the imagination. One of them, the Colorado-Big Thompson project, had been started before the war, its design to take water through a thirteen-mile tunnel under the Continental Divide and dump it into the Big Thompson River near Estes Park—water not for new land, mind you, but for 615,000 acres at present insufficiently irrigated in the Fort Collins-Loveland-Longmont-Greeley-South Platte areas. The war slowed things down and ran costs up toward the $140,000,000 mark. Water sold to farmers and an ad valorem tax on the entire district benefited, chain stores as well as hayfields, will pay back perhaps a quarter of this enormous sum. Power sales from 900,000,000 kilowatt hours of electricity generated annually by seven power plants will bite off another large portion. The rest? Well, there's always Uncle Sam, the theory being that, since prosperity in Colorado will indirectly benefit the whole nation, the whole nation should help bring that prosperity about, just as Coloradoans help pay for Federal developments elsewhere throughout the land.

Slated for the Denver area, whose situation had been relieved but not solved in 1936 by the completion of the city-financed diversion part of the Moffat Tunnel, is the massive Blue River-South Platte project. Designed to be twice as large as the Big Thompson behemoth, it presumably will cost twice as much; it, too, will provide supplemental water, though some new land may be opened. Still farther south, engineers are mapping the Gunnison-Arkansas colossus, which will be three times the size of the Big Thompson, will furnish supplemental water all the way from Pueblo to the Nebraska border, and in addition will open some 360,000 acres of new land. New Mexico, meanwhile, is hungrily eying the San Juan, hoping to scoop part of it over into the Rio Grande. She may not succeed. After all, the three projects outlined above are all transmontane operations bleeding the Colorado River, and Southern California is stirring restively. Under the seven-state compact there must be a specified amount of water for the lower basins.

Where on earth is it coming from? The only possibility is the storage of floodwaters in a bewildering complex of reservoirs which will trap the spring runoff and then let it trickle on down the Grand Canyon as it is needed. This explains, for example, why the Colorado-Big Thompson project necessitated the building of the multimillion-dollar, rock-and-earth-fill Green Mountain dam, 270 feet high and 1000 feet long, on a river scores of miles from the main workings themselves and utterly beyond reach of the diversion tunnel. It is money in the bank for a very sharp-eyed creditor—Los Angeles.

But all this is simple compared with the Central Utah fantasy for the saving of Salt Lake Valley's economic skin. Here was a tough engineering nut to crack; for years men had been trying to figure out how to lift water out of the gorges of the Green into the Uinta Basin and from the Uinta over the Wasatch Range. Oh, it could be done with gargantuan electric pumps and such, but it was so appalling a job that revenues would scarcely meet operating and maintenance costs, let alone repay the construction bill. The only alternative was to tap the many small streams which foam down the southern side of the wild Uinta Mountains. But Uinta Basin farmers had already filed on that water and . . . Never mind; take it anyhow and replace it with water brought from the Green, which was feasible.

Such, in reclamation parlance, is diversion by replacement, the last white hope of salvaging the last precious one of Jonathan Carver's crystals. In the Central Utah plans it means at least three major dams varying from 300 feet in height at Soldier Creek to 529 feet in Echo Park on the Green in Colorado, the last to store 6,400,000 acre-feet of water. It involves a gathering ditch 8000 feet high on the ragged face of the Uinta Mountains, forty-odd tunnels aggregating more than 100 miles in length, the longest being the fourteen-mile Midway–Little Cottonwood bore under the Wasatch. Besides innumerable lesser canals and dams, it will also involve several mammoth power plants and the longest man-made aqueduct (equal to one eighth the air-line distance from New York City to Los Angeles) in irrigating history. Fifteen per cent of the total cost, estimated at $300,000,000, 1940 prices, will presumably be met by water users and the balance by power purchasers.

Beyond this are the plans, big and little, for the rest of the Colorado River, for the Columbia, the Missouri, the Rio Grande, and all their tributaries, plans dryly outlined in tall thick books replete with graphs, charts, and tables which anyone interested may obtain by writing to the United States Department of the Interior, Bureau of Reclamation. They make heavy reading, but their matter-of-fact lines tell the story of a dramatic war: how the nation has set out to rule her largest mountains and through them to rule the life-giving valleys. It is the big story of the West today. With the world's hungry hands reaching to us from every side, some in anger, some in appeal, it may even be one of the big stories of all America.

CHAPTER XV

WELCOME, TOURISTS

WHEN men perform the function of naming great things," cried an early mountain eulogist, "why do they not study to supply a name that shall be characteristic of the object?" His suggestion for Colorado: Utopia.[1]

Comparable grandiloquence is almost as old as the first settlement in the Rockies, and the hurry-scurrying young railroads were quick to abet it with advertising brochures, generally called guidebooks, whose favored descriptives—"awesome," "enchanting," "weird," and "salubrious"—have not been noticeably improved on by later writers. The copy pulled. Tourists rode the westering rails in droves. Though Denver's population in 1878 was hardly 25,000, her four main hotels that summer registered 50,100 visitors, with no one knows how many more quartered in smaller hostelries and boardinghouses.

To help regale these visitors the roads conducted "excursions" without end. Almost as fast as a new section of track was ballasted, up puffed a tourist train, brass a-gleam, red plush seats spotless, Negro porters bustling, and speechmakers in full voice. The Santa Fe's first excursion into the Royal Gorge (before the Denver and Rio Grande won control of that hotly contested gateway) was described in breathless prose: "One glance suffices for a comprehension of the meaning of the word depth never before dreamed of, and never afterward forgotten. . . . A crevice, a huge, awful, crooked crevice through which the miserable little train is timidly crawling . . . Not a word is uttered. The engineer whistles occasionally, and timid folk look for the rocks to fall. It is really a strain on the mind to take it in."

Lest it be such a strain as to frighten away trade, the writer quickly added, "There is no danger apprehended from the masses of rock overhanging the track. Every inch of this wall has been examined and tested."

Another famed canyon, though more remote and hence less visited than the Royal Gorge, was Toltec Gorge on the Denver and Rio Grande's narrow-gauge run from Alamosa to Durango in southwestern

[1] *Illustrated Rocky Mountain Globe*, October 18, 1900.

Colorado. Here the track, instead of hugging the stream bed as is usual, clings to a shelf high above the canyon floor, and trainmen entertain passengers by pointing to tiny objects far below. "Yonder's a rear coach that was just naturally whipped off when the train went around a curve." As a matter of fact, coaches at rare intervals have jumped Toltec's rails. One went over in '82, rolled two hundred feet, smashed itself to flinders against a pine tree, and left ten of its twenty-two occupants dead as doornails.

Still, Toltec Gorge was—and is—a popular run. One noted excursionist, Teddy Roosevelt, delighted the railroad by saying, "This is certainly where Nature spilled her paint pot," and towering Phantom Curve is the site of perhaps the loneliest presidential memorial in the nation. The year was 1881, and James Garfield had just died of an assassin's bullet. A train carrying a load of ticket agents on an excursion to Durango panted to a stop on a flat spot commanding an imposing view of the canyon. It was Garfield's funeral hour. Fittingly, black clouds lowered overhead, wind moaned in the pines. The subdued party held an impromptu service and heaped up stones into a temporary cairn. Back in Denver, they ordered a more enduring monument. Thus today, in one of the most unexpected places in the Rockies, stands a large block of granite inscribed:

In Memoriam
JAMES ABRAM GARFIELD
President of the United States
Died September 19, 1881
Mourned by All the People
Erected by Members of the National Association of
General Passenger and Ticket Agents, Who Held
Memorial Services on This Spot, September 26, 1881.

Also from Durango the Denver and Rio Grande ran its unique Columbine Special to Silverton. The train came back from this annual jaunt all but smothered under masses of the five-petaled, blue-and-white state flower; and the event became so famous that a fraternal organization once requested twenty-five thousand columbines for their convention in Denver. No one was going to count that many blossoms. The exuberant excursionists simply dug up what they thought was a sufficient number and loaded them in tubs. The harvest filled four flatcars— a floral slaughter not likely to be duplicated, since the columbine is now protected. To which naturalists say, "Amen."

These were special events, however. The ordinary outing involved a picnic run up one of the canyons near Denver. Favorite destination was Georgetown Loop, a mid-eighties engineering marvel pictured in geography books alongside Niagara Falls and the Yellowstone Geyser. The Loop came about when the Colorado Central decided to extend its tracks from Georgetown to Silver Plume and found itself faced with the need of gaining a thousand feet of elevation in a mile of distance. This it accomplished by laying four miles of track: a huge U in which the end of one of the steadily rising prongs looped over the other on a trestle three hundred feet high—very titillating, indeed, to passengers who hung goggle-eyed out the windows while wheels squealed on the curves and the laboring engines whooshed forth black billows of smoke laced with steam.

The folk came in hordes—twenty thousand during one summer—the men jaunty in peg-top trousers and beribboned skimmers, the crino-lined women protected from sun, cinders, and mosquitoes by alluring veils draped over straw hats with brims almost as wide as cartwheels. At the lunch stop (either Georgetown or Silver Plume, depending on schedules) the effete ate in depot or town restaurants, one of which, the Hotel de Paris, boasted statuary, couched lions, beveled glass mirrors, beechwood floors, marble-topped tables, and an Italian fountain in the middle of the dining room. More hardy excursionists carried their wicker hampers out under the aspens. Meanwhile merchants sold quantities of hand-colored post cards, paperweights concocted from ore samples, and souvenir teaspoons made from local silver. Then back the groups went, giggling, refreshed, carefree as the wind. Or so we are told. Old-time Coloradoans recall the Georgetown Loop with a nostalgia rendered doubly poignant by the fact that today scarcely a trace of it remains.

Of all the attractions exploited to allure tourist trade, none was so enduring as the mountain hot springs. There are hundreds of them throughout the Rockies; they have given names to dozens of towns. It is small wonder they were focal points. A pailful of heated water, in the era before stoves, was not only a luxury but a labor, and those natural faucets were enough to make rheumatic men—or women—wistfully covetous. Quickly the Indians were dispossessed, the choicest sites homesteaded, quarreled over, sold, and resold.

The prize fountains of all bubbled near the present town of Ther-mopolis, Wyoming, in the northeast corner of the Shoshone reserva-tion—a battery of green-blue pools whose largest, the Big Horn Springs, is twenty-five feet across and pours out over colored terraces of traver-tine more than eighteen million gallons of 135° water each day. The

Shoshone believed that bathing here prolongs a man's life. Perhaps it does. Chief Washakie was almost a hundred years old when he yielded to white insistence and in 1896 called his people together to discuss the government's offer of sixty thousand dollars for ten square miles of the land.

How much money was that? "I tried to count it," said Washakie, "but I could not do it. But as for me I will trust the Great Father." It was trust almost misplaced. The Shoshone sold the ten square miles with a stipulation that Indians always be allowed to bathe there free, but this provision did not appear in the treaty. However, the government gave a portion of the ground to Wyoming for a state park, and in 1899 the legislature restored the right.

Acme of elegance was not at Thermopolis, however, but at the Santa Fe Railroad's Montezuma Hotel and Sanitarium, located five and a half miles up a branch line from once bawdy Las Vegas, New Mexico. In the eighties, during the height of its glory, the Montezuma covered three acres of ground, seated five hundred people in its dining room, one thousand in its casino. There were oak-paneled walls, marble fireplaces, and a menu that included green turtles rushed in tank cars from the Gulf of California. Here, when Captain Manners, future Duke of Rutland and father of Lady Diana Manners, wanted to camp on the grounds in a tent, he was icily reminded by Fred Harvey, savior of the traveling public's collective stomach, that although the hotel was in the wilds it was not of them. (P.S. In spite of the punctilious Mr. Harvey, the captain and his wife jolly well tented on the lawn.)

But the curse of Montezuma was on the resort. It burned down, was rebuilt, burned again, and finally ran into strangling competition from the Santa Fe's own El Tovar at Grand Canyon. Finally it was sold to the YMCA for one dollar, passed into the hands of the Bible Film Company, thence to a Baptist college, and in time became a Roman Catholic seminary.

All of Montezuma's vagaries did not match those of the four-storied, green-and-yellow Antero Hotel, which dominated Heywood Hot Springs at the chalky foot of Mount Princeton, Colorado. For forty years the Antero stood an empty shell while its various owners fought, sold, traded, sickened, and died. At length, just after World War I, Kansas farmers bought enough bonds to finish it and build a fifteen-thousand-dollar golf course. Unfortunately a rancher whose grazing permit embraced the links refused to budge, and at least one guest threatened to sue the resort, since he could not play with cattle obstructing the fairways.

Health, of course, was the main selling point of the hot springs. Their advertisements bristled with chemical analyses of the invigorating carbonates, sulphates, silicates, lithates, and what not in their waters, but even these nostrums paled before the magic ascribed to the climate. Said Fossett's *Tourist Guide to the Rocky Mountains:* "The dryness of the atmosphere, together with the electricity therein contained, combined with, perhaps, other peculiarities of the climate, excites the nervous system. . . . The appetite is keen, the digestion vigorous, and the sleep sound. . . . All lurking ailments are swept away at once, and whatever there is in each individual to enjoy is called into the fullest action. He revels in what might be called an intoxication of good health."

Talk like that was clutched at with frantic eagerness by every sort of invalid, particularly those suffering from pulmonary diseases. During the early seventies Denver was described as harboring "enough asthmatic people to warrant the holding of an asthmatic convention of patients cured and benefited"; and it is said that Chancellor Buchtel helped pull Denver University through its poverty-stricken infancy by a staff of consumptive professors willing to work at half salary for the sake of the climate.

Undoubtedly the preponderance of dry, sunny days helped produce cures. But climate has its limitations. Isabella Bird, traveling horseback through Colorado Territory in the seventies, saw in a wayside inn a sick-looking young man collapsed with grief beside a bed from whose filthy covers protruded two large white motionless feet. The tubercular owner of those feet (and the sick man's brother) was dead. The landlady was annoyed. "It turns the house upside down when they come here and die," she told Isabella, though the half dozen men yarning and playing backgammon in the same room with the corpse seemed unconcerned. "We shall be half the night laying him out."

Poor deluded pair. They and many another in the last stages of consumption had thought that exercise in the pure mountain air would be panacea enough. Too often exercise meant manual labor for earning coarse, greasy meals. Today we know that rest and decent diet are better cures. But such medicines are hard to come by when one's purchasing power consists solely of hope.

To be sure, many an invalid, both actual and hypochondriac, had more in his traveling kit than profitless optimism, and as early as 1870 General William Palmer and his Denver and Rio Grande Railroad hoped to lure the lucrative trade to a tailor-made town near Manitou Hot Springs at the foot of Pikes Peak. They ignored the village which was already there—Colorado City, a freight stop at the mouth of Ute Pass and im-

portant enough, during the first gold rush, to serve for four days as territorial capital. But Colorado City was too rowdy. Perhaps General
Palmer remembered that when the doors of its first church were thrown
open in 1863 only one worshiper had shown up to greet the minister.
The rest of the citizenry were engaged in hanging a horse thief. The job
done, they trooped back to hear a sermon on "the judgment to come."

Avoiding the ungenteel spot, the Denver and Rio Grande's land promoters laid out the town of Colorado Springs on the other side of the
creek and wrote a prohibition clause in the village charter. When one
ingenious entrepreneur endeavored to circumvent the law by means of
a "Katy King Spiritual Wheel" set in a wall and carrying a coin one way
and a glass the other, the city fathers ordered the property forfeit. Industry was also frowned on—too much smoke and grime for delicate
lungs. If mills, smelters, or factories wished to locate nearby, let them
go to Colorado City. (Today the towns have grown so that a traveler
can't recognize the dividing line, and the Colorado Springs Chamber of
Commerce, remembering the effect of the depression of the 1930s on
tourist trade, has apparently decided that industry's smoke and industry's
pay checks are tolerable after all.)

From the start Colorado Springs was a success. By 1874 there were
twenty-five hundred inhabitants, and a hundred and fifty portable buildings had been shipped from Chicago to relieve the housing shortage.
Many Britishers found their way to the resort, partly because William
Bell, Denver and Rio Grande director, was English, and partly because
English capital had always played a part in financing the road. Soon
Colorado Springs was known as "Little Lunnon." Polo, cricket, croquet,
and fox hunting were introduced, with a drag of meat substituting for
the fox, and the second country club in the United States took root just
outside the city limits. A college was founded, arts were fostered—one
grisly touch, in this city of consumptives, being the choice of *Camille*
as the opening play for the new opera house.

Local scenic attractions were boomed to the heavens. Indeed, Colorado Springs, like many another resort center in the Rockies, has suffered
from hyperbole so high-blown that it occasionally leads to a letdown.
For example, Helen Hunt Jackson, author of *Ramona* and resident of
the Springs, touted the nearby Garden of the Gods as a wonderland of
"red rocks of every conceivable and unconceivable size and shape . . .
colossal monstrosities . . . with a strange look of having been stopped and
held back in the very climax of some supernatural joke." Another author,
Julian Street, after reading that and more, was so deflated on seeing the
Garden that he retorted it was nothing but "a pale pink joke." Outraged

Coloradoans ached for revenge—and in typical mountain fashion got it. Street next wrote a derogatory account of Cripple Creek's moral standards (local residents insist he gleaned his information by interviewing a notorious madam through her bedroom window), whereupon the city fathers met in solemn conclave and unanimously changed the name of red-lit Myers Avenue to Julian Street.

Although the hot springs furnished pools wherein guests could puddle, the Rockies, for all their vaunted "we've got everything," lacked one major attraction: water sports. Of the few lakes of any consequence, Jackson and Yellowstone in northwestern Wyoming are too subject to violent squalls for extensive boating and, like Colorado's Grand Lake, which claims the highest yacht regatta in the world, are too cold for comfortable bathing. Only the Great Salt Lake escapes these drawbacks; and to make up for its apparent benignity, it taxes would-be promoters with problems singularly its own.

As a tourist attraction the Salt Lake was a "natural." During the last century all America was curious about the Mormons and their saline sea. Strange legends spread: that a diver would bounce on the water; that it was impossible to drown (not if one's head, the heaviest part of the body, goes under like a lead sinker); and, conversely, that actual swimming was out of the question (an eight-mile marathon from Antelope Island to Saltair was for many years an annual feature). Some bathers reported that the water stung not only their eyes but their skin. Others countered with descriptions of tingling exhilaration. All emerged with hair hoary from precipitated brine and tongues buzzing with accounts of the water's extreme buoyancy.

The lake, however, is farther from the basin towns than tourists even today generally realize. Though the Mormons made occasional day-long excursions to its shores (as early as the Fourth of July, 1851, Salt Lake City moved down en masse, a brass band trumpeting ahead in an overgrown carriage pulled by sixteen mules), resort development lagged until the advent of railroad transportation. Not until 1870 did "Prince John," third of Brigham Young's twenty-five sons, launch a commercial enterprise on the east shore, conveniently near the Utah Central's new tracks. Thereafter, on the completion of their own rails, the Utah Western and the Denver and Rio Grande roared into competition, as did smaller private concerns.

The railroads reaped well—for a time. During the season of '87, sixty thousand visitors paid handsomely for the dancing, swimming, and boating provided by the Denver and Rio Grande at Lake Park. But the shoes of the tourists also trampled the beach's thin layer of sand into a malodorous gluepot of mud (a bane that has always plagued the lake's eastern reaches), and Lake Park went into a decline. Farther to the south, the Utah and Nevada's Garfield Beach lasted longer. Here the sand was firm. Here, too, a huge pavilion, approached by a covered pier and surmounted by an observation tower, had been built on pilings four hundred feet out in the shallow water; but its elegant dressing rooms, restaurant, and saloon blazed spectacularly out of existence in 1904.

Meanwhile Garfield had been outdone by dazzling Saltair, where a railroad ran four thousand feet out from shore to a crescent-shaped platform supporting a two-story pavilion that housed a restaurant on its lower floor, a ballroom on its upper, and bathhouses for a thousand visitors around the edges. To swim, guests had to climb down ladders, but this was a novel attraction rather than a drawback, and the place ran long enough to pay back far more than the $250,000 it had cost. Unlike the Garfield resort, Saltair survived its fire. The blow that crippled came from the lake itself, whose fluctuating waters suddenly pulled in their skirts and in the mid-1930s left pilings and all high and dry.

The erratic lake level has also played hob with various excursion steamboat docks, yacht anchorages, and rowing clubs which have endeavored to find permanent toe hold. As waters receded, docks built during high stages either were choked by cattails or dehydrated entirely, and salt precipitation on the hulls made boatowners tear their hair. When the Federal Government finally helped open a satisfactory harbor in the late thirties, facilities weren't large enough to meet the demand, and in 1946 the aid of Army engineers was solicited for a mile-long breakwater to Fritch Island. This would impound, to a depth of fifteen feet, fresh water discharged into the lake from a series of springs near the old Garfield Beach, would provide safe anchorage for large craft, and would make possible small-boat regattas, outboard-motor races, and other aquatic attractions. Whatever results will cause brow knittings—the briny sea will attend to that—but it seems inevitable that the growing demand of Utah cities for recreational improvements will eventually tame the lake's temperamental antics.

The most widespread water-sport developments are those attendant on the Bureau of Reclamation's irrigation dams. Notable example is Pineview Reservoir, built in 1936 in a canyon east of Ogden, Utah. Its construction presented a headache because Ogden drew domestic water from fifty-one artesian wells located smack-dab under the lake site. The difficulty was solved by a system of underground collecting pipes, so that in effect there are now two reservoirs, one on top of the other. Today the lake's July speed and sailboat races attract some ten thousand spectators. Water skiing, here and elsewhere, is enormously popular; and, as at other dams, the business of providing for participants and their watchers is on the boom.

Indeed, throughout the Rockies the commercial side of recreation is a thorn in the Bureau of Reclamation's flesh. Its projects are supposed to be self-liquidating, and the farmers who help foot the bill are stubbornly opposed to buying more land than the impounded waters will cover. Therefore, stretches along reservoir edges are sometimes left in private hands, and attractive sites are thus open to unattractive forms of exploitation—hot-dog stands, souvenir shops, pony-ride concessions. Aided by recreation experts of the Forest and National Park Services, the Bureau of Reclamation does the best it can to keep offensive commercialism out of these spots by means of moral suasion and the presentation to property owners of "suggested plans for development." Sometimes this works; sometimes it doesn't. It will be interesting to see, ten years from now, the privately owned west shore of Shadow Mountain Reservoir (of the new Colorado-Big Thompson project), which hooks hard up against tourist-happy Grand Lake.

When the first automobile, along about 1906, struggled through the bridgeless streams and miring mud of the old wagon road over Twogwotee Pass, Wyoming, residents of the Wind River Valley were intrigued and even congratulatory. But they were not impressed. The automobile would never faze *that* country.

"What we didn't foresee," explains dude-rancher James Moore of Dubois, "were modern roads. We kept remembering the chuckholes and boulders we used to fight our wagons over, and we knew automobile traffic was impossible on them. But now . . . "

But now hard-surfaced highways have changed the tourists' entire conception of the Rockies. Tenderfeet, once concentrated in some monstrous hot-springs hotel, could now spread far and wide, and the era of dude ranches began. The idea, of course, had been in the air before roads gave it substance. As long ago as 1880 the three Eaton brothers had established a ranch in South Dakota and were keeping it out of the red by entertaining paying guests from their native Pittsburgh. When the trio moved on to Wyoming's Big Horns in 1904, they took the system with them; their ranch on Wolf Creek, with its own post office, store, telephone system, individual cabins, and community hotel, is perhaps the West's oldest and most famous dude hostelry. Among other devices to lure trade, Howard Eaton ran pack trips into Yellowstone, and a 153-mile horseback trail through the park is justly named for him.

Trips to Yellowstone were the germinating force behind other dude outfits. When the Chicago and Northwestern reached Lander in 1906 (the town's slogan is still "Where the rails end and the trails begin"), Charles Moore, brother of James and now president of the National Dude Ranch Association, chartered a Pullman car, filled it to the rafters with well-heeled Eastern high-school boys, and brought them West. In Lander he met his ecstatic charges with two chuck wagons and horses for everyone, trundled them over Twogwotee, quit the wagons near Jackson, toured Yellowstone with pack mules, and then cut straight back across the Wind River Mountains to the Moore ranch near Dubois. When the youngsters went home after this glorious six weeks' trip they were the most vocal publicity agents any organization ever had. Their friends burned with envy; their delighted parents decided that a wonderland capable of evoking such enthusiasm might hold something for old folk too. Yellowstone, however, was a long haul for creaky bones. Many of the elders were content to loaf around the ranch at Dubois while the young fry bounded along the trails. To care for these stay-behinds, short rides and wise wranglers were provided. Comfortable cabins and plenty of hot water, green lawns, cardrooms, and lounges decorated with antlered heads filled the idle hours. When automobile roads killed the horseback trips to Yellowstone, the Moores' CM Ranch and many like it simply retreated to the already well-established home bailiwick and went their tourist-attractive ways with no pain whatsoever.

Catering to youngsters, incidentally, is still a mainstay for many a dude outfit. With massive Western assurance, they do it coeducationally, blandly adding the problems of adolescence to the already fantastic harassments involved in adapting outlanders to a brand-new environment. By way of recompense, however, the boys and girls are more resilient, more co-operative, and far more teachable than are their elders. Young vacationists at Sue and Charlie Beck's Trail Lake Ranch, also near Dubois, have at times so mastered the novel art of whirling through intricate square-dance patterns on horseback that they have gone to the Lander Pioneer Days celebration and there have won as many plaudits as have Indians and professional cowboys.

After one group of Shoshone Indians had seen an automobile, they reported to awed tribesmen that the "rubber wagon runs without horses, without anything drawing it. All it leaves behind is an awful smell." But the Shoshone had not followed the automobile far enough. It also leaves dirty paper plates, fouled springs, trampled flower patches, initial-carved trees, and, most devastating of all, fire. The Forest Service reacted as best it could with neat, attractive camp grounds, policed and.besigned. Meanwhile wilderness lovers, led by the late Bob Marshall, the Forest Service's Chief of the Division of Recreation and Lands, fought the invasion with alarm. Starting in the 1920s, they pushed through Congress a series of laws allowing the Forest Service to set aside certain wilderness or primitive areas into which roads may not penetrate, and where resorts may not be built, though the lands are open to some grazing, mining, and lumbering. There are now upward of seventy of these areas in ten Western states, varying in size from Arizona's seventy-four-hundred-acre Mount Baldy section to the mammoth Selway-Bitterroot wilderness that sprawls nearly two million acres along the Idaho-Montana border. These tracts are not game refuges, as many people suppose. Hunting and fishing are allowed, subject to normal regulations, though ardent protectionists with nightmares of helicopters, which need no roads, are agitating for more stringent limitations.

To guarantee wilderness recreation more had to be done than simply reserve a few million acres of mountainland. The ordinary two-week vacationist cannot contact competent packers and guides, find horses and rustle equipment—or pay for them if he could. Accordingly, in 1933 the American Forestry Association inaugurated its non-profit trail rides, which from a variety of centers conduct summer pack trips into several Rocky Mountain and Pacific coast wilderness areas. Limited in size and, in the main, efficiently run as to safety, comfort, interest, and mountain entertainment, the rides are becoming increasingly popular each year. Those who do not want to fuss with horses take out afoot on the excellent trails maintained by the Forest Service both in and out of the wilderness areas and over the timber-line passes between the peaks. Their equipment they carry on their own backs. War-born materials—light tents, light sleeping bags, concentrated foods—help keep them from foundering. It sounds rigorous—and is, until the walker's muscles harden or when a lashing rainstorm strikes during the before-breakfast doldrums as he is trying to kindle a fire while knees knock and hands shiver so he can scarcely strike a match.

On level trails ten miles a day is no exhausting ordeal, and when the going gets steeper a pause where scenery is exhilarating and a cup of coffee or tea can be brewed on an alcohol stove has its charms as well as its recuperative powers. Three lone females spent the entire summer of 1945 tramping all over the Elk Mountains of Colorado, and there are enough back-pack addicts, male and female, in the Colorado Mountain Club to warrant scheduling regular trips for them. Should you ask why they do it, they'll simply look at you and say: "Why not? We like it."

David Lavender

Summer camp of a western Colorado ranch, Lone Cone Peak in background. As snow melts, cattle and sheep are hurried to the lush pastures of the high country, retreat when winter comes.

During the early 1900s the Argentine Central, in the Georgetown, Colorado, silver district, carried goggle-eyed tourists to the top of Mount McClellan, nearly 14,000 feet high, "the most scenic one-day train ride in the world."

CHAPTER XVI

HIGH JINKS

ASK any old-timer who lives off the mountains, not off the tourists, what the summit of a peak is like, and he'll probably snort, "I ain't lost anything up there." In other words, only damn fools go where there is no reason to go.

Yet the outlanders keep right on climbing, and have since a day late in November 1806, when Lieutenant Zebulon Pike and three others set out on what they thought would be an overnight jaunt up the "Grand Peak" which had been beckoning to them during ten days of traveling across the Colorado plains. However, like other neophyte mountaineers, they misjudged everything: distances, temperatures, even the mountain. After marching the better part of three days and spending a foodless night in a cave, they wallowed, clad only in "light overhauls and no stockings," through the waist-deep snow of the final stretch—and found themselves on the wrong peak. Their goal towered unreachably beyond. "No human being," they consoled themselves, "could have ascended to its summit."

Such is the history of most of America's major mountains. First their conquest is impossible, next difficult, then an interesting scramble, and finally "an easy day for a lady." Chronologically, Pikes Peak led in all departments. In 1820 Edwin James, botanist of Major Long's expedition, and three companions spent two days' hard slogging to reach the "impossible" summit and returned to find their base camp in ashes because they had neglected to put out their breakfast fire. One is tempted to say, "Served them right," except that fire prevention in the mountains was then unknown. Thirty-eight years later, during the early days of the gold rush, along came the inevitable first woman, Anna Holmes (or Homes), who "wore the Bloomer costume, and what is more, she carried a larger pack than her husband." An unusual lady all around was Mrs. Holmes; she and James Holmes, 'tis said, were "religiously or conscientiously free lovers and were married after a style of their own belief."

Longs Peak duplicates the story, although it resisted longer because of its inaccessibility and because early aspirants naturally headed up the closest ridge. This left them staring from the lower summit (known today as Mount Meeker) across a knife-edge so blood-chilling that even now it has been traversed fewer times than you can count on your fingers. After one look at that fearsome stretch, W. N. Byers, founder of the *Rocky Mountain News* and a member of the fifth party to climb Meeker, vowed no one could reach the top of Longs without wings. However, four years later Byers himself, still featherless, teamed up with one-armed Major Powell (who later led the first boat trip through the Grand Canyon), and with five others tamed the untamable peak. They managed it by trudging up the back side via Grand Lake, just as many Indians had done before them in order to trap eagles for their feathers.

Another Anna—this time Anna Dickenson—followed in 1871 with Professor Hayden of the United States Geological Survey. Two years later came Isabella Bird, who wrote a lively tale of all her troubles and then blunted it by adding that mountaineers shouldn't take her too seriously; from the standpoint of pure alpinism the climb was nothing at all. Maybe she was right. It is estimated that since her day Longs has been ascended fifty thousand times by forty thousand different people, including one man eighty-five years old, a boy and girl each five, and at least two persons on crutches. . . . But as a warning against complacency the peak has also killed at least fourteen: six by falling, two by exposure, one each by freezing, lightning, exhaustion, an accidental gunshot, being struck by a falling rock, and one by undetermined cause, the victim's skull having been found nineteen years after his disappearance in 1921.

The miners got around too. There is a jingle that says, "A good silver mine is above timber line ten times out of nine," and this was particularly true in the Mosquito range of central Colorado, where the peaks present nothing more formidable than vast cones of loose rock. Here shaft houses stood almost at the very summits, and on the gentle 14,284-foot peak of Mount Lincoln, prospectors in the course of the years heaped up a cairn of stones twelve feet in diameter and fifteen feet high. On Lincoln, too, Governor Bross, exhilarated by the rare air and the view, burst forth into the Doxology before a large company who previously had put their names in a box and had hoisted it to the top of a large "liberty pole." Enchanted, the assembly promptly named one of the massif's neighboring summits Mount Bross, an appellation it still wears.

The most famous peaks in early times, however, were not Lincoln, Longs, or Pikes, but Colorado's Grays and Torreys, twin mountains of which many a modern tourist never hears. Located in Georgetown's teeming Argentine silver district, the two peaks had horseback trails to their summits while Longs was still deemed impossible and climbers were struggling up Pikes under their own power. By 1869 the journal of the American Geographical Society of New York was advising, "If any of you visit the Rocky Mountains, the best peak for the ladies is . . . Grays,"[1] and at timber line stood Kelso Cabin, "a hostelry of but little less celebrity than the mountain whose climbers it was built to entertain." After the turn of the century the rush of tourists was so great that the Argentine Central Railroad, designed originally to supply the Waldorf mines high on the shoulder of nearby Mount McClellan, extended its tracks clear to the top of the ridge, almost 14,000 feet high.

Short on mileage (15.9 from Silver Plume to McClellan), the Argentine was long on thrills. Its Shay-geared, narrow-gauge engines spent an hour and forty minutes dragging two big-windowed tourist cars over intricate double switchbacks, around curves with a radius as tight as 145 feet, up grades approaching 10 per cent. The altitude reached and the scores of peaks brought into view gave basis to its slogan, "A lifetime in a day," and to its claim of being the highest, most scenic one-day train trip in the world. For a time passenger revenues outstripped freight returns ten to one, but the death of the mines and the opening of automobile roads throughout the Rockies brought on a slow paralysis. In 1918 the unique road followed into limbo the Kelso Cabin and horseback rides up Grays and Torreys. Though the peaks are still frequently climbed afoot over remnants of the old trail, little remains to remind present-day climbers of the flamboyance which preceded them.

In other sections, too, the business of making life easy for altitude gainers, as contrasted to climbers, went on apace. Though many tourists were eager to exult over the lowlands from the "heaven-kissing heights," they quickly discovered that the process of lifting one foot above the other at elevations exceeding two miles can be horrendous. Long ago, Ernest Ingersoll, breasting Wind River Peak in Wyoming with the Hayden Survey, described it thus: "The 'ever-living purity of the air' is becoming a terror. You gasp instead of breathe . . . your tongue protrudes; your stomach rebels; your nerves fail to direct your muscles . . ."

The unhappy Mr. Ingersoll was merely suffering from mountain sickness. This debility arises from the unacclimated body's demand for extra oxygen at altitudes where it is already rare, and the results have given rise to an inelegant mountaineering pun: a sufferer joins the Daniel Boone Club; i.e., he goes out and shoots his lunch.

[1] Speaking of ladies, Mrs. Gray "acquitted herself nobly" in 1872 while climbing the peak named for her botanist husband, as did the daughter of John Torrey, Gray's colleague.

Since visitors were willing to pay to avoid membership, local residents quickly obliged. During the seventies three horseback trails were constructed to the top of Pikes Peak; by 1888 a carriage highway, called the U. S. Grant Road, had been completed, and stage drivers, for one dollar a head, were scaring their passengers as green as Daniel Booners with fifteen-foot snowbanks and sidling curves. Shortly thereafter Zalmon Simmons, of bedding fame, and Dave Moffat spent a million and a quarter dollars building the widely publicized Cog Road to the top (average grade 16 per cent, maximum 25), its picturesque old engines recently replaced by Diesels and its observatory cars roofed in 1947 with shiny new plexiglass domes. Spencer Penrose and the Pikes Peak Automobile Company built a motor highway in 1916, ran it for twenty years as a profitable toll affair, established the breathless Labor Day car races, and then turned the road over to the state at a Pikes-Peak-or-Bust Jubilee attended by a chamber-of-commerce-estimated throng of fifty thousand people.

Not to be outdone, the Denver area secured the nation's highest auto road (a hundred and forty-nine feet loftier than Pikes) by blasting a way to the top of Mount Evans, where the Cosmic Ray Laboratory of the University of Denver stands, reputedly the highest scientific laboratory in the world. Meanwhile Longs Peak, protected by Rocky Mountain National Park and perhaps unsusceptible to the mechanical age anyhow, did the best it could for its panting guests by furnishing a handrail in the form of an iron cable strung along the more exposed stretches of the north face.

All very interesting, say the alpinists, but don't confuse it with mountain climbing, wherein the devotee gets down to grips with his chosen peak and, self-propelled, surmounts it by whatever gymnastics seem necessary at the moment. Followers of this sport also came early to Colorado, many of them attracted during the seventies and eighties by Blanca Peak in the Sangre de Cristos, its 14,363-foot summit for a long time thought to be America's highest. (Actually Blanca is topped by Whitney and Rainier and, in Colorado, by Massive, Elbert, and Harvard, three fat, easy humps in the Sawatch range near Leadville.) Soon a handful of enthusiasts established the region's first mountaineering organization, the short-lived Rocky Mountain Climbers Club. Before it died this club financed the 1898 ascent of the Grand Teton, led by charter member Frank Spalding, and thereby unwittingly precipitated the most acrimonious controversy in American climbing history.

Oddly enough, Wyoming's Teton and Wind River Mountains, the first to be crisscrossed by the fur trappers, long remained the least known to climbers. Here are the country's most truly alpine chains. The first sight of their glaciers and ice-chewed pinnacles is, to one used to other parts of the Rockies, nothing short of astounding.[2] Yet all except a handful of the summits remained frostily virgin long after Colorado's main peaks had been climbed again and again.

To be sure, there had been a few exploratory ascents. In 1833 Captain Bonneville went up Wind River Peak; ten years later Frémont, on his first expedition, sought out what trappers mistakenly believed was the highest point in the Rockies, and with Lucien Maxwell, Kit Carson and two others climbed the peak which now bears his name. Here at least is one "first" to which the Pathfinder can lay uncontested claim. When he stepped onto the summit slab, where the cliff drops under your toes with the suddenness of a gunshot, no previous eyes had widened at the sight of that terrific sweep of ice and rock; and his journal shows that he appreciated not only his victory but also the view. Even then, however, he could not resist making the "grand gesture"—unfurling a special flag of thirteen standard stripes but showing a corner field of white wherein a blue eagle perched on a blue Indian peace pipe, the whole encircled by blue stars.

Now comes a curious thing. In *Scribner's Monthly* for June 1873, Nathaniel P. Langford, who rendered such yeoman service as first superintendent of Yellowstone National Park, published an article purporting to describe his and James Stevenson's successful climb of Mount Hayden, as the Grand Teton was then known. Acclaim followed, but climbers did not—until 1898, when Frank Spalding, William Owen (who had made the first survey of Jackson Hole), Frank Petersen, and John Shive, financed by the Rocky Mountain Climbers Club, found the famous "Cooning Place," wriggled belly-flat along a stony ledge roofed by a massive overhang, and so reached the top. They were puzzled. Where was Langford's cairn? And what about Langford's description of the upper peak, which simply did not jibe with the conditions encountered by the 1898 party? William Owen pondered, rechecked data, photographed a repeat climb two days later, and in the end politely called Langford a liar.

---

[2] Why the most jaggedly spectacular of them all, the Tetons, leaping upward in one breath-taking vault from the sagebrush flats of Jackson Hole, should have been called after a woman's breasts is difficult to imagine; even to a French trapper the resemblance must have been remote. However, the custom was common in the early days. Colorado's steep-slabbed Crestones were also known for a time as Tetons; the Spanish Peaks near Trinidad were called by Indians Wahatoyah, "Two Breasts," a conceit in this case not overly fanciful; and the woods used to be full of lesser summits known as Iron Nipple, Mary's Nipple, Susie's Nipple, etc.

Now Nathaniel Langford was a man with a deserved reputation and many friends. They leaped to his defense (and so did he). Recriminations flew; before long nearly every mountaineer in America was embroiled in the controversy. Yet in spite of all this publicity, the magnificent peak was not climbed again until 1923, when two parties went up.

The next year Paul Petzoldt, then fifteen, followed with a youthful friend on the first of his several dozen ascents. It was nearly Petzoldt's last. Defeated on their initial attempt but refusing to quit, the two boys shivered out the night on a bleak ridge top, went on without food, hacked steps in the ice with their pocketknives, frosted their fingers—and returned to Jackson to find that no one would believe their story. A heated argument developed in the middle of town, a crowd assembled, and someone ran off to fetch William Owen, who happened to be there. The grand old man of the mountain questioned the lads closely, satisfied himself as to their honesty, and turned to the throng with a dramatic gesture and said: "Gentlemen, these boys have climbed Grand Teton!" Now others wanted to go up. Petzoldt took them and so laid the groundwork for his becoming, when Grand Teton National Park was established, the first government-licensed guide in the region.

From the ascents which now became almost commonplace more evidence was adduced to refute Langford's claim. Finally the sound and fury of a quarter of a century reached such a pitch (even now there are climbers familiar with the peak who believe Langford may have succeeded) that the Wyoming legislature ordered an investigation. The upshot was that on February 9, 1927, a joint resolution was passed declaring in Owen's favor. Thus for the first time in history, perhaps, a mountain climb was accorded full legality in the statute books of a sovereign state.

It is hardly coincidence that the legislature delivered itself at this particular time. Climbing was in the air, and during the decades of the 1920s climbers rushed into Wyoming from every side. Gannett Peak, 13,785 feet, toppled in 1922; before another ten years had passed nearly every "impossible" summit in the Tetons and Wind Rivers had heard the crunch of hobnails.

Colorado's easier, more accessible peaks had given up the ghost even earlier. Today, according to the records of the Colorado Mountain Club, at least twenty people have climbed all the state's fifty-two fourteen-thousand-footers. Included in this select circle are one father-mother-daughter trio, one husband-wife combination, and one father-son pair, the last interesting because Carl Melzer and his young son Bob, after hoofing 831 miles along the crest of the Continental Divide from Wyoming to New Mexico in 1936, when Bob was eight, had knocked off the peaks during the lad's ninth summer, and when he was eleven had gone to the Pacific coast and had there finished scaling all sixty-four of the United States' fourteen-thousand-foot peaks.

By the 1920s the era of "walk-ups" was over. Mountaineers wanted to develop—to meet difficulty, to find novelty either in the form of slightly lower but technically more challenging pinnacles, or in the winning of new routes up old favorites. They had, and have, ample room in which to experiment. From Glacier Park in Montana to the Sandias near Albuquerque there is so vast a variety of cracks, chock stones, arêtes, cliffs, *couloirs*, overhangs, bulges, ledges, and what not—to say nothing of the unpredictable weather—that duplication of attacks, methods, and results is all but impossible.

Sometimes a new route was found by accident; way back in 1871, for example, the Reverend Elkanah J. Lamb, clad in a long frock coat, climbed Longs Peak alone after the rest of his party had played out, and then set about finding a shorter route to the bottom. He did. After inching has way along the edge of the stupendous seventeen-hundred-foot east face, he reached an ice sheet now known grandiosely as Mills Glacier. His feet slipped; down he zoomed, coattails flying. By great good fortune he caught hold of a boulder as he hurtled past, checked his wild flight, opened his pocketknife with his teeth, and managed to chip toe holds back to less treacherous rock. Fortified by this and other experiences, the Reverend Lamb became one of the peak's earliest guides, taking pilgrims to the summit for five dollars per trip. "If they would not pay for spiritual guidance," he wrote in his *Memories of the Past and Thoughts of the Future*, "I compelled them to divide for material elevation."

Occasionally the mountaineers tried too hard. Although no member of a guided party has died on Grand Teton, five others have—experienced climbers, too, who made the mistake of underestimating the peak and biting off more than they could chew. Similar misfortune stalked Agnes Vaille, a truly lovely woman and a true lover of the mountains, on the east face of Longs. Three times she had tried without avail to complete that forbidding ascent in winter. On a fourth attempt, after twenty-five hours of climbing, the hardest part of which extended throughout the dead of night, she and Walter Kiener reached the summit. An icy wind met them—fourteen degrees below zero. As the laggard sun of a new day appeared they crept down the easier north face. Suddenly Miss Vaille slipped, rolled a hundred feet or so down a steep slab of rock.

Kiener hurried after her. No, she insisted, she was not injured. But could he help her loosen her pack straps? She couldn't do it herself, she explained apologetically, because for some hours now her hands and feet had been frozen.

Kiener pulled her upright, but after they had gone a few yards she sank back into the snow, saying she had to rest. There was nothing he could do other than make her as comfortable as possible and hurry for help to the Timberline Shelter Cabin. At the cabin he met four men who had come up from an inn below to look for him and Miss Vaille. Leaving one man to keep a fire, the others started out into a sleet storm so severe that frequently they had to stop and wipe one another's faces clear before they could see. Two turned back. One of them lost his way, fell, broke a hip, and froze to death. Kiener and a man named Christian kept on, though by now Kiener, who had no sleep for nearly forty hours, was all but snow-blind and had to be led by the hand. Even so, he found Agnes Vaille. She was dead.

These were the tragedies, which were rare. Besides them one must rack up the multitudinous triumphs. Slowly climbers learned how to anchor the rope with pitons and karabiners and how properly to belay it against falls, so that soon they dared venture where ropeless mountaineers could never have gone with impunity. They saved time, too, descending steep snow fields in a swishing glissade, wherein one slides ski-wise on his feet with an ice ax as rudder and brake; they dropped over sheer cliffs *en rappel* and retrieved the doubled rope by pulling it down after them; and on even the most exposed traverses they nerved themselves to keeping their body out from the wall, their feet planted flat, their ankles supple. Above all, they learned good mountain judgment. With that prime essential fortifying their technique, they have gone, and are still going, up an imposing array of pinnacles, cliffs, and *couloirs* so varied that a mere listing of them is beyond the scope of this work.

As if summer's challenges weren't enough, winter climbing became popular. Of the many brumal ascents taken each year, the most famous is the one started in 1922 by Willis Magee, Harry Standley, and the Morath brothers of Colorado Springs, who conceived the idea of climbing Pikes Peak on New Year's Eve and setting off fireworks. Though mist prevented the first display's being seen from below, the performance attracted wide interest and developed into an annual affair. The climbers call themselves the AdAmAn Club from the fact that one new member is added each year, and their original simple fireworks have given way to rockets taller than a man, hundred-pound flares, and bombs shot from mortars, all carried up the peak on the cog train's last trip and cached in the Summit House. In recent years the doings have been broadcast over nationwide radio hookups. Small wonder, after a century and a half of notoriety ranging from Zebulon Pike to pyrotechnics, that this peak, though exceeded in altitude by twenty-seven others in Colorado alone, is America's most widely known mountain.

Why do climbers do it? Why slither across the ice fields of Gannett while the wind cuts your eyeballs like a file? Why crouch out an electric storm on the knife ridge of Capitol while sparks jump off the tips of your extended fingers and your sizzling hair feels as if moths were fluttering through it? Why should the University of Colorado's recreation department offer facetious "degrees," replete with outrageous puns, for attainment in the field of mountaineering? How does it happen that enough addicts are interested for the Colorado Mountain Club to run extensive summer and winter outings, week-end trips and Sunday hikes, conduct sinew-battering classes in rock climbing and skiing, build and mark trails, sponsor lectures and photographic exhibits, lobby for conservation laws, and dispense reams of information in answer to queries ranging from "Are the columbine out yet?" to "Where can my daughter go on a safe trip?"

Why, indeed, is it necessary to justify mountain climbing any more than trout fishing, say, or golf?

The questions, however, are always asked—and always answered, though rarely to anyone's satisfaction. Scenery is one reason given: superb and indescribable daubs of color and shade, sunlight and cloud, mass and contour. And physical exultation: the good feel of sweat, of tired muscles triumphant, of having gone ahead when one was weary and afraid. There is emotional enjoyment, a vague, pantheistic mysticism which is inescapable among the splintered crags, and the intellectual stimulus of a more intelligent class of people than many sports attract.

On the other hand, it has been said (and by good mountaineers, too) that people often climb because in their youth they were frustrated, unable to measure up in the personal-contact, body-buffeting sports of high school and college; whereas on the peaks no one is trying to beat them at anything, and in their own individual ways they can excel or at least hold their own. Still other critics suggest that all the toil and excitement are but another manifestation of the super-ego of the Anglo-Saxons, the drive to dominate, to set one's self higher than the rest of the world.

No, the reasons given never suit anyone. Knowing that, George

Leigh-Mallory, when asked why men brave Everest, gave the answer which no writer on climbing seems able to avoid: "Because it is there."

To one who has felt the tug of high places, that is enough. To the old-timer who had lost nothing on top, it is no reason at all and never was—unless, perchance, he has grown tired and so has forgotten the nameless stir, half awed, half savage, which ran through his viscera when the great peaks first reared up before his eyes.

CHAPTER XVII

FUN IN THE SNOW

I T TOOK that ubiquitous myth killer, the automobile, to return a final negative to a rhetorical question which, only a few years ago, every summer tourist in the Rockies asked with open commiseration: "Aren't the winters *terrible* up here?" Certainly they were—when all one could do was sit and take them. But today, thanks to rotary plows and cyclopean scrapers, the rubber wheels roll swiftly up from the cities and swiftly back again. Thousands of once timorous people are discovering that no blizzard lasts forever, that avalanches can be understood and avoided, and that even on slopes thirteen thousand feet above sea level there are sun-slashed February days when one is comfortable without a shirt. Moreover, unlike the old-timers, they know how to ski.

To be sure, mountain dwellers of seventy years ago moved across the snow on pieces of wood. They had to, to survive. A yellowed edition of the *Elk Mountain Pilot* tells us that on Saturday afternoons in the eighties there were often as many as fifty pairs of skis stacked outside Mid Gray's store in Crested Butte, Colorado, while miners and their wives were inside buying goods. Mail carriers made regular trips across the passes—and sometimes were abused for their devotion to duty: when one Crested Butte miner ordered a pair of hip boots sent in by parcel post the profane deliverer had to lug the unwieldy articles over the mountains one at a time.

He had reason for profanity. Early skis (they were called "snow-shoes," and what we term snowshoes were known as webs) stretched a prodigious ten to twelve feet, were correspondingly wide, and invariably handmade of spruce, the more durable hardwoods being unobtainable. Fourteen inches of their ponderous tips were boiled in water and curled upward in racks made from rounds of firewood. Since wax was unknown, the snow which balled up in great gobs beyond the wearer's reach was jarred loose with a stick.

To go uphill the owner either had to walk and drag the boards behind with a rope, or sprinkle their bottoms with water, add snow, and allow the mixture to freeze into a leg-killing but slope-gripping anchor. The top gained, he scraped off the frozen mass with a knife, clutched a ten-foot pole he could ride as a brake in case of emergency, and took off. Stemming was impossible, because all that held his feet were leather straps across the toes. To avoid crashing into boulders or missing turns, he often had to leap off his hurtling conveyance into neck-deep snow. His skis were kept from catapulting beyond reach by lanyards tied to his belt.

Whenever possible, regular travelers journeyed between the hours of 2 and 10 A.M., when the crust was frozen hard enough to bear their weight, and occasionally in the bitter darkness trouble was real. Once in a howling blizzard during the early sixties, Father Dyer, a Methodist itinerant who eked out his income by carrying mail into Colorado's South Park, slipped over the edge of a precipice. He checked his fall, but how far the slope extended he could not tell. Still, it was descend or die, for he could not climb back up.

Gingerly he worked his skis loose and grasped a crooked end under each armpit. By trailing the long boards behind, he thought he might keep his feet foremost and so slide to the bottom alive. The prayer he breathed has since become a not altogether facetious byword among Colorado skiers as they stand at the top of some headlong run: "O God, into thy hand I commit my soul, my life, my all." Down he shot, pluming snow, the trailing skis preventing him from bounding end over end. But the long night had frozen his feet. To thaw them he plunged them into the icy water of a spring, redonned his boots, and staggered on to a friend's cabin. There he made a poultice from the bark of a balsam sapling. "Half my toenails sloughed off with considerable skin," but in less than three weeks he was carrying mail again.

In spite of such difficulties a few enthusiasts in Gunnison and in Crested Butte formed ski clubs, the latter of which put on an exhibition in 1886. Old newspapers from Encampment, Wyoming, to Silverton in southern Colorado, reveal that on moonlit nights young people amused themselves by "sliding downhill," and after the turn of the century the Colorado Mountain Club began nurturing outings for the hardy. By 1913, Carl Howelsen, a Norwegian, had established February jumping tournaments at Steamboat and Hot Sulphur Springs in northern Colorado, the first organized winter sports affairs, perhaps, in the West. Children received instruction as part of their school curriculum, the Steamboat Springs band learned to tootle while marching on boards, race horses whisked skijorers along floodlit streets, daredevils leaped through hoops of fire, and after a time Denverites began chugging over the divide on the Moffat Railroad to view the fun.

Somewhat later approximately the same sort of thing went on at

Ecker Hill near Salt Lake City, where jumper Alf Engen, soaring farther and farther each year, at last turned in a booming leap of 287 feet. All this, however, was a spectator sport, with watchers showing little desire to emulate the performers.

In the East, meanwhile, young men and women were discovering that one didn't necessarily have to jump the length of a football field in order to enjoy himself in the snow. Westerners, notably college students, joined them, learned fast, and came home with a revolutionary change: bindings which held their boots solidly to the skis and enabled them not only to turn corners but even to go uphill. Old-timers were horrified. Strapped to the skis! One fall and good-by leg!

Occasionally legs were indeed broken, but the faithful went right on, riding automobiles to the top of Berthoud Pass above Denver or the train to the west portal of the Moffat Tunnel. At both places (and at an infinite number of other spots throughout the Rockies) snow conditions were superb. High altitude made for "powder," light, fluffy, lightning-fast. Indeed, the stuff is so unsubstantial that the best skiing does not come until after the surface has been melted by a few warm spells. Refreezing during the night, this forms a solid base. New "powder" falls on top, and now one can zoom downward in stirring schusses, snow spuming knee-high and the skis singing that dry, sweet *wis-s-s* so dear to an addict's heart.

Later in the year comes "corn" snow, round pellets formed by the thaws of spring and, until it becomes too wet, delectable in its own swift way. In high basins this corn lasts well into summer: a ski tournament is a Fourth of July event on St. Mary's Glacier above Boulder, Colorado, and fair-weather tourists in the Tetons sometimes are startled to see skiers heading upward through grassy meadows with the implements of their sport strapped to their horses.

Skiing country inevitably brings to the visitor indescribable stimuli—snow plumes blowing from peak tops achingly bright against the sky; dusky spruce standing stubborn under their caps of white; a trickle of wind flowing through a narrow pass and abruptly dying into a silence so absolute that one instinctively holds his breath. Perhaps from far across a canyon spiked with trees comes a faint rumble, a faint puff of snow where an avalanche hurtles downward, its titanic terror turned puny on the face of this vaster truth. Simplicity, spaciousness, awe. To an ardent cross-country skier those things are enough.

But to others the stupendous slopes above timber line meant downhill runs. Speed. The perfect control of one's body in the nearest escape from earth's clay chains that unmechanized man has yet achieved . . .

But before one can go down, he must go up, either by putting skins on the bottoms of his skis or by resorting to a muscle-murdering herringbone stride. Three hours to climb to the top of a run, three minutes to descend—wistfully Frank Ashley, a leader in Colorado winter sports development, wrote in the 1936 *American Ski Annual* that, so far as Colorado was concerned, "much is still to be desired."

At Sun Valley, Idaho, the Union Pacific Railroad showed the rest of the Rocky Mountain area what money can accomplish. Furnish well-heeled tourists with mechanical means of reaching the top of a desirable hill, enable them to loaf enjoyably between runs, and the reaction on the cash register is immediate. Ski lifts and winter hotels, however, are fabulously expensive. Despite Sun Valley's success, private capital, during the shaky financial decade of the thirties, remained dubious about the market's extent. All the mountain towns could do was give Sun Valley a jealous glare and proceed to lift themselves by their bootstraps.

The Forest Service helped, as did the WPA and CCC during their days. So, too, did unexpected angels, none of whom looked less cherubic than a certain hard-rock miner who dwelt all alone at Alta, a ghost town high above Salt Lake City.

Once Alta had been Utah's rootin'-tootin'est gold-and-silver camp, with an 1872 population of five thousand and a weird little railroad that worked by horsepower going up and by gravity going down. In the 1930s, however, all this was gone—all save George H. Watson, self-styled mayor of Alta, who for years had been buying up tax titles to old claims in the hope that someday the town would come back.

When Salt Lake skiers began seeking the high country around Brighton, where a summer hotel offered out-of-season accommodations of a sort, "Mayor" Watson found the lese majesty intolerable. A one-man chamber of commerce if ever there was one, he heckled the boys into crossing the ridge and trying *his* slopes. They did and liked what they found—five hundred inches of accumulated snow on sheltered runs ranging from eighty-five hundred to more than 11,000 feet in altitude. Immediately they raised a howl for facilities. In 1935 the Forest Service, aided by state and county funds, managed a road. But lodges and lifts were something else; a wise government ruling forbids the expenditure of public money on private holdings. And Watson, together with three or four lesser owners, controlled the heart of the basin.

It was a fine speculation setup. Yet for a consideration of one dollar, Watson and the others deeded to the government surface rights to eighteen hundred acres of patented claims. Forthwith the Forest Service issued permits for three smallish lifts, the Denver and Rio Grande Western Railroad helped finance a lodge, and the boom would have been on had not the war and its aftermath of high costs slowed construction down to a walk.

Through it all prances George H. Watson, beaming a smile of welcome and wearing a battered hat studded with buttons representing ski organizations from all over the world. In his cabin, snow-buried during winter and reached via a sort of periscope through the roof, he has a "bottle" room decorated with containers that once held every kind of liquor brought into Alta in mining days, a multitudinous array indeed. Here distinguished visitors are rocked on their heels by a steaming, secret concoction known as a ski-ball. To some people the airs are picturesque; others find them smacking of a stunt. But although it is true that Mr. Watson seldom dodges publicity dealing with Mayor Watson, it is likewise true that more than half a million ski fans have already benefited from his generosity; and "romantic Alta," as copy writers seem gruesomely determined to label it, appears destined to become one of the Rockies' major winter resorts.

Aspen, in the eye-dazzling Elk Mountains of western Colorado, is another. Oddly, Aspen's development started in Pasadena, where Tom Flynn and Billy Fiske, Olympic bobsled champion, were recalling how Swedish and Norwegian miners used to amuse themselves by "sliding" down the slopes of Highland Basin. Why, the two asked themselves, couldn't people ski there now? They rushed out to see. The result was the Highland-Bavarian Corporation and golden dreams of a closed aerial tramcar which would lift twenty-five people at a time fourteen thousand feet high on Mount Hayden, from which spectacular runs dive beautifully down in every direction. But it didn't come off. Aspen was hard to reach; money was tight; Billy Fiske, aviator as well as skier, was probably the first American to be killed in action with the RAF.

Still, the germ had been planted. Tom Flynn had already arranged ski instructions for youngsters, and the Aspen Ski Club, containing more women than men, had come into being in 1937. Famed skier André Roche, followed by Otto Schniebs, Dartmouth College's peerless ski leader, extolled the region in book, film, and lecture. WPA-ers began beavering out a run through matted aspens on a hill above the somnolent mining village, and when their efforts weren't enough townspeople seized axes and waded in. But it was slow going until, miraculously, along came an angel haloed with considerably more than old mining claims: Walter Paepcke, board chairman of the Container Corporation of America.

In 1946 Paepcke and others formed the Aspen Corporation, which secured an RFC loan and built, among other things, an engineering cynosure, an orange-towered, quarter-of-a-million-dollar chair lift fourteen thousand feet long, one of the lengthiest, fastest, and steepest in the world. Its terminus, 11,300 feet high on Ajax Peak, points to an octagonal sun deck which commands a wintertime view of snowy peaks that persons suspicious of superlatives won't believe without seeing— and where the flushing of toilets is a superlative of a different sort, since water hauled up from below costs ten cents a gallon. There are no nearby springs; old mine shafts have drained the underground tables. Another natural source, however, is being tapped by means of the sun deck's new funnel-shaped roof. Snow collects in the depression, is melted by heat from the fireplace, and is piped into a storage tank.

But skiing alone was not enough for Mr. Paepcke. Aspen was to be the Salzburg of America—with, of course, American trimmings. Summer concerts, aimed at a grand-opera season, have been inaugurated, along with fly-fishing tournaments, dude ranches, tennis courts, and a plush remodeling of the gay-eighties' Jerome Hotel, where one can live for thirty dollars a day and up, cheaper facilities being available in ski dormitories and motels. To attune the town to new times, residents are offered free paint for refurbishing such mining-style houses as haven't fallen down or burned up. And the idea is taking. Aspen is a lovely spot; a surprising number of artists and even Denver professional people are migrating there to live. Add to them several veterans who trained with the mountain troops at Camp Hale, across the divide, and who are trickling back to the Rockies, and you have the backbone of a phenomenon which half a dozen years ago would not have been credited.

Though Sun Valley, Alta, and Aspen are the glamour spots of Rocky Mountain skiing, a score of other resorts are now bidding for a share of this astonishing new trade which, at least while flush times last, appears to have no limit. Recently the Denver Winter Sports Council sent three experts on a seven-thousand-mile trip to tabulate snowfall, wind crust, slope, and temperature factors in every part of the state. In 1941 Logan, Utah, christened Snow Basin with carnations dropped during a simultaneous jump by Alf and Sverre Engen; and the Colorado Highway Department is considering a tunnel under Loveland Pass, where magnificent Arapaho Basin is coming into rampant popularity. Tiny Pinedale, Wyoming, farther from a railroad than any other town in the United States, is whooping it up for Surveyor's Park. Jackson Hole, her canny eye ever cocked toward the main chance, has sunk a staggering sum into a first-class lift and, like Aspen, is joyfully discovering that summer tourists as well as skiers will pay to ride it.

Even New Mexico, after years of wheedling winter trade by means of enchanted mesas and sunny vistas, has caught the fever. Albuquerque jumped off first with T-bar lifts in the Sandia Mountains; Santa Fe, trying to overhaul her, bumped into one of the oddest problems a ski center has yet met. Her imported expert, Graeme McGowan, located a good site in the Big Tesuque-Aspen Basin wilderness area; but when talk of a road was broached, up popped the Tesuque Indians with an objection which conservationists, by nature opposed to the very word "highway," quickly exploited. The area was sacred; in it young Tesuque men and women received instruction in tribal mysteries, and the hallowed ground should not be desecrated. Skiers retorted that Indians used all that area of the Sangre de Cristos for ceremonials and that no particular significance attached to Aspen Basin. After a few years' stalemate the Indians backed down (who ever heard of a red man's claims blocking for long white man's desires?), and the controversial road is being pushed high above Hyde Park to the marvelous touring regions at timber line. Santa Fe boosters, no more modest than those in other sections, are trumpeting that here is the Rockies' most singular winter-sports center—deep-snow skiing only an hour away from Indian pueblos, Spanish antiquities, and horseback rides under a desert sky.

So it goes. Every Rocky Mountain ski area, from Colorado's Glenwood Springs, where one can swim in a hot, open-air pool after a slalom down the hill, to the lonesome slopes of Wyoming's Big Horns, has the fanciest, fastest, highest, most picturesque something-or-other; and the amount of money being spent to turn boasts into fact would have left the pampered dude ranchers and hunters of olden days pop-eyed with astonishment. Legends are growing: with straight faces skiers will tell you that oxygen tanks are going to be placed on the chair lifts for the solace of low-altitude tourists flying out from the East. A new idiom, with its own brand of humor, has been born. Skiers in swank lounges or in drafty dormitories recognize it with instant delight, though to the uninitiate it approaches incomprehensibility.

But anyone can understand the golden tune. The once dead world of winter has come to life. Ski bums, ranging from youthful trail workers to decorative and often extraordinarily proficient socialites, float from resort to resort. With an echoing bawl of "Track!" the schuss boomer roars down the runs regardless of his own and everyone else's life and limb.

For the most part, however, the slope haunters are ordinary city folk who have hoarded their dollars and their days for a week-end or a week-long fling at a kind of fun that simply did not exist less than a generation ago. The mountain towns can't quite believe it. But they are learning. In their own ways they are beginning to sing out, as Otto Schniebs once did with his incomparable zest:

"Skiing is not a schport—it iss a vay of life."

ACKNOWLEDGMENTS

A BOOK of this kind obviously could not exist without the work of many trail blazers: writers and students both new and old, and those less articulate people who, loving the high country, have made it their particular province. From many of the latter I have received more help than I can adequately acknowledge. Some I unfortunately do not know by name: small-town librarians, newspaper editors, workers on reclamation projects or in district forest offices, resort owners and ranchers, miners and cowboys and sheepherders, storekeepers, fishermen, and chance acquaintances along the mountain trails; all of them more generous with their time, information, and hospitality than I had any right to expect.

Others I can be more specific about, particularly Miss Ina T. Aulls, Mrs. Alys Freeze, and Miss Nelle Minnick of the Western History Department of the Denver Public Library; Dr. LeRoy Hafen of the Colorado Historical Society, and Dr. Arthur Anderson and Miss Evelyn Bauer of the combined libraries of the Museum of New Mexico, the Laboratory of Anthropology, and the School of American Research in Santa Fe.

My own family, too, were helpful beyond the ordinary course of family interest. Three of them, sisters, had lived as young brides in remote sections of the Rockies, and each furnished me not only with rich stores of anecdotes but put me in touch with persons I could not otherwise have contacted. One was my mother, Mrs. E. N. Lavender, who knew the town of Telluride, Colorado, when it was a booming camp; another, Mrs. Kenneth Luman of Salt Lake City, had lived in the storied ranching section near Pinedale, Wyoming; and Mrs. Helen McGrew of Greeley, Colorado, had in the early days of Middle Park watched the struggles of the Moffat railroad.

In Salt Lake City I received cordial help from historian Perry Jenkins, rancher Herb Landis, Richmond Johnson of the Bureau of Reclamation, and F. C. Koziol, supervisor of Wasatch National Forest. On the Hoback Rim, north of Pinedale, Wyoming, Mr. and Mrs. Linn Sargent, pioneers themselves, turned over to me manuscripts which

Mrs. Sargent has been preparing for the Sublette County Historical Society. Superintendent McLaughlin and mountaineer Paul Petzoldt of Grand Teton Park were helpful; and at Dubois, pioneer dude rancher James Moore and Sue and Charlie Beck were more than gracious, as was Mrs. Boyer at Savery, Wyoming.

In northern Colorado, at the lonesome hamlet of Slater on the Little Snake River, was the Rockies' most colorful storekeeper, Mildred MacIntosh, yarn spinner and local historian extraordinary. Particular indebtedness is due also to Charles Leckenby, pioneer newspaper editor of Steamboat Springs, Colorado; to Fred McLaren, Rocky Mountain National Park ranger at Grand Lake; to Francis Thomas of the Estes Park office of the Colorado-Big Thompson project; to Floyd Merrill, editor of the Greeley *Tribune;* to Charles Tutt and Harry McDonald of Colorado Springs; Ben Draper of Georgetown; Frank Ashley and the Ray Maxwells, especially Jean of the *Times,* in Aspen. In my old stamping ground of the San Juans, Franklin Bell of the Camp Bird Mine and Harry Stough, old-time mule skinner of Ouray; Telluride's Frank Wilson, Homer Reid, and H. M. Wooster of the Telluride Gold Mines went out of their way to be of assistance, as did Joe and Mabel Redd of Norwood, Mr. Segerberg and A. M. Camp of Durango. An especial debt is due Josie Moore Crum of Durango for letting me see the fruits of her laborious research into the narrow-gauge railroads of southern Colorado.

In Santa Fe, New Mexico's game warden Elliott Barker, F. A. Koch, and, in particular, K. D. Flock, supervisor of Santa Fe National Forest, were most helpful in digging up pertinent information on a variety of subjects. Other specialists now living outside the Rocky Mountain area patiently bore with my many questions and letters: Ed Pierce of Ventura, California, who knew the San Juans during their most colorful era; Ben Rastall, authority on Cripple Creek; Robert LeMessina, student of the mountain railroads; and F. P. Keenan, special assistant to the United States Attorney General in regard to various Ute Indian matters.

In Denver more people than I can list here provided information or opened the way to sources I could not otherwise have tapped, notably Melvin Griffiths, Evelyn Runette, secretary of the Colorado Mountain Club, and Louisa Ward Arps. Also Jim and Janice McGrew, Gene Broyles, A. H. Crow, David McClain, Dayton Denious, Dr. Henry Buchtel, Jack Kendrick; Ferrington Carpenter, former Federal grazing administrator; George Dodge of the Denver and Rio Grande Railway; D. O. Appleton, editor of the *American Cattle Producer.* Special thanks are due Thomas Hornsby Ferril and Harper & Brothers for permission to quote from *Trial by Time* his lines on water, which also appear in the Colorado State Capitol Building.

It was Howard S. Cady of Doubleday who proposed this book, supplied stacks of material, opened the way to more, and throughout manifested remarkable patience.

But the greatest debt is due my wife, who browsed through dusty newspaper files, abstracted books, helped guard my limited working hours, hauled me back from ill-judged tangents, buoyed my discouragements, and, above all, cheerfully waded through the dreary chore of typing the manuscript.

BIBLIOGRAPHY

BIBLIOGRAPHY

Adams, Andy, *The Log of a Cowboy*. Boston, 1903.

Albright, Horace, and Taylor, Frank J., *Oh, Ranger!*. Stanford University, 1928.

Alter, J. Cecil, *Utah, the Storied Domain*, 3 vols. New York, 1932.

———, *James Bridger*. Salt Lake City, 1925.

Anderson, A. A., *Experiences and Impressions*. New York, 1933.

Atwood, Wallace W., *The Rocky Mountains*. New York, 1945.

Bakeless, John, *Lewis and Clark*. New York, 1947.

Baker, James H., and Hafen, LeRoy R., *History of Colorado*, 3 vols. Denver, 1927.

Bancroft, H. H., *History of Arizona and New Mexico*. San Francisco, 1889.

———, *History of Nevada, Colorado and Wyoming*. San Francisco, 1890.

———, *History of Utah*. San Francisco, 1890.

Banning, Captain William, and Banning, George Hugh, *Six Horses*. New York, 1930.

Bartlett, I. S., ed., *History of Wyoming*, 3 vols. Chicago, 1918.

Beebe, Lucius, *Highball*. New York, 1945.

———, *Mixed Train Daily*. New York, 1947.

Bird, Isabella, *A Lady's Life in the Rocky Mountains*. London, 1881.

Birney, Hoffman, *Zealots of Zion*. Philadelphia, 1931.

Bolton, Herbert Eugene, *Spanish Explorations in the Southwest, 1542–1706*. New York, 1916.

Bradley, Glenn D., *The Story of the Pony Express*. Chicago, 1913.

———, *The Story of the Santa Fe*. Boston, 1920.

Burns, Walter W., *The Saga of Billy the Kid*.

Cairns, Mary L., *Grand Lake: The Pioneers*. Denver, 1942

Chittenden, H. M., *The American Fur Trade of the Far West*, 2 vols. New York, 1902; rev. ed., New York, 1936.

Clay, John, *My Life on the Range*. Chicago, 1924.

Clyman, James, *American Frontiersman, 1792–1881*, ed. by Charles L. Camp. San Francisco, 1928.

Colorado. American Guide Series. New York, 1941.

"The Colorado River," U. S. Department of the Interior. Washington, 1946.

Coman, Katherine, *Economic Beginnings of the Far West,* 2 vols. New York, 1912.

Conrad, Howard, *Uncle Dick Wootton.* Chicago, 1890.

Cooper, Courtney Riley, *High Country.* Boston, 1926.

Cottam, Walter P., *Is Utah Sahara Bound?* Salt Lake City, 1947.

Coues, Elliott, ed., *The Expedition of Zebulon Pike, etc.* New York, 1895.

Coutant, C. G., *The History of Wyoming.* Laramie, Wyoming, 1899.

"Criminal Record of the Western Federation of Miners, Coeur d'Alene to Cripple Creek, 1894–1904." Colorado Springs, 1904.

Crum, Josie Moore, *Rails around Peaks.* Manuscript, author's possession, Durango, Colorado.

Culhane, Albert, *A History of the Settlement of La Plata County, Colorado.* Master's Thesis, University of Colorado, 1934.

Dale, Harrison C., *The Ashley-Smith Explorations and the Discovery of a Central Route to the Pacific.* Rev. ed., Glendale, Cal., 1941.

Daniels, Helen Sloan, *The Ute Indians of Southwestern Colorado.* Durango, Colorado, 1941.

Darrow, Clarence, *The Story of My Life.* New York, 1932.

Davis, Carlyle C., *Olden Times in Colorado.* Los Angeles, 1916.

Dawson, T. F., *Scrapbooks,* 14 vols. Collection of clippings, Colorado State Historical Society, Denver.

Dellenbaugh, F. S., *Breaking the Wilderness.* New York, 1905.

De Voto, Bernard, *Across the Wide Missouri.* Boston, 1947.

———, *The Year of Decision: 1846.* Boston, 1943.

Dick, Everett, *Vanguards of the Frontier.* New York, 1941.

Donnelly, Thomas C., ed., *Rocky Mountain Politics.* Albuquerque, 1940.

Draper, Benjamin P., *Georgetown.* Georgetown, Colo. 1940.

Duffus, R. L., *The Santa Fe Trail.* New York, 1930.

Dunn, J. P., *Massacres of the Mountains.* New York, 1886.

Dyer, John L., *The Snow-Shoe Itinerant.* Cincinnati, 1890.

Farnham, Thomas Jefferson, *Travels in the Great Western Prairies.* Reprinted in Thwaite's *Early Western Travels,* Vol. XXVIII. Cleveland, 1905.

Favour, Alpheus H., *Old Bill Williams.* Chapel Hill., N. C., 1936.

Fenneman, Nevin M., *Physiography of Western United States.* New York, 1931.

Fergusson, Harvey, *The Rio Grande*. New York, 1933.

Fossett, Frank, *Colorado: Tourists' Guide to the Rocky Mountains*. New York, 1879.

Fowler, Gene, *Timberline*. New York, 1933.

Frémont, John C., *The Exploring Expedition to the Rocky Mountains in the Year 1842 and to Oregon, and Northern California in the Years 1843–4*. Washington, 1845.

Fritz, Percy S., *Colorado, the Centennial State*. New York, 1941.

Fryxell, Fritiof, *The Teton Peaks and Their Ascents*. Grand Teton National Park, 1933.

Garrard, Lewis H., *Wah-To-Yah and the Taos Trail*. Ed. by Ralph Bieber, rev. ed., Glendale, Cal., 1938.

Ghent, W. J., *The Road to Oregon*. New York, 1929.

Gibbons, J. J., *In the San Juan*. N.p., 1898.

Grant, Blanche, *When Old Trails Were New: The Story of Taos*. New York, 1934.

Greeley, Horace, *An Overland Journey from New York to San Francisco in the Summer of 1859*. New York, 1860.

Gregg, Josiah, *Commerce of the Prairies, 1831–39*. New York, 1845; reprinted in Thwaite's *Early Western Travels*, Vols. XIX and XX, Cleveland, 1905.

Grinnell, George Bird, *The Fighting Cheyennes*. New York, 1915.

Hafen, LeRoy R., and Ghent, W. J., *Broken Hand*. Denver, 1931.

Hart, J. L. J., and Kingery, Elinor, *Fourteen Thousand Feet*. Denver, 1931.

Hart, Stephen H., and Hulbert, Archer B., *Zebulon Pike's Arkansaw Journal*. Denver, 1932.

Hebard, Grace Raymond, *Washakie*. Cleveland, 1930.

———, and Brininstool, E. A., *The Bozeman Trail*. Cleveland, 1922.

Holbrook, Stewart, *The Story of American Railroads*. New York, 1947.

Hollister, O. J., *The Mines of Colorado*. Springfield, Mass., 1867.

Howbert, Irving, *Memories of a Lifetime in the Pikes Peak Region*. New York, 1925.

Ingersoll, Ernest, *The Crest of the Continent*. Chicago, 1889.

———, *Knocking round the Rockies*. New York, 1883.

Inman, Henry, *The Santa Fe Trail*. Topeka, 1916.

Irving, Washington, *Astoria*. Philadelphia, 1836.

———, *The Adventures of Captain Bonneville*. New York, 1837.

Jackson, Clarence, *Picture Maker of the Old West*. New York, 1947.

Jocknick, Sidney, *Early Days on the Western Slope of Colorado*. Denver, 1913.

Kappler, Charles J., *Indian Affairs, Laws and Treaties*. Vol. 2, Senate Document 452. Washington, 1903.

Keleher, William A., *The Fabulous Frontier*. Santa Fe, 1945.

Lamb, E. J., *Memories of the Past and Thoughts of the Future*. 1906.

Langdon, Emma, *The Cripple Creek Strike*. Denver, 1904.

Larpenteur, Charles, *Forty Years a Fur Trader on the Upper Missouri*. New York, 1898.

Laut, Agnes, *The Overland Trail*. New York, 1929.

Lavender, David, *One Man's West*. New York, 1943.

Leckenby, Charles, *The Tread of the Pioneers*. Steamboat Springs, Colo., 1943.

Logan, Paul S., *History of the Denver and Rio Grande Railway, 1871–1881*. Master's Thesis, Colorado College, 1931.

Magoffin, Susan, *Down the Santa Fe Trail and Into Mexico*. Stella Drumm, ed., New Haven, 1926.

McLean, Evelyn Walsh, *Father Struck It Rich*. Boston, 1936.

McMechen, Edgar C., *The Moffat Tunnel of Colorado*, 2 vols. Denver, 1927.

———, *The Shining Mountains*. Denver, 1935.

Majors, Alexander, *Seventy Years on the Frontier*. Col. Prentiss Ingraham, ed., Chicago and New York, 1893.

Marcy, Randolph Barnes, *Thirty Years of Army Life on the Border*. New York, 1866.

Marsh, Barton W., *The Uncompahgre Valley and the Gunnison Tunnel*. Montrose, Colo., 1905.

Marshall, James, *Santa Fe, the Railroad That Built an Empire*. New York, 1945.

Messer, La Visa Lake, *Reminiscences of the San Juan Basin*. Unpublished manuscript, Durango, Colo., Public Library.

Mokler, Alfred James, *History of Natrona County, Wyoming*. Chicago, 1923.

Monroe, Arthur W., *San Juan Silver*. Montrose, Colo., 1940.

Morgan, Dale L., *The Great Salt Lake*. Indianapolis and New York, 1947.

Neihardt, John G., *The Splendid Wayfaring*. New York, 1920.

Nesbit, Paul, *Longs Peak—Its Story and Guide for Climbing It*. Denver, 1946.

Nevins, Allan, *Frémont, Pathmarker of the West*. New York, 1939.

New Mexico. American Guide Series. Albuquerque, 1945.

Nunn, P. N., *Pioneer Work of the Telluride Power Company*. Transactions, Vol. 2, International Electrical Congress, St. Louis, 1904.

Orchard, Harry, *The Confessions of Harry Orchard*. New York, 1907.
Paden, Irene, *The Wake of the Prairie Schooner*. New York, 1943.
Page, Elizabeth, *Wagons West*. New York, 1930.
Parkman, Francis, *The Oregon Trail*. New York, 1849.
Peake, Ora Brooks, *The Colorado Range Cattle Industry*. Glendale, Cal., 1937.
Pelzer, Louis, *The Cattlemen's Frontier*. Glendale, Cal., 1936.
Pioneers of the San Juan Country, compiled by Sarah Platt Decker Chapter D.A.R., Durango, Colo. Colorado Springs, Vol. I, 1942; Vol. II, 1946.
Quiett, Glenn Chesney, *They Built the West*. New York, 1934.
———, *Pay Dirt*. New York, 1936.
Raine, William McLeod, and Barnes, Will C., *Cattle*. New York, 1935.
Rastall, Benjamin McKie, *The Labor History of the Cripple Creek Districts*. Bulletin of University of Wisconsin, 1908.
Rickard, T. A., *Man and Metals*, 2 vols. New York, 1932.
A Report on Labor Disturbances in the State of Colorado From 1880–1904. Senate Document No. 122, Washington, 1905.
Reports of Explorations for a Pacific Railroad. Vols. I, II, and XI, Washington, D. C., 1855 and 1861.
Rollins, Philip A., *The Cowboy*. New York, 1922.
———, ed., *The Discovery of the Oregon Trail*. New York, 1935.
Rollinson, John K., *Wyoming Cattle Trails*. Caldwell, Ida., 1948.
Russell, Osborne, *Journal of a Trapper or Nine Years in the Rocky Mountains, 1834–1843*. Boise, Ida., 1921.
Ruxton, George Frederick, *Life in the Far West* (fictionized). New York, 1849. Reprinted, 1915.
———, *Wild Life in the Rocky Mountains*. Rev. ed., New York, 1924.
Sabin, Edwin L., *Kit Carson Days*. New York, 1935.
Sage, Rufus B., *Rocky Mountain Life*. Boston, 1857.
Skinner, Constance L., *Beaver, Kings and Cabins*. New York, 1933.
Smiley, Jerome C., *Semi-Centennial History of Colorado*, 2 vols. Chicago, 1913.
Smythe, William, *The Conquest of Arid America*. Rev. ed., New York, 1911.
Spring, Agnes Wright, *Seventy Years Cow Country*. Wyoming Stock Growers Association, 1942.
Statement of the Western Federation of Miners. Senate Document No. 163, Washington, 1905.
Steinel, Alvin H., *History of Agriculture in Colorado*. Fort Collins, Colo., 1926.

Stone, Elizabeth, *Uinta County: Its Place in History*. Laramie, Wyo., 1924.

Story, Isabelle, *Glimpses of Our National Parks*. Washington, 1941.

Sullivan, Maurice S., *The Travels of Jedediah Smith*. Santa Ana, Cal., 1934.

Taylor, Bayard, *Colorado: A Summer Trip*. New York, 1867.

Twain, Mark, *Roughing It*. Hartford, Conn., 1879.

Twitchell, Ralph Emerson, *Leading Facts of New Mexico History*, 3 vols. Cedar Rapids, Ia., 1912.

Utah. American Guide Series. New York, 1941.

Vestal, Stanley, *Kit Carson*. Boston, 1928.

———, *Mountain Men*. Boston, 1937.

Victor, Frances Fuller, *The River of the West*. Hartford, Conn., 1870.

Walker, Tacetta, *Stories of Early Days in Wyoming*. Thermopolis, Wyo.

Ward, Louisa A., *Chalk Creek, Colorado*. Denver, 1940.

Warman, Cy, *Story of the Railroad*. New York, 1898.

Webb, Walter Prescott, *The Great Plains*. Boston, 1931.

Wellman, Paul I., *The Trampling Herd*. New York, 1939.

Westermeir, Clifford P., *Man, Beast, and Dust*. Denver, 1947.

The Westerners' Brand Book. A collection of historical sketches published annually in Denver by The Westerners.

Williston, George F., *Here They Dug the Gold*. Rev. ed., New York, 1946.

Wilson, Rufus Rockwell, *Out of the West*. New York, 1936.

Wissler, Clark, *The American Indian*. New York, 1932.

———, *Indians of the United States*. New York, 1940.

Wyoming. American Guide Series. New York, 1941.

Young, Frank C., *Echoes From Arcadia*. Denver, 1903.

Miscellaneous information abounds in the following periodicals (unfortunately, some of the state historical reviews have not enjoyed continuous publication): *The Colorado Magazine*, published by the State Historical Society of Colorado; *Municipal Facts*, Denver; *The New Mexico Historical Review; New Mexico Magazine; Annals of Wyoming; Utah Historical Quarterly; Improvement Era*, a Mormon Church publication; *Rocky Mountain Life*, Denver; *Reclamation Era*, published by the Bureau of Reclamation, Washington, D. C.; *Trail and Timberline*, published by the Colorado Mountain Club; *The American Alpine Journal*, New York; *American Ski Annual*.

Occasional pertinent information was adduced from random articles in *Year Books of the Colorado Metal Mining Association; The Western Livestock Journal; American Cattle Producer*, published by the American Livestock Association, Denver; *Midwest Wool Growers News; Trains;* bulletins of the Railway and Locomotive Historical Society; *Harper's Magazine; The Atlantic Monthly; The Saturday Evening Post; Field and Stream; Sports Afield; The National Geographic Magazine; Pacific Northwest Quarterly; The Living Wilderness; Ski Illustrated,* etc.

Various publications, bulletins, and mimeographed releases by the Department of the Interior (Bureau of Reclamation, Fish and Wildlife Service, etc.); the Department of Agriculture (Forest Service), and by the Colorado State Agricultural College were often valuable.

Contemporary newspapers were widely, if sporadically, consulted. References in the text itself indicate scope and dates.

INDEX

INDEX

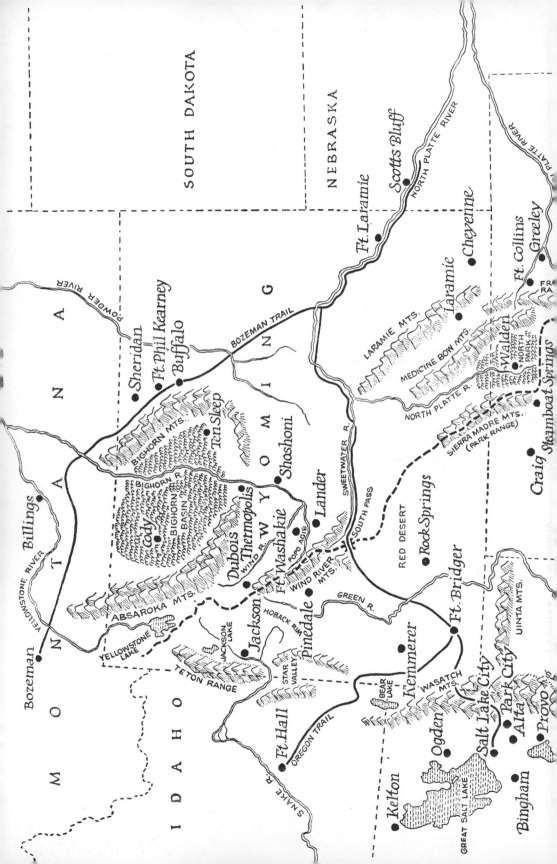